Reforming AGRICULTURAL TRADE FOR DEVELOPING COUNTRIES

AGRICULTURE AND RURAL DEVELOPMENT

Reforming AGRICULTURAL TRADE FOR DEVELOPING COUNTRIES

Volume One: Key Issues for a Pro-Development Outcome of the Doha Round

Alex F. McCalla & John Nash, editors

THE WORLD BANK
Washington, DC

1818 H Street, NW
Washington, DC 20433
Telephone 202-473-1000
Internet www.worldbank.org
E-mail feedback@worldbank.org

1 2 3 4 :: 09 08 07 06

e-ISBN: 0-8213-6497-9 DOI: 10.1596/978-0-8213-6496-3

Library of Congress Cataloging-in-Publication Data

Reforming agricultural trade for developing countries / edited by Alex F. McCalla, John Nash.
p. cm. — (Agriculture and rural development)
Includes bibliographical references and index.
Contents: v. 1. Key issues for a pro-development outcome of the Doha Round negotiations — v. 2. Quantifying the impact of multilateral trade reform.
ISBN-13: 978-0-8213-6496-3 (pbk. : v. 1)
ISBN-10: 0-8213-6496-0 (pbk. : v. 1)
ISBN-13: 978-0-8213-6716-2 (pbk. : v. 2)
ISBN-10: 0-8213-6716-1 (pbk. : v. 2)
1. World Trade Organization—Developing countries. 2. Agriculture and state—Developing countries. 3. Developing countries—Commerce. I. McCalla, Alex F., 1937– . II. Nash, John D., 1953– .
HF1385.R42 2006
382′.41091724—dc22 2006049111

CONTENTS

BOXES, FIGURES, AND TABLES

Boxes

Figures

Tables

PREFACE

This is one volume of a two-volume set titled *Reforming Agricultural Trade for Developing Countries.* The first volume is subtitled *Key Issues for a Pro-Development Outcome of the Doha Round,* because the chapters are for the most part focused on specific concerns that are being encountered in the agricultural negotiations, and on strategies for dealing with them to arrive at a final agreement that will significantly spur growth and reduce poverty in developing countries. The companion volume is subtitled *Quantifying the Impact of Multilateral Trade Reform.* It comprises chapters that take different approaches to modeling trade reform and quantifying the resulting benefits and costs to various players in the negotiations. The overview chapter of that volume explains the differences in results that come out of these different approaches, and compares them to some other recent estimates of the gains from global trade reform.

With few exceptions, the papers in these two volumes were first presented at a workshop, "The Developing Countries, Agricultural Trade, and the WTO," sponsored by the International Agricultural Trade Research Consortium, the World Bank, and Agriculture and Agri-Food Canada, held in Whistler, British Columbia, in June 2002. Most of the papers have been revised and updated for this book. At the time of the workshop the Doha Round of multilateral trade negotiations was in its early days and a negotiating framework had not been proposed, so each paper invented its own scenario for evaluation.

Considering the amount of time that has elapsed since the conference, there might be some concern that the papers are now of limited, mainly historical, value. This is not the case. Progress in the Doha Round has been fitful and slow and is now years behind schedule. The Cancún Ministerial Meeting in 2003 ended without agreement on a negotiating framework as some developing countries walked out because of a lack of movement on agriculture. The next deadline was the Ministerial Meeting in Hong Kong in December 2005. It too ended with a very limited agreement, the most significant accomplishment being the setting of a 2013 deadline for ending agricultural export subsidies. More recently, the WTO was forced to call for a de facto suspension of the Round, due primarily to the failure of members to agree on the next steps in the agricultural negotiations. Agricultural issues remain unresolved and continue to be of central importance to getting the Round back on track.

Such delays are not uncommon in trade negotiations. All recent multilateral trade rounds—Uruguay, Tokyo, and Kennedy—have been delayed, always by impasses on agricultural trade liberalization. Agriculture was pulled from the table to enable the Kennedy Round to reach conclusion, minimal progress was made in the Tokyo Round, and only a last minute deal between the United States and the European Union salvaged the Uruguay Round, three years late. The Doha Round is perhaps more complicated because there are new power blocs at the table, but that may also help to get an agreement in the end. In the Kennedy and Tokyo Rounds, agriculture was essentially a bilateral confrontation between the United States and the European Union. What progress there was made in the Uruguay Round in getting agriculture under the rules of the World Trade Organization (WTO) can be attributed in part to the emergence of a third player, the Cairns Group of agricultural exporters. In the Doha Round more groups—such as the Group of 20 developing countries (G-20), the Group of 33, and the Group of Least Developed Countries—have emerged as developing countries themselves have become major players (see chapter 5 by Rashid S. Kaukab in this volume for a road map). In the G-20, countries like Brazil, China, India, and South Africa are involved in shaping the negotiations and should play a stronger role in determining the ultimate agreement.

Thus, the issues addressed in these two volumes, policy issues for developing countries, country experience, and quantitative analysis of potential gains —are if anything more relevant to developing countries now than they were in 2002. The quantitative analyses involved projections of potential gains into the future at least until 2010, so they remain useful.

Alex F. McCalla
Professor Emeritus of Agricultural and Resource Economics
University of California, Davis

John Nash
Adviser for Trade, Agriculture, and Rural Development
The World Bank

CHAPTER ONE

Agricultural Trade Reform and Developing Countries: Issues, Challenges, and Structure of the Volume

Alex F. McCalla and John Nash

On July 27, 2006, the World Trade Organization's (WTO) Director-General, Pascal Lamy, recommended an indefinite time-out in the Doha Round negotiations. Mr. Lamy warned that the suspension could result in an opportunity missed to integrate more vulnerable members into international trade, thereby forgoing "the best hope for growth and poverty alleviation," and could lead to a resurgence of protectionism. While the time-out is unfortunate for many reasons, it is important to recognize that it does not imply the death of the Doha Development Agenda. The multilateral trading system has faced challenges before, including similar circumstances and fears during the Uruguay Round, and has reemerged with renewed strength. The challenge now is to find the political will to bridge negotiating gaps and resume negotiations promptly. In any case, there should be no backsliding on progress that had already been made in the negotiations—such as the offer to eliminate agricultural export subsidies by 2013 and provide duty-free/quota-free access for exports from least developed countries—nor on other promises made outside the negotiations per se, such as commitments of Aid for Trade in order to help poor countries integrate into the global economy. At a time like this, it should also be kept firmly in mind that regardless of what happens in the multilateral discussions, all countries can benefit from reforming their own trade regimes. Countries should carefully consider stepping up trade reforms as part of strategies to promote economic efficiency and growth and reduce poverty, or to stem budgetary waste.

This chapter provides a summary of some of the issues that are fundamental to the Doha negotiations themselves and to the eventual implementation of an agreement. The first two sections explore two critical questions: Why are agricultural trade reforms important, and what will it take to ensure a pro-development and pro-poor outcome from the Doha negotiations? But it is not only important to reach agreements on trade reform at the global level. The reform programs also have to be properly designed and executed. So the third section shifts the focus from the multilateral negotiations to the design of agricultural trade policy reforms at the country level. The final section of this introduction provides a road map to the rest of this volume.

WHY ARE AGRICULTURAL TRADE REFORMS IMPORTANT?

Among the many reasons that agricultural trade reforms are important, two stand out: the importance of agriculture in developing countries and the slow growth of agricultural trade from developing countries to developed countries.

Agriculture Is Especially Important to Developing Countries

It is now well established that agricultural development is critical to developing countries, especially the least developed. Agriculture remains the largest employer, the largest source of GDP, and the largest source of exports and foreign exchange earnings in most developing countries. About 75 percent of poor people worldwide reside in rural areas, and most of them are dependent on agriculture. The rural poverty rate exceeds the urban rate by a large margin in almost all developing countries for which Poverty Reduction Strategy Papers have been prepared (table 1.1). While agriculture declines relative to the rest of a growing economy as incomes improve, its growth is absolutely critical at early stages of development, and it can often drive export-led growth.

Table 1.1 Rural-Urban Poverty Gap

Poverty Rates	Burkina	Uganda	Mauritania	Tanzania	Mozambique	Niger	Zambia	Gambia	Ethiopia	Ghana	Malawi	Cambodia	Vietnam	Mongolia	Kyrgyzstan	Georgia	Honduras	Nicaragua	Yemen	Nepal	Sri Lanka
Rural	51	46	68	50	71	66	80	61	47	34	67	40	57	33	70	10	51	69	45	44	27
Urban	17	16	25	24	62	52	56	48	37	27	55	21	26	39	49	12	57	31	31	23	15
Difference	34	30	43	26	9	14	24	13	10	7	12	19	31	–6	21	–2	–6	38	14	21	12

Source: Calculations from Poverty Reduction Strategy papers for each country.

A vibrant agricultural sector is therefore crucial to reducing poverty through economic growth, as well as improving global food security and conserving natural resources (Ingco and Nash 2004). Agricultural trade reform to better integrate this sector into global markets is equally crucial to developing countries for a number of reasons. Trade liberalization fuels prosperity (Ingco and Nash 2004 have a brief survey of this literature). Agriculture has the highest levels of trade distortions and therefore the greatest potential for gains from reform. And domestic reforms necessary to implement trade reforms benefit developing countries more than developed countries.

Relatively Slow Growth of Agricultural Trade from Developing Countries to Developed Countries Is a Problem

World trade has been booming over the past two decades, and developing countries share of the total pie has been expanding. The share of developing countries in exports of manufactured goods to industrial countries has risen dramatically, as has their share in exports of manufactured goods to developing countries (table 1.2). Their share of agricultural exports in trade to other developing countries has also risen, although not as much as in manufactured products. But the share of developing countries in agricultural exports to the industrial world has stagnated. Of course, simple statistics such as these cannot prove a causal link, but they are consistent with the hypothesis that developed economies' barriers to agricultural trade have effectively stifled this segment of global trade.

So, developing countries potentially have a lot to gain from global trade reform. Recent estimates are that developing country income would be some 0.8 percent higher by 2015 than it otherwise would be if all merchandise trade barriers and agricultural subsidies were removed between 2005 and 2010, with about two-thirds of the total gain coming from agricultural trade and subsidy reform (Anderson, Martin, and van der Mensbrugghe forthcoming; Hertel and Keeney 2006). The high share of the gains attributable to agriculture may seem

Table 1.2 Share of Developing Countries' Exports in World Trade

	1980/81	1990/91	2000/01
Total agricultural exports	35.4	32.2	36.3
To developing countries	9.5	8.9	13.4
To industrial countries	25.8	23.3	22.9
Total manufacturing exports	19.3	22.7	33.4
To developing countries	6.6	7.5	12.3
To industrial countries	12.7	15.2	21.1

Source: United Nations Statistics Division, Comtrade database.

surprising, since agriculture contributes only about 4 percent of world GDP and 9 percent of merchandise trade. But the sector's importance in trade reform is magnified by the much higher protection of agricultural products than manufactured products in countries all over the world.

Some analysts have pointed out that net agricultural importers—particularly net food importers in Africa—will suffer a static balance of payments loss from the negative terms of trade effect as world market prices rise and that many low-income countries that receive preferential access to developed country markets will see their competitive advantage from the preferences reduced (Panagariya 2004). These points are true, of course, but they are only part of the story. First, liberalization will also change the prices of other goods—manufactured goods imported and exported by these countries, as well as their agricultural exports. General equilibrium simulations (taking into account preferences) of a full global liberalization show that these changes will have a positive impact more than large enough to offset the negative terms of trade effect of the rise in food prices, so the net effect will be small, but positive (Anderson, Martin, and van der Mensbrugghe forthcoming). Second, when trade is liberalized, developing countries will benefit from improvements in their access to markets in other developing countries—particularly important, since these barriers are larger than those in the industrial countries, and developing countries are important markets for developing country exporters. Third, liberalization will benefit the rural sectors of these countries, where poverty is concentrated, because of higher world agricultural prices. Net farm incomes are predicted to rise by an average of 7 percent for Africa as a whole. The bottom line effect on poverty (defined as those earning less than $1 a day) would be to lift almost 32 million people out of poverty worldwide, about two-thirds of them in Sub-Saharan Africa.

Furthermore, the dynamic impact of improved functioning of world markets on overall growth in GDP in countries that liberalize their markets should help even net food importers. Tangermann (2005), in a recent more comprehensive look at the impact of developed country agricultural trade liberalization on least developed net food importing countries, came to similar conclusions.

While preference erosion is a legitimate concern, it is a major issue for only a few countries. Anderson and Martin (2006b) show that preference erosion will have a significant negative impact on only a handful of countries and that the impact is so small for most poor countries that it could be easily compensated by modest increases in aid. Hoekman, Martin, and Braga (2005), in a review of the literature, cite several studies estimating that the aggregate annual income losses to the least developed economies would be on the order of $200–$300 million—not trivial, but not a serious concern for the majority of countries. This consideration does not undermine the case for liberalization, but it does argue that the international community should be ready to provide transitional assistance for negatively affected countries.

WHAT IS IMPORTANT TO ENSURE A PRO-DEVELOPMENT AND PRO-POOR OUTCOME FROM THE DOHA NEGOTIATIONS?

Recognizing the importance of the negotiations, developing countries have emerged as a powerful force. One of the more striking differences between the ongoing Doha Round negotiations and previous multilateral rounds is the much greater leverage of developing countries, due at least in part to their large and growing share of world trade. This became evident, if it had not been before, at the Ministerial Meeting in Cancún in 2003. There the G-20 not only successfully insisted on dropping three of the four "Singapore Issues" (investment, competition, government procurement, and trade facilitation) from the negotiations, but also refused to go along with the proposal on agriculture that had been negotiated in advance by the United States and the European Union (albeit at the behest of other WTO members), leading to the eventual breakdown of the meeting without an agreement. Later, in July 2005, the clout of the G-20 was recognized when other WTO members agreed to accept their proposal on market access, which had been elaborated at a meeting of developing countries in Dalian, China, as the basis for further discussions in this sensitive area.

The voices of the developing countries are clearly being heard. This is certainly as it should be, given that Doha is being billed as a "development round." Nonetheless, it remains to be seen whether this influence will be translated into a final agreement that is truly more development-friendly. What would be the key ingredients in such a final outcome of the negotiations?

A Need for Significant Reductions in Agricultural Barriers and Subsidies in High-Income Countries

The many loopholes in the Uruguay Round Agreement on Agriculture (URAA) and how they were exploited to keep high-income markets heavily protected, are well documented.[1] Tariffs remain much higher in agriculture than in manufactured products (figure 1.1). While this pattern is characteristic of trade regimes in all regional groups, the discrepancy is most remarkable in high-income countries. But the level of tariffs, while high, greatly understates the degree of protection in the trade regimes in high-income countries because many products are afforded even higher levels of support by nontariff measures such as export subsidies and tariff rate quotas, which are applied to products covering close to 30 percent of agricultural production in these countries (figure 1.2). Tariff rate quota systems and the nontransparent mechanisms through which they operate create an additional layer of protection and more difficulties for developing country exporters (de Gorter and Kliauga 2006). The antidevelopment bias of the trade regimes is amplified by the extent to which tariff structures are escalated, with higher rates applied as the degree of processing increases (figure 1.3), discouraging developing country exporters

Figure 1.1 Average Tariffs, by Region, 2003

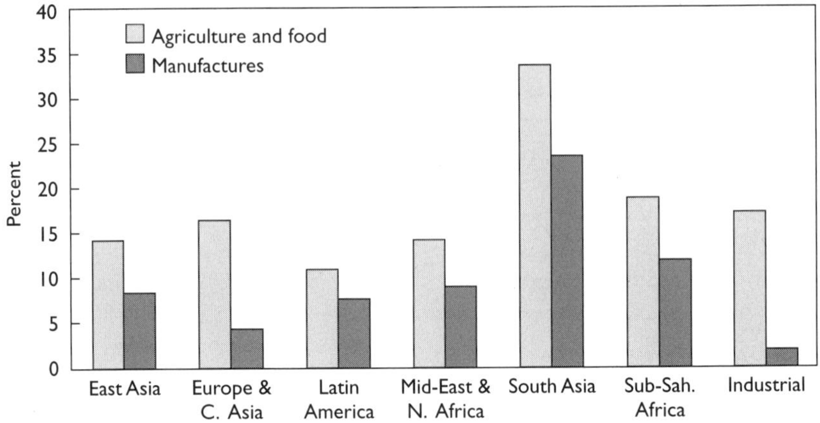

Source: Global Trade Analysis Project, release 6.03.

Figure 1.2 Coverage of Tariff Rate Quotas, 2003

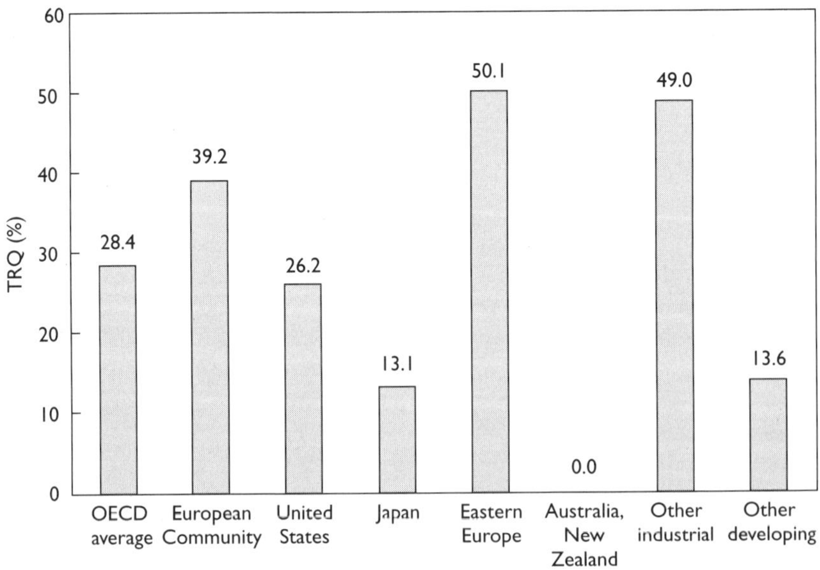

Source: OECD, Agricultural Market Access Database (AMAD).

Figure 1.3 Tariffs Escalate in Final Products

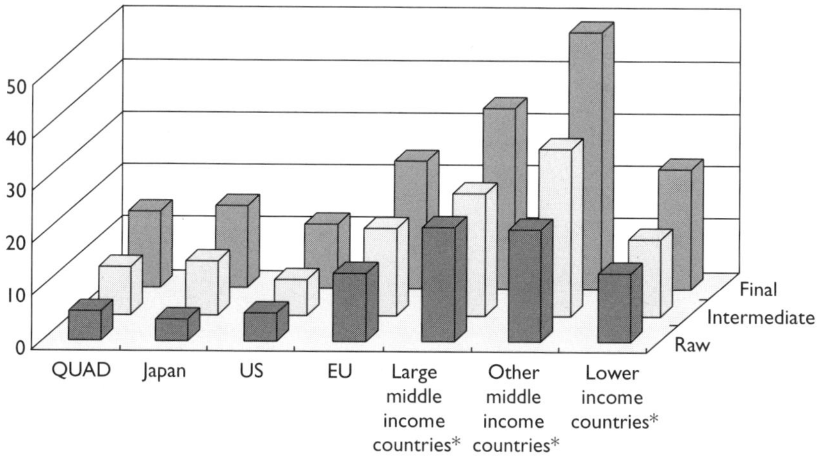

Source: World Trade Organization Integrated Database, 2001.
Note: Tariffs are most recent year reported, 1999–2001.

from moving up the value chain. And finally, while most protection is given through some form of trade measure, substantial additional support is provided by direct budgetary payments to farmers (figure 1.4).

One lesson from implementation of the URAA is that the political economy of agricultural protection in high-income countries is such that when reduction is required in one mechanism of trade-distorting support, another mechanism often pops up to replace it. Given the array of support instruments available, it follows that to guarantee increased trade opportunities for developing countries, the agreement must include strict disciplines on all fronts.

The negotiations produced an early breakthrough on *export competition,* one of the three pillars of agricultural negotiations, agreeing that the target should be a complete phase-out of export subsidies. At the Hong Kong Ministerial Meeting in December 2005 one of the few agreements was to fix the date as 2013. Thus, the value of this reform will be spread over a long time frame and will depend on how disciplines are extended to cover indirect forms of export subsidies, including export credit, the operations of state trading enterprises, and food aid. That food aid is a subject of negotiation is surprising to some, but an examination of historical patterns shows clearly that aid has been used as a means of dumping surplus production. Food aid has been most abundant when it has been least needed (when world market prices are low) and vice versa (figure 1.5).

On *market access,* the second pillar, covering tariffs and nontariff barriers to imports, the basic approach has been to reduce tariffs by a tiered formula that reduces higher tariffs proportionately more than lower tariffs. This is poten-

Figure 1.4 Border Protection and Direct Payments in High-Income Countries, 2000–2002

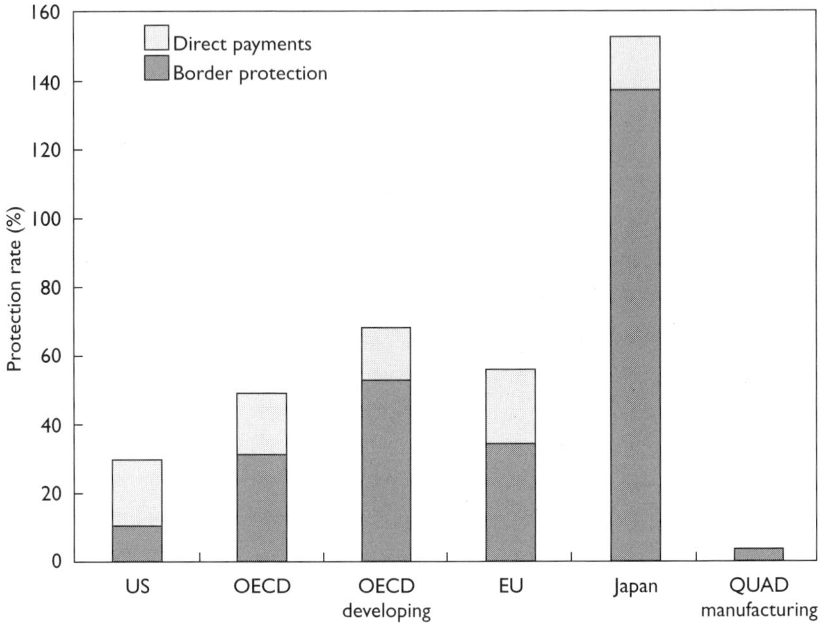

Source: OECD 2003, *Agricultural Policies in OECD Countries: Monitoring and Evaluation.*

Figure 1.5 Food Aid and World Prices

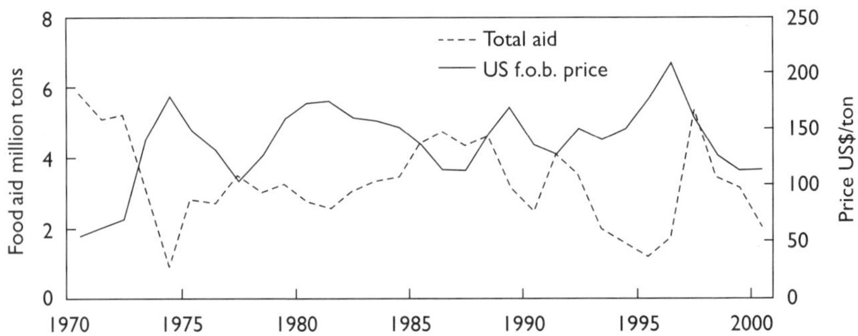

Source: USDA and World Bank.

tially a great improvement over the "average cuts" approach of the URAA, which allowed countries to maintain extremely high tariffs on some crops. But the benefits will be small if the final agreement does not use a numerical formula that requires truly significant cuts in tariffs and forecloses use of the designations "sensitive" and "special" to shield many products from the cuts required under the general formula.

Recent research indicates that if as little as 2 percent of each country's tariffs lines (on the most sensitive products) were shielded and subjected to relatively small cuts, the benefits of the overall reform would be virtually nil (Jean, Laborde, and Martin 2006). Finally, disciplines on the use of tariff rate quotas will need to be improved (de Gorter and Kliauga 2006). Anderson and Martin (2006b) note that the overwhelming majority of the benefits in an agreement will come from improving market access, although the other pillars remain important, if for no other reason than to avoid "re-instrumentation" of protection when market access barriers are reduced.

On the third pillar, *domestic support,* some of the URAA loopholes were implicitly recognized early. Agreement was reached to impose caps and eventually reduce product-specific support (to prevent the support shifting that characterized the URAA implementation) and to review the rules for classifying support as "green box," which exempts it from reduction commitments. There was also an early agreement to cut support through a tiered formula, so the countries with the highest levels of support would make larger cuts. Progress since then has been slow. The key to ensuring that the agreement reduces the antitrade distortions created by the domestic support system will be to force significant cuts in the amber box (with cuts that really "bite" for all products), while also imposing more stringent disciplines on the blue box and the green box—where much future support will be channeled—to ensure that domestic support really is "non- or minimally trade distorting," as it is required to be.

These points are not surprising, but what may not be generally recognized is the magnitude of the cuts that must be imposed to really make much of a difference. The cuts seem likely to be made using as a baseline the end-point values of the URAA. Because this agreement was not very ambitious, most countries are currently using support levels that are far below their allowable ceilings. Thus, simulations indicate that even a cut as seemingly draconian as 75 percent would force the major subsidizing countries to cut their amber box support by relatively small amounts—for example, the European Union by 16 percent and the United States by 28 percent (Jensen and Zobbe 2006).

Liberalization by Developing Countries Is Required as Well

Liberalization is also required by developing countries both because it is in their own direct interest and because it is necessary for progress in the negotiations. Reforms of trade and macroeconomic policies that obstruct trade are incomplete in most developing countries, although many countries have made substantial progress in recent years. The Doha Round represents an opportunity for developing countries to push their own trade policy reform agenda forward, while at the same time increasing their leverage in the negotiations through full engagement. It would be counterproductive for developing countries to try to opt out of all commitments. Ultimately, you get what you pay for in trade talks. A pro-development outcome is more likely in the WTO framework, in which all countries are involved in the negotiations, than in bilateral negotiations with countries with superior negotiating leverage.

That said, however, it is clear that developing countries need to be accorded special treatment in the negotiations based on their development needs. But such "special and differential treatment" should focus on development objectives, with actions linked to specific institutional or capacity-building problems, rather than on blanket exemptions from obligations to reduce trade barriers. It could also focus on positive obligations of developed countries to provide aid to overcome institutional challenges in developing country efforts to comply with their multilateral trade agreements.

Negotiations Need to Recognize that Structural Food Security Is Generally Reduced, Not Enhanced, by Trade Barriers to Food Imports

Food insecurity is a product of poverty and the consequent insufficient purchasing power. It cannot be adequately addressed by trade measures that restrict imports in order to encourage domestic food production. Trade policy can affect structural food security, properly defined, in several ways. First, global liberalization may cause a structural increase in global food prices, thereby reducing the ability of poor people to buy sufficient food. This is a legitimate concern as a long-term issue, although its importance is often exaggerated. Any structural effects will be realized only gradually, as the agreements reached in the Doha Round are implemented, giving significant adjustment time. In addition, there will be a reduction in the volatility of world prices, so both producers and consumers can manage risks better. Nevertheless, this is an issue that should be taken up in the negotiations, with the objective of finding ways to help the poor deal with higher prices.[2] Second, trade liberalization (multilateral and unilateral) should increase the purchasing power of the poor by raising incomes. Liberalization resulting from successful negotiations would lift millions out of poverty, greatly improving food security. Third, trade policy at the national level may increase or reduce the price of food, affecting poor producers and consumers in opposite ways.

Unfortunately, rather than focusing on the first two linkages with the global trading system, the concept of food security has been used in the Doha negotiations primarily to suggest that developing countries should be allowed to maintain high barriers to imports of food products as a means of increasing national production, under the rubric of "special products" or as a component of the "development box."

This kind of import-substitution policy creates an antiexport bias and is unproductive or counterproductive in the long run for a number of reasons:

- By keeping domestic food prices high, it imposes a regressive tax, undermining the food security of urban and rural poor.
- It encourages farmers to continue to plant low-value food crops instead of diversifying into high-value nontraditional exports, which is often a better road out of poverty.[3] In many countries these policies also reduce the demand for labor in rural areas, since import-substitute crops tend to be less labor intensive than exports, particularly nontraditional exports (Valdés and Foster 2003).
- By creating an antiexport bias, it reduces the foreign-exchange earning potential of the country, undermining its structural capacity to import food and other products.
- It diverts attention from methods of support for agriculture that have been proven to be much more productive, such as increased spending on infrastructure or research and extension, and from investments in domestic food distribution systems (Diaz-Bonilla, Diao, and Robinson 2003).
- The rural poor benefit from the protection of food crops less than might appear because the poorest are (in most countries) landless and are therefore harmed in their capacity as net consumers, and the next poorest class are generally self-sufficient (noncommercial) producers, who neither gain nor lose. Of course, to the extent that the rural landless rely for employment on commercial food crop production, raising food prices benefits them as laborers.[4]
- The pure "subsistence" farmers targeted by proponents of "special" products benefit little, if at all, from policies that raise farm prices. They are, by definition, not significant sellers of food.
- It diverts attention from how to use the global trading system to make all consumers more food secure by disciplining the practice of export taxation or controls by food-exporting countries in periods of high world prices and by disciplining abuse of food aid, which has at times made developing countries dumping grounds for the surplus production of rich countries, thereby undermining food production and marketing channels.
- From a global viewpoint, it is particularly damaging for trade among developing countries, which has great potential for many countries.

The Global Cotton Market Requires Special Attention, through Both Trade Reform and Development Assistance

A global deal that curtails trade-distorting subsidies and raises global prices is particularly important for cotton because of its direct effect on improving incomes of some of the world's poorest farmers. But in addition to trade reform, many of these same countries will need technical and financial assistance to ensure a supply response to new price incentives that a pro-poor Doha deal might bring. Some have suggested targeting such assistance at development of downstream industries dependent on cotton, such as textiles and garments, as a way of helping cotton farmers. But it seems unlikely that such a strategy would yield significant benefits, for several reasons. First, unless the demand created by the local industry is sufficient to absorb all domestic supplies of the raw material, the price will be set at the margin by the export sales. That is, the price to cotton producers would not be increased. In fact, the history of attempts to develop processing industries suggests that the opposite might happen, as governments have often placed controls or taxes on exports of primary products to keep domestic prices low as a means of subsidizing development of the downstream industry. In addition, it appears that there is limited potential for textile and garment industry development in the West African countries in the short run because of infrastructural and institutional constraints. A good strategy for donors, therefore, would be to focus initiatives not on downstream industries, but rather on primary cotton production, while also testing the potential for downstream development with appropriate preferential trade policy.

HOW TO DESIGN, SEQUENCE, AND IMPLEMENT TRADE POLICY REFORM AT THE COUNTRY LEVEL

A perennial issue in agricultural policymaking in developing countries is how to design, sequence, and implement trade reforms—whether a result of unilateral decisions or of multilateral or bilateral negotiations—so as to minimize negative effects on losers and ensure a supply response.[5] This issue is not unique to agriculture, of course. But it resonates even more strongly in this sector for two reasons: (1) because of the perception that domestic protection that raises internal agricultural prices reduces rural poverty and improves food security, and (2) that it protects domestic producers from the impacts of depressed and volatile world agricultural commodity prices due largely to protectionism and subsidies by high-income countries. This creates pressure for "reactive protectionism" by some developing countries that would otherwise be able to compete in world markets.

Before the 1980s the trade and macroeconomic policies of developing countries had on average an antiexport and antiagricultural bias, due to overvalued exchange rates, heavy protection of industrial sectors, operation of state-owned enterprises, and explicit taxation of export commodities (Krueger, Schiff, and Valdés 1991). Largely as a result of structural adjustment and stabilization programs since the mid-1980s, these biases appear to be weaker now—perhaps even reversed—although comprehensive empirical evidence awaits collection.

However, implicit barriers—including high tariffs on imports of manufactures—still obstruct primary export sector development in many countries. Although average agricultural tariffs in developing countries have been reduced over the past two decades (from about 30 percent in 1990 to less than 20 percent in 2000), in some countries (especially middle-income countries) relatively high tariffs on agricultural imports still create an antiexport bias in agriculture (see figure 1.1).

In this context, how should developing countries carry out trade reforms? Given the benefits of export-oriented growth, any remaining explicit policy barriers to exports should be removed as a high priority.[6] Possible exceptions may be cases where exporters cannot be taxed through more efficient mechanisms and are not already being implicitly taxed at high rates (for example, through protection of the country's import-competing sectors). A number of behind-the-border measures—including investment, capacity building, and institutional reforms—are also needed in most developing countries to encourage agricultural export development, especially of nontraditional products.

While reform of import barriers is more controversial, it is clear that governments should not as a long-term strategy maintain high import barriers (tariffs or nontariff barriers) in the name of food security or in support of an import-substitution agricultural development strategy, for the reasons set out above.

Still, immediate deep unilateral reduction in agricultural trade taxes is not always appropriate. Policy design will depend on the characteristics and conditions of the country and commodity. Some considerations on which this design may depend include:

- *The size of the sector.* Where the sector is a modest part of the economy, any unemployed labor may be rapidly reabsorbed, so liberalization will be minimally disruptive.
- *The pattern of protection.* Where agricultural protection is uneven (high protection focused on a few "sensitive" commodities), the case for reducing it is stronger, since it will be easier for farmers and laborers to move to the large number of commodities that are not experiencing a reduction in price, subject to technical substitutability and the availability of start-up capital.
- *Effects on labor markets.* Many export crops—especially nontraditional ones—are more labor-intensive than import substitutes, and so the net effect on labor demand should be positive when protection of import substitutes is reduced. (But to facilitate development of these markets, behind-the-border measures may be especially important.) It is also essential to consider whether urban and rural labor markets are well integrated, and whether rural areas have other employment opportunities outside of agriculture. Off-farm employment in food processing and services may have a bigger impact on the wages of unskilled labor than does agriculture (Valdés and Foster 2003).
- *A realistic assessment of the degree of protection needed to compensate for global distortions.* It is often argued that protective tariffs are needed to com-

pensate for world prices that are artificially depressed by protectionist policies in other countries. Since these prices will rise with global liberalization, the argument goes, tariffs are needed until global liberalization occurs in order to avoid irreparably damaging a production base that will be competitive in the long run—or to avoid adjustment costs when capital and labor markets are imperfect. The argument itself is of dubious economic merit, but if it is used to justify tariffs, the size of the tariffs should have some analytical underpinning. For most commodities the price increases with global liberalization are expected to be moderate—on the order of 10 percent or less, so that the tariffs implied by this argument would be fairly modest. For some of the most distorted markets—sugar and dairy are examples—the increases from full liberalization would be larger, but these are unlikely to be fully liberalized soon in any case.

- *Fiscal implications.* In a few countries trade taxes, while an inefficient way to raise revenue, are important. In such cases tariff reductions may need to be more gradual and coordinated with fiscal adjustments.
- *Complementary behind-the-border policies.* Such policies may be needed to provide safety nets and facilitate adjustment. High-income countries have compensated farmers for reductions in protection through direct, decoupled (and WTO-compliant) area-based payments. In countries where this is feasible, tariff reductions (and phase-outs of other subsidies) can be carried out quickly.[7] Mexico and Turkey show that this is a practical approach even in some developing countries.[8] However, in developing countries with liquidity constraints, direct payments may not be affordable, or the necessary institutions (in particular, a land registration system) may not be in place. Reductions in protection may need to be more gradual. Whatever compensatory policies are adopted, other policy reforms and investments—both inside and outside the agricultural sector—should be considered to complement trade policy reforms. Some investments of this kind could be important components of the "Aid for Trade" agenda associated with the Doha Round.
- *The characteristics of the production structure.* When production is mainly by small, resource-poor farmers who will have difficulty adjusting their cropping patterns or diversifying their income sources, reduction of protection may need to be more measured, with greater attention to collateral policies. Where large commercial farmers hire a large quantity of labor, there may be some transient negative impact on the poor, particularly if labor markets are not functioning well. In the medium run, however, commercial farmers would generally be expected to have less difficulty moving into other crops and, as noted above, a switch to export crops should absorb more labor.

ROADMAP FOR THE VOLUME

The remaining nine chapters of this volume provide a rich diversity of analysis and perspectives on developing country interests in agricultural trade liberalization and the Doha Round of WTO negotiations. This round is different. Whereas the General Agreement on Tariffs and Trade (GATT) was historically primarily a developed country club, the WTO is increasingly becoming numerically dominated by developing countries. Because this change potentially gives developing countries more power to set the agenda and to shape and ratify agreements, the focus of the debate on agricultural protection has shifted from bilateral battles between the European Union and the United States to a growing chorus of demands for market access and reduced subsidies. This changing mix of issues and players has influenced how the negotiations have proceeded to date.

This changing context is reviewed in detail in chapter **2.** Tim Josling first examines the legacy of the Uruguay Round, showing how the adoption of a rules-based regime for agriculture has played out in the implementation of the commitments made under the three pillars of market access, export competition, and domestic support. He confirms the conversion of most nontariff barriers to tariffs, but argues that the levels calculated, selected, and bound were in general high, so that mandated reductions had little actual impact. Likewise, ceilings for domestic support were set at generous levels, and reduction commitments were not very ambitious, with the result that in recent years few countries were anywhere close to their ceilings. Export subsidies are issues for only a few countries, with the European Union being the dominant player, and commitments to reduce domestic support were not binding. In looking at developments in the Doha Round to date (circa late 2005), he focuses on proposals and options that were on the table and establishes that progress has been limited. Given very limited forward movement at the 2005 Hong Kong Ministerial Meeting, his analysis remains very relevant. Josling is one of the world's foremost experts on the WTO and agriculture, and the book benefits greatly from his comprehensive introduction.

The rest of the volume is in two parts. The six chapters of the next part address selected issues in Doha, of particular importance to developing countries. The final two chapters examine country experience.

Selected Issues in Doha of Particular Importance to Developing Countries

The remainder of the book comprises an eclectic set of papers, each of which addresses an issue or issues important to developing countries. **Chapter 3,** by Ramesh Sharma, draws lessons from more than 20 FAO case studies of developing country perspectives on which possible outcomes from Doha could have important implications for their own policies. Significant reductions in permissible domestic support will have limited impact because most of these countries do not heavily subsidize domestic agriculture. Similarly, given that most developing countries do not subsidize exports, ending export subsidies would have little direct impact. From their own perspective, it is reductions in domestic protection that worry developing countries most if that leaves their domestic food production sector vulnerable to international prices depressed by subsidies and protection in developed countries. This complicates their position in WTO negotiations because all analyses suggest that developing countries have the most to gain from improved market access.

Chapter 4, by Bernard Hoekman, Francis Ng, and Marcelo Olarreaga, analyzes how subsidies on domestic production and on exports affect developing countries. They conclude that developing countries have differing interests in subsidy removal depending on whether they are exporters or importers and on what they export or import. As rich country subsidies are concentrated in a few products, impacts of the subsidy obviously vary by whether a developing country produces subsidized products.

In **chapter 5,** Rashid S. Kaukab presents an up-to-date analysis of the rapidly evolving patterns of coalitions and alliances that are developing in the WTO, and of potential negotiating strategies. He concludes that, regardless of the final pattern of coalitions, developing countries clearly are going to have increasing influence on WTO outcomes.

Chapter 6, by William Foster and Alberto Valdés, focuses on increased exposure to international price variability and sustained periods of low prices when developing countries open their borders to direct price transmission. They explore possible policy options such as price bands for WTO-consistent ways to prevent import surges from disrupting domestic food markets. An actual example of price risk management and its implications is analyzed in chapter 9 for India.

In **chapter 7,** Tim Josling explores whether the Agreement on Sanitary and Phytosanitary Measures has had a differential impact on developing countries. Evidence to date suggests that progress on implementation has been slow and that the potential to disadvantage poor and small developing countries by increasingly rigorous requirements is real.

Chapter 8, by Philip L. Paarlberg, Maury Bredahl, and John G. Lee, examines multifunctionality from the perspective of developing countries. They explore two dimensions. The first is the potential spillover on developing countries from the implementation of policies to reward agriculture in OECD countries for multifunctional activities. The second dimension concerns the implications of developing countries adopting multifunctionality as a policy approach.

Country Experience

The final two chapters take a country perspective. In **chapter 9,** Ashok Gulati and Sudha Narayanan closely examine India's experience with liberalization, which lowered domestic protection only to be confronted by dramatic world price fluctuations and sustained low prices. The impacts of such reforms on small resource-poor farmers are potentially severe. What is needed are better ways to manage import competition in a previously closed economy.

Chapter 10, by Alberto Valdés and William Foster, presents a recently completed comparison of policy reforms in three Latin American countries and examines the potential gains from trade liberalization. Their analysis is detailed and thorough and provides rich lessons about the potential gains from domestic and international liberalization, with insights on a number of other issues that are raised in other chapters of the book. It provides a fitting conclusion to this volume.

NOTES

1. Both World Bank (2004b) and Ingco and Nash (2004) document and quantify this in detail. See also the World Bank Trade website www.worldbank.org/trade, especially de Gorter and others (2003); de Gorter, Ingco, and Ignacio (2003); de Gorter, Ingco, and Ruiz (2003); and Martin (2004).
2. At the end of the Uruguay Round, when this problem was recognized, the WTO convened a committee to seek solutions. While this has not been an urgent issue, given that the URAA did not lead to sweeping liberalization, it may become more pressing if the Doha Round does.
3. See World Bank (2003, pp. 48–50) for a discussion of export and food crop production.
4. This is not to say that such support increases the aggregate demand for labor, since it also reduces employment in other industries. The net effect is not obvious.
5. For discussions of the World Bank's trade policy advice for agricultural trade, see World Bank (2004a).
6. For a recent discussion of the advantages of export-oriented agricultural growth to accelerate sectoral growth and reduce poverty, see Valdés and Foster (2003).
7. To the extent possible, this needs to be done with a credible commitment to keep tariffs low. Otherwise, it may set up perverse incentives for lobbying to raise tariffs in the future not only to collect the initial rents, but also to collect the compensation when the tariffs are later reduced.
8. Care must be taken to ensure that these do not become permanent drains on the budget or distract from more productive forms of public expenditure in the sector. The medium-term vision should be a phase-out of such payments and gradual integration of poor farmers into a national targeted safety net system. Baffes and de Gorter (2005) examine lessons of experience in direct income support, which can be useful in designing new schemes.

BIBLIOGRAPHY

Aksoy, M. A., and J. Beghin, eds. 2005. *Global Agricultural Trade and Developing Countries.* Washington, DC: World Bank.

Anderson, K., and W. Martin, eds. 2006a. *Agricultural Trade Reform and the Doha Development Agenda.* Washington, DC: World Bank.

———. 2006b. "Agriculture, Trade Reform, and the Doha Agenda." In K. Anderson and W. Martin, eds., *Agricultural Trade Reform and the Doha Development Agenda.* Washington, DC: World Bank.

Anderson, K., W. Martin, and D. van der Mensbrugghe. Forthcoming. "Would Multilateral Trade Reforms Benefit Sub-Saharan Africans?" *Journal of African Economies* 15.

Baffes, J., and H. de Gorter. 2005. "Experience with Decoupling Agricultural Support." In M. A. Aksoy and J. Beghin, eds., *Global Agricultural Trade and Developing Countries,*. Washington, DC: World Bank.

De Gorter, H., and E. Kliauga. 2006. "Reducing Tariffs versus Expanding Tariff Rate Quotas." In K. Anderson and W. Martin, eds., *Agricultural Trade Reform and the Doha Development Agenda.* New York: Palgrave Macmillan with the World Bank.

De Gorter, H., M. Ingco, and L. Ignacio,. 2003. "Domestic Support for Agriculture: Agricultural Policy Reform and Developing Countries." Trade Note 7, Trade Department, World Bank, Washington, DC.

De Gorter, M. Ingco, and L. Ruiz. 2003. "Export Subsidies: Agricultural Policy Reform and Developing Countries." Trade Note 8, Trade Department, World Bank, Washington, DC.

De Gorter, H., M. Ingco, L. Ignacio, and J. Hranaiova. 2003 "Market Access: Agricultural Policy Reform and Developing Countries." Trade Note 6, Trade Department, World Bank, Washington, DC.

Diaz-Bonilla, E., X. Diao, and S. Robinson. 2003. "Thinking Inside the Boxes: Protection in the Development and Food Security Boxes versus Investments in the Green Box." In E. Diaz-Bonilla, S.E. Frandsen, and S. Robinson, eds., *WTO Negotiations and Agricultural Liberalization: The Effect of Developed Countries' Policies on Developing Countries.* Oxford, U.K.: CABI Publishing.

Hertel, T. W., and R. Keeney. 2006. "What's at Stake: The Relative Importance of Import Barriers, Export Subsidies and Domestic Support." In K. Anderson and W. Martin, eds., *Agricultural Trade Reform and the Doha Development Agenda.* New York: Palgrave Macmillan with the World Bank.

Hoekman, B., W. Martin, and C. A. P. Braga. 2005. "Preference Erosion: The Terms of the Debate." In R. Newfarmer, ed., *Trade, Doha, and Development: A Window Into the Issues,* ed. R. Newfarmer. Washington, DC: World Bank.

Ingco, M., and J. Nash. 2004. *Agriculture and the WTO: Creating a Trading System for Development.* Washington, DC: Oxford University Press and the World Bank.

Jean, S., D. Laborde, and W. Martin. 2006. "Consequences of Alternative Formulas for Agricultural Tariff Cuts." In K. Anderson and W. Martin, eds., *Agricultural Trade Reform and the Doha Development Agenda.* Washington, DC: World Bank.

Jensen, H. G., and H. Zobbe. 2006. "Consequences of Reducing Limits on Aggregate Measurements of Support." In K. Anderson and W. Martin, eds., *Agricultural Trade Reform and the Doha Development Agenda.* New York: Palgrave Macmillan with the World Bank.

Krueger, A., M. Schiff, and A. Valdés. 1991. *The Political Economy of Agricultural Pricing Policy.* Baltimore: Johns Hopkins University Press for the World Bank.

Martin, W. 2004. "Market Access in Agriculture: beyond the Blender." Trade Note 17, Trade Department, World Bank [www.worldbank.org/trade], Washington, DC.

Newfarmer, R., ed. 2005. *Trade, Doha, and Development: A Window into the Issues.* Washington, DC: World Bank.

Panagariya, A. 2004. "Subsidies and Trade Barriers: Alternative Perspective 10.2." In B. Lomborg, ed., *Global Crises, Global Solutions.* Cambridge, U.K. and New York: Cambridge University Press.

Tangermann, S. 2005. "Organization for Economic Cooperation and Development Area Policies and the Interests of Developing Countries." *American Journal of Agricultural Economics* 87 (5): 1128–44.

Valdés, A., and W. Foster. 2003. "The Positive Externalities of Chilean Agriculture: The Significance of Its Growth and Export Orientation.": A Synthesis of the Roles of Agriculture Chile Case Study. Food and Agriculture Organization." FAO, Rome. www.fao.org/es/ESA/ROA.

World Bank. 2003. *Reaching the Rural Poor: A Renewed Strategy for Rural Development.* Washington, DC: World Bank.

———. 2004a. *Agriculture Investment Sourcebook.* Washington, DC: World Bank.

———. 2004b. "Agricultural Policies and Trade." In *Global Economic Prospects 2004: Realizing the Development Promise of the Doha Agenda.* Washington, DC: World Bank.

CHAPTER TWO

An Overview of the WTO Agricultural Negotiations

Tim Josling

Talks in the World Trade Organization (WTO) on the further reform of agricultural trade began in March 2000. The mandate for the negotiations was Article 20 of the Uruguay Round Agreement on Agriculture (URAA) of 1994, which committed members to initiate further negotiations by the end of 1999.[1] Thus the talks continued in Geneva despite the failure of the Seattle Ministerial Meeting in December 1999. The agricultural negotiations were given a significant boost by the decision at the Doha Ministerial Meeting in November 2001 to initiate a new general round of trade talks.[2] An ambitious timetable for completion of the talks was to culminate in an agreement by January 2005.[3] The timetable soon came into question as intermediate deadlines passed without agreement. The WTO Ministerial Meeting in Cancún in September 2003 gave countries the opportunity to get back on track, but trade ministers failed to reach consensus. A Framework Agreement for the Doha Round was reached in August 2004, and the next step is to conclude an agreement on the modalities of the negotiations. It was hoped that this would take place at the time of the WTO Ministerial Meeting in Hong Kong, China, in December 2005.

This chapter assesses the situation in agricultural trade policy in light of the adoption of the URAA rules and the need for further reform. It discusses the developments in the Doha Round of WTO negotiations and the options facing countries in the final stages of that round, drawing particular attention to issues related to the interests of developing countries in the agricultural talks.

A brief concluding section looks at the conditions for an eventual positive outcome of the agricultural talks.

THE LEGACY OF THE URUGUAY ROUND AND THE CURRENT SITUATION IN AGRICULTURAL TRADE POLICY

The Uruguay Round was the first multilateral negotiation on agricultural policy. The URAA imposed rules and quantitative limits on both trade and domestic policy instruments (box 2.1). It also provided a negotiated framework into which both trade policies for agricultural products and domestic farm policies must fit if conflicts and penalties are to be avoided. Nontariff barriers were replaced by bound tariffs, and minimum market access commitments were agreed. Export subsidies were limited both in expenditures and in the quantity that can benefit from subsidies. Domestic support was categorized as minimally distorting (green box), linked to production controls (blue box), or output-increasing (amber box), with amber box support subject to agreed limits that have been reduced over time.

At first, this framework appeared rather permissive, requiring few changes in farm policy by the major industrial countries. Over time the noose has tightened somewhat. The current agricultural trade negotiations are to decide in essence whether to continue this process or to loosen the constraints to allow countries more flexibility to pursue domestic objectives.

How effective has this framework been in modifying agricultural trade and domestic policies? An important side-effect of the URAA has been greater transparency in agricultural policies, as countries notify their trading partners of policy changes. Notification requirements have created a large body of quantitative and qualitative information on agricultural policies in WTO member countries.[4] This information facilitates comparisons of policies and evaluations of policy change.

Institutional changes have also been important. The establishment of the WTO Agricultural Committee has given countries a forum for challenging the policy notifications of other members. The Agricultural Committee also provides a sounding board for ideas about further reform of the rules and has enabled preparations for the current negotiations to continue in a relatively informal setting. Meeting in special session, the Agriculture Committee is the main negotiating body for the agricultural component of the Doha Development Round.

Whether the new WTO rules and procedures have improved the situation in agricultural markets is of interest to countries as they try to wrap up the current negotiations. This first section looks at the commitments made in the Uruguay Round and the changes that those commitments have stimulated. For convenience, the triad of market access, export competition, and domestic support, which provide the structure of the URAA, are used to frame the discussion.

Box 2.1 Accomplishments of Uruguay Round Agreement on Agriculture

- Converted nontariff border measures to tariffs and bound all tariffs (tariffs cannot be increased without negotiation with other countries).
- Reduced tariffs by 36 percent (on average) over six years from a 1986–88 base with a minimum reduction of 15 percent per tariff line (with 24 percent reduction over 10 years for developing countries).
- Established rules for the application of additional (safeguard) duties (up to one-third of normal duties) if imports surge or if world prices fall below preset trigger prices for goods subject to tariffication.
- Created minimum access commitments as a share of domestic consumption for products subject to tariffication.
- Reduced domestic support—as measured by the total aggregate measurement of support from a 1986–88 base—by 20 percent over six years. Domestic support considered minimally trade distorting (green box) was not included. Direct payment for production-limiting program (blue box) was not included under certain conditions
- Banned new export subsidies and introduced constraints on existing subsidies. Budget expenditures for export subsidies were reduced by 36 percent and volume by 21 percent over the six-year implementation period.
- Subjected developing countries to only two-thirds of the agreed cuts in tariffs, domestic support and export subsidies and over a period of 10 years

Source: IATRC (1994).

Implementation of Market Access Commitments

The primary test of the effectiveness of the new rules for market access is whether countries have converted nontariff border measures to bound tariffs and whether these tariffs have been reduced to remain within maximum agreed (bound) levels. This has generally been the case. With a few exceptions, WTO members have imposed bound tariffs on their agricultural products. The major exception was removed when Japan replaced its quantitative import restriction on rice with a tariff in 1999, though the Republic of Korea has yet to follow suit. Several complaints have alleged that importing countries have violated the requirement not to maintain, resort to, or revert to nontariff measures (URAA Article 4.2), where the justification has involved balance of payments problems.[5] On the other hand, there are many cases, mainly in developing countries, where tariffs are below bound levels and so the bound rates are not the constraining factor on trade (Tangermann and others 1997). Only a small number of complaints have been made to the WTO that a country has used an import regime in violation of its tariff binding.[6]

The nearly universal binding of agricultural tariffs has not, however, completely eliminated measures that resemble the nontariff barriers that existed before the Uruguay Round. Some countries have established sophisticated tariff regimes that act like nontariff barriers. The European Union's post-Uruguay Round entry price regime for fruit and vegetables is similar to its former reference price system (Grethe and Tangermann 1999). Variable tariffs used in Latin America have effects similar to variable levies (Tangermann and others 1997). The European Union's maximum duty-paid import price regime for cereals (also called a margin of preference), established at the request of the United States as a result of the Blair House II agreement, effectively continues the variable levy (Tangermann and others 1997). It is important, though, to note that none of these policies is legally inconsistent with tariff bindings agreed during the Uruguay Round and that the variable tariffs in Latin America and the European Union are below the bound tariff rates.[7]

An innovative, if controversial element of the URAA rules on market access is the special safeguard provision that protects goods subject to tariffication from surges in imports or from the effects of falling world prices. However, the special safeguard provision has been used selectively, and there has been only one dispute involving the provision.[8] Equally controversial has been the administration of the many tariff rate quotas in agriculture, under which countries specify import quantities that incur duties below the bound rates. Including the WTO banana case, which raised many other issues, only three complaints have addressed administration of tariff rate quotas. But there is clearly more dissatisfaction with tariff rate quotas than is apparent from formal WTO complaints, as their administration has been a major point of contention in the Agriculture Committee.

Tariffs in Agricultural Markets

Did the Uruguay Round significantly liberalize trade in agricultural products? Undoubtedly, some market opening was achieved. But despite the adherence to the commitments made in the Uruguay Round to reduce agricultural tariffs, duties on farm products remain very high. In a comprehensive comparative analysis of post-Uruguay Round tariff rates by country and commodity, Gibson and others (2001) estimate the global average of post-Uruguay Round agricultural tariffs at 62 percent.[9] Regional average tariffs for WTO members range from an ad valorem tariff equivalent of 25 percent to 113 percent (figure 2.1). With the exception of the high tariff region of non-EU Western Europe (104 percent), the highest tariffs are in developing country regions: Africa, the Caribbean, and South Asia have average tariffs ranging from 71 percent to 113 percent—all above the global average of 62 percent. Organisation for Economic Cooperation and Development (OECD) economies with agricultural tariffs below the global

Figure 2.1 World Agricultural Tariff Averages, by Region

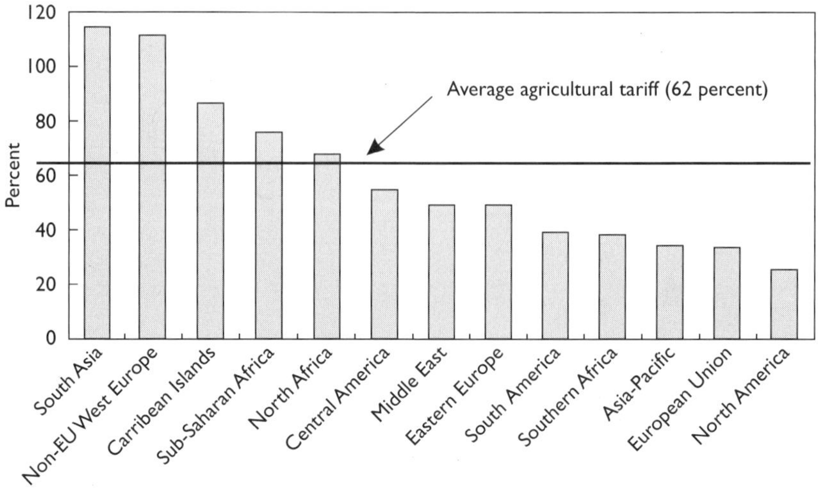

Source: Gibson and others (2001).

average include Canada (24 percent), the European Union (30 percent), Japan (33 percent), Mexico (43 percent), and the United States (12 percent).

The distribution of tariffs across commodities is also revealing. Gibson and others (2001) aggregated agricultural commodities into 46 groups and found that average tariffs for these groups varied from 50 percent to 94 percent. While there are countries with low levels of tariffs, there are few commodities that are not subject to high import tariffs. The average tariff for 18 of the commodity groups (including tobacco, dairy, meats, sugar, sweeteners, and several categories of vegetables, grains, grain products, and breeding animals) exceeded the average for all products (figure 2.2). Tariffs on the remaining 28 commodity groups fell below the 62 percent average tariff. Even the commodity groups with the lowest tariffs (coffee, fiber, several fruit categories, spices, and live horticulture) have a high degree of protection, with an average tariff of 50 percent.

The full impact of these high tariff levels on trade depends on how the tariffs are distributed across countries. OECD tariff protection is very high in many sectors including dairy (116 percent), grains (78 percent), livestock (82 percent), and sugar and sweeteners (64 percent). These are the sectors in which some OECD countries use megatariffs (tariffs higher than 100 percent) and in which notified tariff rate quotas are concentrated. OECD tariffs are relatively low in other sectors. Because tariff spikes for sensitive commodities characterize OECD tariff profiles, there is a large dispersion, or variation, in tariffs across commodities. Non-OECD countries tend to have higher average tariffs than OECD countries, but with less variation across commodity groups. They have high protection for the same commodities as OECD countries, except that

Figure 2.2 World Agricultural Tariff Averages, by Commodity

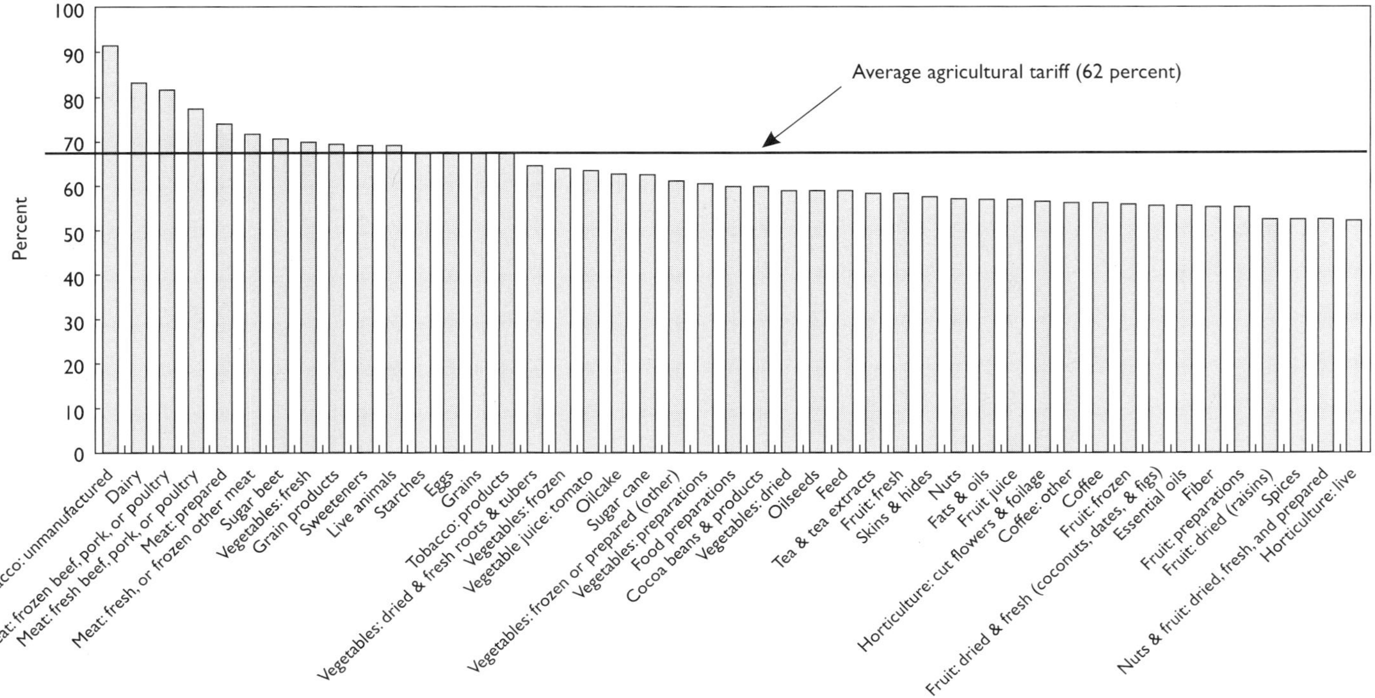

Source: Gibson and others (2001).

tobacco, rather than dairy, has the highest average tariff. Non-OECD countries use megatariffs more than OECD countries. Many of the megatariffs were not subject to reduction under the URAA because they were established as ceiling bindings. However, many developing countries have applied tariff rates that are considerably lower than the bound rates in the WTO schedules.[10]

Tariff Dispersion and Escalation

In addition to the high level of tariffs on agricultural products, variations in levels across countries and commodities are striking. Nonuniform tariffs introduce relative price distortions within countries that can worsen resource misallocation. Similarly, a wide dispersion of tariffs for the same commodity across countries distorts trade and lowers the efficiency and responsiveness of world markets. There is also a concern, especially among developing countries, that tariff dispersion often reflects tariff escalation—low rates on intermediate inputs (such as bulk farm products) and high rates on final products (such as processed foods). This results in high effective rates of protection for value added, and less opportunities for economically viable processing in the countries producing the raw material.[11]

Tariff escalation is a major problem for the agricultural and food systems. The location of processing is important for economic development, particularly since the growth in trade is concentrated in processed products. But the pattern of tariff escalation is itself significant. Wainio, Gibson, and Whitley (2001) find that in both the United States and the European Union, tariffs have a U-shaped distribution over commodity categories that are classified by level of processing. Rates of protection are higher on bulk commodities than on intermediate products and highest on consumer-ready items.[12] This suggests that first-stage processors of raw materials do not get much benefit from tariff protection but those farther up the processing chain may benefit considerably. Japanese tariffs are highest on bulk products, indicating that the tariff structure penalizes its processing sector, while Canada appears to exhibit the same type of tariff escalation as the European Union and the United States, with the tariff structure protecting processing activities.

Comparing tariffs across broad commodity groups is only a rough indicator of the extent of tariff escalation since it does not capture input-output relationships among commodities. More research on a commodity-specific basis is needed to estimate more precisely the extent of tariff escalation.

Tariff Rate Quotas in Agriculture

Tariff rate quotas were introduced to open up markets controlled by nontariff border measures. They have, however, become a controversial aspect of the trade regime for agricultural products. Although tariff rate quotas cover only 6 percent of tariff lines, they are prevalent in sensitive sectors such as meat, dairy, sugar, and cereals. In all, 1,371 tariff rate quotas had been notified to the WTO by 1999, covering a wide variety of bulk and processed products. Tariff rate quotas are used primarily by developed countries: only 37 of the 137 WTO members use them. Abbott and Morse (2000) examined tariff rate quotas for 14 developing countries and found only a few cases of binding quotas. Many countries applied tariff rate quotas as a simple tariff (no higher over-quota tariff was levied, and hence the quota was ineffective). Eastern European countries also appear to be using tariff rate quotas frequently as simple tariffs, enforcing only 65 percent of their tariff rate quotas. Iceland and Norway account for 322 tariff rate quotas, but 90 percent of them are administered as simple tariffs. In fact, quota restrictions are applied for only half of the tariff rate quotas notified to the WTO. As a result, enforcement is concentrated in a relatively small number of developed countries that use them to protect sensitive products.

Although tariff rate quotas were designed to increase market access for commodities that previously faced quantitative barriers, high in-quota and over-quota tariffs imply that tariff rate quotas can still be an impediment to trade.[13] Across all WTO members the average over-quota tariff is 123 percent, suggesting that the tariff rate quotas work in much the same way as the quantitative restrictions that they replaced. Five countries have average over-quota tariffs of at least 150 percent, and in certain instances the over-quota tariffs exceed 1,000 percent (for example, the Japanese tariff on dried peas). Across WTO members the simple average in-quota tariff is 63 percent, similar to that for all types of agricultural tariffs—or even lower, at 50 percent if a few very high tariffs are excluded. High in-quota tariffs have led to low quota fill rates, often below 65 percent. In addition, tariff rate quotas have been administered in different ways, causing exporters to argue for more uniformity.[14] Tariff rate quotas regimes may provide less market access than the architects of the URAA wished.

Special Agricultural Safeguards

Among the other innovations in the market access rules of the URAA, those that relate to safeguards have a particularly significant role in convincing countries that are reluctant to open markets that severe disruption can be avoided. The URAA allows countries to apply special safeguard duties to counter import surges for products whose border protection was "tariffied" and included in the country schedules. Rules governing special safeguards differ from those governing general safeguards in two important respects: actions are exempt from the obligation to compensate and from the threat of suspension of equivalent concessions or other obligations (Perkins 1996), and special safeguards may be invoked only during the reform process, as detailed in the preamble to the URAA. However, if the reform process extends beyond the initial six-year period envisioned in the URAA, the special safeguard would be available during that extended period.

The special safeguard provision allows the imposition of an additional tariff when certain criteria are met: a specified rapid surge in imports (volume trigger) or, on a shipment-by-shipment basis, a fall in the import price below a specified reference price (price trigger). For the volume trigger higher duties apply only until the end of the year in question. For the price trigger an additional duty can be imposed only on the shipment concerned. Additional duties cannot be applied to imports within tariff rate quotas.

Of the 137 WTO members that notified tariff rate quotas, only 38 reserved the right to use special safeguards in their URAA schedule of commitments. The share of agricultural tariff lines covered by special safeguards ranges from less than 1 percent for many developing countries to 9 percent for the United States, 12 percent for Japan, 31 percent for the European Union, 49 percent for Norway, 59 percent for Switzerland, and 66 percent for Poland. The number of tariff items that could potentially be protected by special safeguards ranges from 10 for Australia to 961 for Switzerland.

The coverage across product categories reflects the degree of sensitivity to liberalization in each economy. Product coverage is concentrated in dairy for the United States; cereals for Japan; and meat, dairy products, fruits, and vegetables for the European Union. The United States declared coffee and tea to be covered by special safeguards to prevent the entry of sugar in dry or powdered beverage preparations. Norway and Switzerland reserve the right to use special safeguards across almost all products.

Despite the broad coverage across products, few special safeguard actions have been taken.[15] Since 1995 only the European Union, Japan, and the United States have notified special safeguard actions in almost all years. Of 436 price-based actions reported during 1995–99 the United States accounted for more than a half, Poland for a third, and the European Union for about a tenth. Price-based actions tended to be directed at relatively small volumes of imports from specific sources. Of 213 volume-based actions the European Union and Japan combined accounted for more than 90 percent, with the European Union alone accounting for almost 60 percent. The European Union used the volume-based special safeguards for fruits (particularly citrus) and vegetables (particularly tomatoes).

In practice the special safeguard provision appears to have been used to balance internal markets by Japan, the European Union, and the United States. The US application of price-triggered special safeguard duties on relatively small quantities of individual dairy product imports signaled to exporters that their products would face routinely applied special safeguard duties when trying to gain access to the US market. The European Union used the special safeguard, in concert with other policies and regional agreements, to balance internal markets for perishable fruits and vegetables by restricting imports. Only Poland seems to have resorted to special safeguards on several occasions to counteract inflows of products. The United States has used the price-trigger to place duties on dairy products, peanuts, and sugar-containing powder and dry beverages. Overall, the special safeguard provisions of the URAA appear not to have been used as a haven for countries seeking to avoid their liberalization commitments.

Disciplines on Export Competition

Many observers consider the rules on export subsidies to be the most important element of the URAA, by establishing effective constraints on agricultural policies and affecting trading conditions. Implementation of the rules on export competition should therefore be an important test for the effectiveness of the URAA.

Based on this criterion the URAA appears to have worked rather well, though it should be noted that export subsidies were high in the base period and the first few years of the URAA saw higher world prices and thus lower export subsidies. Above all, the URAA prohibited any new export subsidies and increases in existing export assistance programs. The number of countries that are able to grant export subsidies and the products that they can subsidize are now limited (table 2.1). These limits have generally been observed: there has only been one case in which a country flagrantly exceeded its commitments on the volume of subsidized exports or budgetary outlays or granted export subsidies on products not specified in its schedule.[16] The operation of the export

Table 2.1 Countries Able to Use Export Subsidies and Number of Eligible Products

Country	Number of eligible products
Australia	5
Brazil	16
Bulgaria	44
Canada	11
Colombia	18
Cyprus	9
Czech Republic	16
European Union	20
Hungary	16
Iceland	2
Indonesia	1
Israel	6
Mexico	5
New Zealand	1
Norway	11
Panama	1
Poland	17
Romania	13
Slovak Republic	17
South Africa	62
Switzerland-Liechtenstein	5
Turkey	44
United States	13
Uruguay	3
Venezuela, R.B. de	72

Source: WTO (2000c).

competition rules has been without major controversy, with the exception of the case of Canadian dairy policy, discussed below.[17]

But these data give a misleading picture of the extent of export subsidies. Overall, WTO members used less than 40 percent of their allowable export subsidy outlays on aggregate from 1995 to 1998 (table 2.2). Many agricultural policy developments underlay this phenomenon, and high world market prices for some agricultural commodities during the URAA implementation period (in particular for cereals in 1995 and 1996) also helped. Moreover, there was "water" in the export subsidy commitments, as the base period chosen for setting the constraints was characterized by particularly large expenditures. Nonetheless, based on the aggregate quantitative experience with the export subsidy commitments, this part of the URAA appears to have been implemented with few problems.

It is also important to note that the mere existence of this new type of rule for agricultural trade policies, and the expectation that further reductions will be negotiated in future WTO negotiations, have been important in the domestic agricultural policy debate in the European Union. Cuts in support prices agreed in 1999 (the so-called Agenda 2000 reforms) were intended to make it possible for the European Union to reduce, if not eliminate, export subsidies for some products. One of the major objectives of the mid-term review of the Common Agriculture Policy, agreed in June 2003, was to further reduce the dependence of EU agricultural policies on export subsidies. Other countries also changed policies to meet export subsidy limits. Canada eliminated its rail subsidies for grains in 1995. Switzerland began reforms in 1999 to eliminate state trading of dairy products. Australia replaced dairy export subsidies with rebates of a new production levy and then eliminated that levy in 2000.

WTO rules are the product of negotiation but sometimes need to be tested in the dispute settlement process. These challenges can occur in somewhat unlikely commodity markets and result in decisions with wider significance.

Table 2.2 Export Subsidy Commitments, Outlays, and Utilization (US$ millions)

	1995	1996	1997	1998	1995–98
All WTO members					
Commitments	21,036	19,800	17,432	12,987	71,255
Notifications[a]	6,812	7,857	5,931	5,533	26,134
Utilization (percent)	32.4	39.7	34.0	42.6	36.7
European Union					
Commitments	14,573	13,870	12,100	8,333	48,876
Notifications	6,058	7,088	5,262	4,849	23,257
Utilization (percent)	41.6	51.1	43.5	58.2	47.6

Source: Calculated from figures in WTO (2000c).

a. Reported subsidy outlays are not comprehensive for 1996, 1997, and 1998 as some countries had not yet notified their export subsidies by the time the WTO Secretariat produced its background paper on export subsidies.

The most important challenge to an agricultural trade policy has focused on Canada's dairy regime, which some countries felt was inconsistent with Canada's WTO obligations, particularly on export subsidies.[18] The issue was whether the price pooling regime in Canada amounted to an export subsidy as defined in Article 9 of the URAA, and hence whether Canada had violated its obligations by exporting dairy products in excess of its export subsidy commitments. The panel found that Canada's regime amounted to a producer-financed export subsidy, and the Appellate Body agreed. Canada accepted the outcome and adjusted its policy. However, a WTO panel later ruled that the steps taken were insufficient.

The outcome of the dispute has implications that go far beyond the Canadian dairy regime. The dispute has led to other challenges, such as that by Australia, Brazil, and Thailand on EU sugar policy. The Canada dairy case therefore has the potential to contribute significantly to strengthening the export subsidy provisions of the URAA and their application through the dispute settlement route in parallel to that through negotiations. One need only to compare this outcome with the ineffective disputes over Article XVI:3 of the General Agreement on Tariffs and Trade (GATT) prior to the Uruguay Round to see how much the URAA has strengthened the legal disciplines on agricultural policies (Josling and Tangermann 2003).

Current Extent of Export Subsidies

Though the URAA has curbed export subsidies, they remain a major factor in world commodity markets. Between 1995 and 2000 WTO members spent more than $36 billion subsidizing exports, with the European Union accounting for nearly 90 percent, Switzerland for 5 percent, and the United States for less than 2 percent (table 2.3). The European Union is the largest user of export subsidies in both value and volume terms.[19] According to WTO notifications, the European Union spent an average of $6 billion annually from 1995 to 1998 on export subsidies, though expenditures fell in 2000 with firmer prices (and weaker currencies).

Export subsidies are focused on relatively few commodities. Total expenditures on export subsidies by WTO members have been greatest for dairy products—accounting for 34 percent of all export subsidy expenditures from 1995 to 1998. Among individual commodities beef has the largest subsidy expenditures at 21 percent, averaging $1.4 billion a year. Grains, sugar, and processed products together accounted for 35 percent of expenditures.

From 1995 to 1998 the European Union subsidized nearly all of its exports of coarse grains, butter and butter oil, beef, skim milk powder, and much of its wheat and other dairy exports. Switzerland subsidizes exports of breeding cattle and horses, dairy products, fruit, potatoes, and processed products. Dairy products account for 65 percent of Swiss subsidy expenditures and nearly 80 percent of subsidized export volume—averaging nearly $230 million and 59,000 tons per year. Nearly 98 percent of US export subsidy expenditures have

Table 2.3 Total Expenditure on Export Subsidies by Country, 1995–2000 (US$ millions)

Economy	1995	1996	1997	1998	1999[a]	2000[a]
European Union	6,495.9	7,470.3	4,856.7	5,989.0	5,853.7	2,516.6
United States	25.6	121.5	112.2	146.7	80.2	15.3
Switzerland	454.6	355.4	294.5	292.8	268.9	187.7
Norway	83.9	77.9	99.9	76.9	116.0	44.0
Rest of world	267.0	227.5	194.6	162.3	177.4	442.8

Source: US Department of Agriculture, Economic Research Service calculations based on WTO notifications.

a. Not all countries had notified as yet for these years.

been for dairy products, just under 2 percent for poultry, and less than 1 percent for coarse grains.

The URAA did not explicitly restrict per unit subsidies; consequently, the size of subsidies has varied greatly across countries and commodities. Subsidy expenditures on a dollar per ton basis have been largest for such high-value products as alcohol, wine, and fresh flowers. However, those commodities account for less than 1 percent of subsidized export expenditures and subsidized export volume. In terms of sectors, dairy has had the largest subsidies per ton. Such subsidies would be expected to have decreased over the implementation period of the URAA, because both permissible volume and value limits were declining. Generally, export subsidies have trended downward recently, due both to market conditions and exchange rates and to reductions in the difference between domestic and world prices.

Use of Export Credits in Agriculture

Export subsidies are not the only policies to distort commodity export markets. Subsidies given through advantageous credit terms have also come under scrutiny. The Uruguay Round was unable to deal with this issue, and subsequent negotiations in the OECD did not bear fruit. This has become an important element in the current trade talks, as the European Union has insisted that the use of export credits (mainly by the United States) be disciplined if the European Union is to reduce its use of export subsidies.

Short-term export credit is important to many international transactions. Governments are commonly involved in export credit activity, both for agriculture and for other commodities. This "officially supported export credit," as it is termed by the OECD and the WTO, can include state agencies (including state traders) that offer credit, interest rate subsidies offered by government, government assumption of default risk for private loans, and publicly supported or subsidized insurance offered to private lenders. For agricultural commodities, default risk guarantees are the most common form of officially supported export credit. Insurance schemes and credit offered by state trading agencies are also used. Explicit interest rate subsidies are uncommon.

Officially supported export credit can act as a subsidy if the terms of the loans are more favorable than those available in the market. For example, if the interest rate does not fully reflect country risk premiums, a subsidy element is present. The extent of the subsidy depends on interest rates relative to market rates (appropriately reflecting risk), fees charged, down payments required, and the term of the loan. The longer the term for a given interest rate, down payment, and fee structure, the greater the subsidy element. Since risk premiums reflect default risk (at least in theory), the subsidy element of programs that involve default risk guarantees can be gauged from the extent to which government budgetary outlays are required to pay off guarantees.

A detailed OECD (2000) study on officially supported export credit programs indicates that the use of export credits in agricultural markets increased from $5.5 billion in 1995 to $7.9 billion in 1998. Credits represented 3.6 percent of the value of total agricultural exports in 1995 and 5.2 percent in 1998. That expansion was likely to have been caused by deteriorating financial market conditions, especially the Asian financial crisis in 1997. Interest rates increased substantially during 1998, reflecting the continuing financial crisis.

Few countries used export credits to any significant extent. Only four countries had subsidies that exceeded 1 percent: 6.6 percent in the United States, 3.8 percent in Norway, 3.8 percent in France, and 1.2 percent in Canada. The distortions to trade patterns due to export credits are therefore likely to be relatively small.

Less than half of the loans offered under officially supported export credit programs are for a term of more than one year, and more than 96 percent of these are from the United States, which accounts for 88 percent of the estimated subsidy value of these programs. The European Union accounts for 7 percent of export credit subsidies, Canada for 4 percent, and Australia for 1 percent. Thus, the potential use of export credits as subsidies is largely a US issue. Since the URAA the United States has relied largely on export credits rather than direct export subsidies, whereas the European Union has relied on direct export subsidies.

Bulk cereals are the most important commodity group that benefit from subsidized export credits. More than one-third of subsidies in 1996–97 went to cereals, and up to 14.5 percent (in 1997) of cereal exports received credit subsidies. However, officially supported export credit programs exist for a wide variety of commodities. The OECD report also notes that most subsidized credits are applied to trade between its member countries. The least developed countries accounted for only 0.2 percent of export credits, and food-importing developing countries for only 8.9 percent. For this reason the OECD concludes that disciplines on agricultural export credits would not greatly harm poorer food importing countries. The OECD suggests that this is indirect evidence that liquidity constraints for such countries are not being relieved. However, the study shows increasing use of export credits during the Asian financial crisis, when liquidity constraints were likely to be binding.

Domestic Support

The URAA was most innovative in the area of domestic support, establishing new rules that strongly distinguish agriculture from industry. Despite that, this is the area in which country commitments are the weakest and the effectiveness and workability of the URAA have been least tested. The URAA established bindings on domestic agricultural support mainly through limits on the total aggregate measurement of support. Reduction commitments were intended to constrain domestic support measures that encourage agricultural production or raise consumer prices and are therefore considered to distort trade (amber box policies). The URAA also specifies measures that are not subject to reduction. Countries are not required to include direct payments under certain production-limiting programs (blue box policies) in their aggregate measurement of support. More widely applicable are the green box exemptions for policies that are considered to have minimal or no trade-distorting effects or effects on production. In addition there are *de minimis* provisions that allow countries to omit from their reduction commitments a fraction of specific and nonspecific support payments.

Developing countries can exempt a somewhat larger set of policy instruments from commitment and reduction. It was recognized that government assistance for agricultural and rural development is an integral part of the development programs of developing countries, and investment subsidies for agriculture and input subsidies for low-income or resource-poor producers in these countries are exempt from reductions. In addition, support to encourage diversification away from illicit narcotic crops is exempt. These provisions are known collectively as Article 6.2 exemptions.

Since 1995 levels of domestic support, as measured by the current total aggregate measurement of support, have remained considerably below allowed levels in many countries. Only two countries exceeded the commitment level in any individual year, and both were special cases.[20] In all years since 1995 for which notifications are available, around half of WTO members with domestic support notifications used less than 60 percent of their domestic support commitments.

To some extent, this significant slack is due to the use of a generous base period. In the European Union, and in the past in the United States, it also reflects the importance of the blue box, which shelters a large part of actual support to farmers in the form of direct payments. In other cases, though, the low utilization of domestic support commitments reflects policy changes, with support decoupled from production and moved into the green box. The US Federal Agricultural Improvement and Reform (FAIR) Act of 1996 is the most prominent example of such a shift, though subsequent "emergency" legislation introduced in 1998 and enshrined in the 2002 Farm Security and Rural Investment Act "re-coupled" some of the support. Asian countries, especially Japan and the Republic of Korea, also made considerable changes in agricultural policy in response to WTO commitments.

The fact that domestic support commitments have not (yet) proved restrictive may explain why there has been only one WTO complaint.[21] That case reinforced the methodology for calculating the aggregate measurement of support and in that sense showed that the URAA is effective and operational in this area. Another part of the URAA rules on domestic support, though, still remains to be tested—the eligibility of policies for inclusion in the green box. There have been no legal challenges to countries' decisions to place their policy measures in the various boxes.[22] Either the system is working well or the rules are deemed to have inadequate teeth to make a challenge worthwhile. If most countries are well within their allowable total aggregate measurement of support levels, it makes little sense to challenge green box policies to have them declared amber.

To ensure that policies that qualify under the green box are not subject to challenge by rules that apply to nonagricultural subsidies, the URAA provided for "due restraint." The peace clause, as this provision is known, specified that domestic support measures that conform to the green box provisions are nonactionable subsidies under the Agreement on Subsidies and Countervailing Measures and were consequently exempt from countervailing duties and from challenge under the WTO doctrine of protection against "nullification or impairment" of benefits (table 2.4). Other domestic support was also protected against similar actions unless support levels were raised above those in place in 1992.[23] For this reason, challenges to domestic support policies during the life of the peace clause were unlikely to have succeeded (Steinberg and Josling 2003). The peace clause expired at the end of 2003, however, and any rebirth will depend on agreement in the current negotiations that it is necessary and desirable to shelter agricultural subsidies from the Agreement on Subsidies and Countervailing Measures.

If the URAA is judged purely on the basis of the total level of support for agriculture, its impact appears limited. Domestic support levels in the European Union and the United States were as high in the late 1990s as in the 1986–88 base period (OECD 2001a). In the weak market conditions of 1998–2001 developed country support for agriculture was at levels comparable to those at the beginning of the Uruguay Round, although there were modest declines in 2002 in some countries (OECD 2003). Support levels remain high in large part because of a few key sectors, such as dairy and sugar, where adjustments to less production- and trade-distorting outcomes have yet to take place. In these sectors domestic prices are high relative to international prices and transfers from consumers and taxpayers are substantial.

The URAA scores somewhat better on the nature of domestic support (table 2.5). It has reinforced the shift from nonexempt (amber box) to exempt (green box or blue box) domestic support, even if it has not ensured that total support has been reduced. Countries have considerable flexibility under the provisions of the green and blue box categories as well as under the *de minimis* provisions. An evaluation of the impact of the domestic support rules in the

Table 2.4 Extent of Protection of Domestic Support by the Peace Clause

	Countervailing duties	Subsidies and countervailing measures, Articles 5 and 6	GATT 1994 Article XVI	Nonviolation of nullification or impairment of benefits
Green box	Not actionable	Not actionable	Not actionable	Not actionable
Amber and blue box subsidies that conform	Actionable but with "due restraint"	Not actionable (if subsidies do not exceed 1992 levels)	Not actionable (if subsidies do not exceed 1992 levels)	Not actionable (if subsidies do not exceed 1992 levels)

Source: Steinberg and Josling (2003).

URAA must therefore rest on the effectiveness of this shift in reducing trade distortions.

Effectiveness of Amber Box Constraints

In meeting total aggregate measurement of support commitment levels agreed in the URAA, WTO members were required to notify agricultural support to the WTO Committee on Agriculture. Domestic support is highly concentrated in a few countries. Together accounting for nearly 95 percent of domestic support notified to the WTO, the United States, the European Union, and Japan "used" only 85 percent, 69 percent, and 18 percent, respectively, of their "available" aggregate measurement of support in 1999 (table 2.6).[24] Canada, as a result of substantial changes in policy, notified subsidies to the extent of only 17 percent of its ceiling, and Mexico reported subsidies amounting to only 14 percent of its agreed limits.[25] Norway, Switzerland, and the Republic of Korea made fuller use of their "available" aggregate measurement of support, as did Argentina, but whether this means that the support would have been greater in the absence of the limits or that the limits provided a target expenditure for support is not always apparent from the numbers.

To meet their URAA commitments, some countries have reduced their aggregate measurement of support levels by shifting domestic support from nonexempt to exempt categories. More than 60 percent of the domestic support in OECD countries is now excluded from reduction commitments under the green box, ranging from all support in the green box category in New Zealand to less than 25 percent of support in that category in the European Union (OECD 2001b).

Table 2.5 Total Agricultural Support, United States, European Union, Japan, and All Others 1995–99 (US$ millions)

		Amber box	Blue box	Green box	Total
United States	1995	6,214	7,030	46,041	59,285
	1996	5,898	0	51,825	57,723
	1997	6,238	0	51,252	57,490
	1998	10,392	0	49,824	60,216
	1999	16,862	0	49,749	66,611
European Union	1995	66,524	27,720	24,972	119,217
	1996	64,815	27,345	28,120	120,280
	1997	55,896	22,765	20,230	98,891
	1998	52,394	23,012	21,513	96,919
	1999	49,933	20,638	20,783	91,354
Japan	1995	36,767	0	33,219	69,986
	1996	29,765	0	25,192	54,957
	1997	25,851	0	21,616	47,467
	1998	5,911	387	23,150	29,448
	1999	6,689	829	24,022	31,541
All others[a]	1995	12,064	1,156	28,011	41,231
	1996	10,402	1,119	42,573	54,094
	1997	9,487	1,019	24,094	34,600
	1998	8,301	1,039	16,281	25,621
	1999	4,079	967	10,970	16,016

Source: US Department of Agriculture, Economic Research Service calculations based on WTO notifications.

a. The number of countries included varies by year, depending on notifications of January 1, 2003.

Blue Box and Green Box Exemptions

The URAA reductions in domestic support applied to elements of farm programs that were deemed to be the most trade distorting. Other programs were exempted from the reduction commitments. The principal exemptions for developed countries were for programs in the blue and green boxes. The European Union argued in the Uruguay Round for the blue box as a way of sheltering its compensatory payments, under the 1992 reform of the Common Agricultural Policy, from reduction commitments. The United States used the blue box for its 1995 deficiency payments for similar reasons, but the blue box became of little significance to the United States subsequent to the Farm Act of 1996. Japan placed its rice policies in the blue box in 1998, replacing the rice support formerly subject to reduction in the amber box. Other countries using this provision include Norway and, in the past, Iceland and the Slovak Republic. In 1995, $35 billion of blue box support was notified to the WTO, 77 percent of it by the European Union. With the elimination of US deficiency payments,

Table 2.6 Current Aggregate Measurement of Support as Share of Ceiling, Selected Countries (percent)

Year	United States	European Union	Japan	Canada	Norway	Argentina	Korea, Rep.	Mexico	Switzerland
1995	26.9	63.6	73.1	15.0	70.7	143.8	95.1	4.8	83.3
1996	26.5	66.8	71.8	12.3	78.8	99.9	93.4	3.2	73.8
1997	29.0	67.8	70.9	10.8	81.7	99.9	95.5	11.5	71.9
1998	50.2	65.1	17.8	16.9	87.8	99.4	80.1	13.8	71.0
1999	84.7	68.9	18.1	—	90.4	99.6	82.8	—	—

Sources: WTO notifications and US Department of Agriculture, Economic Research Service website.

Note: Table excludes *de minimis* exceptions.

—, not available.

the total dropped to roughly $27 billion in 1996, 96 percent of which was in the European Union.

The use of green box measures has expanded over the implementation period for the URAA. Several countries, including Australia, Canada, the Republic of Korea, and the United States notified new or modified green box measures to the WTO. A total of 63 new green box measures were notified for 1995–98. In 1996, $127 billion of green box support was notified to the WTO. The two leading categories of support were domestic food aid (32 percent) and infrastructural and general services (28 percent). Other forms of support, such as investment aids, environmental programs, and decoupled direct payments, each accounted for 6–8 percent of total green box support. However, not all green box measures are equally trade neutral, and not all countries accept that the shift to green box support removes the problem of subsidized production. This issue surfaced at the WTO Ministerial Meeting in Cancún as a point of contention between developed and developing countries.

Food Aid and the WTO

Of interest to many developing countries is the treatment of food aid in the WTO. Though the WTO as an institution is not involved in setting food aid policies, there is a clear overlap with trade rules, particularly in the area of export competition. Both the URAA and a Ministerial Decision included in the Marrakesh Treaty address food aid. Article 10.4 of the URAA states that food aid shall not be tied to commercial exports of agricultural products to recipient countries, must be carried out in accordance with the Food and Agriculture Organization's Principles of Surplus Disposal and Consultative Obligations, and be provided fully in grant form or meet concessional terms, as provided in Article 4 of the 1986 Food Aid Convention. The Ministerial Decision on Measures Concerning the Possible Negative Effects of the Reform Programme on Least Developed and Net Food Importing Developing Countries committed the WTO to:

- Review the level of food aid established by the Committee on Food Aid under the Food Aid Convention 1986 and to initiate negotiations in the appropriate forum to establish a level of food aid commitments sufficient to meet the legitimate needs of developing countries during the reform period.
- Adopt guidelines to ensure that an increasing percentage of basic food stuffs is provided to least developed and net food importing developing countries fully in grant form or on appropriate concessional terms in line with Article IV of the Food Aid Convention of 1986.
- Give full consideration to requests for the provision of technical and financial assistance to least developed and net food importing countries to improve their agricultural productivity and infrastructure.

A mix of national and multilateral agencies provides food aid. The United States is the largest donor, providing 40–60 percent of total donations in the 1990s. Multilateral agencies have delivered 28–42 percent of food aid since 1994. Most multilateral aid is delivered through the United Nations World Food Programme. Actual deliveries of food aid exhibit substantial variability. Food aid was nearly 13 million metric tons (mmt) in 1994, declined to 7.2 mmt in 1996, and rose to 14.5 mmt in 1999. While a variety of foods are used as food aid, cereals continue to account for about 87 percent of the total (WFP 2000). Cereal food aid averaged less than 0.5 percent of world cereal production, or about 9 percent of cereal imports by low-income food deficit countries.

The delivery of food aid has been, and to some extent remains, greatly influenced by availability. For recipients, the role of surplus disposal in donor food aid programs has resulted in less food aid during times of global food shortage, when prices are high and stocks are low. In an attempt to better address recipient needs, donors commit to provide a minimum amount of food aid for a specified period of time through Food Aid Conventions. The first Food Aid Convention, negotiated in 1967, guaranteed minimum commitments of 4.5 mmt of food aid. This rose to 7.5 mmt in 1986, although actual donations exceeded the minimum in many years. In 1999 donors decreased their pledged commitments to 4.8 mmt—the lowest amount since the initiation of the program—though actual donations were nearly three times the commitments. Current donor obligations are expressed in terms of tons of food, not dollars, which should assist the maintenance of minimum food aid levels regardless of cereal prices. However, in recent years the United States has continued its historical pattern of varying its food aid donations in line with its wheat and other cereal stocks.

Food aid was one of the concerns expressed by least developed and net food importing countries, which anticipated difficulties in importing adequate supplies of food under reasonable terms during implementation of Uruguay Round reforms. The Ministerial Decision has not entirely met those concerns. One problem is the ambiguity of its language, making it difficult for the parties to agree whether commitments have been met. Eleven developing countries stated in their WTO position paper that "Despite the promises, there has been no political will to activate the Marrakesh Decision in order to address the problems of net-food-importing developing countries (NFIDC). This had been the avenue developing countries had expected to receive compensation for the negative effects of liberalization" (WTO 2000a).

State Trading in the WTO

Treatment of state trading enterprises is the subject of ongoing discussion in the WTO. State trading comes under the purview of the Uruguay Round Understanding on Interpretation of Article XVII, which established a working definition of a state trading enterprise and notification requirements, as well as under the URAA, which subjects such enterprises to rules on market access and subsidies.

Over the past several years, notification requirements have been tightened, generating information to judge the impact of state trading enterprises on trade flows. Thirty countries have notified the WTO of the existence of nearly 100 state trading enterprises. Because of differing interpretations and ambiguities in definitions, it is likely that not all state trading enterprises have been notified. State trading enterprises are generally used for politically sensitive commodities—grains, sugar, and dairy—a reflection of the importance of domestic agricultural policy objectives as the underlying reason for this type of institution.

The importance of state trading enterprises in agricultural trade has generally been declining in recent years. While nearly 90 percent of rice and wheat trade was handled by state traders in the 1970s (Schmitz and others 1981; Falcon and Monke 1980), the share fell to between 33 percent and 50 percent by the late 1990s (Abbott and Young 1999; Young 1999). The decline is due largely to the impact of structural adjustment programs. Implementing the redistributional objectives of these agencies is costly, in both domestic resources and foreign exchange, and contributed to the macroeconomic imbalances that led to structural adjustment programs. Pressure from international institutions prompted reform of these institutions. Many Asian countries avoided the pressures through better management of debt and foreign exchange, and so less reform occurred in that region.

To date, the WTO has had very little to do with the reform or elimination of state trading. Countries have resisted elimination of state trading enterprises since they are used to implement domestic policy. A common reform has been to permit private trading entities to coexist with public agencies. In some cases state trading enterprises continue to manage imports of lower quality products targeted toward poorer consumers, while private agents handle trade for higher quality products. The coexistence of state trading enterprises with private traders is likely to reduce the monopoly power of the state trader. However, the state trader may retain certain special privileges. Reform has also been accomplished through privatization. An example of this is the reform of the Australian Wheat Board, which has become similar to a producer cooperative and is required to operate without government subsidization.

PROGRESS, OPTIONS, AND PROPOSALS IN THE CURRENT TALKS

The agricultural negotiations, at the time of writing, have reached the crucial stage at which compromises must be made. This section describes the range of options that faced negotiators at the start of the talks and the way in which they have been consolidated during negotiation. An understanding of the options discussed is an important part of assessing whatever conclusions may be reached at the end of the negotiations.

The stages of the talks and the timetable for their completion are summarized in table 2.7. The initial stage of the talks involved seven meetings of the Agriculture Committee (meeting in special session) at which an impressive array of proposals were tabled.[26] These proposals were contained in 45 documents representing the opinions of 85 percent of the WTO membership.[27] Notably different from the Uruguay Round was the high level of interest and involvement by developing countries. After a stocktaking meeting in March 2001, a second phase began that focused on particular topics. Few new proposals were generated at that time, and for the most part countries put their ideas in "non-papers" that have not been released by the WTO Secretariat. The third phase, that of negotiating the modalities, began in June 2002 and was due to end in March 2003.[28] It did not prove possible to agree on the text of the modalities by the end of March. A short period of six months had been set aside for the submission of draft schedules based on the modalities agreement, which would then have been discussed at the Ministerial Meeting in Cancún in September 2003. The timetable slipped significantly, as agreement on the modalities before the Ministerial Meeting proved elusive. Instead, the task at Cancún was revised to the more limited aim of reaching an agreement on a framework for the modalities, with the nature of the reductions and the depth of cuts in tariffs and subsidies to be added later.

In the lead-up to the Cancún Ministerial Meeting considerable progress was made in clarifying issues and options. The chairman of the Agriculture Committee, Stuart Harbinson, presented an overview paper in December 2002 that listed options raised by countries in the course of the negotiations and looked

Table 2.7 Timetable of the WTO Agricultural Negotiations

Date	Stage
March 2000	The negotiating committee is established and the chairman is appointed
March 2000–March 2001	Phase I. Initial position papers are presented by many countries
March 2001–February 2002	Phase II. Countries elaborate on specific topics and discuss alternatives
November 2001	Doha Ministerial Meeting confirms objectives and sets timetable for agricultural negotiations
March 2002–March 2003	Modalities were to be developed for further trade reform steps, but the deadline is missed. Harbinson draft not found acceptable
March 2003–September 2003	Negotiations focus on a framework for approval at Cancún rather than modalities. No framework agreed before Cancún
September 2003	WTO Ministerial Meeting in Cancún takes stock of progress on agriculture, but fails to agree on a framework for agriculture
July 2004	Framework agreed for the Doha Round, including for agriculture
December 2005	WTO Ministerial in Hong Kong failed to agree on modalities for negotiations
December 2006	Schedules due to be verified and agreement reached to signal end of negotiations (unlikely)

Source: Author's compilation based on information on the WTO website (www.wto.org).

for similarities in these positions (WTO 2002). Following this overview and discussions with the delegates in January 2003, the chairman prepared a draft of the modalities that could form the basis for an agreement. The "Harbinson draft" was presented to delegates for discussion at the February meeting of the Agriculture Committee and revised for the March meeting (WTO 2003). Though not universally accepted as a basis for negotiations, the draft stimulated intensified talks. In July the chairman reported to the WTO Trade Negotiating Committee, giving his own interpretation of the issues to be decided.

A flurry of activity in the month leading up to Cancún gave some hope that a Framework Agreement would emerge from the Ministerial Meeting. On August 13, 2003, the European Union and the United States tabled a joint proposal in an effort to focus on a feasible modalities framework before Cancún. In response, on August 20 Brazil, China, India, South Africa, and 16 other developing countries, eventually to be known as the Group of 20 or G-20, presented their version of the framework for the agricultural modalities.[29] Taking into account these new proposals, the Trade Negotiating Committee included an outline of a framework in the draft document for Cancún that it presented to the General Council in late August. The chairman of the General Council, Caros Pérez del Castillo, presented his suggestions to the ministers at Cancún as the Draft Ministerial Declaration.

At Cancún much of the time was taken up by trying to resolve the agricultural issues. The G-20 insisted that its draft be discussed along with the Castillo draft, as that paper was seen as too close to the EU-US joint proposal. A facilitator, George Yeo, appointed to attempt to forge a compromise, produced a draft modalities framework that was incorporated into another version of the ministerial draft, presented by Luis Ernesto Derbez Bautista, the chairman of the General Council at the ministerial level. The Derbez draft, though widely criticized, remained on the table when the Ministerial Meeting was closed. The combination of the original proposals, the Harbinson draft, the Harbinson report to the Trade Negotiation Committee, the US-EU agreement, and the subsequent set of suggestions from G-20 offered a reasonable range of options from which an eventual settlement could have emerged at Cancún. Indeed, the Derbez draft included elements of most of these earlier proposals. But the ministers failed to close the gap between the G-20 and EU-US positions on key aspects of domestic support reduction.

In the first few months of 2004 another effort was made in Geneva to find common ground in the agricultural positions of the various groups. Eventually, as a result of the work of the "Five Interested Parties," a compromise was reached in the early hours of August 1.[30] The new document, referred to as the "July Framework Agreement" because it was largely negotiated in that month, covered all the main areas of the Doha Agenda (WTO 2004). But it was in agriculture that the most specific language was crafted.[31]

The next step, and one originally scheduled for the period before the Cancún Ministerial Meeting, was to move from the framework of an agreement to the modalities.[32] The target for such modalities was set as the Hong Kong Ministerial Meeting in December 2005. This would have given time for the modalities to be translated into draft schedules of tariffs and subsidies by country and for those schedules to be checked and verified. Final agreement would then take place by June 2007, when the US "fast track" authority (now known as "trade promotion" authority) expires.[33]

The slow progress on developing the modalities continued in the months following the Framework Agreement. The end of July deadline for agreement on a "first approximation" of the modalities was missed, both for agriculture and for other tariff negotiations. A high-level meeting in Dalien, China, and a discussion among several countries in Paris at the time of a September OECD meeting gave some signs that the hard bargaining was about to start. But it was the circulation of a proposal from the G-20 along with the tabling of proposals from the United States and the European Union at a mini-ministerial at Zurich in Switzerland in October 2005 that finally gave some impetus to the talks. Nevertheless, by July 2006 negotiations had once again stalled.

In the absence of any new and more radical ideas, a final agreement will likely reflect some combination of these EU, US, and G-20 suggestions, modified by the reaction to them of the G-10 and other groups. The options discussed below reflect this tentative convergence toward an eventual modalities agreement.

OPTIONS FOR IMPROVING MARKET ACCESS

The negotiations on market access are the most significant and contentious aspect of the agricultural talks. A major reduction in tariffs could revitalize agricultural markets and rationalize trade patterns. However, many countries are concerned about the effect on their uncompetitive industries and have argued for more modest approaches to market opening. The talks have therefore been about the methods and the extent of cuts to tariffs, the level and administration of tariff rate quotas, and the use of safeguards against import surges. Several options have been suggested for resolving these questions, and the final choice will go a long way toward defining the nature of the post-Doha agricultural trade regime.

Choosing a Tariff-Cutting Method

If tariff cuts are at the heart of trade negotiations, the way in which such cuts are made determines the ultimate distribution of benefits and costs. In the "request and offer" technique, used in the first five rounds of GATT negotiations, participants tried to balance their "concessions" against those that they sought from others.[34] The problem is that the request and offer approach had a tendency to focus on a few easy sectors, since highly protected sectors have nothing to gain from concessions in export markets. The result is that dispersion in levels of protection increases, and the reduction in the average rate of protection can be modest.

Another form of negotiation takes a sectoral approach, in the current context usually associated with zero-for-zero agreements. All countries agree to drop tariffs to zero for a particular sector (and often to eliminate export subsides as well). The advantage is the opportunity to increase market access for specific commodities with low levels of protection (Meilke, Wensley, and Cluff 2001). But this approach is also unlikely to open heavily protected markets and may even entrench protection, since there are fewer gains to be had in return for concessions in sensitive products. On the other hand, the approach does allow trade liberalization to proceed to nearly free trade in some sectors.

A third negotiating approach, and the one that has been agreed for this current round, involves formula cuts in tariffs. Formula reductions can be as simple as a given percentage across the board cut in all tariffs over a given period or as complicated as the negotiators' imaginations allow. The approach can produce very different results depending on the formula adopted. There are two generic types of formulas: linear or across the board reductions that target the level of tariffs, and harmonization formulas that reduce both the level and the dispersion of tariffs (including tariff peaks and tariff escalation) by reducing high tariffs proportionately more than low tariffs (Wainio, Gibson, and Whitley 2001).[35] Harmonization formulas are flexible enough that negotiators can achieve any degree of tariff liberalization they wish. Given the tariff profiles in agriculture, the Swiss formula, which allows for a ceiling tariff and the elimination of nuisance tariffs, would seem to be the most effective. But the use of an across-the-board cut as in the Uruguay Round has also been suggested. More complex tariff-cutting schemes, which Josling and Rae (1999) refer to as a "cocktail" approach, have also been suggested that use different formulas for different tariff levels.

Agreement on the method of tariff cutting has been difficult to reach. The major players have championed different approaches to tariff cutting. The main division has been between those that favor a Swiss formula approach, led by the United States, and those that prefer a Uruguay Round approach, as suggested by the European Union.[36] As a compromise, the 2003 Harbinson draft proposed different cuts depending on the initial height of the tariff, a banded approach that mimicked, though less directly, the impact of a Swiss formula that brings high tariffs down rapidly to a predetermined level. Cuts would be made from bound rates, and specific and variable tariffs would be reduced by calculating an ad valorem equivalent.[37]

The Harbinson suggestions for tariff cutting still left the United States and the European Union unsatisfied, the one arguing that the proposals were not ambitious enough and the other indicating that they penalized countries that started with higher tariffs. The US-EU proposal of August 13 compromises in a different way, by dividing agricultural commodities (tariff lines) into three groups. One group would be reduced on a Swiss Formula basis, one would be reduced on the basis of the Uruguay Round cuts, and one would be granted duty-free entry. This would allow all countries to shelter some sensitive products from sharp cuts in tariffs.[38] In addition there would be a tariff cap, with the option of increasing tariff rate quotas to have an equivalent effect.

The G-20 broadly supported this three-method approach for developed countries but added the requirement of a steady increase in tariff rate quotas and the reduction of within-quota tariffs to zero. Their formulation would also have allowed developing countries to choose between a Uruguay Round cut, a formula, or tariff elimination for a certain percentage of their tariff lines, but not be subject to a tariff cap. The G-20 formulation would also have removed the special agricultural safeguard for developed countries. In addition, they insisted on the development of a special safeguard mechanism for developing countries and the creation of a category of special products, as in the Harbinson draft.

The General Council chairman's draft in the lead-up to the Cancún Ministerial Meeting closely followed the EU-US paper on developed country obligations, but was significantly more lenient on developing countries. The special product category was retained from the Harbinson draft, and developing countries were allowed to keep tariffs above the cap. The Derbez draft of September 13, 2003, adopted the EU-US formula for three reduction methods, suggested a target for the average tariff cut, retained the notion of a tariff cap with a tariff rate quota option, and agreed with the Harbinson proposal to reduce tariff escalation.

Negotiations on the tariff cutting formula proved difficult, but eventually some progress was made. The Framework Agreement of July 2004 specified that conditions of market access be improved through significant tariff cuts, using a tiered formula that imposes higher percentage cuts on items with higher levels of current tariffs. The notion of tiers, like the banded approach of Harbinson, did not end the dispute over how reductions were to be made within the bands. The G-20 proposed in July 2005 that a linear cut be made within each of five tariff bands (for developed countries) and that the issue of flexibility be addressed after agreement on these cuts. This proposal was given a cautious reception by the United States and the European Union and became in essence the basis for their October proposals. The United States proposed on October 10 at the Zurich mini-ministerial that four bands be established, with cuts of 55–90 percent for developed countries, and that tariffs be capped at 75 percent. The EU proposal aimed at more modest cuts of 20–50 percent, with a tariff cap of 100 percent for developed countries. The G-20 suggested a compromise formula with four bands and tariff cuts of 45–75 percent. The G-10, a group of reluctant importers, rejected the notion of a cap and argued for more flexibility among commodities, suggesting a "credit" system by which deeper cuts could "pay" for less painful cuts in other products. The final modalities were not agreed before Hong Kong, but the convergence on the method of cutting tariffs and the shift of emphasis to the depth of cuts marks a significant stage in this crucial aspect of the talks.

The issue of flexibility to shelter some commodities from the full impact of a formula cut has been a significant part of the discussion of tariff cuts. It has been generally agreed that developing countries could shelter a few commodities as being of special significance in domestic production and development from import competition. The products would be designated as "special products," and countries could reduce the height of their tariff protection on these products less rapidly. But the Derbez proposal also introduced a new element (in brackets, denoting further discussions) that would allow a "very limited" number of products to be chosen on the basis of nontrade concerns. These products would not be subject to the tariff formula (or tariff cap). All WTO members could take advantage of this exception. The selection of these "sensitive" products would be at the discretion of the country concerned.

The concept of special products has been incorporated into the Framework Agreement, although the issue of defining such products is still under discussion. But the Framework Agreement also endorsed the designation of sensitive products, with the option of increasing tariff-rate quotas in these products to have an equivalent effect on improving market access. By the October Zurich meeting the disagreements had narrowed to the percentage of tariff line items that could be so designated: the G-10 favored 10–15 percent, the European Union seemed to be willing to settle for 8 percent, and the United States insisted that sensitive products be limited to 1 percent of tariff lines.

By agreement, tariff cuts will be made from the bound levels and focus on most favored nation tariffs. As preferential tariffs under various regional trade agreements are much lower (and in many cases are zero), the impact on trade might not be as great as the tariff reductions would suggest. Moreover, the preference margins themselves would be reduced, of course, which could allow some developing country agricultural produce to enter presently protected markets.[39]

Expanding and Improving Tariff Rate Quotas

What options were open to countries as they negotiated on the level and administration of tariff rate quotas? Should tariff rate quotas be treated as a transitional mechanism? Should there be a uniform method of allocating them so that all countries abide by the same set of transparent rules? Even if the best long-run solution is to eliminate tariff rate quotas, exporting countries that enjoy preferential access under tariff rate quotas may not agree to their elimination. An alternative approach is a steady expansion of the minimum access commitment or a progressive reduction in the over-quota tariff, eventually eliminating the problems of a tariff rate quota.

If tariff rate quotas cannot be eliminated, increasing the minimum access commitment becomes crucial. Josling (1998) and Anderson (1999) advocate expanding the size of the minimum access commitment as the only practical method of overcoming the entrenched protection inherent in the tariff rate quota system. Expanding the minimum access commitment is useful when imports equal the quota, indicating that there is excess demand for the import. In addition, quota rents would be reduced.[40] Quota rents are important because of their potential to bias trade.

The effectiveness in opening markets and the distribution of rents are influenced by the administration of tariff rate quotas. Market-based allocation methods such as quota auctions and unrestricted resale of quota rights capture quota rents and remove the incentive for biased trade.[41] Determining the best allocation method to ensure maximum fill when there is excess demand at the in-quota tariff is more challenging. Complete fill should occur as long as economic rents exceed transaction costs. Administered techniques—historic access, state trading enterprises, and the like—may be less complex than auctions and may involve lower transaction costs for importers and exporters. However, these methods are not responsive to market conditions and may involve less transparent transaction costs, such as those due to political preferences. Unfortunately for convenient rule making, the best choice of quota administration method, in the face of transaction costs, is specific to the product traded.[42]

The issue of tariff rate quotas was covered by many countries in their negotiating proposals. The United States argued for an expansion of tariff rate quotas to 20 percent of consumption and elimination of within-quota tariffs. The Cairns Group also wanted substantial increases in market access and improved rules on administration. The European Union was less forthcoming but has not blocked discussion on expansion. The Harbinson proposal called for a doubling of the tariff rate quotas, from 5 percent to 10 percent of consumption, though there is some suggested flexibility: countries that wish to limit this access to 8 percent for up to one-quarter of their tariff rate quotas can give additional access in other markets. Developing countries again would get a longer period for implementing these changes. In-quota tariffs would not be controlled unless quota-fill was below 65 percent or the good was a tropical product or a substitute for narcotics production. The US-EU draft revived an earlier idea (put forward by Canada) that countries could choose expansion of tariff rate quotas as an alternative to some part of their tariff reductions. The General Council chairman's pre-Cancún draft picked up this idea of offering countries a choice between tariff reductions and greater market opening through tariff rate quotas. The Derbez draft, however, reverted to earlier formulations, including the reduction of in-quota tariffs and the negotiation of an expansion of tariff rate quotas.

A general expansion of tariff rate quotas appears to be unlikely at this stage of the talks. But the Framework Agreement identifies the expansion of tariff rate quotas as an alternative way to open up markets protected by high tariffs that are not likely to be subjected to the tariff cutting formula. The Framework Agreement mentions the possibility of some reductions in within-quota tariffs and improvements in administration of tariff rate quotas as part of the balance of concessions, but these elements are not mentioned in the G-20, EU, or US proposals tabled at the Zurich meeting of October 2005. So the expansion of tariff rate quotas will probably be restricted to products that individual importing countries designate as "sensitive" and thus wish to exclude from the general tariff-cutting formula.

Revising the Special Safeguards

In almost all WTO members some sectors are politically sensitive, and members reserved the right to take action quickly through the special safeguards of the URAA if imports threaten domestic producers. The first issue is whether the special safeguards should be continued. One interpretation of the URAA is that the safeguards will continue as long as the reform processes continues, and so will continue if further reform is undertaken. Opponents of extending the special safeguards point to the "emergency safeguard" (Article XIX) provisions that allow members to take action if increased imports cause or threaten to cause serious injury to a domestic industry. They argue that this safeguard is sufficient for agricultural trade. They see the elimination of special safeguards as an important step toward subjecting agricultural trade to the same rules that apply to other goods.

The political reality of agricultural reform in developed countries is that stakeholders demand some discretionary control of trade flows. They need assurance that they can counter large, price-depressing inflows of products if necessary. Special safeguards are inherently distorting, so accepting the mechanism as a compromise to obtain further tariff liberalization requires rules to ensure that special safeguards do not become more distorting than the measures they replace. Providing smaller offsets (tariff increases) for a fall in domestic prices or shortening the period for the quantity trigger would tighten the current criteria. Negotiators should keep the mechanism as transparent as possible, so that affected parties receive adequate notification and information about additional duties. The use of the special safeguards provision could be time limited and regulated, with renewals and extensions judged by a technical committee, and possibly involve an injury test.

Developing countries have made only limited use of special safeguards. The issue is whether the provision represents a satisfactory alternative to such devices as price bands. The expanded use of special safeguards in agricultural trade could contribute significantly to a compromise in the negotiations, in particular if it allows developing countries to open markets to imports.

The proposals on special safeguards laid out in the Harbinson draft envisage that they would be phased out for developed countries but suggest a possible new mechanism "to enable developing countries to effectively take account of their development needs." This new safeguard is under technical discussion along with possible disciplines on state trading importers and rules for the administration of tariff rate quotas.[43] The notion of a developing country safeguard has been a feature of several pre-Cancún proposals. The EU-US draft argued for the creation of such a safeguard for some products, and the G-20, Castillo, and Derbez drafts all call for the negotiation of such a safeguard.

The Framework Agreement called for the creation of a modified safeguard for developing countries, known as a special safeguard mechanism, that would apply to a defined range of products and involve both price and quantity triggers. Such a safeguard could not be used together with Article XIX safeguards or the special safeguard provision of the URAA but could be combined with antidumping and countervailing actions consistent with WTO agreements. The fate of the special safeguard is still under negotiation.[44]

Options for Improving Export Competition

Negotiations on export competition have focused on the reduction or elimination of export subsidies, the need for disciplines on export credit, the curbing of any misuse of food aid, and the disciplining of the activities of state trading enterprises. As in the case of market access, these issues form an integrated package in the negotiations, though they can be discussed separately from an analytical perspective.

Eliminating Export Subsidies

The inclusion of disciplines on export subsidies was a major accomplishment of the URAA. The question in current negotiators was whether to set a date for eliminating export subsidies and, if such a date were set, how to continue cuts in permitted expenditures and volumes from the final 2000 bound levels. The use of both value and volume commitments constrains export subsidies in times of both low and high prices, weakening the ability of export subsidies to maintain fixed internal price supports.[45] When world prices are low, the value limit becomes more constraining because the wedge between the domestic support price and the competitive export price becomes larger. Volume limits prevent exports of excess supply when domestic prices are low. When world prices are high, the value constraint becomes less binding, but the volume constraint can still be effective.

Country proposals on export subsidies showed a general desire to see their rapid elimination. The European Union was initially among the few WTO members to argue against this position. Its main contribution was to insist that export credits and food aid, along with the activities of monopoly state exporting agencies, be disciplined. The United States agreed with the European Union about the need to curb state trading agencies in the export field and on the need for rules for export credit. The Cairns Group argued for a "down-payment" in the form of immediate cuts in volume and expenditure.

In search of a compromise, the Harbinson draft suggested further sharp reductions and elimination within a few years, albeit with some flexibility. The longer time period for half of the export subsidies is a concession to the European Union, which has claimed that it would be difficult to remove export subsidies on dairy products in the short term. There would be no carryover of unused subsidy entitlements from year to year. The United States is no longer dependent on such subsidies and so can argue strongly for their removal.[46] The different schedule for developing countries is an almost empty gesture, as export subsidies are rarely used as a development tool. The US-EU proposal elaborates on the Harbinson notion of flexibility by suggesting elimination of export subsidies on "products of interest to developing countries" and reductions in subsidies on other products using both quantity and expenditure limits, as in the URAA. The suggestion by the G-20 is more explicit: all export subsidies should be eliminated, even if those on products of interest to developing countries go first. The Castillo draft and the Derbez text agree with the EU-US formulation, though they include the provision that the date for the eventual elimination of all subsidies can be discussed.

A major turning point in this aspect of the agricultural talks came when the European Union agreed to the setting of a date for elimination of export subsidies, providing that other forms of export assistance were also eliminated, notably subsidized export credits, export-displacing food aid, and the implicit subsidies given by state exporters. This shift in position was incorporated into the Framework Agreement, which calls for the negotiation of a credible date for eliminating export subsidies and similar export aids, though that date may be several years away. The proposals for the Zurich meeting took this a stage further, with the United States suggesting a date of 2010 for the elimination of subsidies and agreeing to put limits on export credit guarantees and food aid. Finally, at the Hong Kong ministerial in December 2005, a date was agreed of 2013 for the end of export subsidies, subject to the conclusion of other parts of the negotiations.

Disciplining Export Credits, Food Aid, and State Trading Enterprises

Though it was agreed at a political level that "parallel" disciplines on export aids other than export subsidies are needed, the modalities in this area are more problematic. Negotiations on the need to discipline officially supported agricultural export credits has raised issues related to the extent to which export credit programs contain subsidies, the extent to which they distort trade, and how disciplines on credit programs would limit distortions. According to OECD (2000) estimates, the subsidy value of existing programs is relatively low. Only for US programs are subsidy values above 4 percent and credit terms longer than one year. In all cases the relatively low subsidies are likely to create small trade distortions. Evidence from the literature suggests that programs may create additional demand, and to the extent that this is true their negative impact on competing exporters is likely minimal.

Disciplining officially supported export credit programs is more likely to be accomplished by limiting the term of loans offered and by constraining government budgetary outlays than by adjusting program parameters such as minimum interest rate requirements. The Framework Agreement of July 2004 goes some way toward this by calling for the elimination of export credits, guarantees, and insurance programs with repayment periods of more than 180 days. Constraining interest rates or other program parameters risks interfering with commercial relationships and may negate the value of a program to importers. Special and differential treatment of credit programs for developing countries is already mandated by the URAA.

Difficult issues arise where credit programs overlap other subsidies, such as food aid. The most prominent food aid program that operates on a concessional basis is the US PL 480 Title I Program, which uses subsidized credit and has the stated goal of promoting US agricultural exports. Thus it has elements of both food aid and export credit. Food aid programs are also mandated to provide terms favorable for least developed countries and net food importing countries. Including PL 480 Title I in the context of export credit negotiations may meet the desires of both donors and recipient countries to eliminate unclear distinctions between food aid and export credit programs.

Sometimes food aid is used as an export subsidy to reduce unwanted surpluses. This is most explicit when aid is tied to the requirement that the recipient import only from the donor. The URAA prohibits this, but it does not discipline more implicit subsidies, such as those for which disciplines are being sought by the European Union. Adequate (increased) levels of food aid guaranteed in advance by donors and delivered through the World Food Programme would solve some of the problems. By weakening the link between surplus production and food aid, such a change could help to ensure that food aid was available in times of shortage. For countries concerned about the impact of food aid on world markets, such a change would divorce food aid from sporadic surplus disposal. Political realities may make this solution unworkable, however. To secure the necessary political support to pay for food aid programs, donor governments, particularly the United States, rely on food aid to achieve both producer support and humanitarian objectives. Insisting on the ideal solution could further reduce the amount of food aid supplied by the United States. It seems necessary that food aid programs continue to meet multiple objectives in order to sustain the level of provision.

Questions remain on the definition and treatment of emergency food relief and whether food aid should have to be triggered by UN agencies (Food and Agriculture Organization, United Nations Development Programme, or World Food Programme). In addition, there is still disagreement on whether food aid should always be given as a grant (the EU position) and whether more complete reporting of food aid to the WTO is necessary (as the United States suggests).

Concerns have been raised about the monopsony and monopoly power exercised by state trading enterprises, in particular in the context of export crops. Their ability to use price discrimination among markets and to engage in price pooling has been challenged in the WTO negotiations, especially in the face of the lack of transparency in their operations. The possibility of state trading importers discriminating against imports even when tariff rate quotas are in place has caused concern for exporting countries. However, disciplines on the action of such entities, though they exist in the WTO (in Article XVII of the GATT), have been hard to enforce. In many countries state trading enterprises are charged with achieving a broad set of domestic policy goals. To the extent that domestic constituencies support these goals, there can be high political costs in abandoning these institutions.[47] In some cases the politically costly process of reform has resulted in the implementation of new methods to achieve the same domestic policy goals. In other cases public monopolies have been replaced by private monopolies, doing little or nothing to alleviate concerns about market power, transparency, and price discrimination.

The most sensitive issue facing the WTO in the discussion of state trading is that of single-desk sellers of temperate zone agricultural products and more particularly the conduct and status of the Canadian Wheat Board. The Framework Agreement included an obligation to eliminate trade-distorting practices of state trading enterprises but merely anticipated "further negotiation" on the use of monopoly powers. That question is unlikely to be resolved except as part of a more comprehensive package.

Consideration of changes in the treatment of state trading enterprises under Article XVII of the GATT has not progressed far. Developing countries have a major stake in this issue and could benefit from an agreement that reduces conflicts between domestic decisions on marketing agencies and agricultural trade rules on market access and export competition.

Each of these three export policy instruments—export credits, food aid, and state trading—has been discussed extensively in the negotiations. The Harbinson modalities draft supported the notion of disciplining export credits (no hidden support) and food aid (no commercial advantage). In addition, it picked up on the notion of private competition with state trading exporters and other disciplines on state trading exporters (no exports at less than the purchase price, and no special financing). The US-EU proposal of August 2003 also addressed export competition issues as a package, in accord with the EU suggestion to introduce disciplines on export credits in parallel, while also avoiding export credits on products that developing countries export. Disciplines would also be applied to food aid, and state trading exporters would have to relinquish their monopoly positions. The G-20 draft called for rules to discipline export credits and for the elimination of the subsidy element of such credits. State trading enterprises would be similarly disciplined. The Castillo draft would eliminate the trade-distorting element of export credits in parallel with export subsidies on products of interest to developing countries and would phase out the subsidy provided by state trading enterprises. The Derbez text picked up on each of these issues, indicating the possibility of agreement once the more divisive question of the elimination of export subsidies is settled.

The Framework Agreement confirmed the link between export subsidy elimination and the removal of subsidies provided through these other export policies. A key provision was inserted that there be parallel treatment for the export subsidy component of export credits (long time periods and below-market interest rates) and of state trading exporters (low-interest loans and government underwriting of losses). Food aid is to be disciplined to avoid disruption of commercial trade flows. The goal is set as the elimination of food aid that is not in conformity with disciplines still to be agreed. These disciplines will be aimed at preventing commercial displacement, but the thorny problem of how to translate this aim into practical rules has yet to be tackled. The framework added another component to the export competition talks. Export taxes and restrictions are also to be subject to tighter rules.

The Zurich proposals of October 2005 clarify somewhat the steps that can be taken in this area. The United States accepted the idea of a maximum repayment period of 180 days on export credits and the establishment of specific disciplines to bring credits in line with commercial practices. The US paper suggests adopting new disciplines on state trading entities that would end monopoly export privileges, prohibit indirect export subsidies, and expand transparency.[48] The United States also agreed to discipline food aid to guard against commercial displacement, but added that countries should remove obstacles to emergency shipments to chronic food deficit countries.[49] Assuming that agreement on these parallel issues emerges, the European Union indicated that it stood ready to fix a date for the elimination of export subsidies in Hong Kong.

Options for Reforming Domestic Support

Reducing the level of domestic support has proved to be among the most controversial elements of the agricultural negotiations, even though the economic impact is limited to a few countries and the overall gains to the trade system are not as great as for improved market access. The initial proposals highlighted a range of issues, including the accommodation of "nontrade" concerns, the role of the blue box, possible limits on green box subsidies, the role of the peace clause, provisions for special and differential treatment for developing countries, and reductions in aggregate support (including refinement of the definition and criteria for exempt policies, consideration of inflation and exchange rate changes in measuring support, the desirability of the *de minimis* provisions, and whether to have total or product-specific aggregate measurement of support commitments).

One challenge facing negotiators has been to identify ways to reduce trade-distorting domestic support while providing flexibility for achieving important societal goals. The urgency of this issue has increased as the amount of support allowed within the amber and blue boxes has declined. Over time, criteria must be refined to provide clearer definitions of acceptable minimal trade distorting domestic policy measures that allow countries to pursue important societal objectives for environmental standards, rural development, food security, poverty alleviation, and others. In essence, the tension is between countries that consider domestic support a form of subsidy that should be controlled by international rules and those that consider it a legitimate aspect of domestic policy-making that should not be overly constrained by international bodies. The compromise between these positions is reflected in the differential treatment of the URAA boxes in the Doha Round and the weight given to domestic support relative to the other two pillars of the agricultural negotiations.

Further Reducing Limits for Trade-Distorting Support

The URAA placed limits on individual countries' total aggregate measurement of support and specified reductions, resulting in a final, bound support level. The main issue for the current negotiations is how much further to reduce those levels. The bound aggregate measurement of support varies greatly among countries, with most having a zero commitment but some having high levels in relation to the size of their agricultural sectors. In addition, negotiators have had to consider the modalities of reductions. Should support be reduced by a given amount or to a particular level? Reducing support by a given amount provides advantages to countries with high levels of support. Reducing support to a particular level would result in a more level playing field among countries but would impose greater adjustments on countries with high levels of support.[50]

A number of other issues are significant in the renegotiation of the disciplines on domestic support. The current *de minimis* rules specify the level of support that is exempt for developed and developing countries. Negotiators are considering whether such exemptions should be retained, in particular whether and by how much (or to what level) the *de minimis* threshold should be reduced.[51] Some countries have proposed that developing countries be allowed to increase the level of support provided under the *de minimis* provision. Currently, aggregate measurement of support commitments and levels are reported in nominal terms. Negotiators are considering the development of criteria that account for inflation or exchange rate fluctuations in determining a country's aggregate measurement of support level.

Since the URAA was implemented, a number of countries have shifted significant portions of their domestic support from the nonexempt category to the green and blue boxes. At issue is whether all domestic policies currently categorized as exempt truly fit the criteria of the current agreement. The next agreement will seek more specific criteria to determine the status of domestic support policies. And finally, there is the question of product specificity. Under the URAA, countries have the flexibility to adjust the level of support among products in the amber box, provided that the total aggregate measurement of support does not exceed their commitment. Setting aggregate support limits on a product-specific basis would increase the discipline of the URAA.

Country proposals have reflected a range of opinions. Some have argued for expanding the scope for trade-distorting support on the grounds that such support of the "multifunctional" nature of agriculture can lead to the rapid elimination of all such support. The Cairns Group proposal argued for the reduction and eventual elimination of amber (and blue) box support, with an "early harvest" reduction of 50 percent at the start of any transition period. The United States proposed a reduction in the level of amber box domestic support to no more than 5 percent of agricultural GDP (but retaining the *de minimis* provisions).[52] The European Union proposed the reduction of all amber box payments (by 55 percent) but rejected the need to tie payments to the level of agricultural GDP.

The domestic support reductions suggested by the Harbinson draft were even more ambitious. They would have cut the aggregate measure of support by 60 percent from the 1999–2000 average over 5 years (but only 40 percent over 10 years for developing countries) while still aggregating support across all products. Amber box payments by commodity would not be allowed to rise relative to the 1999–2000 base. Developed countries would have their *de minimis* allowance (currently 5 percent) reduced by one-half percentage point each year over 5 years. Developing countries could include a "negative" element in their aggregate measurement of support in cases where there are taxes on agricultural production.

The US-EU proposal of August 2003 introduced a new idea, that of using bands analogous to the Harbinson market access formulation to limit domestic support. Countries with high levels of support would reduce them by a higher proportion. This, together with the proposed reduction in the *de minimis* exemptions, would require significant reductions in domestic support. The G-20 proposal agreed on banding, but suggested product-specific reductions in the aggregate measurement of support and a limit on domestic support for export crops. The Castillo draft did not include these refinements and followed the formulation of the EU-US draft, but the Derbez draft reinstated the notion of a cap on product-specific aggregate measurement of support levels.

The Framework Agreement of July 2004 introduced a new notion into the discussion of domestic support. The Framework Agreement calls for harmonization of levels of the "overall trade-distorting domestic support," comprising the total aggregate measurement of support (or amber box payments), the blue box, and *de minimis* levels. Overall trade-distorting domestic support would be reduced progressively, with higher levels coming down by a greater percentage. A "down-payment" of a 20 percent cut in the first year would be followed by annual cuts. In addition, there would be substantial cuts in the individual components of this overall trade-distorting domestic support, with the aggregate measurement of support itself reduced, also on a harmonization formula, that would bring the highest levels down by more.

The G-20 announced its own ideas in July 2005, which built on the Framework Agreement. The reductions in the overall trade-distorting domestic support and the aggregate measurement of support would differ depending on the current level of a country's support. Three bands would be distinguished, and the cuts would be higher for countries in the top band (80 percent for both overall trade-distorting domestic support and the aggregate measurement of support) and less for countries in the lowest band (70 for overall trade-distorting domestic support and 60 percent for the aggregate measurement of support). In practice, the European Union would be in the highest band, with the United States and Japan also making large cuts in support. The October 2005 proposals by the United States and the European Union are along similar lines, but the United States requested an 83 percent cut in overall trade-distorting domestic support by both the European Union and Japan, while the European Union envisaged only a 70 percent cut in its trade-distorting support. Some distance still separates the main parties, but as with tariff cuts the emphasis is now on numbers rather than on different methods of reduction.

Determining the Future Role of the Blue Box

The intent of the blue box category in the URAA was to make it easier for the European Union and the United States to meet their domestic support reduction commitments. Some argue that the blue box was transitional and should be phased out, encouraging countries to adopt measures that fit green box criteria. Blue box payments are not included in the aggregate measurement of support calculation and are exempt from reduction commitments. However, blue box policies can have output and trade impacts, which exporting countries may want to discipline.

The key issues are whether the blue box should be eliminated and, if so, at what rate. The European Union and Japan have insisted that the blue box plays a useful role and should be retained. Other countries are unconvinced and have argued for reduction commitments for the blue box, at a minimum. The Cairns Group has argued for its eventual elimination, and the United States, by seeking to bring the blue box under amber box limits, also appears to envisage its eventual demise.

The G-20 paper proposed the elimination of the blue box. The Harbinson plan called for either capping the blue box and reducing it by 50 percent in 5 years (33 percent in 10 years for developing countries) or including it in the aggregate measurement of support (the amber box) immediately for developed countries and after 5 years for developing countries. The US-EU proposal of August 2003 argued for a redefinition of the blue box and a limit of 5 percent of agricultural GDP.[53] The Castillo draft adopted the US-EU approach, including a declining budget ceiling for the newly defined blue box. These provisions were also incorporated in the Derbez draft. This compromise between the two parties with the greatest interest in the issue might have been expected to prove acceptable for other countries, but this was not the case. Disagreement over the fate of the blue box was one of the points of contention when the Cancún Ministerial Meeting ended.

The Framework Agreement moved this discussion forward somewhat. The blue box criteria would be modified to include payments on fixed acres and yields but not linked to production cuts, and the total blue box would be limited to 5 percent of the value of production. Such a redefined blue box would have the direct effect of allowing the United States to notify the countercyclical payments introduced in the 2002 Farm Bill as blue box payments.[54] The US proposal of October 2005 offered to reduce the blue box limit to 2.5 percent: the European Union indicated that it was prepared to consider some reduction from the 5 percent limit in the Framework Agreement. That flexibility depends in part on the results of discussions on other aspects of domestic support.

Limiting Green Box Subsidies

The URAA placed no limits on the level of support within the green box framework, which is supposed to include measures that have no, or at most minimal, distorting effects on trade or production. Any support must be government funded (not involving transfers from consumers) and must not provide price support to producers. A number of policy-specific criteria and conditions also apply. However, the imprecise nature of the criteria has left considerable room for interpretation. Beyond requests for clarification of acceptable green box policies, several countries have called for limits on the amount of support. While limiting green box expenditures will be a contentious issue, the agreement could involve improved definition of policies that have no, or at most minimal, trade-distorting effects or effects on production.

The European Union has been the most enthusiastic proponent of a more capacious green box that would include payments for programs linked to animal welfare, the environment, food security, and rural development programs. This approach is supported by several countries interested in "multifunctionality" (the so-called Friends of Multifunctionality) and has its parallel in the concern among developing countries that WTO constraints may limit development policies. The Cairns Group would by contrast prefer to strengthen and clarify the criteria for the green box, particularly by moving safety net, investment, and some forms of direct payment into the amber box. (Canada would include green box subsidies in a comprehensive subsidy cap.) The United States has essentially argued to keep the green box intact, as it too seeks to shift the emphasis of farm spending from commodities to decoupled producer payments and to rural development programs.

The Harbinson draft modalities paper suggests no change in green box criteria, except to add compensation payments for animal welfare regulations to allowed environmental payments and to ease the categories applying to developing countries. The US-EU draft of August 2003 suggests no major changes to the green box. It was left to the G-20 to suggest a cap on certain green box expenditures (including direct payments, crop insurance, and disaster relief). The Castillo draft did not mention these restraints but left the green box criteria open for discussion. The Derbez draft also followed this path, leaving open the possibility of further restricting green box policies by tightening the rules rather than by reducing the level of payments. There has been no convergence of opinion between the developing and the industrial countries on this issue.

Under the Framework Agreement, there would be a review of the green box criteria and an effort to improve surveillance and monitoring. But there would be no quantitative restrictions on this (minimally trade-distorting) support. Closer analysis (along with implementation of the outcome of the cotton panel) could yet cause some adjustments in green box policies, even with no changes in the definitions.

Deciding on the Peace Clause

The peace clause provides an incentive for countries to shift domestic policy instruments toward the green box in order to eliminate the threat of countervailing duties and other actions. It also shelters policies that exporters could otherwise challenge under the Agreement on Subsidies and Countervailing Measures. Steinberg and Josling (2003) conclude that several EU and US farm policies could be vulnerable to such challenges, and recent cases such as that involving US cotton policy confirm that Brazil and some other exporters consider the legal route to policy change to be potentially productive.

Agreement on some form of extension of the peace clause seems probable if there is substantial progress in the Doha Round. No specific proposal has been made on this issue in recent months, though the European Union has argued vigorously for its extension. The Harbinson draft provides no guidance, and the chairman's report to the Trade Negotiating Committee is also silent on the issue. Neither the EU-US proposal nor the G-20 paper includes any suggestions on the peace clause, and it is not mentioned in the Castillo draft. But the Derbez draft discussed at Cancún did suggest the possibility of a continuation of the clause.

The Framework Agreement is silent on the question of the peace clause as are the October 2005 proposals from the G-20 and European Union presented at Zurich. Only the US proposal mentions the reintroduction of the peace clause, as a way of discouraging other members from taking legal action to further restrict US domestic policies. If it were to be extended, countries would have to decide on the terms of the extension. One question is the form that it should take to encourage the greatest shift toward support that does not distort trade. Should the clause be permanent or of limited duration? Should it cover only green box policies or include other support? If the peace clause were not reintroduced, would this eliminate much of the meaning of the "boxes" as the main criteria would be whether a policy caused serious prejudice to other WTO members?

DEVELOPING COUNTRIES AND THE AGRICULTURAL NEGOTIATIONS UNDER THE DOHA DEVELOPMENT AGENDA

One lesson of the failed Ministerial Meeting in Seattle in 1999 was that developing countries were unwilling to participate in another round of trade negotiations in which their views were not fully considered (Stiglitz 2000). This lesson was resoundingly reinforced by the breakdown of the Cancún Ministerial Meeting. However, developing countries are not a homogeneous block. Several developing country food exporters are members of the G-20 and share the aim of rapid agricultural trade liberalization. Other G-20 members are food importers and remain skeptical of the benefits of opening their domestic agricultural markets. However, all developing countries share three major concerns about the current trading system: the structure of the WTO, the perceived lack of benefits from the Uruguay Round negotiations, and the need for special rules and disciplines for developing countries.

Participation and Decision making in the WTO

Developing countries dominate the membership of the WTO. Since the conclusion of the Uruguay Round roughly 40 new developing countries have joined the WTO. Despite their majority position, most developing countries feel that important debates and decisions at the WTO take place without their full participation. As former US Trade Representative Charlene Barshefsky commented following the Seattle Ministerial Meeting: "The WTO has outgrown the processes appropriate to an earlier time. We needed a process which had a greater degree of internal transparency and inclusion to accommodate a larger and more diverse membership."

The WTO has responded to some of these concerns by making most documents publicly available and by providing technical assistance and training for developing country representatives. WTO institutional reform remains a key issue in making developing countries an integral part of the decision-making process. Though developing countries have not complained that they were excluded from decision-making at Cancún, there is still the widespread perception that their participation was not as effective as it might have been. Institutional reform is back on the agenda at the WTO.

Benefits from the Uruguay Round

Many developing countries feel that the benefits promised by the URAA have not been forthcoming. Their list of grievances is long, and only a partial review is provided here. First, they feel that they have not benefited from market access to the degree expected from liberalization of developed country markets for agriculture, clothing, and textiles. Further, they fear that when they do become competitive in developed country markets, they are subjected to antidumping actions that are generally too costly for them to block effectively. They also realize that because of the URAA, their domestic markets continue to face competition from subsidized agricultural exports from developed countries. In addition, the URAA largely constrains developing country domestic support for agriculture to *de minimis* levels, while developed countries continue to pour huge sums of money into their domestic agricultural sectors through the amber, green, and blue boxes. Poor developing countries feel that they have no chance to compete effectively in agricultural markets against the deep pockets of the rich and powerful countries of the world. Finally, developing countries fear the inclusion of environmental and labor standards in trade agreements.

For many developing countries border measures are the only policy instrument available to provide income support to their farmers. Given budget realities, taxpayer-funded support measures such as those in developed countries are not an option. This provides one rationale for allowing developing countries to retain some slack in their tariffs and to have access to a special agricultural safeguard mechanism. More creativity may be needed to make it possible for developing countries to adapt their domestic fiscal policies so that they do not have to distort trade patterns in order to raise revenue.

Special Treatment for Developing Countries

There are conflicting concerns that negotiators face as they attempt to develop rules for special and differential treatment of developing countries. Many of the poorest developing countries have 60 percent or more of their labor force in agriculture, and agriculture often accounts for more than 40 percent of their GDP. Opening up their economies may have significant consequences for their rural population. However, developing countries have a large stake in trade liberalization given that 43 percent of developing countries are net agricultural exporters, including 28 of the world's poorest countries (McCalla 2001). So the issue for many developing countries can be framed as one of gaining market access overseas but increasing the competition facing domestic farmers. Special and differential treatment is a way of ensuring market access gains in the products of interest to developing countries as exporters while easing the burden on domestic farmers through lesser tariff cuts and more time to adjust.

The extreme form of special and differential treatment is the proposed policy toward the world's 48 poorest countries, known collectively as the least developed countries. The European Union has recently eliminated both tariffs and quotas on all products, except arms, for the least developed countries. This policy, known as the Everything But Arms agreement, has put considerable pressure on other developed countries to follow suit. The United States has implemented a trade act (the African Growth and Opportunities Act) that grants many of the same benefits to African countries, many of which are in the least developed country category, but with conditions related to "good governance." It should be possible in the Doha Development Round to agree on a general policy of opening up markets to the least developed countries and of allowing them to avoid making concessions with their own tariffs and subsidies (known as "a round for free"). The fact that the least developed countries may not be required to reduce tariffs and subsidies does not imply that it is not in their best interest to do so, however.

Developing countries should make sure that developed countries grant them major tariff concessions on all agricultural products of export interest to them, including import-sensitive products, during this round of negotiations. Without such access there will be no deal. But in return, developing countries should agree to liberalize their agricultural markets, albeit with a longer transition period for tariff reductions. They could in many cases pursue their development and food security concerns using instruments that are consistent with less border protection. This approach may require additional financial aid from developed countries and perhaps even new international institutions. However, additional financial support to address nontrade concerns in developing countries would be a small price to pay for obtaining meaningful reductions in agricultural trade barriers in developed countries.

Creation of a special safeguard for developing countries will be an important consideration for the large number of developing country products whose bound tariff rates substantially exceed applied tariffs.

Developing countries also will receive special and differential treatment under the URAA for domestic support. This includes a smaller reduction commitment, higher *de minimis* level, longer implementation period, and exemption for the least developed countries from all reduction commitments. Continuation of these special and differential treatments seems both likely and appropriate. In addition to determining what special and differential treatment will be granted, the current negotiations should develop specific criteria to determine which WTO members will qualify as developing countries. The application of special and differential treatment to transition economies will also need to be addressed.

NEGOTIATION OUTCOMES AND INTERESTS

The Framework Agreement of July 2004 signaled a determination to restart the negotiations on the modalities for agriculture, services, and nonagricultural tariffs after the setback at Cancún. The Framework Agreement also triggered the start of talks on the wider Doha Development Agenda.[55] Agriculture was not the only lagging issue: the timetable for services negotiations was also behind schedule, as many countries saw them moving in parallel with the talks on agriculture.[56] Similarly, discussions on nonagricultural tariffs were slowed by the lack of agreement in agriculture.[57] As important, several other issues that were built into the Doha timetable are proving difficult to resolve. One of the key aspects of the Doha agreement, on the application of the Agreement on Trade-Related Aspects of Intellectual Property Rights (TRIPS) to pharmaceuticals needed by developing countries, which missed the December 2002 deadline for agreement, has since been settled, but the issue of special and differential treatment for developing countries remains on the table.[58] But for most countries it is agriculture that holds the key to the pace and the level of ambition of the round.[59]

The packaging of possible outcomes to the agricultural negotiations has to reflect balance in at least four dimensions. First, it has to meet the major aspirations of both developed and developing countries. The Cancún Ministerial Meeting showed that developing countries will not agree to a negotiating conclusion that ignores their interests. Proposals by developing countries make their concerns explicit, and proposals by developed countries have indicated a willingness to take those concerns into account. But agreement will require substantial market access in products of interest to developing countries, recognition of special development needs in domestic policies, some allowance for safeguard action in the event of market disruption, and a stronger commitment to action on food security in times of high world prices. In turn, developed countries will expect full involvement by developing countries (though not the least developed) in market opening commitments and perhaps some further restrictions on the activities of state trade importing agencies. Though the agricultural talks could proceed alone, this package will be easier to achieve in the context of a larger round because other benefits such as improved market access for textiles could be included, along with better access for developed countries in the manufacturing markets of developing countries.

Second, the package has to be balanced between importing and exporting countries. Despite the restraints on export subsidies agreed in the Uruguay Round, the feeling is widespread that such subsidies and the domestic farm programs in exporting countries remain a major distortion in world markets. Importing countries have often claimed that their own policies reflect the need for protection against erratic world prices that are depressed by the activities of the exporters. It would not be possible to craft a deal if the only changes in export policy were further reductions in EU export subsidies. But importers will not be able to avoid painful cuts in their tariffs and in their own domestic subsidies. As usual in trade negotiations, the pace and level of market opening depend on the willingness of importing governments to inflict adjustment on their less competitive industries. The European Union, both the largest importer of farm products and a major exporter, in many ways holds the key. The change in EU trade strategy from a defensive to an offensive approach has been slow. There are signs that the European Union is finally beginning to argue for open markets rather than for the right to keep markets protected. A key to the current talks will be the extent to which this attitude is manifest in EU behavior in the negotiations.[60]

A third aspect of the package is the balance among commodities. It is well understood that the URAA left some commodities, notably sugar and dairy products, virtually untouched. By contrast, serious discussions were held on virtually free markets for oilseeds and malting barley. Some countries are in favor of trying again with zero-for-zero agreements, though this could exacerbate distortions across agricultural markets.[61] The question is whether this round of talks can conclude without significant liberalization of dairy and sugar markets. The answer is shrouded in the domestic politics of the European Union and the United States, but the G-20 will also have a say. Countries such as Australia and New Zealand have a strong incentive to see that dairy trade is not treated lightly in this round. Dairy markets have shown some signs of recovering from the disarray caused by unrestricted export subsidies, but they are still distorted by high tariffs. Further domestic reforms by the European Union and a move toward a more liberal North American policy on dairy products could set the scene for significant liberalization. The same may not be true in the sugar market. The low-cost suppliers, particularly Australia and Brazil, will push hard for sugar to be included in the tariff reductions in the next round. However, some developing countries benefit from preferential access for this product into EU and US markets, which complicates negotiations on market access.

The fourth element is balance among the various parts of the package. The balance among instruments is difficult to define. Clearly, some of the measures are connected: lower tariffs restrict the ability of countries to use export subsidies, reduce the potential trade diversion impacts of free trade areas, and cut the quota rents from tariff rate quotas. But there are also links between the use of safeguards by importing countries and control of export subsidies. It is likely that the market access and export competition components will have to be considered as a whole. Just as important is the connection between domestic support and export competition. Subsidies have an impact on competitive exporters whether paid at home to domestic farmers or at the border to traders. The extent to which domestic policies can be reformulated to have less impact on other countries is a key to the acceptability of tighter subsidy rules for agriculture. Again, a balance will have to be sought that represents a domestically acceptable set of international constraints.

Negotiators have faced a difficult task of keeping alive the momentum and the spirit of compromise that characterized the Doha Ministerial Meeting in November 2001. The Ministerial Meeting in Cancún in September 2003 was an opportunity to keep that process moving forward, but it failed to deliver. Some progress was made in 2004, as the framework for the talks was finally agreed. The Ministerial Meeting in Hong Kong made limited progress. The key role of the agricultural talks in the round has been repeatedly demonstrated, and the discussion of agriculture has absorbed much of the negotiations. Recognition of the importance of developing countries in the WTO has been equally essential to progress in the round and to the cohesion of the WTO. Developing countries are vitally interested in agriculture, but they also have widely different interests. So the question may come down to the ability of developing countries to keep a focus on some of the key agricultural issues, of improved market access and the curbing of subsidies, and hence both to improve the trading system for agricultural goods and to advance the ability of the multilateral trade system to support and energize their economic development.

ANNEX. BACKGROUND PAPERS

This chapter synthesizes and updates a series of papers prepared for the International Agricultural Trade Research Consortium (IATRC). Four IATRC task forces were set up at the end of 2000, and each was asked to prepare a commissioned paper. The papers were presented at the conference, WTO Negotiations on Agriculture: Review of Progress, held in Washington, D.C., on May 18, 2001. The original synthesis paper (IATRC 2001a) was prepared by Praveen Dixit (US Department of Agriculture, Economic Research Service), Tim Josling (Stanford University), and David Blandford (Pennsylvania State University). This current update, by Tim Josling, takes into account developments after the conference in 2001 and up to October 2005.

The papers prepared for the IATRC conference, and their authors, are as follows:

"Market Access: Issues and Options in the Agricultural Negotiations" (Commissioned Paper 14)

Maury Bredahl, University of Missouri

Mary Burfisher, US Department of Agriculture, Economic Research Service

Karl Meilke, University of Guelph (principal author)
James Rude, University of Saskatchewan

"Export Competition: Issues and Options in the Agricultural Negotiations" (Commissioned Paper 15)
Philip Abbott, Purdue University
Susan Leetmaa, US Department of Agriculture, Economic Research Service
Linda Young, Montana State University (principal author)

"Domestic Support: Issues and Options in the Agricultural Negotiations" (Commissioned Paper 16)
Lars Brink, Agriculture and Agri-Food Canada
John Dyck, US Department of Agriculture, Economic Research Service
Lynn Kennedy, Louisiana State University (principal author)
Donald MacLaren, University of Melbourne

"The Role of Product Attributes in the Agricultural Negotiations" (Commissioned Paper 17)
Julie Caswell, University of Massachusetts
David Orden, Virginia Tech
Tsunehiro Otsuki, World Bank
Donna Roberts, US Department of Agriculture, Economic Research Service (principal author)
Ian Sheldon, Ohio State University
Laurian Unnevehr, University of Illinois
John Wilson, World Bank

Two other papers were also presented at the conference, and some of their conclusions are included in this synthesis:
"Agriculture in the WTO: Background to Current Negotiations"
Stefan Tangermann, University of Göttingen
"Future Research Needs and Prospects and Role of the IATRC"
Tim Josling, Stanford University
Praveen Dixit, US Department of Agriculture, Economic Research Service
These papers are available on the IATRC website (www.agtrade.org).

NOTES

The author thanks all who participated in the original series of commissioned papers in 2001 (listed in the appendix), particularly Praveen Dixit, Chief, Asia and Western Hemisphere Branch, Economic Research Service, US Department of Agriculture, and David Blandford, Head of the Department of Agricultural Economics and Rural Sociology, Pennsylvania State University, who were coauthors of the IATRC (2001a) synthesis report. None of these people bear any responsibility for this current paper.

1. Article 20 is explicit on the objectives of the talks but allows several issues to be taken into account that somewhat blunt its ambitious tone. It reads as follows (WTO 1996):

   > Recognizing that the long-term objective of substantial progressive reductions in support and protection resulting in fundamental reform is an ongoing process, Members agree that negotiations for continuing the process will be initiated one year before the end of the implementation period, taking into account:
   >
   > - the experience to that date from implementing the reduction commitments;
   > - the effects of the reduction commitments on world trade in agriculture;
   > - non-trade concerns, special and differential treatment to developing-country Members, and the objective to establish a fair and market-oriented agricultural trading system, and the other objectives and concerns mentioned in the preamble to this Agreement; and
   > - what further commitments are necessary to achieve the above mentioned long-term objectives.

2. The relevant part of the Doha Declaration reads:

   > Building on the work carried out to date and without prejudging the outcome of the negotiations we commit ourselves to comprehensive negotiations aimed at: substantial improvements in market access; reductions of, with a view to phasing out, all forms of export subsidies; and substantial reductions in trade-distorting domestic support. We agree that special and differential treatment for developing countries shall be an integral part of all elements of the negotiations and shall be embodied in the schedules of concessions and commitments and as appropriate in the rules and disciplines to be negotiated, so as to be operationally effective and to enable developing countries to effectively take account of their development needs, including food security and rural development. We take note of the non-trade concerns reflected in the negotiating proposals submitted by Members and confirm that non-trade concerns will be taken into account in the negotiations as provided for in the Agreement on Agriculture.

   Details can be found on the WTO website, at www.wto.org.

3. The commitment was made as follows:

   > Modalities for the further commitments, including provisions for special and differential treatment, shall be established no later than 31 March 2003. Participants shall submit their comprehensive draft Schedules based on these modalities no later than the date of the Fifth Session of the Ministerial Conference. The negotiations, including with respect to rules and disciplines and related legal texts, shall be concluded as part and at the date of conclusion of the negotiating agenda as a whole.

   Details can be found on the WTO website, at www.wto.org.

4. The WTO Secretariat has been summarizing this information and making it available to the general public. The US Department of Agriculture, Economic Research Service, has a website that collects WTO notifications (www.ers.usda.gov).

5. This account of complaints and disputes is based on the document "Overview of the State-of-play of WTO Disputes," accessed on the WTO website on 23 March 2001 (http://www.wto.org).

6. See Tangermann (2000) for details of these complaints.
7. In the early phase of the implementation of the URAA there was some discussion between the United States (and Canada) and the European Union about how the European Union implemented its variable tariffs on cereals. However, the fundamental approach was not in question, only "technical" aspects of it. The issue was settled when the European Union adjusted its regime. More recently, Chile's price band regime was challenged in the WTO, but at the time of writing that case has not yet been settled; see *Chile–Price Band System and Safeguard Measures Relating to Certain Agricultural Products,* complaint by Argentina (WT/DS207/1).
8. *European Communities–Measures Affecting Importation of Certain Poultry Products,* complaint by Brazil (WT/DS69).
9. Their analysis is based on tariff data from several sources, in particular the Agricultural Market Access Database (AMAD), of post-Uruguay Round bound tariffs, tariff rate quotas, and some applied tariffs for about 40 WTO members (www.AMAD.org). Other tariff data are from the WTO Secretariat and UN Conference on Trade and Development. The 62 percent simple (unweighted) average of post-Uruguay Round–bound agricultural tariffs includes the ad valorem equivalents of specific tariffs, which are in some cases very high and whose values depend on prices. It also includes the over-quota tariff in tariff rate quota regimes.
10. For example, the 1998 average applied rate for agricultural tariffs for Latin American countries, at 13 percent, is less than one-third of the average bound rate of 45 percent.
11. Value added refers to the contribution of primary factors (labor, capital, and land) to a sector's output and can be roughly calculated by subtracting the costs of intermediate inputs from the value of production.
12. However, the category of consumer-ready items includes some unprocessed products such as apples and bananas.
13. More details about the economics and administration of the tariff rate quota system are found in IATRC (2001b).
14. The WTO identifies seven methods that are used to administer tariff rate quota access: simple applied tariffs at the within-quota rate, first-come first-served, licenses on demand, auctioning of licenses to importers, historical allocation, state trading importers, and import licenses to producer groups. Applied tariff administration, allowing unlimited imports at the in-quota tariff, accounted for 47 percent of tariff rate quotas in 1999. A first-come first-served method allows the earliest imports to enter at the in-quota tariff rate up to the quota level. In 1999, 11 percent of tariff rate quotas were administered using this method. License on demand (if demand for import licenses exceeds the quota, the amount allocated to each applicant is reduced proportionately) is the most popular administration method, after applied tariffs, with 25 percent of tariff rate quotas allocated in this manner. In 1999 only 4 percent of tariff rate quotas were administered by auction, and fill rates were low (under 40 percent in 1995 and 1996). Historical allocation accounted for 5 percent of tariff rate quota administration methods in 1999. Assigning quota rights to state trading enterprises or domestic producer groups is potentially the most distorting method of administering quota; it has not been a frequent choice. In 1999 state trading enterprises administered 2 percent of the tariff rate quotas; producer groups administered 1 percent. Both state traders and producer groups have generally filled their quotas.
15. However, for a period after implementation of the URAA, international and national prices for many agricultural products were high by historical standards and so would not have triggered efforts to limit imports.

16. The country concerned was Hungary, which claimed that it had erroneously overlooked some export subsidies that had actually been granted in the base period, and hence had wrongly specified commitments in its schedule. The case resulted in long and heated debates in the Committee on Agriculture, and a complaint was brought before the WTO. In the end, Hungary was granted a waiver that allowed it to exceed its commitments on export subsidies by given margins, for an interim period ending in the year 2001. From 2002 on Hungary would have to hold its export subsidies to the levels originally bound in its schedule.
17. There was a debate in the Committee on Agriculture on whether the "credit" provisions in Article 9.2(b) should allow countries to exceed their annual commitments on export subsidies if they had "underutilized" them in previous years. This practice was finally accepted and used in a number of cases (particularly by the European Union).
18. *Canada–Measures Affecting the Importation of Milk and the Exportation of Dairy Products,* complaint by the United States (WT/DS103/1), and *Canada–Measures Affecting Dairy Products,* complaint by New Zealand (WT/DS113/1).
19. The European Union and Switzerland rely on export subsidies more than most WTO members do because they support producers through high internal prices, which stimulate production above domestic needs and commercial export possibilities. Both also employ import barriers to keep cheaper imported products out of the domestic market. The size of export subsidies changes with fluctuations in world prices and exchange rates, as the price gap between the domestic and world price is the per unit export subsidy.
20. In one case (Argentina 1995) the point was made that the original schedule had been established erroneously. In the other case (Iceland 1998), "excessive inflation" was given as a reason. See WTO (2000a) and the WTO documents mentioned therein.
21. *Korea–Measures Affecting Imports of Fresh, Chilled, and Frozen Beef,* complaint by the United States (WT/DS161/1), and the related case *Korea–Measures Affecting Imports of Fresh, Chilled, and Frozen Beef,* complaint by Australia (WT/DS169/1) examined by the same panel.
22. The Brazilian challenge to the US cotton policy is in part a test of the domestic support provisions of the URAA, but it also involves the issue of whether the cotton subsidies rose to such an extent that they were no longer sheltered by the peace clause.
23. The peace clause also protects export subsidies that conform to the URAA commitments against challenge under the Agreement on Subsidies and Countervailing Measures and GATT Article XVI.
24. The sharp fall in the Japanese notifications in 1998 reflects policy shifts away from a reliance on administered prices, as well as substantial reductions in those prices. The equally dramatic rise in the US amber box category reflects the "emergency" payments that started in 1998.
25. The Canadian and Mexican figures are for 1998, as the 1999 notifications had not been reported to the WTO.
26. The Agriculture Committee meets in special session as the negotiating body for agriculture, in addition to performing its regular monitoring functions.
27. The WTO website has links to these documents, along with various notes and technical submissions, at www.wto.org.
28. The modalities of the agricultural negotiations refer to the methods by which tariffs, export subsidies, and domestic support are to be cut and by extension to any rule changes that may also be agreed in the negotiations. They are translated later

into national schedules that become part of the obligations and to new or amended articles in the URAA.

29. Many Cairns Group countries associated themselves with the proposal, as did several other WTO members. The group was initially 20 countries, but three other countries associated themselves with the group (and one country left) giving rise to the less common name of G-22.
30. The economies concerned—the European Union, United States, Brazil, India, and Australia—were careful not to be regarded as a "group," with common views. Rather, they claimed that their common link was a desire to see the talks move forward and to provide the economic and political weight to ensure such movement. As the talks on the Framework Agreement moved ahead, an extended meeting of the Five Interested Parties was instituted that included members of the G-10, China, and some other developing countries.
31. This agricultural framework constitutes Annex A of the Framework Agreement.
32. In the language of trade negotiations, a framework defines the components of the final agreement and the modalities are the specific measures that will be taken along with any necessary rule changes. After that, the agreement has to be translated into legal terms, the WTO members have to produce draft schedules implementing the modalities, and a final decision has to be taken.
33. Under this authority the US executive branch can negotiate trade agreements that then have to be implemented by congressional action. Congress agrees to vote such legislation up or down, rather than offer amendments.
34. Request and offer techniques are still used, for instance, in the services negotiations.
35. The best-known formula is the Swiss formula, which was applied in the Tokyo Round. This formula is designed to achieve deeper cuts in high tariffs and to specifically address the problem of tariff peaks. The formula is $T_1 = aT_0/(a + T_0)$, where T_0 is the initial tariff, T_1> is the new tariff, and a is a parameter that determines the depth of cut. The reduction parameter, a, used in the Tokyo Round was 16, but this reduction method was designed for initial tariffs that were less than 50 percent (Laird 1998). With the parameter $a = 16$ a tariff of 350 percent is reduced to 15 percent; with $a = 60$ the reduced tariff is 51 percent; with $a = 140$ the reduced tariff is 100 percent.
36. Under the original US proposal, high agricultural tariffs would have converged on a level of 25 percent. The use of such a formula does not reduce low tariffs as much as the across-the-board reductions employed in the Uruguay Round.
37. In addition, the draft includes a suggestion that tariff escalation be reduced by cutting tariffs on processed goods by a greater amount that those on raw materials.
38. The US-EU joint proposal also includes a greater reduction in tariffs on goods of interest to developing countries.
39. The Harbinson draft is sympathetic to the notion that preference margins be maintained "to the maximum extent technically feasible" including the slower liberalization of access where "long-standing preferences" are present.
40. With an inelastic demand rents will decline as the quota is increased, but with an elastic demand quota rents will increase as the import quota is expanded.
41. Auctions have the additional benefit that auction prices can identify the true tariff equivalent of the quota, and this could be used to set the initial, bound over-quota tariff, which could be gradually reduced. An alternative approach would be to establish resale markets for quota rights. This would avoid the need to develop a potentially expensive bureaucratic structure. If resale markets were monitored, this would provide information on the true tariff equivalents for the products traded. These options are appealing because they would minimize disruptions to markets

by gradually reducing trade barriers, while at the same time providing meaningful market access opportunities.

42. In addition to the administrative issue, a new set of domestic consumption figures and current access commitments may have to be developed so that all countries are working from a common base for minimum access commitments. Simultaneously, negotiators will have to determine the level of product aggregation to which the new commitments will apply.
43. These technical discussions took place throughout the summer leading up to the Cancún Ministerial Meeting. A report on their progress was given to the Trade Negotiating Committee in July 2003.
44. The G-20 proposal on market access of July 2005 does include the removal of the special safeguards. Neither the US nor the EU papers for the Zurich meeting mentioned the issue of special safeguards, but this does not mean that they will not be a part of the market access package.
45. Some countries argue that market promotion activities should be subject to export subsidy disciplines. However, Article 9, Section 1d exempts widely used export promotion and advisory services from export subsidy reduction commitments.
46. The United States still subsidizes dairy product exports, through the Dairy Export Incentive Program.
47. In the Canadian case support exists on the part of some Canadian producers for elimination of the Canadian Wheat Board.
48. Canada and other exports with state trading entities have not yet signaled a willingness to change policies in this area. It is likely that such a move will have to wait until the "package" is considered.
49. For this, the United States suggests that an objective test be developed to identify commercial displacement by food aid.
50. The prospect of a significant tightening of the rules for allowable domestic support was diminished earlier in the negotiations by the generous subsidies of the 2002 US Farm Bill. Though technically not breaching WTO commitments, the bill reduced the credibility of the United States as an advocate for the reduction of such payments. As the European Union also has an interest in maintaining considerable flexibility for domestic subsidies, pressure from the G-20 has been needed to keep a focus on further reductions. The expiration of the peace clause at the end of 2003 and the rulings of the WTO panel in the case of US cotton subsidies have given some leverage to their position.
51. It could be questioned why *de minimis* thresholds are needed in the aggregate measurement of support rules but not in other parts of the URAA. Such a provision does not save time and effort: calculating and monitoring the aggregate measurement of support is still needed to justify a *de minimis* claim. It merely weakens the impact of the constraints on support.
52. The rationale, similar to that behind the use of the Swiss formula to eliminate tariff peaks, however, runs up against the negotiating principle that all participants must share in the "pain" of an agreement. For a full comparison of the Cairns Group, US, and EU proposals (and also one from Canada) see Brink (2002).
53. Recent changes in the EU Common Agricultural Policy have made it more possible to limit the blue box in this way without necessitating major changes in domestic policy.
54. The countercyclical payments do not easily fit in the green box as they are tied to the level of market prices. But they are also not tied to supply controls, and therefore are not eligible for the current blue box.

55. This wider agenda included the so-called Singapore issues of investment, competition, transparency in government procurement, and trade facilitation, where working parties engaged in some "pre-negotiations" to identify the key topics to be addressed. But pressure from developing countries, and lack of strong support from several developed countries, persuaded negotiators to drop all the Singapore issues except for trade facilitation (addressing customs procedures). The ministers also were to have considered suggested "interpretations and clarifications" to such contentious trade issues as antidumping policies at Cancún. These "rules" issues are still under discussion. The topic of trade and labor, however, is not on the agenda, and the environment issues will be addressed primarily in a report from the Committee on Trade and the Environment.
56. The services negotiations also had a deadline of March 31, 2003, for the submission of final offers. This deadline passed with relatively few offers being tabled. A significant increase in these offers may be necessary if ministers are to agree to a package of modalities.
57. Draft modalities on nonagricultural tariffs (nonagricultural market access) were supposed to have been tabled by March 31, 2003, with agreement by May 31. The Framework Agreement of July 2004 included some options for an agreement, but the modalities have also not yet been decided.
58. Negotiations are also proceeding on "improvements and clarifications" to the dispute settlement process, on the "establishment of a multilateral system of notification and registration of Geographical Indications for wines and spirits," and on the ways in which least developed countries might be helped in their accession to the WTO. This third set of talks is among the few that have progressed on target, and several least developed countries are in the process of joining the WTO.
59. Negotiations are said to have "positive linkages" when progress in one area encourages movement in another and "negative linkages" when the slow progress is contagious. Cairns Group countries have in particular indicated an unwillingness to move on nonagricultural issues when there is no progress on agriculture.
60. It is ironic, if not inexplicable, that the EU member with the most defensive position with respect to the talks (France) is also one of the main agricultural exporters in the European Union. The change of heart mentioned here is largely dependent on changes in French policy.
61. See Josling and Rae (1999) for a discussion of the drawbacks of sectoral negotiations that can lead to imbalances.

BIBLIOGRAPHY

Abbott, P., and B. A. Morse. 2000. "Tariff Rate Quota Development and Administration by Developing Countries." *Agricultural and Resource Economics Review* 29 (1): 115–24.

Abbott, P. C., and L. M. Young. 1999. "Wheat-Importing State Trading Enterprises: Impacts on the World Wheat Market." *Canadian Journal of Agricultural Economics* 47: 119–36.

Anderson, K. 1999. *Cairns Group Perspective: Getting Ready for the Millennium Round—2020 Focus I.* Washington, DC: International Food Policy Research Institute.

Brink, Lars. 2002. "Assessing the Proposals of the Cairns Group, Canada, and the United States for WTO Disciplines on Domestic Support." Paper presented to the International Agricultural Trade Research Consortium Annual Meeting, Monterey, California, Dec. 15–17.

Falcon, W. P., and E. A. Monke. 1980. "International Trade in Rice." *Food Research Institute Studies* 17 (3): 279–304.

Gibson, P., J. Wainio, D. Whitley, and M. Bohman. 2001. "Profiles of Tariffs in Global Agricultural Markets." AER 796. U.S. Department of Agriculture, Washington, DC.

Grethe, H., and S. Tangermann. 1999. "The EU Import Regime for Fresh Fruit and Vegetables after Implementation of the Results of the Uruguay Round." Diskussionsbeitrag 9901, Institut für Agrarökonomie, Göttingen.

IATRC (International Agricultural Trade Research Consortium). 1994. "Bringing Agriculture Into the GATT: The Uruguay Round Agreement on Agriculture—An Evaluation." Commissioned Paper 9, Minneapolis, MN.

———. 2001a. "The Current WTO Agricultural Negotiations: Options for Progress." Commissioned Paper 18, Minneapolis, MN.

———. 2001b. "Issues in Reforming Tariff-Rate Import Quotas in the Agreement on Agriculture." Commissioned Paper 13, Minneapolis, MN.

Josling, T. 1998. *Agricultural Trade Policy: Completing the Reform.* Washington, DC: Institute for International Economics.

Josling, T., and A. Rae. 1999. "Market Access Negotiations in Agriculture." Paper prepared for the World Bank Conference on Developing Countries and the New Agricultural Negotiations, Geneva, October 1–2.

Josling, T., and S. Tangermann. 2003. "Production and Export Subsidies in Agriculture: Lessons From GATT and WTO Disputes Involving the US and the EC." In *Transatlantic Economic Disputes,* ed. Ernst-Ulrich Petersmann and Mark Pollack. New York: Oxford University Press.

Laird, S. 1998. "Multilateral Approaches to Market Access Negotiations." Trade Policy Review Division Staff Working Paper TPRD-98-92, WTO, Geneva.

McCalla, A. F. 2001. "What the Developing Countries Want from the WTO." *Estey Centre Journal of International Law and Trade Policy* 2 (1): 165–77.

Meilke, K. D., M. Wensley, and M. Cluff. 2001. "The Impact of Trade Liberalization on the International Oilseed Complex." *Review of Agricultural Economics* 23 (1): 2–17.

OECD (Organisation for Economic Co-operation and Development). 2000. "An Analysis of Officially Supported Export Credits in Agriculture." COM/AGR/TD/WP(2000)91/FINAL, OECD, Paris.

———. 2001a. *Agricultural Policies in OECD Countries: Monitoring and Evaluation.* Paris: OECD.

———. 2001b. *The Uruguay Round Agreement on Agriculture: An Evaluation of Its Implementation in OECD Countries.* Paris: OECD.

———. 2003. "Agricultural Policies in OECD Countries: Monitoring and Evaluation." OECD, Paris.

OECD/DAC (Development Assistance Committee). 2001. *Aid Flows from Development Assistance Committee Members.* Paris: OECD/DAC.

Perkins, Coie. 1996. "The Special Safeguard Mechanism Under the WTO Agreement on Agriculture." Paper presented at the Symposium on Anti-Dumping and Safeguard Systems, Taipei, Feb. 28–29.

Schmitz, A., A. McCalla, D. Mitchell, and C. Carter. 1981. *Grain Export Cartels.* Cambridge: Ballinger Press.

Steinberg, Richard H., and Timothy E. Josling. 2003. "When the Peace Ends: The Vulnerability of EC and US Agricultural Subsidies to WTO Legal Challenge." *Journal of International Economic Law* 6 (2): 369–417.

Stiglitz, J. E. 2000. "Two Principles for the Next Round, or How to Bring Developing Countries in from the Cold." *The World Economy* 23 (4): 437–53.

Tangermann, S. 2000. "Agriculture on the Way to Firm International Trading Rules." Paper prepared for the University of Minnesota Law School Conference on the Political Economy of International Trade Law Honoring Professor Robert E. Hudec, University of Minnesota, Sept. 15–16.

Tangermann, S., T. Josling, M. Honma, J. Lee, D. MacLaren, D. McClatchy, D. Miner, G. Pursell, D. Sumner, and A. Valdés. 1997. "Implementation of the Uruguay Round Agreement on Agriculture and Issues for the Next Round of Agricultural Negotiations." IATRC Commissioned Paper12, Minneapolis, MN.

Wainio, J., P. Gibson, and D. Whitley. 2001. "Background Paper on Options for Reducing Agricultural Tariffs." In "Agricultural Policy Reform in the WTO: The Road Ahead." Report ERS-E01-001, U.S Department of Agriculture, Washington, DC.

WFP (World Food Programme). 2000. Annex. *Annual Report.* WFP/EB.A/2000/3-A, Rome: WFP.

WTO (World Trade Organization). 1996. *The Results of the Uruguay Round of Multilateral Trade Negotiations: The Legal Texts.* Geneva: WTO.

———. 2000a. *Agreement on Agriculture: Special and Differential Treatment and a Development Box, Proposal to the June 2000 Special Session of the Committee on Agriculture by Cuba, Dominican Republic, Honduras, Pakistan, Haiti, Nicaragua, Kenya, Uganda, Zimbabwe, Sri Lanka and El Salvador.* Geneva: WTO

———. 2000b. "Domestic Support." Background paper by the Secretariat. G/AG/NG/S/1, WTO, Geneva.

———. 2000c. "Export Subsidies." Background paper by the Secretariat. G/AG/NG/S/5, WTO, Geneva.

———. 2002. "Negotiations on Agriculture: Overview." TN/AG/6, 18. WTO, Geneva.

———. 2003. "Negotiations on Agriculture: First Draft of Modalities for the Further Commitments" (Revision). TN/AG/W/1/Rev.1, WTO, Geneva.

———. 2004. "Doha Work Programme: Decision Adopted by the General Council on 1 August 2004." WT/L/579, WTO, Geneva.

Young, L. 1999. "Prevalence and Reform of State Trading Importers in World Grain Markets." *Canadian Journal of Agricultural Economics* 47 (4): 351–62.

CHAPTER THREE

Developing Country Experience with the Key Policy Issues of the Uruguay Round Agreement on Agriculture

Ramesh Sharma

Reviewing countries' experiences with implementation of the Uruguay Round Agreement on Agriculture (URAA) can provide important guidance for negotiating the new round effectively. Article 20 of the URAA calls on World Trade Organization (WTO) members to review their experience in preparation for the new negotiations. The main source for reviewing implementation experience is the reports of the WTO Committee on Agriculture, which meets regularly. The WTO's national Trade Policy Review reports also provide helpful insights. Many civil society organizations have also made valuable contributions to this analysis in recent years. And there is a growing literature on the subject by individual researchers and agencies. In 1999 the Food and Agriculture Organization (FAO) commissioned 14 case studies to review country experiences with implementation of the URAA, changes in trade flows, and other effects of trade liberalization.[1] Subsequently, the FAO completed nine other country case studies.[2]

This chapter summarizes experience with implementation of the rules and country-specific commitments of the URAA, focusing on its three main pillars: domestic support, market access, and export competition. It reviews trends in agricultural exports and food imports since 1995 and draws some conclusions on negotiating and policy issues.

On domestic support measures it finds that levels of trade-distorting domestic subsidies have been very low on the whole relative to what the URAA permits, and so the rules and commitments have not constrained policies or outlays. The interest of developing countries might be better served by focusing more on reducing high levels of support to developed country agriculture than on obtaining additional flexibility for themselves. With applied tariffs much lower than the bound rates on average, developing country experience with border measures has been positive on the whole, though there were many instances of countries facing particular difficulties in basic foods. With the limited range of feasible policy instruments available to developing countries at this stage of their economic development, "appropriate" levels of bound tariffs are of particular significance. Export subsidies are not an implementation issue for most developing countries, but their use by other trading partners is a matter of considerable concern. The net agriculture trade position of developing countries as a whole worsened between 1990–94 and 1995–99 despite marked increases in agricultural exports because of sharp increases in food imports.

HOW SHOULD IMPLEMENTATION EXPERIENCES WITH THE URUGUAY ROUND AGREEMENT ON AGRICULTURE BE EVALUATED?

The URAA focused on disciplining policies that were considered to distort production and trade. The URAA prohibits very few policies—a notable one being quantitative restrictions on trade. Most policies are disciplined by setting upper limits on actions, such as how much tariffs may be raised or what trade-distorting subsidies can be granted. The commitment to implement policies within some limit applies to all WTO members.

One criterion for reviewing experiences would be to see how countries have complied with the general rules and country-specific committed limits. For example, did all agricultural trade take place under a tariff-only regime or were there exceptions? Did domestic and export subsidies remain within permitted limits at all times? But it is unlikely that there will be much to review on the basis of this criterion because there have been very few reports of breaches in basic rules and commitments. A more relevant question is whether countries have been able to live comfortably within the set limits. Thus, the issue is one of degree of flexibility in policy choices. To what extent do commitments appear to be binding?

Especially among trade negotiators and policymakers there is a tendency to associate less binding commitments with "positive" experience, and rules and commitments that have restricted action with "negative" experience. This is the predominant view. Another view is that the URAA encourages best practices and provides an opportunity for countries to lock-in policy reforms. From this standpoint binding commitments—for example, forcing countries to shift domestic support outlays away from trade-distorting subsidies—would be reckoned as a positive experience because it contributes to greater efficiency in resource allocation. Yet the primary interest of trade negotiators (often unspoken) seems to be achieving or maintaining some degree of flexibility.[3] Therefore, the margin of policy flexibility is a key criterion for evaluating experiences.

Other experiences should also be reviewed. These include, for example, difficulties in meeting notification obligations, preparing statistics for these notifications, and defending these numbers and policies to other members at the WTO Committee on Agriculture. Finally, a review of experience with actual trade flows since 1995 is a useful complement to the analysis of policies.[4]

DOMESTIC SUPPORT MEASURES

With respect to domestic support measures the key issue is the extent to which developing countries are constrained in their policies and support outlays by general rules and by their own commitments. The URAA limits outlays on measures considered to be trade-distorting (included in the aggregate measurement of support or AMS) but not other measures, such as those under the green box. The two components of the AMS, product-specific and non-product-specific, are disciplined separately. Five main issues are being addressed in this area in the ongoing negotiations and are briefly discussed below.

Some 80 Percent of Developing Country WTO Members Have Provided No Information on Trade-Distorting Support Levels

Considering that the most important debate in this area has been on policy flexibility, it is striking that there is no information for 96 of the 118 developing countries to verify the extent to which their policies have been constrained (box 3.1). Without an AMS reduction commitment their support measures fall, by default, under exempted categories (green box, Article 6.2 development measures, and within the 10 percent *de minimis* level of the AMS). Although this lack of information on policy flexibility for these countries is a handicap for the debate, some inference can be drawn on the basis of information available for other developing countries (reviewed below).

Product-Specific Aggregate Measurement of Support—Fewer Commodities Receiving Price Support, but Mixed Experience on Binding

There is a trend in national agricultural policies toward removing price supports, so that product-specific AMS is relevant for fewer commodities now

Box 3.1 Availability of Information on Trade-Distorting Domestic Support Measures (Aggregate Measurement of Support)

136 WTO members (as of April 2000)

- 18 developed countries all with detailed information on AMS
- 118 developing countries
  - 96 with no information on AMS
  - 22 with some information on AMS[a]
    - 21 with information on product-specific AMS
    - 11 with information on non-product-specific AMS

a. Of these, 13 have total AMS reduction commitments and 9 do not.
Source: Compiled from WTO (2000b).

than in 1986–88 (the Uruguay Round base period) or even in 1995. For example, Pakistan had product-specific AMS on 10 crops in 1986–88, but for only 3 by 1995/96 and for only 1 (for wheat) in the following two years. Brazil had 22 crops with product-specific AMS in 1986–88 but only 3 (cotton, rice, and sugarcane) in 1997/98. These policy changes were not due to the URAA, which permits countries to continue these policies. Rather, they reflect policy reforms in most developing countries since about mid-1980s under structural adjustment or similar programs. This observation also applies to developing countries for which there are no WTO notifications in this area.[5]

While fewer commodities are receiving price support, experience is mixed on whether commitments are binding. In several cases actual support levels were high relative to the committed levels. For example, product-specific AMS levels were 60 percent of the committed level in 1996 and 79 percent in 1997 for Thailand, 33 percent in 1996 and 12 percent in 1997 for Morocco,[6] and about 25 percent in both 1996 and 1997 for Brazil. For countries without reduction commitments the limit is the *de minimis* level (10 percent of the value of production of that commodity). There are also several cases where the product-specific AMS levels were closer to the 10 percent limit, but most are relatively low (about 2–5 percent). While this information is not available for most developing countries, in general terms 10 percent of the value of production (not value-added) is a large amount for most major commodities to constrain product-specific subsidies.

Finally, a potential problem for countries without reduction commitments is that they cannot provide price support to any commodity beyond the 10 percent level, which could be a binding constraint for some countries. For countries with reduction commitments the rules allow shifting total AMS across commodities, and so support can be concentrated in two to three commodities (the 10 percent limit can be exceeded if the total AMS limit permits).

Non-Product-Specific AMS Offers Greater Promise for Developing Countries, but More Flexibility Is Needed

To the extent that developing countries cannot politically afford to maintain high domestic prices (through support prices and tariffs) for reasons of food insecurity and lack of resources, providing some support to farmers through input subsidies (fertilizers, credit, electricity) is an attractive option. That makes rules on non-product-specific AMS more important for developing countries than rules on product-specific AMS.

Of the 22 developing countries with information on AMS, only 11 have data on non-product-specific AMS. Four of them (India, Pakistan, Peru, and Uruguay) do not have a commitment to reduce total AMS.

The data provide some insight on whether the 11 countries have been constrained by rules on non-product-specific AMS (table 3.1). In only one country was the ratio of non-product-specific AMS to the value of total agricultural production closer to the 10 percent limit (Peru, at 6.2 percent). This ratio was also very high (at 7.5 percent) for India for 1995, but from 1996 onward India notified most of these outlays on input subsidies under Article 6.2, rather than under non-product-specific AMS. This is reflected in the high ratio of Article 6.2 outlays to value of production (table 3.2). The weighted average for the 11 countries was only 1.3 percent. The message is simple: the non-product-specific AMS has not constrained any of these countries so far, and except for Peru there is considerable scope for providing additional support.

Many developing countries have called for additional flexibility, with proposals to increase the *de minimis* level, to permit combining product-specific and non-product-specific AMS in applying the 10 percent rule, and to exempt from the AMS support to food crops designated as essential to food security.

Since lack of flexibility does not seem to have been a problem so far, why have so many proposals expressed apprehensions and called for greater flexibility? One reason could be fear for the future. The Egypt case study (in FAO 2000) notes that Egypt may need to reassess its food strategy, especially for wheat, under the assumptions that food aid will shrink, export subsidies will dry up, and import costs will rise as trade is further liberalized globally. One study estimates that raising Egypt's self-sufficiency ratio for wheat from the 1994/95 level of 48 percent to 60 percent would require product support of more than the 10 percent *de minimis* level, which is Egypt's current limit (Kheralla and others 2000).

Another reason for concern could be that some 100 developing country WTO members do not have any subsidy notifications, although many of the countries are known to provide some subsidies to agriculture.[7] How close they are to the limit is therefore not known. So far, there has been little scrutiny in

Table 3.1 Non-Product-Specific Aggregate Measurement of Support and Value of Total Agricultural Production

Country	Year	Commitment to total AMS reduction?	Non-product-specific AMS (millions US$)	Value of agricultural production (millions US$)	Non-product-specific AMS as share of total agricultural production (percent)
Brazil	2000	Yes	740	38,409	1.93
Chile	2000	Yes	39	4,144	0.94
India	1997	No	1,003	91,113	1.10
Jordan	2001	Yes	3.1	777	0.04
Korea, Rep.	2000	Yes	365	28,140	1.30
Mexico	1995	Yes	51	20,875	0.24
Pakistan	1999	No	13	11,094	0.12
Peru	1997	No	277	4,448	6.23
Tunisia	2001	Yes	8	2,453	0.33
Uruguay	1999	No	7	2,327	0.30
Venezuela	1998	Yes	115	4,237	2.71
Total	n.a.	n.a.	2,621	208,017	1.26

Sources: Author's computation using data in WTO notifications. Agricultural production values for Egypt, Pakistan, and Venezuela are from FAO and for the Republic of Korea and Mexico from OECD.
Note: n.a., not applicable.

the WTO Committee on Agriculture of policies not notified, but this could change at any time. Since WTO commitments once made are difficult to revise, developing countries would prefer more flexibility in the rules.

Subsidies under Article 6.2 Are Potentially Valuable for Developing Countries but Require Greater Clarity

Article 6.2 of the URAA exempts from inclusion in the AMS "investment subsidies which are generally available to agriculture in developing country Members and agricultural input subsidies generally available to low-income or resource-poor producers in developing country Members," where these measures are an integral part of agricultural and rural development. Since these are the same types of subsidies as those covered by non-product-specific AMS, Article 6.2 provides additional scope for subsidizing agriculture under some criteria. Between 1995 and 2002, 25 developing country WTO members used this provision (table 3.2).[8] Only four countries (India, Malaysia, Tunisia, and Turkey) had Article 6.2 outlays exceeding 2 percent of the value of production, six countries had outlays of 1–2 percent, and the rest had outlays of less than 1 percent.[9] The weighted average for the 25 countries was 2.2 percent.

Table 3.2 Outlays on Article 6.2 Development Measures and Total Value of Agricultural Production

Country	Year	Article 6.2 outlay (millions US$)	Value of agricultural production (millions US$)	Ratio of Article 6.2 outlay to production (percent)
Bahrain	1996	2.5	—	—
Brazil	2000	332	38,409	0.86
Chile	2000	3.2	4,144	0.08
Colombia	1998	45	7,783	0.58
Costa Rica	1997	14	1,111	1.26
Cyprus	1997	3.8	493	0.77
Egypt	1998	2.4	11,313	0.02
Fiji	1997	1.8	286	0.63
Gambia	1997	0.25	70	0.36
Honduras	1999	1.9	1,993	0.10
India	1997	5,172	91,113	5.68
Jordan	2001	6	777	0.77
Korea, Rep.	2000	51	28,140	0.18
Malaysia	1997	220	10,118	2.17
Mexico	1998	40	27,981	0.14
Morocco	2001	134	7,048	1.90
Namibia	1997	3.7	288	1.28
Pakistan	1995	1	11,094	0.01
Philippines	2000	74	24,704	0.30
Sri Lanka	1997	26	2,030	1.28
Thailand	1997	170	12,917	1.32
Tunisia	2001	61	2,453	2.49
Turkey	1996	671	28,762	2.33
Uruguay	1999	5.4	2,327	0.23
Venezuela	1998	47	4,237	1.11
Total	n.a.	7,089	319,591	2.22

Sources: Author's computation using data in WTO notifications. Agricultural production values are from WTO notifications, FAO, and OECD.

Note: n.a., not applicable; —, not available.

Some of the key terms in Article 6.2 are not defined clearly, such as what are "low-income" and "resource-poor" farmers or "generally available" subsidies? Subsidies granted under this provision are currently low, which may explain why use of this provision has not received much scrutiny by other WTO members. This may change, however, if developing countries raise these outlays substantially. This provision is potentially very useful for developing countries, so there is a need for greater clarity.

Review Meetings of the WTO Committee on Agriculture Have Identified Many Practical Difficulties Facing Developing Countries

Besides Article 6.2, other issues of definition and methodology arose in the Committee on Agriculture. They include accounting for the effects of inflation and currency depreciation in calculating the AMS; revisions in the AMS calculation methodology from that originally used; definition of "eligible" production in computing the AMS; treatment of negative AMS; confusion over the logic of using fixed, historical external reference prices for computing current AMS levels; definition of reference prices if a country changes its trade status during the implementation period (from net importer to net exporter, for example); and treatment of recovery (or lack of it) of investment and operating costs (for example, on irrigation projects). These and other issues are discussed in detail in the FAO (2000) case studies.

Some of these issues also reflect particular difficulties of low-income agricultural economies. For developing countries as a whole, and for all WTO members, it is important to resolve these ambiguities, definitional problems, and practical difficulties.

MARKET ACCESS

The main instruments of market access for which rules have been written and commitments made are bound tariffs, tariff rate quotas, and special agricultural safeguards.[10] For developing country implementation experience, however, tariffs are the most relevant because most developing countries are unable to use special safeguards (discussed later), and few have used tariff rate quotas. Developing country experiences are summarized here under four main points.

Compliance with the Tariffs Only Rule for Border Measures and with Committed Bound Tariff Rates Has Not Generally Been a Problem

With a few exceptions, lack of compliance on the use of tariffs only for border protection has not been an issue. By the time the URAA was implemented, most developing countries had already abandoned quantitative trade restrictions.

A major accomplishment of the Uruguay Round was tariff binding, with developing countries binding almost 100 percent of their agricultural tariff lines. For most developing countries, applied tariff rates are much lower than bound rates. For a sample of 32 developing countries the simple average applied rate is 20 percent, while the average bound rate is 84 percent (table 3.3).[11] Most developing countries went through a series of trade policy reforms before conclusion of the Uruguay Round and had consequently eliminated most non-

Table 3.3 Average Bound and Applied Tariffs on All Agricultural Products in 32 Developing Countries

	Bound rate (percent)	Applied rate (percent)	Ratio of applied to bound rate (percent)
Argentina	35	13	37
Brazil	36	11	31
Colombia	87	22	25
Costa Rica	42	17	40
Ecuador	26	16	62
El Salvador	41	13	32
Guatemala	49	11	22
Mexico	63	20	32
Nicaragua	61	11	18
Panama	43	12	28
Paraguay	35	10	29
Peru	30	13	43
Uruguay	32	13	41
Venezuela	52	15	29
Average (14)	45	14	31
Coefficient of variation (14)	36	25	70
Bangladesh	200	25	13
Fiji	50	15	30
India	114	26	23
Indonesia	48	16	33
Korea, Rep.	66	50	76
Pakistan	102	22	22
Philippines	34	19	56
Sri Lanka	50	20	40
Thailand	36	32	89
Average (9)	78	25	32
Coefficient of variation (9)	69	43	62
Egypt	28	19	68
Kenya	100	17	17
Malawi	125	18	14
Morocco	65	19	29
Mozambique	400	21	5
Tanzania	240	28	12
Tunisia	110	35	32
Zambia	125	19	15
Zimbabwe	150	27	18
Average (9)	149	23	15
Coefficient of variation (9)	74	27	36
Average (all 32)	**84**	**20**	**23**
Coefficient of variation (all 32)	**92**	**43**	**46**

Sources: Author's compilation from FAO (2000); Agricultural Market Access Database (www.amd.org); Gibson and others (2001); Southern Africa Development Community Secretariat.

Note: Bound and applied rates are simple averages for all agricultural tariff lines. Bound rates are mostly for 2004 and applied rates mostly for 1999 and 2000. Coefficient of variation is standard deviation*100/mean.

tariff barriers and reduced applied rates considerably, capping them unilaterally (in many cases as part of loan conditionality). The bound rates that were typically set as ceiling bindings during the Uruguay Round tended to be on the high side, but not for all countries.[12] In several cases applied rates were low because of the adoption of a common external tariff of a customs union. And for many developing countries, especially those with large populations at or near the poverty line, it is not politically feasible to use high tariffs to maintain high domestic prices on basic foods.

Many Countries Have Had Serious Difficulty with Ordinary Tariffs, Notably for Basic Foods

Developing country tariffs, especially on basic foods, are often higher than average and in many instances are supplemented by additional measures such as surcharges and price bands. Examples include Peru's price band policy, Morocco's threshold-price-based formula for determining import tariffs, Kenya's suspended duties (surcharges), Jamaica's additional stamp duties, and India's quantitative restrictions on balance of payments grounds and use of state trading enterprises for imports and exports (FAO 2000 and chapter 9 in this volume). Several other countries in Latin America also use variants of price bands. These measures were generally implemented for good reasons and probably with good effect. In Peru's case the 30 percent tariff (the bound rate for most agricultural products) would not have been adequate to stabilize domestic markets for sugar, wheat, and dairy products, where applied tariffs reached as high as 46–54 percent during 1995–99 (the bound tariff is 68 percent for these products). In Mexico all agricultural lines are subject to ad valorem duties with the exception of products containing sugar, which are subject to either specific or compound rates.

How should one judge these cases? It is tempting to dismiss these measures as not being in the spirit of the URAA or of falling short of "first-best" policy. But managing border measures for basic foods has not been an easy task for many developing countries, where these commodities play an important economic role (see also chapter 9 by Gulati and Narayanan in this volume). Most small farmers grow these products, and so their food and livelihood security are at stake. Because these are staple foods, market stability is an important public policy goal. These are also products whose global markets are the most distorted because of high levels of subsidies and protection. These issues need to be addressed both in the arena of food policy analysis and in WTO negotiations.

Tariffs Are Often the Primary Trade Instrument for Stabilizing Domestic Markets and Safeguarding Farmers' Interests in the Face of External Shocks

With virtually no safety net measures, no access to the special agricultural safeguard, and practical difficulties in resorting to general WTO safeguards, developing countries often have to rely on tariffs to cope with sharp swings in world market prices or changes in exchange rates.[13] Developed countries, by contrast, have a variety of nontariff instruments for coping with price and other risks, such as extra payments to farmers when prices are depressed, subsidized emergency loans and insurance programs, and risk management instruments. Because of the more important role that tariffs play in developing countries, the "appropriate" level of bound tariffs is of special concern. Lower bound rates have some benefits but also many risks.

Despite Reports of Surges in Food Imports and Other Negative Effects, Few Countries Have Applied for Formal Trade Remedy Measures in the WTO

Import surges and associated negative effects on farmers are a sensitive matter for all countries, rich and poor. Many such incidents have been reported in recent years (several are discussed in FAO 2000 and 2003). National and international nongovernmental organizations have been active in documenting such cases. Specific conditions have to be met to trigger WTO trade remedy measures, notably demonstrating a causal link between the surge and negative economic effects. During 1995–2001 only seven developing countries initiated or implemented emergency safeguards (the most popular form of trade remedy measure in agriculture) for a total of 16 agricultural products (table 3.4).[14]

This is a relatively small number compared with the many cases of import surges reported in the press and the literature. Part of the reason could be that some import surges did not have negative effects. But the main reason seems to be the complexity of the process, including the need to establish a causal link between the surge and the negative effect. As a result, many countries simply do not take formal action (see the Jamaica case in FAO 2000). The problems arising from import surges can be serious for vulnerable agriculture sectors, and therefore there is an urgent need to study this aspect carefully, documenting known cases and analyzing the sources and nature of the problem. This is also essential for devising appropriate response mechanisms for countries that lack the institutional capability to use the formal WTO trade remedies.

EXPORT COMPETITION

Very few developing countries subsidize agricultural exports, so there is little implementation experience in this area.

A few of the FAO (2000) case studies report that countries have taken advantage of the special provision for subsidies on internal transport and international freight (Article 9.1 of the URAA). But this has been used on a limited scale and selectively for high-value, low-weight products like cut flowers, fresh fruit, and vegetables. There have been no proposals to the WTO concerning this provision, and developing countries will likely continue to find it useful.

Table 3.4 Emergency Safeguards on Agricultural Products Initiated by Developing Countries, 1995–2001		
Country	**Product**	**Date initiated**
Chile	Wheat and wheat flour, cane/beet sugar, edible vegetable oils	September 1999
	Liquid and powdered milk	June 2000
Egypt	Powdered milk	September 2000
El Salvador	Pork and rice	January and June 2000
Korea, Rep.	Soybean oil	1995
	Dairy products	1996
	Garlic	1999
Morocco	Bananas	June 2000
Argentina	Peaches	January 2001
Brazil	Coconuts	August 2001

Source: Author's compilation from annual reports of the WTO Safeguards Committee.

More widespread, however, are export incentive measures such as tax breaks, currency retention schemes, and duty drawbacks. These schemes are not referred to in the URAA but in Annex 1 of the Agreement on Subsidies and Countervailing Measures. The status of such subsidies for agricultural products is unclear, however, considering that the URAA prohibits all forms of agricultural subsidies for countries with a zero percent export subsidy commitment. The issue requires some clarification, though it has not yet provoked any consultation or dispute, probably because the scale of the subsidy granted is so small.

Finally, developing countries have a record of regulating agricultural exports through quantitative restrictions and taxes, both to promote agro-industries and to generate tax revenue. By the time the URAA was signed, export regimes had been substantially liberalized, and few countries still regulate exports. Many developing countries favor some form of regulation of exports of primary products to promote industrialization, however, and tariff escalation in export markets is said to be one justification for such regulation.

EXPERIENCE WITH AGRICULTURAL EXPORTS AND FOOD IMPORTS SINCE 1995

Trade expansion is a goal of most countries and a key motivation for WTO membership. Thus there is considerable interest in information on the impact of the Uruguay Round, especially the URAA, on trade. Yet, it is analytically difficult to quantify the impact ex post, notably to isolate the effect of the Uruguay Round reforms from many other developments taking place simultaneously—which is not a problem in ex ante model-based impact assessments. Nevertheless, it is useful to know whether recent experience with agricultural trade has been positive or negative. The question should be, what has experience been since 1995 rather than what has the impact of the URAA been since 1995?

Trade experience is derived from FAOSTAT trade statistics on total agricultural exports and total food imports and on a few products defined as basic foods—cereals, dairy and meat products, oilseeds and vegetable oils, fruit and vegetables, and sugar. Basic foods are the main commodities whose markets are highly distorted by subsidies and protection, and so the impact of the URAA should be felt primarily in these markets. These products are produced in both developed and developing countries, and the products are the main concern of many of the URAA-related issues. For basic foods, trade statistics were also constructed in constant prices (average 1989–91 export and import unit values), to give an indication of the change in trade volume.

A simple approach for reviewing the trade data is to compare the average values of exports and imports for the post-Uruguay Round period, 1995–99, with those for the pre-Uruguay Round period, 1990–94. When a series is trending upward, as with trade data, the second period average is obviously higher than the first period average. The value of this comparison lies rather in the relative changes experienced by various country groups. In addition, actual 1995–99 values are compared with extrapolated values for this period derived from a linear trend estimated with the data for nine prior years, 1986–94. With the extrapolated values for 1995–99 assigned to represent some form of a counterfactual scenario, this comparison would show departures from that baseline.

Statistics are presented for five country groups:

- Least developed countries, as classified by the United Nations (49 countries in 2002).
- Cairns Group-14, the developing country members of the Cairns Group (14 countries).[15]
- Other developing countries—all remaining developing countries (about 120 countries).
- Developed countries (about 30, counting the EU-15 as one, as classified in FAOSTAT).
- World total.

Agricultural Exports

For total agricultural products in current prices, export performance between the two periods was similar for the two major country groups, with a 38 percent increase for developing countries and 31 percent for developed countries (table 3.5).[16] The performance of the Cairns Group-14 stands out, with a 50 percent rise. The least developed countries had the smallest gain, at 24 percent. All country groups performed better relative to the historical trend. The least developed countries appear to have done much better than the other groups, with 40 percent more exports in 1995–99 than predicted by the trend level.

In volume terms (constant prices) exports of the seven basic foods increased by about 24 percent for both the developing and developed countries. The least developed countries performed relatively better (23 percent increase, the same as in current prices). The smallest increase was for the rest of the developing countries, at 14 percent. This group also performed poorly compared with the historical trend (a 3 percent fall), the only group to suffer a decline. Only developed countries and Cairns Group-14 performed markedly better, at 9 percent above trend values.

Changes in relative shares in world agricultural exports are also informative (last two columns of table 3.5). For the seven basic foods in constant prices, only the Cairns Group-14 increased its share notably, from 18 percent in 1990–94 to 20 percent in 1995–99, while other developing country groups experienced slight declines in their shares, despite the increases in absolute terms noted above. The change was marginally positive for developed countries.

Several FAO (2000) case studies attempted to relate the change in trade flows at the individual commodity level to changes in market access or other factors. For example, the rapid growth in Brazil's agricultural exports in recent years (such as in soybeans and soybean products, sugar, and poultry) was attributed to a large extent to the remarkable and consistent rise in crop yields—to competitive advantage led by productivity growth. The export performance for poultry was particularly impressive (26 percent increase in volume) despite little change in market access terms for poultry in the URAA. Similarly, Sri Lanka's notable increase in agricultural exports between the two periods was not attributed to the URAA because expansions took place in products that had faced few access problems even before the Uruguay Round (such as, tea, coconut, and rubber) and because trade had expanded to Persian Gulf countries that were not members of the WTO.

Many case studies identified fruits and vegetables as the principal nontraditional products with good export prospects. In some cases there were reports of positive effects, though minor, such as for Bangladesh, Guyana, Jamaica, and Pakistan. In other cases, preferential access, rather than improved access terms negotiated multilaterally, was said to explain the growth, such as for Egypt and Morocco.

While these analyses provide useful information, a thorough analysis of agricultural export performance, relating export performance to changes in market access, is yet to be undertaken.

Food Imports

On the import side the seven basic foods comprise about 90 percent of all food in the FAOSTAT category "food (excluding fish)," so the results for basic foods are similar to those for all foods. Imports of basic foods increased sharply for

Table 3.5 Comparison of Food and Agricultural Exports, 1990–94 and 1995–99

	Values (billions US$)		Change (percent)		Share in world total (percent)	
	1990–94	1995–99	Between periods	From trend[a]	1990–94	1995–99
Total agriculture, in current prices						
All developing countries	95	132	38	15	41.5	42.7
Least developed countries	3.9	4.9	24	40	1.7	1.6
Cairns Group-14	41	61	50	18	17.6	19.7
Other developing countries[b]	51	66	30	11	22.1	21.5
Developed countries[c]	135	177	31	2	58.5	57.3
World total[c]	230	309	34	7	100	100
Basic foods, in current prices[d]						
All developing countries	50	69	39	9	39.3	40.7
Least developed countries	1.0	1.2	23	8	0.8	0.7
Cairns Group-14	23	35	52	11	18.2	20.8
Other developing countries[b]	26	33	27	6	20.3	19.2
Developed countries[c]	77	101	31	4	60.7	59.3
World total[c]	127	170	34	6	100	100
Other agricultural products, in current prices						
All developing countries	45	63	38	23	44.1	45.1
Least developed countries	3.0	3.7	25	54	2.9	2.7
Cairns Group-14	17	25	46	31	16.9	18.3
Other developing countries[b]	25	34	34	15	24.3	24.2
Developed countries[c]	58	76	32	1	55.9	54.9
World total[c]	103	139	35	10	100	100
Basic foods, in constant 1989–91 prices[d]						
All developing countries	50	61	23	3	39.0	38.8
Least developed countries	1.1	1.4	23	2	0.9	0.9
Cairns Group-14	22	29	31	9	17.3	18.3
Other developing countries[b]	26	30	14	–3	20.8	19.2
Developed countries[c]	78	96	24	9	61.0	61.2
World total[c]	127	157	24	7	100	100

Source: Author's computation using FAOSTAT database.

a. Actual 1995–99 value compared with extrapolated value for this period computed from a linear trend estimated with 1986–94 data.

b. Includes all developing countries except the least developed countries and Cairns Group-14.

c. Excludes intra-EU trade.

d. Basic foods include cereals, meats, dairy products, oilseeds and oils, fruit, vegetables, and sugar.

developing countries—by 44 percent in current prices between the two periods (table 3.6). This was in marked contrast to the case of developed countries as a group, which experienced only a 16 percent increase. Among developing countries food imports rose the most for Cairns Group-14 (89 percent), but they also rose markedly for the rest of the developing countries (37 percent) and the least developed countries (29 percent). Thus, while the experience of the two main country groups was similar for total agricultural exports, it was considerably different for food imports.

In volume term (constant price) as well, imports of basic foods by developing countries increased markedly, by about 25 percent for both the least developed countries and the rest of the developing countries, 67 percent for Cairns Group-14, and 32 percent for all developing countries. For developed countries, however, the increase was only 10 percent. Compared with trend values, food imports in 1995–99 were higher by 11–17 percent for developing country groups but 3 percent lower for developed countries.

Thus, on the whole, food imports by developing countries increased markedly since 1995, both between the two periods and relative to trend levels. Many factors explain these changes, but it is difficult to identify their individual contributions. In particular, there is a heightened interest in whether (and to what extent) trade liberalization by importing countries themselves was a major factor.[17]

Overall Performance: Net Trade in Basic Foods and Total Agriculture

What can be said of experience with agricultural trade on balance? For developing countries as a whole the net deficit in basic foods rose by $6 billion between 1990–94 and 1995–99, reflecting the combined loss of $11 billion for the rest of the developing countries and least developed countries and the gain of $5 billion for Cairns Group-14 (table 3.7). Developed countries experienced a net gain of $10 billion. A notable difference between results in current and constant prices is that the surplus for the Cairns Group-14 was much smaller in constant prices ($1 billion rather than $5 billion).

While developing countries gained $4 billion in net exports of agricultural products other than basic foods, this surplus was not sufficient to offset the deficit in basic foods. For developed countries, however, the trade surplus in basic foods more than offset the $3 billion deficit in other agricultural products.

Thus the overall trade experience has been positive for developed countries and negative for developing countries, especially for basic foods. If the URAA had any influence on trade flows during 1995–99—a big "if" given the modest extent of reform—the outcome was not what many global trade models had projected back in 1995 and earlier, when there was an expectation that production and export would shrink somewhat in countries that subsidize agriculture and expand elsewhere following URAA reforms.[18]

Table 3.6 Comparison of Food Imports, 1990–94 and 1995–99

	Values (billions US$)		Change (percent)	
	1990–94	1995–99	Between periods	From trend[a]
All foods, in current prices				
All developing countries	66	95	44	11
Least developed countries	5.2	6.6	27	5
Cairns Group-14	9	18	95	26
Other developing countries[b]	51	70	36	8
Developed countries[c]	100	120	21	–2
World total[c]	166	215	30	3
Basic foods, in current prices[d]				
All developing countries	58	84	44	11
Least developed countries	4.8	6.1	29	5
Cairns Group-14	8	16	89	23
Other developing countries[b]	45	62	37	9
Developed countries[c]	87	101	16	–5
World total[c]	145	185	27	2
Other foods, in current prices[e]				
All developing countries	8	11	44	5
Least developed countries	0.4	0.5	13	4
Cairns Group-14	0.9	2.3	149	45
Other developing countries[b]	7	9	31	–2
Developed countries[c]	13	19	51	17
World total[c]	20	30	48	12
Basic foods, in constant 1989–91 prices[d]				
All developing countries	58	77	32	12
Least developed countries	4.8	6	25	11
Cairns Group-14	9	14	67	17
Other developing countries[b]	45	57	26	11
Developed countries[c]	88	97	10	–3
World total[c]	146	175	20	4

Source: Author's computation using FAOSTAT database.

a. Actual 1995–99 value compared with extrapolated value for this period computed from a linear trend estimated with 1986–94 data.

b. Includes all developing countries except the least developed countries and Cairns Group-14.

c. Excludes intra-EU trade.

d. Basic foods include cereals, meats, dairy products, oilseeds and oils, fruit, vegetables, and sugar.

e. Other agricultural products include all agricultural products except basic foods as listed here.

Table 3.7 Net Trade Balance in Food and Agricultural Products, 1990–94 and 1995–99

	Net exports (billions US$)[a]		
	1990–94	1995–99	Change
Total agriculture, in current prices			
All developing countries	0	–2	–2
Least developed countries	–2	–3	–1
Cairns Group-14	26	34	8
Other developing countries[b]	–23	–33	–10
Developed countries[c]	–23	–17	6
Basic foods, in current prices[d]			
All developing countries	–8	–15	–6
Least developed countries	–4	–5	–1
Cairns Group-14	15	19	5
Other developing countries[b]	–19	–29	–10
Developed countries[c]	–10	0	10
Other agricultural products, in current prices[e]			
All developing countries	9	13	4
Least developed countries	1	2	0
Cairns Group-14	11	15	4
Other developing countries[b]	–4	–4	0
Developed countries[c]	–13	–16	–3
Basic foods, in constant 1989–91 prices[d]			
All developing countries	–9	–16	–7
Least developed countries	–4	–5	–1
Cairns Group-14	13	14	1
Other developing countries[b]	–19	–27	–8
Developed countries[c]	–10	–1	10

Source: Author's computation using FAOSTAT database.

Note: FAOSTAT reports exports at f.o.b. values and imports at c.i.f. values. As a result, at the global level the value of imports exceeds the value of exports.

a. Net exports equal exports minus imports. Negative numbers imply net imports.

b. Includes all developing countries except the least developed countries and Cairns Group-14.

c. Excludes intra-EU trade.

d. Basic foods include cereals, meats, dairy products, oilseeds and oils, fruit, vegetables, and sugar.

e. Other agricultural products include all agricultural products except basic foods as listed here.

CONCLUDING REMARKS

Several conclusions and lessons can be drawn from experience with agricultural trade reform.

Export Subsidies

Export subsidies are not an implementation issue for developing countries, but they are nonetheless a matter of considerable concern. Few developing countries grant direct export subsidies, but there is considerable concern about this practice by some developed countries. Even large net food importers that benefit from the lower food costs resulting from such subsidies have taken positions against the practice in view of negative effects on their exports and agriculture.

Developing countries have used the special provision allowing them to subsidize internal and external transport costs, which they consider useful for selectively promoting niche exports. But the overall subsidy level is not likely to be large in coming years. Developing countries also use some export incentive measures referred to in the Subsidies Agreement. There is a need to clarify the legality of these measures under the URAA.

Domestic Support Measures

Developing countries may be better served by focusing more on eliminating high levels of support to agriculture in OECD countries than on obtaining additional flexibility for themselves. Disciplines on domestic agricultural support measures have not been binding and so have not affected agricultural policies or constrained support outlays. WTO negotiating proposals from developing countries emphasize two positions: more flexibility for supporting their agriculture, and sharp curtailment of support to OECD agriculture. Although information on aggregate measurement of support levels is missing for some 80 percent of developing country WTO members, the experience of other developing countries likely applies to most of them.

No developing country has been constrained in providing additional subsidies within the non-product-specific aggregate measurement of support category. Only one or two countries were closer to the 10 percent *de minimis* level, but even then Article 6.2 provision provides additional space for subsidies. Thus, non-product-specific aggregate measurement of support is unlikely to be a major issue for most developing countries under current rules for the next 10–15 years.

Product-specific aggregate measurement of support is a different matter. Some developing countries are close to committed levels (for those with reduction commitments) or to the 10 percent *de minimis* limit (for those without reduction commitments). However, the trend is toward price supports on fewer commodities, and in coming years policymakers may decide to concentrate support on a few "sensitive" products. On the whole, 10 percent of the value of production of a commodity is unlikely to be a constraint in most cases. Nevertheless, there is some concern among developing countries without reduction commitments (the majority) because 10 percent is the limit for them while other countries can exceed the 10 percent level by concentrating their total aggregate measurement of support on a few sensitive commodities.

Thus, for developing countries additional flexibility seems less important than is sometimes claimed, whereas the high level of support to OECD agriculture is a more serious concern. Many negotiating proposals by developing countries have drawn attention to this side of the problem. There are important unresolved issues in this area, and much is at stake. Subsidies that meet specified criteria are exempted from reduction, yet subsidies that are only partially decoupled, if large enough, can generate significant distortions overall since it is the level of total distortion that matters for competitive trade. Moreover, a measure may be decoupled in that it does not increase production, while still helping to maintain production at the status quo level. Where the status quo is one of structural surplus, additional export opportunities for nonsubsidizing countries are unlikely to arise.

Market Access—Border Measures

The level of bound tariffs, especially on basic foods, is important for developing countries because of the greater vulnerability of their agriculture and small farmers and their limited institutional and financial capability to resort to general WTO safeguards and domestic policy instruments to offset external shocks. A central objective of the ongoing agricultural negotiations is to lower border protection through negotiated reductions in bound tariffs. Tabled proposals range from deep cuts on all products to smaller cuts on all commodities to achieve a given average reduction. Special treatment for developing countries is to be an integral part of the process.

Proposals for special treatment generally call for lower rates of reduction for developing countries and special treatment for selected sensitive products (mainly basic foods),[19] from full exemption from reduction to freedom to set "appropriate" levels of bindings and tariff "rationalization" (upward adjustment, where current bound rates are low).

Developing countries have had some flexibility with border measures because applied tariffs are much lower on average than bound rates. But basic foods have presented difficulties. Developing countries appear not to have much tariff protection of agriculture, nor could many of them politically afford to keep food prices high with tariffs. Therefore, higher bound rates than applied rates are essential for enabling developing countries to use the tariff as a safeguard against such external shocks as depressed import prices and import surges.

Those who support special treatment argue for the overriding importance of market stability of basic foods for developing countries, the relative vulnerability of agriculture and small farmers, the lack of financial and institutional capability to apply first-best domestic and border measures, the need to offset the distortions in global food markets arising from high levels of support and protection, and pessimism about the prospects for ending these distortions through Doha Round negotiations.

Those who oppose special treatment see high bound rates as undesirable in any context, both for developing countries and WTO reforms. They are concerned that this sets a bad example and fear damage to the spirit and tradition of the WTO if lower bound rates are rationalized upward. They argue that high bound rates hinder trade and investment by creating uncertainty, that tariffs are not the best policy for addressing problems in domestic sectors, and that appropriate tariffs would be very low or even zero under the optimum tariff theory.

The special safeguard provision was designed to respond to the types of problems that these negotiating proposals attempt to resolve, including depressed import prices and import surges. With special safeguards the ideal set of instruments for managing border measures would be relatively low tariffs, to provide some protection where needed, and the special safeguards, to respond to shocks. The Uruguay Round made access to special safeguards conditional on tariffication, resulting in their availability for products that also had high bound rates, rather than the other way around. The Doha Round provides an opportunity to rationalize border measures, making them fairer (by making special safeguards available to developing countries) and inducing countries to lower bound tariffs, with access to special safeguards conditional on that.[20]

Should developing countries fail to obtain access to the special safeguards or a similar safeguard, it would make sense for them to bind tariffs at appropriate levels, as discussed above. Table 3.8 provides a rough order of magnitude for the maximum tariffs that would be required to stabilize domestic prices at some reasonable, predetermined level when world prices are depressed.[21] The tariffs range from about 30 percent for lamb to 100 percent for coconut oil, with a simple average for all 18 foods of 54 percent. Most of the tariffs lie within a 45–55 percent range. These levels are in line with actual tariffs applied by many developing countries in recent years, especially during 1998–2000, when world prices of basic foods were severely depressed.

These tariffs do not include any protective tariff that may be in place (typically in the 10–15 percent range on average in recent years). These would need to be added to the tariffs in table 3.8 to establish the maximum tariffs required for complete price stabilization. In practice, it is difficult to separate the permanent protective tariff from the temporary safeguard component. In any case, the full maximum tariff would be required only when world prices dip very low and stay there for a prolonged period. Thus most of the time there would still be considerable "water" in the tariff. Maximum tariffs would be considerably lower when these extreme cases are not included, again highlighting the desirability of the combination of lower bound rates (25–35 percent) plus a safeguard.

If developing countries are allowed to rationalize tariffs in this way, what would be some of the implications? In most cases tariff bindings of about 50 percent will mean substantive reductions from current bound levels. In reducing bound rates, this outcome would benefit other WTO members as well as the developing countries that gain the necessary policy space to stabilize

Table 3.8 Maximum Tariff Rates for Complete Price Stabilization (percent)

	Assumed reference prices					
	Trend values[a]	1990–2000 average[b]	1990–94 average[b]	36-month moving average[c]	24-month moving average[c]	Simple average
Rice (average)	50	47	37	43	40	43
Thai A1	59	50	36	46	39	46
Thai 100	51	56	51	46	44	49
California	39	34	27	34	39	35
Wheat (average)	50	55	43	58	42	50
Argentina	80	87	66	66	50	70
US[d]	36	41	35	59	41	42
Australia	34	38	27	48	36	37
Maize	43	49	42	56	39	46
Sugar, raw	75	101	106	86	75	89
Sugar, white	53	81	88	56	42	64
Milk powder (skim)	52	65	51	31	37	47
Milk powder (whole)	39	53	38	26	27	37
Butter	47	45	28	48	49	43
Beef	29	34	58	40	37	39
Lamb	26	30	26	30	37	30
Poultry	29	57	73	52	41	51
Pork	50	49	44	53	48	49
Vegetable oils (average)	80	70	55	68	64	67
Soybean oil	64	63	56	61	47	58
Palm oil	113	81	52	97	85	86
Sunflower oil	68	61	551	67	52	60
Rapeseed oil	60	54	44	54	49	52
Coconut oil	119	107	73	96	99	99
Groundnut oil	56	55	51	34	51	50
All commodities, simple average	**56**	**59**	**51**	**55**	**49**	**54**

Source: Sharma (2002a).

a. Linear trend fitted with monthly world market price data for 1990–2000.

b. Single reference prices; simple averages for the two periods shown.

c. Moving averages of world prices.

d. United States hard winter wheat no. 2.

domestic markets. The other form of "rationalization" is to allow countries to raise tariffs currently bound at lower rates to the levels computed in table 3.8. While this approach runs counter to the WTO tradition of tariff reduction, sometimes even an established tradition may need to be "rationalized" if there are good reasons to do so.

Agricultural Exports and Food Imports

Despite marked increases in global agricultural exports the net trade position of developing countries as a whole worsened between 1990–94 and 1995–99 due to sharp increases in food imports. Increased imports of foods are not necessarily detrimental provided that the means to import food also grows. For developing countries as a group this does not seem to be the case within agriculture because their net deficit on total agricultural trade also increased. While their exports of nonagricultural products and services may have increased to more than offset the deficit in agriculture, that was not examined in this study.

NOTES

1. The 14 countries covered were: Bangladesh, Botswana, Brazil, Egypt, Guyana, India, Jamaica, Kenya, Morocco, Pakistan, Peru, Senegal, Sri Lanka, and Thailand. The individual case studies along with a synthesis chapter was published in 2000 (FAO 2000).
2. In addition to updating the 2000 case studies, the subsequent publication (FAO 2003) covered nine additional countries: Costa Rica, Côte d'Ivoire, Fiji, Honduras, Indonesia, Malawi, Philippines, Uganda, and Zimbabwe.
3. If all WTO members were instead competing with each other to lock-in first-best economic policies, trade negotiations would be over in a few weeks, not years.
4. An Organisation for Economic Co-operation and Development publication analyzes the implementation experience of OECD countries, asking some of the same questions as here (OECD 2001).
5. The annual FAO publication *Cereal Policies Review* documented and reviewed national cereal policies with a global coverage during 1991–2000. Since 2001 this has been replaced by *Review of Basic Food Policies* (FAO 2001a).
6. The Morocco chapter in the FAO case studies (FAO 2000) presents an interesting example of sharp annual fluctuations in AMS levels as a result of fluctuations in production due to weather. That has not created a problem so far because the degree of flexibility is high, but it could do so were the AMS to get close to the limit. How to address fluctuations in production from the standpoint of compliance with AMS could be an issue to consider.
7. There is also some evidence from FAO technical assistance projects that computed AMS levels showing that the levels are not necessarily always negative or very low in all low-income countries, as is generally assumed.
8. No limits are placed on these outlays, unlike with the non-product-specific AMS. Nevertheless, statistics on these outlays as a share of production values are useful to gauge how extensively this provision is used and to compare it with non-product-specific AMS.
9. The only two countries with very high (closer to the 10 percent limit) non-product-specific AMS relative to the value of agricultural production were Peru in general and India in 1995. Beginning in 1996, India shifted most of the input subsidies previously notified as non-product-specific AMS to the Article 6.2 category, thus creating significant room for additional AMS outlays. India had claimed in its WTO Schedule that it has the option of transferring almost 80 percent of the input sub-

sidies to the Article 6.2 category, stating that about 80 percent of the land is farmed by low-income, resource-poor farmers. Peru, on the other hand, has not used Article 6.2 provision but has a right to do so.

10. This is a review of the implementation experience of individual developing countries, and therefore the focus is on their border measures and not on those of their trading partners.
11. For developed countries applied rates are closer to the bound rates. See Gibson and others (2001) for detailed statistics and analysis on applied and bound tariffs for both the developing and developed countries.
12. There are several exceptions. Egypt, Sri Lanka, and several countries in Latin America have relatively low bound rates. This is also the case for new WTO members.
13. During the period of the cereal price spikes in 1995–96, the most common policy response was to lower tariffs to provide price relief to consumers (Sharma 1996). During 1998–2000 when the world market prices of basic foods were depressed tariff increases were widespread (FAO 2001b; Sharma 2002b).
14. Also, seven developed countries initiated or implemented emergency safeguards in this period for a total of 22 products, 15 of them agricultural products. There have been few cases of antidumping actions on agricultural products, and the peace clause may discourage countervailing actions until the end of 2004.
15. The 14 countries are Argentina, Bolivia, Brazil, Chile, Colombia, Costa Rica, Fiji, Guatemala, Indonesia, Malaysia, Paraguay, Philippines, Thailand, and Uruguay. The other four Cairns Members (Australia, Canada, New Zealand, and South Africa) are considered developed countries and are included in the developed country group.
16. Fishery and forestry products were excluded as these were not covered by the URAA.
17. This is also an issue related to the Marrakesh Ministerial *Decision on Measures Concerning the Possible Negative Effects of the Reform Programme on Least-Developed and Net Food-Importing Developing Countries.* See FAO (2001c) for related issues and analysis in the context of this Decision.
18. See Sharma, Konandreas, and Greenfield (1996) for an overview of these model-based studies and their results.
19. See WTO (2000a, 2001) and analysis by Green and Priyadarshi (2001).
20. See FAO (2001b) and Valdés and Foster (2002) for analysis of the problem of import competition and the importance of a feasible safeguard mechanism for developing countries.
21. These estimates are from Sharma (2002a). Maximum tariffs were estimated using a simple expression for domestic price, $Pd = Pw\ (1+t)$, and solving for tariff t every time the world market price (Pw) changes, for five assumed domestic reference prices (see notes to table 3.8). The world market prices used were monthly prices of the 18 basic foods for the period January 1990 to December 2000.

BIBLIOGRAPHY

FAO (Food and Agriculture Organization). 2000. "Synthesis of the Country Case Studies." In *Agriculture, Trade, and Food Security: Issues and Options in the WTO Negotiations from the Perspective of Developing Countries.* Vol. II, *Country Case Studies.* Rome: FAO. www.fao.org/trade.

———. 2001a. *Review of Basic Food Policies.* Rome: FAO. www.fao.org/es/ESC/esce/escb/rbfp/rbfp.htm.

———. 2001b. "A Special Agricultural Safeguard (SAS): Buttressing the Market Access Reforms of Developing Countries." Discussion Paper 1, FAO Geneva Round Table on Selected Agricultural Trade Policy Issues, FAO, Geneva. www.fao.org/trade.

———. 2001c. "Towards Improving the Operational Effectiveness of the Marrakesh Decision on the Possible Negative Effects of the Reform Programme on Least-Developed and Net-Food Importing Developing Countries." Discussion Paper 2, FAO Geneva Round Table on Selected Agricultural Trade Policy Issues, FAO, Geneva. www.fao.org/trade.

———. 2003. *WTO Agreement on Agriculture—The Implementation Experience: Developing Country Case Studies.* Rome: FAO. www.fao.org/trade.

Gibson, P., J. Wainio, D. Whitley, and M. Bohman. 2001. "Profiles of Tariffs in Global Agricultural Markets." Agricultural Economic Report 796, U.S. Department of Agriculture, Economic Research Service, Washington, DC. www.ers.usda.gov/publications/aer796/.

Green, D., and S. Priyadarshi. 2001. "Proposal for a 'Development Box' in the WTO Agreement on Agriculture." CAFOD Policy Paper, Catholic Agency for Overseas Development, London. www.cafod.org.uk/policy/devbox.htm.

Kherallah, M., H. Lofgren, P. Gruhn, and M. Reeder. 2000. "Wheat Policy Reform in Egypt: Adjustment of Local Markets and Options for Future Reforms." Research Report 115, International Food Policy Research Institute, Washington, DC.

OECD (Organisation for Economic Co-operation and Development). 2001. *The Uruguay Round Agreement on Agriculture: An Evaluation of Its Implementation in OECD Countries.* Paris: OECD.

Sharma, Ramesh. 1996. "Review of Cereal Price Situation in Selected Developing Countries in 1995–96 and Policy Measures to Offset the Price Rise." ESCP Research Paper 1, FAO, Commodity Policy and Projections Service, Rome.

———. 2002a. "Quantifying Appropriate Levels of the WTO Bound Tariffs on Basic Food Products as in the Context of the Development Box Proposals." Commodity and Trade Research Working Paper 3, FAO, Rome. www.fao.org/es/ESC.

———. 2002b. "The Transmission of World Price Signals: Concepts, Issues and Some Evidence from Asian Cereal Markets." Paper presented at the OECD Global Forum on Agriculture: Agricultural Trade Reform, Adjustment, and Poverty, Paris, May 23–24.

Sharma, Ramesh, Panos Konandreas, and Jim Greenfield. 1996. "An Overview of Assessments of the Impact of the Uruguay Round on Agricultural Prices and Incomes." *Food Policy* 21 (4/5): 351–63.

Valdés, A., and W. Foster. 2002. "Reflections on the Policy Implications of Agricultural Price Distortions and Price Transmission for Producers in Developing and Transition Economies." Paper presented at the OECD Global Forum on Agriculture: Agricultural Trade Reform, Adjustment, and Poverty, Paris, May 23–24.

Wainio, J., P. Gibson, and D. Whitley. 2001. "Options for Reducing Agricultural Tariffs." In "Agricultural Policy Reform in the WTO: The Road Ahead." Report ERS-E01-001, U.S Department of Agriculture, Washington, DC. www.ers.usda.gov/publications/aer802/.

WTO (World Trade Organization). 2000a. "Committee on Agriculture, Special Session: Agreement on Agriculture: Special and Differential Treatment and a Development Box—Proposal by Cuba, Dominican Republic, Honduras, Pakistan, Haiti, Nicaragua, Kenya, Uganda, Zimbabwe, Sri Lanka, and El Salvador." G/AG/NG/W/13, Geneva, WTO. www.wto.org.

———. 2000b. "Committee on Agriculture, Special Session, 'Domestic Support': Background paper by the Secretariat." G/AG/NG/S/1, WTO, Geneva. www.wto.org.

———. 2001. "Committee on Agriculture, Special Session: Negotiations on WTO Agreement on Agriculture—Proposals by India in the Area of: i) Food Security; ii) Market Access, iii) Domestic Support; and iv) Export Competition." G/AG/NG/W/102, WTO, Geneva. www.wto.org.

CHAPTER FOUR

The Impact of Agricultural Support Policies on Developing Countries

Bernard Hoekman, Francis Ng, and Marcelo Olarreaga

This chapter provides an overview of agricultural subsidies—domestic support and export subsidies—across World Trade Organization (WTO) members and of the impact on developing countries' trade. It shows that the ratio of subsidies in industrial countries to total developing country exports of the commodities concerned is very high, severely distorting competition and reducing trade opportunities for developing countries with a comparative advantage in the subsidized products.

National export and import shares of products affected by agricultural subsidies vary considerably across developing countries. Because subsidies are likely to lower the world price of affected products and exacerbate price volatility, the short-run impact of global subsidy reform will largely depend on whether a country is a net importer or net exporter of the products concerned. Countries such as Argentina, for which products subject to export subsidies in some WTO members constitute a large share of exports (29 percent) and a small share of imports (3 percent) are likely to benefit greatly from a removal of export subsidies. Conversely, countries such as Bangladesh that export virtually no products that are subsidized in industrial countries but import a substantial share of such products (13 percent of imports) are unlikely to benefit in the short run from removal of export subsidies. In fact, net importers of subsidized products may benefit from subsidies to the extent that they provide access to the subsidized commodities at lower prices.[1] Thus, national interests regarding reform of industrial countries agricultural trade and support policies can differ substantially.

Although the Quad economies—Canada, the European Union, Japan, and the United States—are by far the largest subsidizers, several developing countries have also notified their use. Indeed WTO notifications (commitments) reveal that middle-income countries perceive an interest in having the ability to use export subsidies. However, the absence of information on actual use of subsidies poses a problem—it is not known to what extent notifications lead to the actual application of subsidies. Thus, notifications by developing countries are perhaps a better indicator of intent or preferences than of actual subsidy practices.

This does not make the analysis that follows redundant. To the contrary, even if in practice the countries concerned have not implemented much in the way of export subsidies, the fact that commitments were made suggests that there is an additional rationale for seeking to discipline the use of export subsidies: to prevent the gradual expansion of the use of these instruments. As discussed below, the poorest countries in particular appear to have a strong incentive to seek such disciplines because the notified subsidy commitments by middle-income countries pertain much more to commodities that low-income developing countries either export or import. Indeed, on average, the pattern of trade of developing countries is such that Quad subsidies appear to have less of a net negative impact on the poorest countries than do the notified agricultural support policies of middle income countries. Thus an additional reason for disciplining the use of agricultural support policies is that, to the extent that middle-income developing countries have begun to follow the example of the Quad, the potential impact on low-income developing countries may be particularly negative. Thus the benefits of pursuing multilateral reform in Quad policies include both the direct impacts on (potential) net exporters and the indirect gains associated with preventing the extension of support policies to middle-income countries.

WHO SUBSIDIZES WHAT?

WTO negotiations on interventions in agricultural markets focus on both subsidy policies and border protection (tariffs and tariff rate quotas). An important policy question for developing countries is to determine which instruments of agricultural protection are most detrimental to their interests and which policy reform proposals are likely to benefit them most. This chapter explores that question by analyzing the pattern and incidence of agricultural subsidies across countries and products, focusing on how they affect the export and import bundle of developing countries.

There are 158 commodities at the six-digit level of the Harmonized System (HS) that benefit from direct domestic support in at least one WTO member.

Total support reported to the WTO for 1995–98 averaged some $104 billion (table 1). Domestic support[2] is used primarily by industrial countries, which account for 88 percent of domestic support payments notified to the WTO. The Quad economies alone account for 84 percent and their share of world support is greater than 99 percent in several products (such as products used in milling, oilseeds and oleaginous fruits and other grains, vegetable preparations, fruits and nuts, beverages and spirits, silk, and certain vegetable textile fibers and yarn).

Developing countries have also become users of subsidies—they accounted for 12 percent of total support reported to the WTO during 1995–98 (see table 4.1). Major subsidizers included Brazil, Thailand, and Venezuela. Not surprisingly, the least developed countries report no direct domestic support. Developing countries reporting domestic support target many of the same commodities as high-income countries, but they also support other products, such as live trees and flowers; coffee, tea, and spices; gums, resins, and other vegetables; cocoa; and edible preparations. Subsidies for these products totaled $1.1 billion during 1995–98.

Cereals, meat, dairy, and sugar account for almost 82 percent of all reported nonexempt domestic support, 78 percent of domestic support reported by the Quad, 97 percent of that reported by other industrial countries, and 93 percent of that reported by developing countries. This high product concentration across regions is reflected in high correlation coefficients across products for domestic support in the Quad and domestic support provided by developing countries (0.87) and other industrial countries (0.67).

Export subsidies are also concentrated in a limited number of commodities. There are 208 tariff lines at the HS six-digit level that are subject to export subsidies in at least one WTO member. Export subsidy commitments by WTO members amounted to $10 billion in 2000—or 10 percent of the value of direct domestic support—with industrial countries accounting for 80 percent, developing countries for 20 percent, and the least developed countries not reporting any export subsidies. The Quad share is 76 percent (table 4.2).

Export subsidies are concentrated in the same four products as domestic support: cereals, meat, dairy, and sugar account for 80 percent of total export subsidies, more than 90 percent of Quad export subsidies, 75 percent of other industrial countries export subsidies, and 40 percent of developing country export subsidies. The correlation coefficients for export subsidies across regions is lower than for domestic support, but still high and positive at 0.56 for Quad and other industrial countries and 0.51 for Quad and developing countries.

Thus the largest users of agriculture subsidies are the Quad countries. Virtually all regions are engaged in subsidizing a small set of products (cereals, meat, dairy, and sugar) through domestic support and export subsidies. By far the greatest share of subsidies goes to cereals, which receive more than 40 percent of total domestic support and about 30 percent of export subsidies. Middle-income developing countries are also engaged in subsidizing products, and they are the only countries providing subsidies for some commodities—plants, cut flowers, coffee, teas, and spices. Developing countries also account for a large share of total domestic support and export subsidies notified to the WTO for live animals, cereals, oilseeds and grains, fruits and vegetables, and sugar.

WHO IS AFFECTED?

The impact of the global pattern of agricultural protection and support depends on whether a country is a net producer or net consumer of the commodities affected. The relative importance of subsidized products in a country's exports and imports provides a good indication of the likely impact of support policies and their removal. Such a simple trade share-based analysis yields short-run results that are quite consistent with the conclusions that emerge from model-based analysis, taken up below. And analysis of affected trade on a country-by-country basis has the advantage of allowing a determination of which countries' policies have the greatest impact on specific low-income economies.

The Impact of Domestic Support

Calculations of affected trade shares suggest that least developed countries may be more affected than other countries, since 18 percent of their exports on average are goods that are subsidized by at least one WTO member, compared with an average of 3–4 percent for other countries (table 4.3). A similar observation holds for imports—9 percent of the imports of least developed countries are subsidized products, compared with 3–4 percent for other countries. For many least developed countries the potential effect of subsidies is great. Thus, for countries such as Benin, Burkina Faso, Burundi, Chad, Malawi, Mali, Rwanda, Sudan, Tanzania, Uganda, and Zimbabwe, 60–80 percent of exports are goods that are subsidized in one or more WTO members. These countries also tend to have preferential (mostly duty-free) access to the European market (through the Generalized System of Preferences and Everything but Arms initiative), making subsidies an important issue for WTO negotiations (subsidies are not covered by preferential access agreements).[3]

For countries whose ratio of imports of subsidized goods to total imports is higher than the ratio of subsidized exports to total exports (table 4.3), global liberalization may have short-run negative effects on terms of trade and welfare to the extent that the subsidies lower the price of imports. Countries where the balance is tilted toward imports of subsidized commodities have diverse levels of per capita income: Bangladesh, Comoros, Egypt, Gambia, Guinea, Jordan, the Republic of Korea, Maldives, Mauritania, Morocco, Nigeria, Oman, Saudi Arabia, Senegal, Taiwan (China), Tunisia, and Venezuela.

Table 4.1 Domestic Support by Product and Selected Country Groups, 1995–98 Average

Product at Harmonized System two-digit level	Domestic support (US$ million)				Share of domestic support by country group (percent)			
	All countries (90)	Quad countries (4)	Non-Quad industrial countries[a] (5)	Developing countries (81)	All countries (24)	Quad countries (3)	Non-Quad industrial countries (5)	Developing countries (16)
01 Live animals	365	245	0	120	100.0	67.1	0.0	32.9
02 Meat and edible meat offal	19,505	17,192	1,961	351	100.0	88.1	10.1	1.8
04 Dairy products; birds' eggs; honey	15,494	12,749	1,754	992	100.0	82.3	11.3	6.4
06 Live trees and other plants, bulbs; cut flowers	15	0	0	15	100.0	0.0	0.0	100.0
07 Edible vegetables and roots and tubers	5,307	5,059	113	136	100.0	95.3	2.1	2.6
08 Edible fruit and nuts; melons	4,731	4,624	28	80	100.0	97.7	0.6	1.7
09 Coffee; tea; maté; and spices	101	0	0	101	100.0	0.0	0.0	100.0
10 Cereals	41,230	32,367	690	8,173	100.0	78.5	1.7	19.8
11 Milled products; malt; starches	191	190	0	1	100.0	99.3	0.0	0.7
12 Oil seed; oleaginous fruits	663	550	0	113	100.0	83.0	0.0	17.0
13 Lac; gums, resins, and other vegetables	0	0	0	0	100.0	0.0	0.0	100.0

15 Animal and vegetable fats and oils and products	2,159	2,154	0	5	100.0	99.8	0.0	0.2
17 Sugars and sugar confectionery	8,530	6,702	63	1,766	100.0	78.6	0.7	20.7
18 Cocoa and cocoa preparations	0	0	0	0	100.0	0.0	0.0	100.0
20 Preparations of vegetable, fruit, and nuts products	1,069	1,068	0	1	100.0	99.9	0.0	0.1
21 Miscellaneous edible preparations	3	0	0	3	100.0	0.0	0.0	100.0
22 Beverages, spirits, and vinegar	2,388	2,387	0	1	100.0	99.9	0.0	0.1
23 Residues and waste from food industry	486	387	0	100	100.0	79.5	0.0	20.5
24 Tobacco and manufactured tobacco substitutes	968	890	7	71	100.0	91.9	0.7	7.4
50 Silk	20	20	0	0	100.0	99.2	0.0	0.8
51 Wool, fine and coarse animal hair	27	23	4	0	100.0	85.7	13.4	0.9
52 Cotton	991	946	0	44	100.0	95.5	0.0	4.5
53 Other vegetable textile fibers and yarns	141	140	0	1	100.0	99.4	0.0	0.6
All agricultural products listed above	104,385	87,691	4,619	12,076	100.0	84.0	4.4	11.6

Source: Based on WTO (2000).

Note: Numbers in parentheses are number of countries in the group (European Union is counted as one). Domestic support is defined as the sum of WTO DS4–DS9 categories; see text.

a. Includes non-Quad high-income OECD countries.

Table 4.2 Agricultural Export Subsidy Commitments by Product and Country Group, 2000

Product at Harmonized System two-digit level	Commitments for export subsidies (US$ million)				Share of export subsidies by country group (percent)			
	All countries (24)	Quad countries (3)	Non-Quad industrial countries[a] (5)	Developing countries (16)	All countries (24)	Quad countries (3)	Non-Quad industrial countries (5)	Developing countries (16)
01 Live animals	57	12	13	32	100.0	20.8	23.2	55.9
02 Meat and edible meat offal	1,710	1,442	28	239	100.0	84.4	1.6	14.0
04 Dairy products; birds' eggs; honey	2,664	2,304	259	102	100.0	86.5	9.7	3.8
05 Products of animal origin	1	0	0	1	100.0	0.0	0.0	100.0
06 Live trees and other plants, bulbs; cut flowers	22	0	0	22	100.0	0.0	0.0	100.0
07 Edible vegetables and roots and tubers	144	16	1	127	100.0	11.0	1.0	88.0
08 Edible fruit and nuts; melons	208	49	10	150	100.0	23.4	4.8	71.7
09 Coffee; tea; maté; and spices	13	0	0	13	100.0	0.0	0.0	100.0
10 Cereals	3,059	2,789	0	269	100.0	91.2	0.0	8.8
11 Milled products; malt; starches	337	0	0	337	100.0	0.0	0.0	100.0
12 Oil seed; oleaginous fruits	78	51	0	27	100.0	65.7	0.0	34.3
13 Lac; gums, resins, and other vegetables	0	0	0	0	100.0	0.0	0.0	100.0
14 Vegetable plaiting materials; vegetable products	0	0	0	0	100.0	0.0	0.0	100.0
15 Animal and vegetable fats and oils and products	113	66	0	47	100.0	58.1	0.0	41.9

16 Preparations of meat, fish or mollusks	94	0	4	90	100.0	0.0	4.4	95.6
17 Sugars and sugar confectionery	667	461	0	206	100.0	69.1	0.0	30.9
18 Cocoa and cocoa preparations	33	0	0	33	100.0	0.0	0.0	100.0
19 Preparations of cereal, flour, starch/ milk products	25	0	0	25	100.0	0.0	0.0	100.0
20 Preparations of vegetable, fruit, and nuts products	166	8	0	158	100.0	4.6	0.0	95.4
21 Miscellaneous edible preparations	78	0	68	10	100.0	0.0	87.0	13.0
22 Beverages, spirits, and vinegar	168	125	0	43	100.0	74.4	0.0	25.6
23 Residues and waste from food industry	4	3	0	1	100.0	85.7	0.0	14.3
24 Tobacco and manufactured tobacco substitutes	67	37	0	30	100.0	55.2	0.0	44.8
33 Essential oils and resins	0	0	0	0	100.0	0.0	0.0	100.0
35 Albuminoidal substances; modified starches	8	0	0	8	100.0	0.0	0.0	100.0
41 Raw hides and skins (other than fur)	3	0	0	3	100.0	0.0	0.0	100.0
43 Furs, skins, and artificial fur	0	0	0	0	100.0	0.0	0.0	100.0
50 Silk	0	0	0	0	100.0	0.0	0.0	100.0
51 Wool, fine/coarse animal hair not elsewhere specified	7	0	0	7	100.0	0.0	0.0	100.0
52 Cotton	66	0	0	66	100.0	0.0	0.0	100.0
98 Other incorporated products	412	397	0	15	100.0	96.4	0.0	3.6
All agricultural products listed above	10,206	7,760	384	2,062	100.0	76.0	3.8	20.2

Source: Based on WTO (2001).

Note: Numbers in parentheses are number of countries in the group (European Union is counted as one). Export subsidies are based on budgetary outlay commitments from 24 WTO member countries' notifications.

a. Includes non-Quad high-income OECD countries.

Table 4.3 Trade Shares of Products Benefiting from Domestic Support, 1995–98 Average (percent)

Country or group	Total domestic support		Quad domestic support		Other industrial country support[a]		Developing country domestic support	
	Exports	Imports	Exports	Imports	Exports	Imports	Exports	Imports
Albania	8.8	8.2	3.7	5.6	0.1	3.8	8.7	7.6
Algeria	0.0	20.0	0.0	13.3	0.0	4.5	0.0	17.2
Angola	0.3	7.2	0.0	4.5	0.0	1.9	0.1	6.8
Antigua and Barbuda	6.0	2.8	4.3	1.8	1.7	0.6	5.0	2.4
Argentina	25.6	2.3	20.1	1.4	7.5	0.3	23.7	2.1
Australia	17.0	1.4	11.5	0.5	5.4	0.3	11.1	0.9
Bahrain	0.1	3.7	0.1	2.1	0.1	1.0	0.2	3.8
Bangladesh	2.2	12.7	0.3	11.3	0.1	7.8	1.8	13.3
Barbados	21.9	5.9	0.8	4.0	0.1	1.4	20.6	5.1
Belize	46.6	5.9	13.9	2.8	0.7	1.4	35.1	4.0
Benin	84.7	5.9	72.4	5.3	0.1	3.8	84.5	5.0
Bolivia	11.3	5.2	9.9	3.6	0.1	2.0	12.6	4.5
Brazil	13.1	6.7	5.8	5.3	1.9	3.1	13.1	6.3
Brunei	0.0	1.8	0.0	1.3	0.0	0.9	0.0	1.8
Bulgaria	6.9	5.4	6.1	3.2	1.3	1.1	5.3	4.7
Burkina Faso	75.5	7.9	68.1	4.1	0.0	3.0	75.5	7.7
Burundi	72.8	10.9	2.0	2.4	0.4	1.2	72.1	8.6
Cameroon	24.7	8.6	11.5	4.1	0.0	2.8	26.4	6.2
Canada	3.4	2.1	2.8	1.2	1.2	0.3	3.5	1.5
Central African	24.8	4.4	12.4	1.2	0.1	0.7	24.6	4.2
Chad	82.5	3.5	82.4	2.0	0.0	1.0	82.4	3.3
Chile	14.2	3.2	15.1	2.3	8.3	0.8	10.7	3.1
China	1.9	4.0	0.9	3.9	0.3	1.4	1.4	4.1
Colombia	32.0	7.2	7.4	5.5	0.3	2.4	32.4	6.5

Congo, Dem. Rep.	10.6	8.6	0.3	5.8	0.1	3.2	6.7	8.8
Congo, Rep.	1.1	3.9	0.0	2.8	0.0	1.7	1.0	3.5
Costa Rica	37.5	5.9	24.0	4.1	0.2	1.2	38.4	5.4
Côte d'Ivoire	48.7	11.0	7.3	9.9	0.0	4.0	51.3	12.1
Croatia	2.2	5.0	1.4	2.5	0.4	1.2	1.7	3.9
Cuba	50.7	13.4	2.7	11.5	0.2	7.7	51.4	12.9
Cyprus	24.5	4.2	7.1	2.4	1.1	1.3	16.3	3.0
Czech Republic	1.9	3.6	1.1	1.6	0.6	0.4	1.5	2.2
Djibouti	9.5	9.9	1.3	6.2	0.7	2.0	9.1	12.1
Dominica	57.7	7.1	28.5	1.8	0.5	0.7	30.4	2.7
Dominican Republic	10.2	7.4	3.1	6.5	1.1	1.5	9.9	7.2
Ecuador	31.2	5.7	29.5	4.1	0.7	2.1	36.1	5.2
Egypt, Arab Rep.	11.0	17.1	5.0	9.2	0.9	5.6	8.2	12.0
El Salvador	42.0	8.3	0.9	6.4	0.3	1.8	23.9	8.9
Estonia	6.3	6.3	1.8	2.4	1.2	1.2	2.1	2.9
European Union 15	2.2	4.9	1.8	2.8	0.8	0.8	2.0	4.1
Fiji	37.9	6.5	0.1	4.4	0.0	2.7	31.9	5.6
Gabon	0.1	4.9	0.0	3.3	0.0	1.7	0.1	4.4
Gambia, The	11.0	17.5	2.1	3.5	0.0	2.3	2.7	8.0
Ghana	32.4	4.7	0.9	3.8	0.0	3.1	31.6	4.5
Grenada	14.5	7.2	6.3	5.1	0.7	3.0	15.3	6.5
Guatemala	48.6	7.2	8.2	5.5	1.0	1.9	37.7	7.6
Guinea	7.8	19.1	1.3	2.8	0.0	2.3	7.5	3.8
Guinea-Bissau	39.8	4.2	2.5	3.0	0.0	1.0	39.7	3.0
Guyana	33.1	6.7	6.2	5.0	5.3	2.8	32.3	6.5
Haiti	12.2	14.9	0.1	11.0	0.0	8.6	12.2	16.3
Honduras	43.9	9.0	9.1	3.7	0.2	1.8	23.7	5.2
Hong Kong, China	0.1	1.5	0.1	0.8	0.0	0.4	0.2	1.2
Hungary	5.6	2.3	3.4	0.9	1.2	0.3	4.1	1.4

(continued)

Table 4.3 (Continued)

Country or group	Total domestic support		Quad domestic support		Other industrial country support[a]		Developing country domestic support	
	Exports	Imports	Exports	Imports	Exports	Imports	Exports	Imports
Iceland	7.9	2.6	7.5	1.2	0.1	0.5	0.4	1.5
India	8.4	2.4	3.6	0.7	2.7	0.3	7.1	3.9
Indonesia	2.8	8.9	0.6	6.2	0.1	2.8	3.9	6.7
Iran, Islamic Rep.	1.0	10.3	0.5	8.2	0.4	5.5	0.9	9.3
Israel	4.1	3.3	2.1	2.2	0.2	1.0	4.2	2.7
Jamaica	12.1	5.5	3.8	4.5	0.0	2.6	12.1	5.2
Japan	0.1	4.9	0.0	3.5	0.0	0.9	0.1	4.4
Jordan	6.2	12.3	1.3	8.1	0.2	5.0	4.6	13.8
Kazakhstan	0.0	0.0	9.6	1.2	6.1	0.5	9.8	1.7
Kenya	48.7	8.4	9.7	6.4	0.6	3.6	34.6	8.9
Korea, Rep.	0.3	3.6	0.1	2.8	0.0	0.6	0.3	3.4
Kuwait	0.0	4.0	0.0	2.3	0.0	1.5	0.0	3.9
Kyrgyz Republic	24.1	4.7	20.3	2.6	4.0	1.9	21.9	4.2
Latvia	2.0	5.7	2.0	2.2	0.3	1.0	2.2	3.0
Lithuania	6.7	5.0	4.1	2.5	2.6	0.7	4.0	3.1
Macao	0.3	2.5	0.1	1.2	0.0	0.4	0.1	2.1
Madagascar	26.6	7.8	2.1	2.4	6.4	2.1	23.4	3.6
Malawi	75.7	4.4	67.6	4.3	59.9	1.1	75.3	5.5
Malaysia	0.5	3.4	0.2	1.9	0.1	0.8	3.3	2.7
Maldives	2.1	8.3	0.1	3.7	0.0	0.7	0.2	4.3
Mali	84.5	5.8	83.1	3.9	0.1	1.5	84.0	5.8
Malta	1.2	3.0	0.1	1.4	0.0	0.7	0.4	1.8
Mauritania	0.7	13.8	0.7	10.0	0.0	4.0	0.1	13.6
Mauritius	24.6	8.5	0.1	4.6	0.0	1.9	24.0	5.3
Mexico	3.0	4.3	1.6	4.3	0.2	1.3	3.0	4.7

Mongolia	12.0	2.2	11.7	1.5	0.5	1.2	10.7	2.1
Morocco	9.0	13.8	7.5	7.5	0.0	4.1	8.5	9.6
Mozambique	0.0	0.0	14.5	7.9	1.8	4.5	38.8	10.8
Myanmar	23.6	1.0	15.4	0.4	3.6	0.1	22.7	6.5
New Zealand	24.1	3.0	14.5	1.3	9.5	0.5	15.8	1.9
Nicaragua	40.0	8.7	4.6	10.4	1.2	3.7	33.9	15.0
Niger	17.2	12.9	1.7	5.2	0.1	1.3	2.1	11.0
Nigeria	1.8	7.5	0.2	6.6	0.0	5.2	1.9	7.1
Norway	0.3	2.8	0.2	1.4	0.0	0.4	0.1	1.8
Oman	0.7	5.8	0.1	1.9	0.0	0.7	0.1	3.7
Pakistan	7.0	6.7	6.1	5.0	3.4	4.2	6.9	13.4
Panama	38.8	4.1	16.9	0.5	0.2	0.2	19.0	0.8
Papua New Guinea	15.1	2.6	0.0	1.7	0.0	0.8	15.2	2.6
Paraguay	55.1	3.5	48.3	2.4	1.5	0.9	49.1	3.0
Peru	19.3	9.6	15.4	8.3	0.1	4.0	7.4	9.8
Philippines	5.6	4.5	2.5	3.7	0.1	2.4	4.6	4.2
Poland	2.7	4.9	1.5	2.4	1.1	0.9	1.9	3.2
Qatar	0.0	2.3	0.0	1.1	0.0	0.4	0.0	2.2
Romania	4.9	3.8	3.1	2.2	1.8	0.8	4.2	3.4
Russian Federation	1.4	6.9	1.3	4.2	0.3	1.4	1.2	5.3
Rwanda	59.0	18.2	0.4	9.5	0.1	1.9	58.6	19.9
Saudi Arabia	0.1	6.3	0.1	4.6	0.1	2.9	0.1	6.3
Senegal	7.6	16.1	6.3	10.3	0.0	4.8	7.0	15.9
Sierra Leone	6.6	8.7	0.4	6.1	0.2	4.9	6.5	8.6
Singapore	0.6	1.2	0.1	0.7	0.0	0.4	0.3	1.2
Slovak Republic	2.1	3.0	1.2	1.3	0.4	0.5	1.7	2.2
Slovenia	0.9	3.6	0.7	1.9	0.4	0.9	0.9	3.3
Solomon Islands	9.1	1.7	0.1	1.1	0.0	0.3	9.1	1.8
South Africa	6.4	3.2	5.8	2.5	2.4	1.6	6.6	3.3
Sri Lanka	2.1	9.1	1.1	6.4	0.9	3.3	2.0	9.3
St. Kitts and Nevis	77.5	5.6	0.1	1.5	0.0	1.0	30.2	2.7

(continued)

Table 4.3 (Continued)

Country or group	Total domestic support		Quad domestic support		Other industrial country support[a]		Developing country domestic support	
	Exports	Imports	Exports	Imports	Exports	Imports	Exports	Imports
St. Lucia	63.8	5.3	57.9	2.8	0.4	1.1	59.3	3.2
St. Vincent and Grenadines	57.3	10.5	28.5	6.0	4.4	4.7	28.8	6.7
Sudan	60.1	8.6	30.4	4.8	4.0	3.6	61.3	8.1
Suriname	11.6	5.5	8.7	1.8	4.0	0.8	9.5	2.6
Switzerland	0.5	3.2	0.2	1.2	0.1	0.4	0.6	1.8
Taiwan, China	0.2	3.6	0.1	3.1	0.0	0.6	0.2	3.1
Tanzania	67.8	5.0	24.3	2.6	5.9	1.6	61.7	8.0
Thailand	7.0	2.8	3.5	1.9	3.1	0.7	6.4	1.9
Togo	42.5	6.3	29.8	5.6	0.0	4.3	41.8	9.8
Trinidad and Tobago	2.1	6.4	0.2	5.5	0.1	2.6	2.3	6.9
Tunisia	4.0	6.9	4.2	4.6	0.0	2.5	4.3	5.4
Turkey	10.5	5.0	5.8	3.0	1.9	1.3	10.5	4.1
Uganda	63.3	7.5	4.7	1.7	1.6	1.1	84.0	4.8
United Arab Emi	1.0	3.1	0.4	1.6	0.2	0.9	0.8	3.2
United States	5.2	1.8	4.4	0.9	1.2	0.2	4.8	1.5
Uruguay	23.0	6.2	17.1	3.3	11.6	0.4	21.1	4.3
Venezuela	0.8	8.0	0.4	6.0	0.1	1.8	0.8	8.0
Zambia	8.1	4.0	3.5	3.1	1.0	1.0	7.2	4.2
Zimbabwe	59.3	3.0	37.8	2.8	23.6	1.1	46.7	3.0
All countries (129)	3.6	3.7	2.4	2.4	0.8	0.9	3.4	3.3
Industrial countries (9)	3.1	3.3	2.5	2.0	0.9	0.5	2.8	2.9
Developing countries (90)	4.2	4.2	2.3	3.0	0.8	1.3	4.1	3.8
Least developed countries (30)	17.8	8.9	9.0	6.2	2.3	3.8	17.6	9.3

Source: Based on partners' data from UN Comtrade statistics.
Note: Numbers in parentheses are number of countries in the group (European Union is counted as one).
a. Includes non-Quad high-income OECD countries; excludes intra-EU trade.

On average, the least developed countries appear to be more negatively affected by domestic support in Quad countries than other developing countries are. On average, 9 percent of their exports are affected by domestic support in the Quad, rising to peaks of 82 percent in Chad and 72 percent in Benin (see table 4.3). An average of 6 percent of their imports are affected by domestic support in the Quad, with levels exceeding 10 percent in many countries (including Bangladesh, Haiti, Mauritania, and Senegal). For other developing countries, affected trade flows are much smaller, with a slightly larger share of exports (2 percent) affected by domestic support in the Quad than imports (3 percent). But the variation is substantial, with shares exceeding 20 percent on the export side for Latin American countries such as Argentina, Dominican Republic, Ecuador, and Paraguay.

The pattern of impacts of subsidy programs by other industrial countries is similar to that of the Quad, although the share of trade affected is much lower. For terms of trade effects the impact on least developed countries of agricultural subsidy policies in developing countries is similar to that due to Quad policies (see table 4.3). In part this reflects the commodity composition of developing country support programs, which include products that are produced only by developing countries.

As a first approximation of whether domestic support policies hurt poorer economies disproportionately, it is useful to compare the relative importance of subsidized products in a country's export and import bundle using the following index:

$$I = s^x - s^m \qquad (1)$$

where s^x is the share of exports affected by domestic support across WTO members or in the Quad and s^m is the share of imports. The index varies between 100 and –100. High positive values of I suggest that the country is likely to benefit from a reduction in domestic support, as this will probably improve its terms of trade. Negative values of I suggest that the country will probably see its terms of trade deteriorate after a reduction in domestic support.

Plotting the relationship between I and the log of GDP per capita across all 128 countries in the data set for all domestic support (figure 4.1) and for domestic support provided by the Quad (figure 4.2) shows that many developing countries—mostly the least developed countries and countries in Central and South America—have I values above zero, with many more such countries in the case of all domestic support than for domestic support provided by the Quad. This suggests that the support policies of non-Quad industrial countries and middle-income developing economies target more of the commodities that are produced and exported by low-income nations.

The statistically significant negative correlation between I and GDP per capita for all domestic support suggests that reductions in domestic support across all WTO members would be likely to improve the terms of trade of the

Figure 4.1 Relationship Between Trade Shares Affected by Total Domestic Support in All WTO Members and GDP per Capita

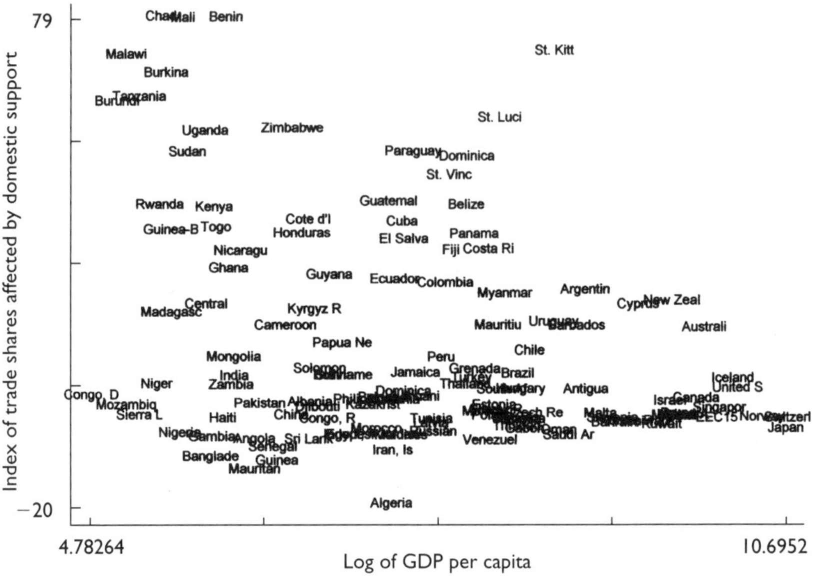

Figure 4.2 Relationship Between Trade Shares Affected by Quad Domestic Support Policies and GDP per Capita

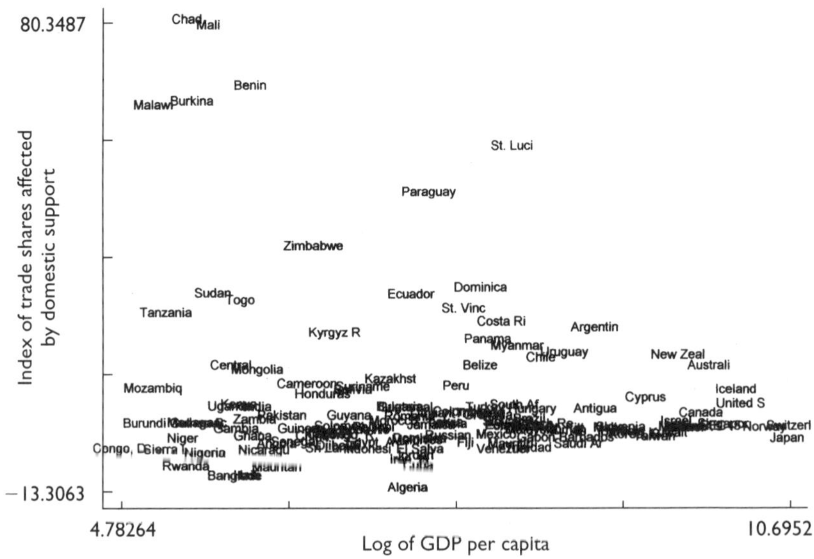

poorest countries. There are also a few countries whose I values are far below zero, suggesting that there will be a few large losers. However, the value of I for developing countries as a whole is close to zero, suggesting that the removal of domestic support is unlikely to result in important gains for developing countries as a whole in the short run.

For the incidence of Quad domestic support policies only, there is no clear negative relationship between I and the log of per capita income. Indeed, if the five Sub-Saharan African countries in the top left corner of figure 4.2 are excluded, there is a slight positive (but not statistically significant) relationship between Quad domestic support and incomes. The implication is that Quad domestic support policies do not appear to be biased against the poorest countries.

The Impact of Export Subsidies

The export subsidy picture differs only slightly from that for domestic support. Products receiving export subsidies in one or more WTO members account for about 17 percent of the value of least developed country exports, 5 percent of the value of developing country exports, and 4 percent of the value of industrial country exports (table 4.4). More than half the exports of many African countries (Benin, Burkina Faso, Burundi, Chad, Côte d'Ivoire, Malawi, Mali, Rwanda, Tanzania, and Uganda) are affected by export subsidies in some WTO member. Most of these subsidies are associated with notifications by other developing countries (see table 4.4). Overall, only 1 percent of the exports of developing countries and least developed countries are affected by an export subsidy in the Quad, compared with 2 percent and 6 percent; respectively, of their imports. Algeria, Cuba, Egypt, Iran, Jordan, and Mauritania have more than 10 percent of their imports subject to an export subsidy in at least one industrial country.

As was done for domestic support, an index was created to explore whether poorer countries gain more than richer countries from the removal of export subsidies, with the s^x and s^m of equation 1 here referring to the shares of exports and imports affected by an export subsidy (a large value of I suggests that the country is likely to benefit from removal of export subsidies). Plotting the relationship between I and the log of GDP per capita for the countries in the sample for all export subsidies (figure 4.3) and for export subsidies of Quad members only (figure 4.4) shows that the share of exports relative to imports affected by an export subsidy seems to decrease with GDP per capita, suggesting that poorer countries are disproportionately hurt by export subsidies. This result is driven mostly by export subsidies in developing countries themselves. The relationship between I and the log of GDP per capita shows that the share of exports relative to imports that is affected by an export subsidy in one or more Quad countries increases with GDP per capita (see figure 4.4). This suggests again that poorer countries tend to be hurt less than richer ones by Quad export subsidies.

Table 4.4 Trade Shares of Agricultural Products Benefiting from Export Subsidies, 1995–98 Average (percent)

	Total export subsidies		Quad export subsidies		Other industrial country export subsidies[a]		Developing country export subsidies	
Country or group	Exports	Imports	Exports	Imports	Exports	Imports	Exports	Imports
Albania	10.6	22.0	3	4	0	2	11	22
Algeria	0.1	23.8	0	14	0	2	0	23
Angola	0.1	16.2	0	4	0	2	0	16
Antigua and Barbuda	6.0	5.2	3	1	0	1	6	5
Argentina	29.3	3.0	18	0	2	0	22	3
Australia	16.3	1.7	7	0	2	0	16	2
Bahrain	0.2	7.3	0	2	0	1	0	7
Bangladesh	0.4	13.3	0	9	0	0	0	13
Barbados	20.9	8.1	0	3	1	1	21	7
Belize	47.5	7.3	3	3	1	1	45	7
Benin	78.2	12.8	0	4	0	0	78	13
Bolivia	19.9	7.4	10	3	0	0	10	7
Brazil	20.1	6.7	5	4	0	1	15	6
Brunei	0.0	3.7	0	1	0	0	0	4
Bulgaria	9.5	6.3	5	2	1	1	9	6
Burkina Faso	73.8	9.2	0	3	0	0	74	9
Burundi	72.2	10.8	0	2	0	1	72	11
Cameroon	27.4	8.5	0	4	0	0	27	8
Canada	3.9	2.8	2	1	0	0	4	3
Central African	24.8	12.2	1	1	0	0	25	12
Chad	82.7	13.5	0	2	0	1	83	13
Chile	12.6	4.2	4	2	3	0	13	4
China	2.1	4.6	0	2	0	0	2	4
Colombia	34.2	7.7	0	5	0	1	34	7

Congo, Dem. Rep.	7.3	13.8	0	5	0	0	7	14
Congo, Rep.	1.0	7.2	0	2	0	0	1	7
Costa Rica	44.5	4.7	0	3	0	0	44	5
Côte d'Ivoire	57.2	13.0	0	4	0	0	57	13
Croatia	2.8	6.2	1	1	0	1	3	6
Cuba	53.8	17.1	2	12	0	2	54	15
Cyprus	20.0	8.8	1	2	1	1	19	8
Czech Republic	3.1	3.4	1	1	1	0	3	3
Djibouti	10.1	20.9	1	5	0	1	10	21
Dominica	32.4	8.6	1	1	1	1	32	8
Dominican Republic	12.0	9.3	1	7	0	1	12	8
Ecuador	38.3	6.6	1	4	0	0	38	6
Egypt, Arab Rep.	9.1	12.8	1	9	0	1	9	12
El Salvador	24.7	10.7	1	6	1	1	25	10
Estonia	3.5	7.8	2	2	1	1	3	8
European Union 15	4.3	5.0	1	1	1	0	4	5
Fiji	36.1	7.7	0	3	0	1	36	8
Gabon	0.1	6.7	0	3	0	1	0	7
Gambia, The	3.3	20.6	0	3	0	1	3	21
Ghana	39.0	7.1	0	4	0	0	39	7
Grenada	23.3	12.4	0	5	1	1	23	12
Guatemala	42.0	9.0	0	4	0	1	42	8
Guinea	7.8	17.2	0	3	0	0	8	17
Guinea-Bissau	39.6	12.7	0	3	0	0	40	13
Guyana	33.2	10.4	1	5	0	1	33	10
Haiti	17.9	22.7	0	8	0	1	18	23
Honduras	26.7	6.2	0	4	0	1	27	6
Hong Kong, China	0.6	2.3	0	0	0	0	1	2
Hungary	6.7	2.1	2	1	1	0	7	2
Iceland	0.7	4.3	0	1	0	0	1	4

(continued)

Table 4.4 (Continued)

Country or group	Total export subsidies		Quad export subsidies		Other industrial country export subsidies[a]		Developing country export subsidies	
	Exports	Imports	Exports	Imports	Exports	Imports	Exports	Imports
India	9.9	2.5	4	0	0	0	8	2
Indonesia	4.0	7.9	0	4	0	1	4	7
Iran, Islamic Rep.	0.7	14.5	0	9	0	1	1	13
Israel	5.0	3.6	0	1	0	0	5	4
Jamaica	13.8	7.9	0	5	0	1	14	7
Japan	0.2	6.2	0	2	0	0	0	6
Jordan	5.3	15.4	0	9	0	1	5	14
Kazakhstan	12.3	5.9	6	1	1	1	12	6
Kenya	36.2	10.5	1	6	0	0	36	10
Korea, Rep.	0.6	4.1	0	2	0	0	1	4
Kuwait	0.1	6.5	0	2	0	1	0	6
Kyrgyz Republic	25.1	8.6	8	2	2	0	25	9
Latvia	3.8	7.2	1	1	1	1	4	7
Lithuania	7.1	7.5	3	1	4	1	6	7
Macao	0.5	6.7	0	1	0	1	0	7
Madagascar	25.8	6.2	1	2	6	0	26	6
Malawi	77.0	9.6	6	4	0	0	77	9
Malaysia	1.4	3.2	0	1	0	0	1	3
Maldives	0.2	10.8	0	3	0	0	0	11
Mali	84.3	10.6	0	4	0	0	84	11
Malta	0.6	3.4	0	1	0	1	1	3
Mauritania	0.1	28.9	0	10	0	1	0	29
Mauritius	25.4	7.5	0	4	0	1	25	7
Mexico	4.5	4.3	0	2	0	1	5	4
Mongolia	12.5	10.6	0	1	0	0	12	11
Morocco	9.7	11.0	0	7	0	1	10	11

Mozambique	36.5	18.2	3	7	0	1	36	18
Myanmar	17.1	6.7	4	0	0	0	17	7
New Zealand	25.3	3.3	13	1	15	0	22	3
Nicaragua	35.2	15.8	2	4	1	1	35	16
Niger	2.3	13.4	0	5	0	1	2	13
Nigeria	2.0	10.9	0	6	0	0	2	11
Norway	0.5	2.6	0	1	0	0	0	3
Oman	0.2	5.7	0	2	0	1	0	6
Pakistan	9.1	7.3	3	4	0	0	9	7
Panama	19.9	1.4	0	1	0	0	20	1
Papua New Guinea	12.0	3.0	0	1	0	1	12	3
Paraguay	27.0	11.9	11	2	0	0	19	12
Peru	9.4	11.8	0	8	0	1	9	11
Philippines	3.6	6.6	0	4	0	1	4	6
Poland	3.9	4.4	1	2	1	0	4	4
Qatar	0.0	4.3	0	1	0	1	0	4
Romania	4.4	5.5	2	1	1	0	4	5
Russian Federation	1.5	12.4	0	2	0	3	1	12
Rwanda	59.2	18.5	0	7	0	1	59	18
Saudi Arabia	0.2	9.0	0	4	0	1	0	9
Senegal	7.8	19.1	0	7	0	1	8	19
Sierra Leone	6.8	15.8	0	6	0	0	7	16
Singapore	0.7	2.3	0	1	0	0	1	2
Slovak Republic	2.7	4.2	1	1	0	0	3	4
Slovenia	1.6	5.1	0	1	1	0	2	5
Solomon Islands	3.3	5.1	0	1	0	0	3	5
South Africa	7.6	4.0	2	2	1	0	8	4
Sri Lanka	3.6	10.5	0	6	0	0	4	10
St. Kitts and Nevis	31.2	6.8	0	1	0	1	31	7
St. Lucia	61.2	10.2	0	2	0	2	61	9
St. Vincent and Grenadines	34.4	8.8	3	6	0	1	34	8

(continued)

Table 4.4 (Continued)

Country or group	Total export subsidies		Quad export subsidies		Other industrial country export subsidies[a]		Developing country export subsidies	
	Exports	Imports	Exports	Imports	Exports	Imports	Exports	Imports
Sudan	48.6	12.5	4	5	0	0	49	12
Suriname	9.6	6.8	2	2	0	0	10	6
Switzerland	1.4	3.1	0	1	0	0	1	3
Taiwan, China	0.6	3.7	0	2	0	0	1	4
Tanzania	60.0	7.8	2	2	0	0	60	8
Thailand	8.0	2.5	3	1	0	0	8	2
Togo	41.8	13.7	0	5	0	0	42	14
Trinidad and Tobago	3.6	7.6	0	4	0	1	3	7
Tunisia	4.5	7.3	4	5	0	0	4	7
Turkey	8.1	4.8	3	1	0	0	8	5
Uganda	83.6	7.4	0	1	0	0	84	7
United Arab Emirates	1.8	4.9	0	1	0	1	2	5
United States	5.2	2.5	2	0	0	0	5	2
Uruguay	25.2	6.4	11	2	5	0	24	6
Venezuela	1.2	8.7	0	5	0	0	1	8
Zambia	7.1	5.6	0	3	0	0	7	6
Zimbabwe	48.8	3.7	7	1	0	0	49	4
All countries (129)	4.4	4.4	1	1	0	0	4	4
Industrial countries (9)	4.0	3.9	2	1	0	0	4	4
Developing countries (90)	5.0	5.0	1	2	0	0	5	5
Least developed countries (30)	16.7	13.1	1	5	0	1	17	13

Source: Based on partners' data from UN Comtrade statistics.

Note: Numbers in parentheses are number of countries in the group (European Union is counted as one).

a. Includes non-Quad high-income OECD countries; excludes intra-EU trade.

Figure 4.3 Relationship Between Trade Shares Affected by Export Subsidies in All WTO

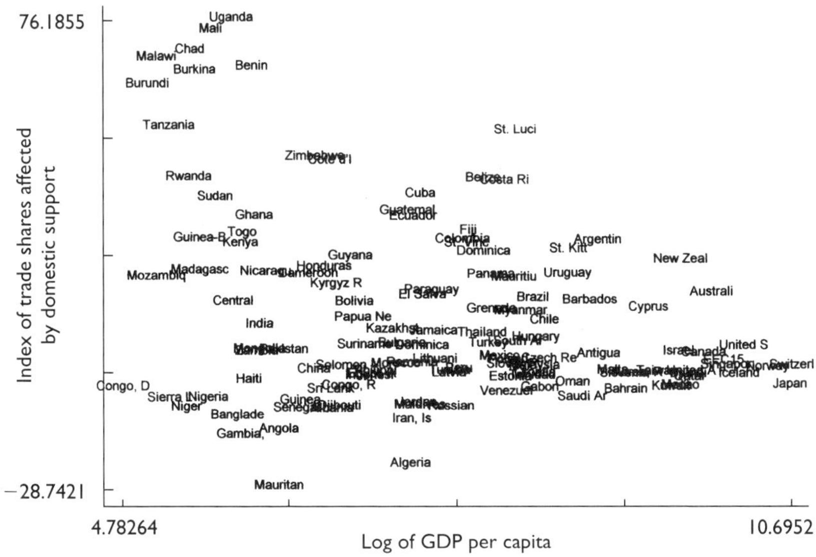

Figure 4.4 Relationship Between Trade Shares Affected by Quad Export Subsidies and GDP per Capita

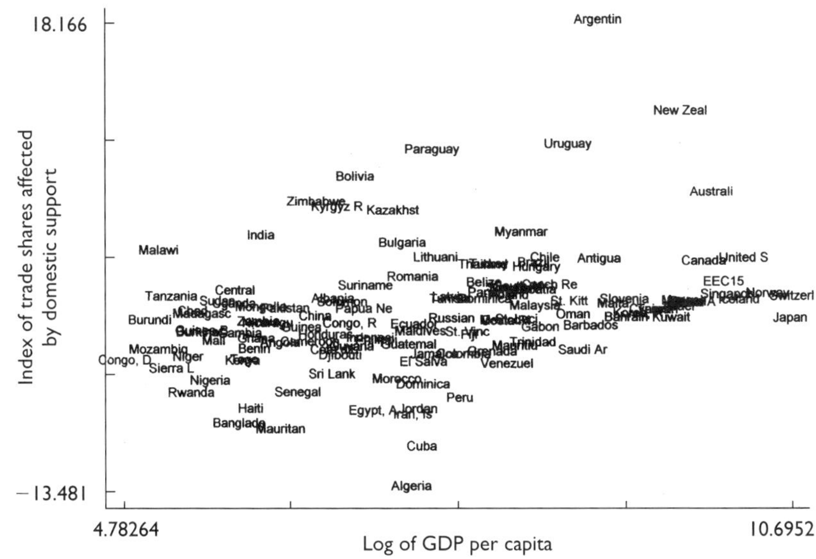

For the Cairns Group,[4] a strong supporter of the elimination of export subsidies, *I* is very high, at around 15. This suggests that the Cairns Group as a whole will probably experience large gains from the elimination of export subsidies. However, there is diversity within the group. Indonesia, Malaysia, and the Philippines all have a negative value of *I*, suggesting the possibility of losses from the removal of export subsidies.

Summing up, the pattern of trade suggests that removal of export subsidies by industrial countries is unlikely to have a large positive impact on developing countries as a group. There will be a number of significant gainers, but also a number of losers. This is also the case among the least developed countries. While some should benefit (Chad, Mali, and Uganda), others may lose because of the increased price of their import bundle.

THE IMPORTANCE OF COMPLEMENTARY TRADE POLICY REFORM

While domestic support and export subsidies are clearly inefficient at the global level, the impact of their removal will differ by country just as their incidence does. Many countries could lose in the short run if support levels drop abruptly and steeply. One way to attenuate any such negative effects is through complementary reforms. One area to consider is tariffs.

The average tariff (including the ad valorem equivalents of specific tariffs, as calculated by the OECD 2000 and Stawowy 2001) in Quad countries is 48 percent for products receiving domestic support and 17 percent for agricultural products as a whole (defined as HS 01–24; table 4.5). The average level of protection for the most heavily subsidized products (beef, dairy, cereals, and sugar) is even higher, at about 70 percent, with peaks of more than 100 percent not uncommon—and some as high as 500 percent. Other industrial countries also have some high tariff peaks for products subject to domestic support in those countries.[5] Tariffs on products subject to domestic support are also higher in developing countries, although the average tariff on such products is only 21 percent.

As with domestic support, the average tariff in Quad countries on products subject to export subsidies (37 percent) is much higher than the average tariff on all agriculture products (17 percent; table 4.6). The average tariff for products subject to large export subsidies in the Quad (beef, dairy, cereals, and sugar) is even higher. Developing countries also have relatively higher tariffs for products subject to export subsidies in developing countries (23 percent) than for agricultural products as a whole, but the difference is not significant. A reduction in these high tariffs is not only likely to bring the classic welfare (efficiency) gains from liberalization but may also mitigate the potential losses from removal of agriculture subsidies in countries where a large share of the import bundle is affected by the subsidies.

Both partial and general equilibrium model-based analyses find that removal of tariffs is likely to bring about the largest gains for developing countries. Using a partial equilibrium approach to analyze the impact of joint policy reform, Hoekman, Ng, and Olarreaga (chapter 3 in volume 2) find that a 50 percent cut in agricultural domestic support across WTO members may result in a welfare loss for developing countries as a whole, although the least developed countries would experience modest gains. They conclude that there is likely to be considerable variation across countries. Argentina, for example, would experience an increase in welfare ($7 per capita), whereas large net importers such as Taiwan, China, would lose ($2 per capita).

For both developing countries and least developed countries a 50 percent tariff reduction by all WTO members—thus including countries' own liberalization—would have a positive effect on welfare. For the least developed countries these gains would be at least 50 percent larger than the gains from a 50 percent cut in domestic support. For no country in which there is an increase in welfare associated with a cut in domestic support is a loss associated with a cut in tariffs. Conversely, many countries that experience a loss from a cut in domestic support experience a welfare gain from a cut in tariffs. The conclusion is that domestic support should be accompanied by cuts in tariffs for the majority of countries to benefit from global agricultural policy reforms.

General equilibrium-based analyses reach a similar conclusion. Beghin, Roland-Holst, and van der Mensbrugghe (2002), using a dynamic general equilibrium model, find that two-thirds of the gains accruing to low- and middle-income countries from agricultural policy reforms are generated by the removal of border protection. For Sub-Saharan Africa—which includes a large number of least developed countries—77 percent of the gains come from the removal of border protection. Similarly, Dimaranan, Hertel, and Keeney (2002) and Anderson and Martin (2005), also employing a global general equilibrium model, find that the removal of price support measures matters more than removal of domestic support, although the welfare effects on individual developing countries are likely to be diverse.

Summing up, the literature suggests that the gains from a reduction in agriculture tariffs will outweigh the gains from a reduction in agricultural subsidies. As important, a reduction in agricultural tariffs may reverse what would otherwise have been a welfare loss for net food importers.

CONCLUSION

Most agricultural subsidies—direct domestic support and export subsidies—are concentrated in a few products. In addition, developing countries' agricultural exports of some $70 billion face $90 billion in domestic support in industrial country markets (excluding non-product-specific green box support) and agricultural exports of $20 billion face $8 billion in export subsidies in indus-

Table 4.5 Average Most-Favored-Nation Tariff and Maximum Tariff on Agricultural Products with Domestic Support, 1995–98 Average (percent)

Product at Harmonized System two-digit level	Quad (4)		Other OECD countries[a] (5)		Developing countries (76)	
	Average tariff	Maximum tariff	Average tariff	Maximum tariff	Average tariff	Maximum tariff
01 Live animals	6	6	..	..	9	73
02 Meat and edible meat offal	36	69	..	..	25	43
04 Dairy products; birds' eggs; honey	126	329	32	350	22	70
06 Live trees and other plants, bulbs; cut flowers	..	..	..	..	10	20
07 Edible vegetables and roots and tubers	17	65	0	0	31	458
08 Edible fruit and nuts; melons	30	219	1	5	30	239
09 Coffee; tea; maté; and spices	..	..	..	..	11	25
10 Cereals	75	557	0	0	11	391
11 Milled products; malt; starches	94	94	..	..	48	293
12 Oil seed; oleaginous fruits	17	125	..	..	25	530

13 Lac; gums, resins, and other vegetables	..	..	..	..	25	25
15 Animal and vegetable fats and oils and products	6	8	..	..	14	20
17 Sugars and sugar confectionery	78	78	..	..	36	135
18 Cocoa and cocoa preparations	..	..	..	..	13	15
20 Preparations of vegetable, fruit, and nuts products	43	163	..	..	22	25
21 Miscellaneous edible preparations	..	..	..	..	25	90
22 Beverages, spirits, and vinegar	8	8	..	..	14	15
23 Residues and waste from food industry	0	1	..	..	15	15
24 Tobacco and manufactured tobacco substitutes	19	68	0	0	12	25
50 Silk	118	236	..	..	20	56
51 Wool, fine and coarse animal hair	28	46	..	..	14	15
52 Cotton	10	20	..	..	6	15
53 Other vegetable textile fibers and yarn	0	0	..	..	8	15
All products listed above with domestic support	48	557	24	350	21	530
All agricultural products	17	1403	37	609	17	1750

Source: UNCTAD TRAINS data (through World Bank and UNCTAD WITS, various years), OECD (2000), and Stawowy (2001).

Notes: Numbers in parentheses are number of countries in the group (European Union is counted as one); .. indicates a negligible value.

a. High income OECD countries, excluding Quad countries, for which support data are available (Australia, Iceland, New Zealand, Norway, and Switzerland).

Table 4.6 Average Most Favored-Nation Tariff and Maximum Tariff on Agricultural Products with Export Subsidies, 1995–98 Average (percent)

Product at Harmonized System two-digit level	Quad (4)		Other OECD countries[a] (5)		Developing countries (76)	
	Average tariff	Maximum tariff	Average tariff	Maximum tariff	Average tariff	Maximum tariff
01 Live animals	0	0	77	385	13	97
02 Meat and edible meat offal	29	119	91	480	26	362
04 Dairy products; birds' eggs; honey	91	275	83	506	24	265
05 Products of animal origin					13	65
06 Live trees and other plants, bulbs; cut flowers					21	80
07 Edible vegetables and roots and tubers	4	6	20	106	23	814
08 Edible fruit and nuts; melons	4	8	1	3	24	255
09 Coffee; tea; maté; and spices					22	559
10 Cereals	42	123			18	467
11 Milled products; malt; starches					20	496
12 Oil seed; oleaginous fruits	1	3			12	51
13 Lac; gums, resins, and other vegetables					15	199
14 Vegetable plaiting materials, not elsewhere specified					12	68
15 Animal/vegetable fats and oils and products	13	81			19	152

16 Preparations of meat, fish, or mollusks			85	385	25	100
17 Sugars and sugar confectionery	16	31			27	143
18 Cocoa and cocoa preparations					19	70
19 Preparations of cereal, flour, starch/milk products					22	70
20 Preparations of vegetable, fruit, nuts	15	17			25	146
21 Miscellaneous edible preparations			125	609	20	70
22 Beverages, spirits, and vinegar	8	12			39	1,200
23 Residues and waste from food industries	1	3			14	80
24 Tobacco and manufactured tobacco substitutes	21	44			37	907
33 Essential oils and resinoids					13	70
35 Albuminoidal substances; modified starches					13	70
41 Raw hides and skins (other than fur)					7	19
43 Furs, skins, and artificial fur					14	45
50 Silk					14	80
51 Wool, fine/coarse animal hair not elsewhere specified					8	25
52 Cotton					7	35
All products listed above with export subsidies	37	275	70	609	23	1,200
All agricultural products (HS 01–HS 24)	17	1,403	37	609	17	1,750

Source: UNCTAD TRAINS data (through World Bank and UNCTAD WITS, various years), OECD (2000), and Stawowy (2001).
Note: Numbers in parentheses are number of countries in the group (European Union is counted as one).
a. Includes non-Quad high-income OECD countries.

trial country markets. Middle-income developing countries have also become participants in the subsidy game.

Export and import shares of products affected by support and subsidy policies reveal large differences across developing countries in the impact of these policies. Because subsidies are likely to lower the world price of affected commodities, an important determinant of the direct impact of global subsidy reform in the short run is whether a country is a net importer or net exporter of the products concerned.

Although the trade share analysis provides a qualitative answer to the question of who is likely to gain or lose in the short run from large-scale global agricultural policy reform, a model-based analysis is required for a detailed assessment of the interaction between agricultural support and complementary reforms. The ultimate impact of global agricultural policy reform depends on domestic and foreign supply responses to an increase in the world price of the products concerned after the subsidy is removed. And that response depends on the incentives to engage in agricultural production relative to other sectors of the economy. These incentives are a function of many factors, including the level of tariff protection for agricultural and manufacturing products.

Tariffs on agricultural products that benefit from subsidies tend to be higher than tariffs on agricultural products overall. The elimination of such high levels of protection is likely to bring the traditional consumer gains in liberalizing countries and to mitigate losses in net importers arising from the removal of subsidies. Because the primary instrument used by developing countries to intervene in agricultural markets is the tariff, trade liberalization offers the greatest source of potential gains for these countries.

A major political economy problem confronting WTO negotiators is how to create incentives for countries to liberalize agricultural trade. Many developing countries oppose further agricultural trade liberalization as long as industrial countries continue to provide large-scale support to their farmers. Experience has demonstrated that the gains from countries' own liberalization may be attenuated by the market segmenting effect of industrial country subsidy policies. In India agricultural liberalization proved politically unsustainable because farmers were subjected to large world price swings and import surges of subsidized commodities (chapter 9 in this volume). Substantial reductions in industrial country agricultural support are therefore important not only for the direct benefits generated for the many economies that are (potential) net exporters but also for the support of efforts by developing country governments to pursue domestic reforms and thus to reap significant gains from the current WTO negotiations on agriculture.

The analysis here also shows that industrial country agricultural support policies have set a detrimental example, now being followed by developing countries. While the subsidies are much smaller than those of the Quad countries, their effects are more harmful because they affect products produced only or primarily by developing countries. Global agricultural support policy reform is therefore also important for the poorest countries by introducing disciplines on the use of support programs by middle-income countries.

ANNEX. DATA SOURCES

All trade data are from the United Nations Statistics Division's Commodity Trade Database (Comtrade) (both value figures and unit prices). For countries that did not report trade data to Comtrade, notifications by their trading partners are used to mirror their data. Tariffs are drawn from UNCTAD and WTO as provided in the World Bank and UNCTAD World Integrated Trade Solution (WITS) system. This database does not include the ad valorem equivalents of specific tariffs, which come from Stawowy (2001) for Canada, the European Union, Japan, and the United States and from OECD (2000) for other industrial countries. For tariff rate quotas the average of within- and outside-quota tariffs is generally taken, although in some cases only the outside-quota tariff is available. The industrial countries' ad valorem equivalents of specific tariffs use exclusively outside-quota tariffs. This may bias results of some estimates since some import prices may be higher if exporters benefit from lower within-quota tariffs.

The source for domestic support data is WTO (2000). National currency data were converted to US dollars using the period average exchange rate reported in the International Monetary Funds' *International Financial Statistics.* Product classifications, which differed by country, were mapped to the HS six-digit classification, generally in a one-to-one mapping. In cases where reported domestic support covers several six-digit tariff lines, the subsidy was distributed across the tariff lines using the share of the reporting country's exports as weights. The concordance file is available from the authors on request.

Exempt subsidies, which are not product specific, were mapped into product-specific subsidies using as weights the product-specific commitments that each country made in the Uruguay Round. Non-product-specific support is divided evenly into all products exported by the country concerned. All products shown in notifications to the WTO are included, even when the support is below the *de minimis* level for the member concerned. Thus, the total aggregate measurement of support for a country may exceed its total WTO commitments. GDP (in US dollars) and population data are drawn from the World Bank's World Development Indicators database.

NOTES

This paper is based on notifications made by WTO members on domestic support and export subsidies in 2000. The most recent notifications were made in 2002. These were not used in this paper because data for that year were only reported for a subset of WTO members. As a number of major countries did not report data for more recent years in 2002, we were not able to undertake the analysis for a more recent period.

The authors are indebted to Lili Tabada for assistance in constructing the agriculture subsidy database from WTO member notifications, to Bijit Bora and Wojciech Stawowy for estimates of ad valorem equivalents on specific tariffs in Quad countries, and to Morvarid Bagherzadeh for information on OECD estimates of ad valorem equivalents.

1. This potential national welfare benefit is offset by the higher price volatility created by support policies since country-specific shocks may be transferred to world markets. The analysis in this chapter ignores the extent to which price volatility is transmitted to world markets.
2. Domestic support includes subsidies that are not exempt from WTO reduction commitments—the so-called green box support measures. These subsidies are excluded from the analysis here, however, because of the difficulty of associating such support with particular crops. The measure of direct domestic support includes only five of the eight categories of support distinguished by the WTO Agreement on Agriculture: nonexempt support that is below the *de minimis* level (DS4), market price support (DS5), nonexempt direct payments (DS6), other product-specific support (DS7), and any support measured using the equivalent measurement of support methodology (DS8). For details, see Chapter 3 in Volume 2.
3. It is difficult to assess to what extent the Everything but Arms initiative offers actual preferential access to least developed countries, as rules of origin and other nontariff barriers may erode the preferential access granted on paper. Brenton and Manchin (2002) show evidence that EU preferential access schemes have offered limited benefits because of restrictive rules of origin. For the US African Growth and Opportunity Act (AGOA), publicly available data show small actual gains for African countries (Mattoo, Roy, and Subramanian 2002).
4. Members of the Cairns Group are Argentina, Australia, Bolivia, Brazil, Canada, Chile, Colombia, Costa Rica, Guatemala, Indonesia, Malaysia, New Zealand, Paraguay, the Philippines, South Africa, Thailand, and Uruguay.
5. These average tariffs are heavily influenced by excessive levels of agriculture protection in Norway. According to OECD (2000) estimates, the average level of agriculture protection in Norway is above 150 percent.

BIBLIOGRAPHY

Anderson, Kym, and Will Martin. 2005. "Agricultural Trade Reform and the Doha Development Agenda." *World Economy* 28 (9): 1301–27.

Beghin, John, David Roland-Holst, and Dominique van der Mensbrugghe. 2002. "How Will Agricultural Trade Reforms in High-Income Countries Affect the Trading Relationships of Developing Countries?" World Bank, Washington, DC.

Brenton, Paul, and Miriam Manchin. 2002. "Making EU Trade Agreements Work: The Role of Rules of Origin." Working Document 183, Center for European Policy Studies, Brussels.

De Gorter, Harry. 2002. "The AMS and Domestic Support in WTO Trade Negotiations on Agriculture: Issues and Suggestions for New Rules." World Bank, Washington, DC.

Dimaranan, Bettina, Thomas Hertel, and Roman Keeney. 2002. "OECD Domestic Support and the Developing Countries." Purdue University, West Lafayette, IN.

Fontagné, Lional, J. L. Guérin, and S. Jean. 2002. "Multilateral Trade Liberalization: Scenarios for the New Round and Assessment." Centre d'Etudes Prospectives et d'Informations Internationales, Paris.

Hoekman, Bernard. 2002. "Strengthening the Global Trade Architecture for Development: The Post-Doha Agenda." *World Trade Review* 1 (1): 23–45.

Hoekman, Bernard, and Michel Kostecki. 2001. *The Political Economy of the World Trading System: The WTO and Beyond.* New York: Oxford University Press.

Hoekman, Bernard, Francis Ng, and Marcelo Olarreaga. 2002. "Eliminating Excessive Tariffs on Exports of Least Developed Countries." *World Bank Economic Review* 16 (1): 1–21.

IMF (International Monetary Fund). Various years. *International Financial Statistics.* Washington, DC.

Mattoo, Aaditya, Devesh Roy, and Arvind Subramanian. 2002. "The Africa Growth and Opportunity Act and Rules of Origin: Generosity Undermined?" World Bank, Washington, DC.

OECD (Organisation for Economic Co-operation and Development). 2000. *Post-Uruguay Rounds Tariff Regimes: Achievements and Outlook.* Paris: OECD.

Schiff, M., and A. Valdés. 1998. "Agriculture and the Macroeconomy." Policy Research Working Paper 1967, World Bank, Washington, DC.

Stawowy, Wojciech. 2001. "Calculation of ad-valorem Equivalents of Non-ad-valorem Tariffs: Methodology Notes." UNCTAD, Geneva.

UNCTAD (United Nations Conference on Trade and Development). Various years. "Trade Analysis and Information System (TRAINS)." Geneva. http://r0.unctad.org/trains.

World Bank and UNCTAD (United Nations Conference on Trade and Development). Various years. "World Integrated Trade Solutions (WITS) Data Consultation and Extraction Software," Washington, DC. http://wits.worldbank.org/witsweb.

WTO (World Trade Organization). 2000. "Committee on Agriculture, Special Session, 'Domestic Support.'" Background paper by the Secretariat. G/AG/NG/S/1, WTO, Geneva.

———. 2001 "Committee on Agriculture, Special Session, 'Export Subsidies.'" Background paper by the Secretariat, G/AG/NG/S/5/Rev.1, WTO, Geneva.

CHAPTER FIVE

Coalitions and Alliance Strategies for Developing Countries in the Doha Round of Agricultural Negotiations

Rashid S. Kaukab

Many developing countries were disappointed with the results of the Uruguay Round Agreement on Agriculture (URAA) and with the less than satisfactory outcome of multilateral trade negotiations since then. This chapter examines the objectives of developing countries in the current round of World Trade Organization (WTO) agricultural negotiations based on their experience with past negotiations and considers possible coalitions and strategies for them in the ongoing WTO negotiations on agriculture. The chapter concludes that developing countries need to build themselves into an effective third force if they want to avoid a repeat of Uruguay Round agricultural negotiations and achieve outcomes that reflect their interests and not just those of the United States and the European Union.

DEVELOPING COUNTRY POSITIONS AND GROUPS IN AGRICULTURAL TRADE NEGOTIATIONS

Agriculture negotiations remain at the heart of the Doha Round. It was the promise of fundamental reform of agricultural support and protection systems in developed countries that persuaded many developing countries to agree to the launch of a new round of multilateral trade negotiations at the Doha Ministerial Conference in November 2001. This allowed the agricultural negotiations, under way since early 2000 under Article 20 of the URAA, to proceed on the basis of a clearer and more comprehensive mandate.

Developing countries' frustrating experience with the URAA has shaped their approach to the WTO agricultural negotiations, before and since Doha. While the URAA brought agriculture back inside the fold of multilateral trade disciplines, the rules established under the URAA and their implementation by some major developed countries were far from satisfactory to nearly all developing countries. For major agricultural producers, particularly the developing country members of the Cairns Group,[1] and for many other developing countries interested in increasing their agricultural exports to developed country markets, the major disappointment was the lack of any meaningful new market openings. The failure to implement the Marrakech Ministerial Decision in Favor of Least Developed Countries and Net Food Importing Developing Countries was a major cause of concern for countries in those two groups. And almost all developing countries complained bitterly about the double standard under the URAA that allowed the major developed countries to continue their protectionist and production- and trade-distorting policies, but further constrained the limited flexibility available to developing countries. Developing countries were also generally displeased with the special and differential treatment provisions, which were often irrelevant and ineffective.[2]

This experience with the Uruguay Round agricultural negotiations and implementation has determined the negotiating position of many developing countries in the Doha Round. Many developing countries consider the URAA to be based on a compromise between the United States and the European Union, to the neglect of other interests. The Blair House deals between the two major powers allowed them to accommodate one another's key interests. The essentially bilateral nature of the URAA deal led to the legalization and continuation of massively subsidized and protected agriculture in developed countries while constraining the use of similar measures by developing countries. Thus most developing countries do not trust the United States and the European Union to strike a compromise favorable to all in the current negotiations. They see truly multilateral negotiations as the best way to accommodate their interests, in discussions involving three equal partners: the United States, the European Union, and developing countries.

While developing countries share the general objective of fundamental reform of agricultural support and protection systems in developed countries, their positions differ in several respects. These positions can be broadly categorized as offensive, defensive, and a combination of the two, based on countries' interests and positions at the start of Doha Round. Although these interests have emerged from countries' articulation of their interests within and outside the WTO, these broad categories are not represented by well-defined and organized groups, either formal or informal. Moreover, there is considerable overlap among the three categories, as the following discussion makes clear. The broad categories discussed in this section help to clarify developing countries' main negotiating interests in agriculture at the start of Doha Round. Later sections discuss actual negotiating alliances and coalitions of developing countries in multilateral agricultural negotiations.

Developing Countries with Mainly Offensive Interests

Except for Australia, Canada, and New Zealand, all members of the Cairns Group are developing countries. They are major agricultural producers and exporters and thus favor liberalization of trade in agriculture. The group generally pursues its liberalization objectives quite aggressively. It would like to see major reform of the agricultural trading system through the elimination of export subsidies and the disciplining of export credits, substantial reduction in trade distorting domestic support, and major improvements in market access. These countries support targeted special and differential treatment for developing countries and are generally hostile to nontrade concerns such as eco-labeling or the use of environmental measures for trade restrictive purposes, as expounded by the European Union, Japan, and some other countries.

It would be a mistake, however, to assume that all developing country members of the Cairns Group share the same aggressive liberalization agenda. Some developing country members, particularly from Asia, are apprehensive that further opening of their own agricultural markets without massive reductions in agricultural subsidies by major developed countries and without effective safeguard instruments at their disposal might play havoc with their domestic agriculture. In this sense these countries share many of the interests and concerns of the developing countries in the middle category (see below).

Developing Countries with Mainly Defensive Interests

Another broad category of developing countries can be perceived to have largely defensive interests in agriculture. This category includes many net food-importing countries and preference-receiving countries. The net food importers are concerned that removal of subsidies will lead to an increase in prices, raising their food import bills in the immediate to medium term. Since almost all of these countries have current account deficits, rising prices could have a major adverse impact on them. This consideration, together with their frustration at the failure to implement the Marrakech Ministerial Decision in Favor of Least Developed Countries and the Net Food Importing Developing Countries at the time of high cereal prices in the mid-1990s, has prompted some of them to favor a slower pace of liberalization and to argue for establishing effective compensatory mechanisms to assist them in the immediate to medium term.

The other group in this broad category consists of countries that are currently the major beneficiaries of preferential market access to some developed country markets, particularly the European Union under the Cotonou Agreement. Many of these countries are small and dependent on a few agricultural exports to a major developed country market and benefit from preferential access to that market. Immediate and complete liberalization of these markets on a most favored nation basis would mean the loss of their preferential status, which could be a large shock for them. Their major concern therefore is for a process that allows them to adjust gradually to a loss of preferential market access without causing major economic disruptions.

Developing countries in this broad category of defensive interests are not against reform of agricultural production and support systems in developed countries. Their concerns are more often about the pace and direction of liberalization as well as the need for compensatory and adjustment mechanisms.

Developing Countries in the Middle

The interests of the third broad category of developing countries are somewhere in between those of countries in the other two categories. Most developing countries fall into this category, which includes some members of the Cairns Group, some net food importing countries, and some preference-receiving countries as well.

The main objective of developing countries in this category is to achieve substantial reform of agricultural trade by remedying the shortcomings of the current URAA disciplines and providing effective special and differential treatment for developing countries that protects their subsistence agriculture and large agrarian populations. They also seek mechanisms to assist the net food importing countries and small preference-receiving countries. Many countries in this category also believe that developing countries should have their own agenda and platform instead of simply following one or the other major power in agricultural negotiations.

EXPERIENCE OF COALITIONS OF DEVELOPING COUNTRIES IN THE MULTILATERAL AGRICULTURAL TRADE NEGOTIATIONS

Developing countries' participation in the multilateral agricultural trade negotiations can be described as a struggle to match the negotiating power—political, economic, trade, technical, and human capacity—of the major developed countries. Experience in the Uruguay Round showed developing countries that they could not trust the United States and the European Union to safeguard developing countries' interests while these two powerful economies cut bilateral deals. Experience also showed that individually no developing country could match the negotiating power of the United States or the European Union. Thus developing countries have tried to come together with other like-minded countries to form formal and informal negotiating alliances and coalitions. Some of these alliances have included developed countries as well.

These coalitions and alliances have increased in number and importance and can now be considered a key element of a developing country strategy in the ongoing agricultural negotiations. The discussion here makes no attempt to cover all the coalitions and alliances of developing countries nor to provide a detailed analysis of those that are covered. Rather, it offers a brief description of some of the important coalitions and alliances with a view to identifying major lessons for developing countries as they continue to strive for a fair, equitable, and balanced outcome of the Doha Round of agricultural trade negotiations.

Developing countries have worked through various formal and informal groups and coalitions in the multilateral trade negotiations.[3] These include such formal regional groups as the African Group and the Caribbean Regional Negotiating Mechanism; criteria-based formal groups that share common characteristics or are linked through common agreement with others, such as the least developed countries and the African, Caribbean, and Pacific (ACP) countries[4]; and formal and informal issue-based alliances and coalitions such as the Cairns Group, the Friends of the Development Box group, the Group of 20 (G-20), and the Group of 33 (G-33).

Formal Regional Groups

Formal regional groups of developing countries have often been established outside the WTO and without any initial intention to employ them in the multilateral trade negotiations. These formal regional groups have elaborate governance structures, and their agendas are often much broader than international trade. Two such groups have been active in the WTO, the African Group and the Caribbean Regional Negotiating Machinery.

African Group

Arguably, the African Group is one of the most active regional groups of developing countries in the WTO.[5] While this regional group is not new, its activities and internal coordination have improved over the years. That is no small feat considering the number of countries involved, the diversity of interests among members, and the very limited human and technical resources of most member countries. A strong political commitment based on a shared sense of African identity has helped this group overcome these drawbacks.

Understandably, the group has not always taken a joint negotiating position in agricultural negotiations. Members of the African Group are quite disparate, including a member of the Cairns Group (South Africa), many least developed countries, net food importing countries, and preference-receiving countries. But the group has been useful as a platform for sharing information, exchanging knowledge and experience, and articulating African concerns. On occasion, the group has also presented joint proposals to the negotiations, particularly of an agenda-setting nature.

Important developments in the organization and effectiveness of the African Group have taken place since it began working in the WTO in late 1990s. It has developed coordinated and well-structured systems of operation. Overall coordination of the group is rotated among African countries, normally on a six-month basis. The coordinator chairs the weekly group meetings and provides general guidance. In addition, issue-specific coordinators, who work at the level of technical delegates, are responsible for coordinating, presenting, and defending the group's position on specific issues such as agriculture and services. These positions are also rotated, though with less frequency.

The technical support arrangements for the African Group in Geneva have improved considerably. The local office of the African Union provides technical backstopping and logistical facilities such as equipped meeting rooms. Similarly, the UN Economic Commission for Africa has established a small office in Geneva with technical expertise on trade issues.

Despite these positive developments, the African Group, with its large size and diversity of interests, may have difficulty becoming an effective negotiating group in the WTO agricultural negotiations, though it may occasionally present common African negotiating proposals on selected issues in the agricultural negotiations. Its strengths lie as a coordinating and information sharing mechanism for African countries and as a political force for broad agenda setting for the negotiating process.

Caribbean Regional Negotiating Mechanism

The Caribbean Regional Negotiating Mechanism is perhaps the only example of a formal, common negotiating mechanism among developing countries.[6] Seventeen small states have pooled their resources to create this mechanism, which allows them to coordinate among their capitals and between their capitals and Geneva missions, provide political guidance and technical inputs to their trade negotiators, and improve their negotiating power. Because of the close political and economic ties among its members, this is probably the only group of developing countries that can be an effective negotiating force across several issues, including agriculture.

However, while the Caribbean Regional Negotiating Mechanism is a promising initiative with substantial potential, several constraints may impede full realization of this potential in the Doha Round agricultural negotiations. Its members have limited resources, spread thinly across several sets of bilateral and regional trade negotiations in addition to those in the WTO. Even more constraining is the treatment of these small states in the WTO, where they tend to be ignored by the bigger powers. Also, the members of this group generally have a narrow and defensive agenda in the agricultural negotiations. Their main concern is the maintenance of preferential access to the protected EU market.

Formal Criteria-Based Groups

Like the formal regional groups, the formal criteria-based groups of developing countries have been established outside the WTO, and international trade negotiations are only one of the issues in their mandates. These formal interregional groups include the least-developed countries and the ACP countries. Both groups are well established and have political and institutional governance structures. They bring to the WTO negotiations a history of working together and often a common agenda.

Group of Least Developed Countries

This group has certain clear advantages.[7] First, the group is based on well defined criteria, so members share economic development indicators, which should be helpful in defining common negotiating objectives in the WTO. Second, various WTO agreements provide for legal recognition of the group and for differentiated rights and obligations for them. Third, while the group has no dedicated secretariat of its own, the secretariats of both the WTO and the United Nations Conference on Trade and Development (UNCTAD) provide logistical and technical support. The group also receives technical support from many other intergovernmental and nongovernmental organizations. Fourth, the countries in this group are considered the "poorest among the poor" and so are the first to be offered any preferential treatment in the WTO. This gives the group much more political and negotiating space than other groups of developing countries.

These advantages are somewhat offset by the large number of members and the very limited human and technical resources of the group. Several least developed country members of the WTO still have no missions in Geneva. Of those that do, many have only one or two negotiators to deal with all WTO negotiations.

For the Doha Round agricultural negotiations the least developed countries, like the African Group, have established a regular system of coordination, with rotating coordinators for both general and issue-specific concerns. This has allowed the pooling of resources to improve the understanding and participation of all group members in the negotiations. The group also holds a general weekly meeting in addition to issue-specific meetings. Very important, the 2004 Framework Agreement for agriculture adopted by the General Council exempts least developed countries from the requirement to undertake any tariff or subsidy reduction commitments.[8] This has been interpreted to mean that the group, at least in the immediate future, does not need to take an active role in the agricultural negotiations and should instead focus on safeguarding these exemptions.

This may not be the best approach, however. Even if these countries do not make any reduction commitments of their own, the commitments made by other developed and developing countries will have important bearing on the trade of the least developed countries. The rules elements of the negotiations are also important for them, such as the special safeguard mechanism for developing countries.[9] Finally, maintaining a one-point defensive agenda is not a good negotiating strategy. The least developed country group should use its commonality of interests to present and defend its own proposals in the agricultural negotiations.

Group of African, Caribbean, and Pacific Countries

The common denominator among the countries in this very large group of ACP countries is their relationship—economic, social, political and cultural—with former European colonial power.[10] The trade and economic ties, particularly the preferential market access for certain commodities in the protected EU market, are important components of the institutional relationship embodied in various Lome-Conventions and now in the Cotonou Agreement. These ties often determine the negotiating positions of these countries in the WTO, where their main concern is to safeguard their preferential market access to the EU market.

For historical and institutional reasons, the ACP countries have their main office in Brussels. They had no Geneva presence until recently. A small ACP mission established in Geneva before the Doha Ministerial Conference has improved coordination among members of the group. The Geneva mission provides logistical and technical support, often with the help of other intergovernmental and nongovernmental organizations. The ACP group, like the African Group and the least developed countries, has established rotating general and issue-specific coordinatorships. All these developments have improved the functioning of the group, and it is now much more active than it had been even a few years ago.

The major constraint for the group is its size. The ACP has more than 70 members, many of them small states without any representation in Geneva. Another constraint has been the strong interest of the group in maintaining its preferential market access to the European Union. Finally, while the WTO negotiations have brought members of the group closer together, negotiations with the European Union to conclude the regional Economic Partnership Agreements that will succeed the Cotonou Agreement have split the ACP. These challenges raise a question mark over the long-term viability of the ACP as a cohesive negotiating group in the WTO.

However, in the current agricultural negotiations the ACP countries generally have a strong common interest: maintaining their preferential market access to the European Union to the extent possible. Admittedly, there is also a growing desire among many ACP countries to enlarge their agenda beyond safeguarding their preferential access. These two factors would mean that the ACP countries can be expected to play an important role in the Doha Round agricultural negotiations.

Issue-Based Alliances and Coalitions

Relatively more important in the WTO agricultural negotiations than the regional groups have been the issue-based alliances and coalitions of developing countries. In focusing exclusively on agricultural negotiations, such alliances allow like-minded countries to come together within the context of these negotiations while maintaining their different positions on other issues. These groups are also much more fluid—joining or leaving the group does not usually require formal procedures. These issue-based alliances and coalitions are playing an increasingly important role in the Doha Round agricultural negotiations.

The Cairns Group

Before the creation of the G-20 in August 2003, the Cairns Group was the most important coalition engaged in the agricultural negotiations that included both developing and developed country members. The Cairns Group was formed during the Uruguay Round as a third force to push for the liberalization of agricultural trade in the face of a standoff between the two major powers, the United States and the European Union. It played an important role in setting the agenda for the Uruguay Round agricultural negotiations and in participating in the negotiations. Despite some internal differences, the Cairns Group has kept the focus of the WTO membership on agricultural negotiations. Among its successes can be included its own survival and expansion, its transformation from an agenda-setting to a negotiating group, and some limited success in achieving its negotiating objectives during the Uruguay Round.

Several reasons have been advanced for the group's success. One is management. Australia has provided inspired and committed leadership, essential to building up the group and working out internal differences. Australia also provided the resources for research and analysis, providing crucial technical support during the negotiations. Also important is the political commitment of members to their cause, which gave them the courage to selectively employ blocking strategies during the Uruguay Round. The group also boasted a clear and proactive agenda, which was different from the negative or reactive agendas of many other developing country coalitions. The group fulfilled an important need at the time, pointing the way to compromise as the two major economic powers were locked in a mutually destructive subsidies war. The group was a bridge builder between the feuding United States and European Union and has to some extent benefited from the tacit or even open support of the United States.

Nonetheless, viewed in the context of its negotiating objectives during the Uruguay Round, the Cairns Group could be said to have had only limited success. The rules established during the round and implementation of commitments did not lead to meaningful reform of agricultural trade. It can also be argued that the group was more successful as an agenda-setting coalition than as a negotiating group. Finally, the ambition of the group to be the effective third force in agricultural negotiations did not really materialize: the final deal on agriculture in the Uruguay Round was mainly between the United States and the European Union. The Cairns Group, along with the other WTO members, was presented with a fait accompli at the end. The hold of the major powers on the agenda and outcome of negotiations in the multilateral trading system has so far frustrated many attempts by smaller countries to fully assert their interests.

The establishment of the G-20, which includes many developing country members of the Cairns Group, seriously weakened the group, which can no longer claim to be the foremost representative of developing country interests in the negotiations. Despite this setback, the Cairns Group retains some of its influence because of its agenda (overtly aggressive liberalization), history and image, research capacity, and the negotiating skills of some of its members, particularly Australia. It is expected to continue to play a role in the Doha Round agricultural negotiations.

Friends of the Development Box

An informal group of developing countries known as the Friends of the Development Box was active at the start of current WTO negotiations on agriculture.[11] The group came together during the submission to the WTO of a series of negotiating proposals on agriculture in 2000 and 2001. The group derived its name from its proposal for the creation of a development box to provide effective special and differential treatment for developing countries. The group's political profile reached its peak at the time of the Doha Ministerial Conference, when it held a ministerial-level meeting and press conference.

The group has had some influence in agenda setting. The need for binding and effective special and differential treatment for developing countries in agriculture has been recognized in the Doha Declaration, and several elements of its proposal on a development box are still being discussed. The group also provided a forum for many developing countries to coordinate their positions on agricultural issues and present a common front in the WTO. Pakistan, informal coordinator of the group, played a role similar to that of Australia in the Cairns Group, in building the group and providing leadership.

Despite initial successes, the group gradually disintegrated. Like many other developing country groups it failed to transform itself from a political agenda-setting forum to an effective negotiating bloc. A major factor in the group's decline was its lack of effective leadership after Pakistan gave up that role. Without committed leadership, informal coalitions and alliances have little chance of survival in the demanding negotiating environment of the WTO.

Arguably, the group was successful in putting forth an agenda that has since been pursued by other groups of developing countries. For example, some elements of the G-20 agenda on export subsidies and domestic support have their roots in the initial proposals by the Friends of the Development Box. A stronger link can be observed between the agenda of the G-33 and the development box proposal of the Friends of the Development Box. Informal alliances and coalitions may disappear for reasons unrelated to the strength and validity of their agendas, which may outlive them.

Group of 20

The establishment of the G-20 may be the most important development of the Doha Round of agricultural negotiations.[12] Before the emergence of the G-20, the Friends of the Development Box group had practically disappeared as an active group and the Cairns Group was the main option for developing countries wishing to present their concerns in the agricultural negotiations. However, the emphasis of the Cairns Group on agricultural exports to the neglect of the issues important to small and subsistence farmers alienated the majority of developing countries that had either a more defensive or a more balanced position, effectively leaving them out of the negotiations. The G-20 filled this gap and brought many key interests of developing countries to the negotiations.

The need for a group like the G-20 had been felt for a long time. But the immediate impetus for its establishment was the presentation of a joint agricultural trade proposal by the United States and the European Union on August 13, 2003, that essentially left their own export and domestic subsidy programs intact while shifting the burden of reform to developing countries in the form of ambitious tariff reductions. An effective response was necessary if a repeat of the Uruguay Round were to be avoided. The response came from a new group of developing countries, led by Argentina, Brazil, India, and South Africa. The group was initially called the G-17, but the number of members changed almost daily in the initial period. Many developing countries joined immediately before and during the Cancún Ministerial Conference of September 2003, while some Central and Latin American developing countries left under US pressure at the time of the conference. The name could not keep up with the changing membership, and so the group settled on the name G-20, no matter what the number of members.

The G-20 was a major actor in the agricultural negotiations at Cancún. G-20 proposals and counterproposals were well researched and internally coordinated. The technical soundness of the proposals was reinforced by the combined political weight of the G-20 members. Even this early in its existence, the G-20 showed considerable maturity and negotiating skills. This was the first time that a developing country alliance had worked as an active negotiating group instead of as a broader agenda-setting coalition. The United States and the European Union were no longer able to ignore the demands of developing countries.

Most important to this early success was Brazil's leadership. Brazil used its substantial human and technical resources to provide substantive backup to the group and, even more important, became an honest and active broker balancing interests within the group. Maintaining the cohesiveness of a group that represented all three of the broad interests of developing countries (as described earlier) required diplomatic skills, commitment, and hard work. Also important to the G-20's success was the combined political and economic weight of its members, the backing it received as an effective alliance of developing countries against the might of the United States and the European Union, and its effective use of media to publicize its views.

Many had expected the G-20 to wither following the excitement at Cancún. It has not. In fact, the group has become more settled. Its membership has stabilized. Brazil continues as a committed leader, and G-20 members seem to realize that they can have their greatest influence on the agricultural negotiations by participating as a group. Internal coordination processes are working smoothly. Individual members are encouraged to take the initiative by preparing negotiating texts on issues of interest to them for discussion within the group. The G-20 has also held several ministerial-level meetings, which help to cement the political commitment of members to the group and send a strong signal to others.

The G-20 has been one of the main actors in the agricultural negotiations since Cancún. It is now considered as given that any final agreement on agriculture will not be possible without the support of the G-20. Two of its members, Brazil and India, are part of the so-called Five Interested Parties, along with the United States, the European Union, and Australia, a group at the center of the agricultural negotiations. It was these five countries that reached agreement on the July 2004 Framework Agreement, before it was brought to the WTO for approval by all the members.

These are impressive gains. But there are at least two potential risks to the group. Balancing interests within the group will remain a major challenge. If that task is not managed properly, one of the major countries could leave the group as negotiations move into a more technical and intensive phase, weakening the group's influence and credibility. The group's relationship with other developing countries is a second area of concern. Many smaller developing countries argue that the G-20 does not represent them. While they acknowledge the important role that the G-20 is playing in the agricultural negotiations as a counterweight to the United States and the European Union, they demand a seat at the main negotiating table. The G-20 is cognizant of these issues and has never claimed to speak on behalf of all developing countries. It has also tried to reach out and communicate with other groups of developing countries. In all likelihood the G-20 will continue as a major power in the Doha Round agricultural negotiations.

Group of 33

While the Friends of the Development Box group was fading away, another developing country alliance, the G-33, was emerging, led by Indonesia and the Philippines.[13] It focused on a few central elements of the former group's agenda: special products (SP) and the special safeguard mechanism (SSM) (the group was originally called the SP/SSM Alliance).[14]

The SP/SSM Alliance retained its cohesion and focus even after the creation of the G-20 in August 2003, which included several SP/SSM Alliance countries as members (Cuba, Indonesia, Nigeria, Pakistan, the Philippines, and Venezuela). The G-20 offered these countries an opportunity to be part of a stronger alliance with a comprehensive position on all issues in the agricultural negotiations. But because of the influence of some export-oriented members (Argentine, Chile, and Costa Rica), the G-20 was unable to take a very strong position on special products and the special safeguard mechanism, and for that reason countries maintained their membership and deep interest in the SP/SSM Alliance.

The narrow focus of the SP/SSM Alliance meant that countries whose interests in other areas of agricultural negotiations differed widely could still come together if they had the same position on special products and the special safeguard mechanism. This has allowed the group to continue to grow. Its membership reached 33 soon after the Cancún Ministerial Conference, giving rise to its current name of the G-33 (its membership has since reached 42 countries).

The G-33 played an active role at the time of the Cancun Ministerial Conference. It presented common negotiating proposals on special products and the special safeguard mechanism and held several press briefings. While it was not at the center stage occupied by the G-20, it became clear that any final deal on agriculture would have to accommodate the concepts of special products and the special safeguard mechanism. The Agriculture Annex of the Framework Agreement of 2004, which relaunched the Doha Round of negotiations after the setback at Cancún, included both concepts.

Indonesia had been chosen as the spokesperson for the G-33 before Cancún. This role has now unofficially been consolidated into that of group coordinator. Indonesia has provided committed leadership and also hosted a ministerial-level meeting of the group in Jakarta in the first half of 2005.

Wide acceptance of the concepts of special products and the special safeguard mechanism is not enough, however. Real success for the G-33 will come only when these concepts are effectively operationalized in the agriculture modalities of the WTO. Thus, considerable work remains for this group in the Doha Round of agricultural negotiations. So far, it has shown resilience and the capacity to work jointly on special products and the special safeguard mechanism even when its members do not share a wider agenda in the agricultural negotiations. Maintaining this pragmatism will be key to achieving the group's objectives.

ELEMENTS OF POSSIBLE STRATEGIES FOR EFFECTIVE ALLIANCES AND COALITIONS IN THE CURRENT AGRICULTURAL NEGOTIATIONS

Developing countries clearly have had wide and varied experience with coalitions in the multilateral agricultural negotiations—from very informal coordination to formal groups, from small regional mechanisms to very large groups with members from different regions, from issue-based alliances on selected issues to broader political and economic alliances, from exclusive groups among developing countries to coalitions involving developed countries as well, and from agenda-setting coalitions to common negotiating mechanisms. Some of these coalitions have been more successful than others, and while a few have disappeared, several others have shown remarkable resilience in adapting to changed circumstances. They have also faced immense challenges. Coordination among large numbers of countries with diverse interests is never easy. The technical and human resources required to build and provide intellectual backstopping to the groups have not always been available. This experience, with its successes and challenges, provides useful lessons for successful developing country alliances and coalitions in the current multilateral negotiations on agriculture.

Developing country coalitions and strategies in multilateral agricultural and other trade negotiations were successful when they had the following characteristics:

- The coalition shared a common and well-defined agenda. All the successful negotiating alliances and groups (for example, the G-33, G-20, Caribbean Regional Negotiating Mechanism) have exhibited this feature. Their common agenda has been based on a clear perception of interests and objectives shared by all the members of the group. There has also been a willingness to work together to resolve any internal differences. Moreover, some of the more successful groups have pursued a proactive agenda rather than a negative or reactive one. This characteristic is often important in establishing the credibility of the group and ensuring its survival. Two examples include the Cairns Group and its pursuit of agricultural reform during the Uruguay Round, and the G-20 and its efforts to present a balanced agenda for agricultural negotiations in the Doha Round.
- The structure of the group was efficient and flexible, with good coordination mechanisms. Creating the right balance between some formal coordination mechanism and the efficiency of informality was often important to the effectiveness of the coalition. The importance of dedicated and well-respected leaders cannot be overemphasized. The evolution of developing country alliances and coalitions shows that they have come a long way in building efficient group structures. The examples range from the more formal coordination of the ACP countries, the African Group,

and the group of least developed countries to the more informal mechanism of the G-33. And all the successful groups, particularly issues-based in formal alliances, have relied on good and dedicated leadership—Pakistan for the Friends of the Development Box and Brazil for the G-20, for example.

- The successful coalitions had recourse to good support systems. This not only ensured the pooling of limited human and technical resources, but also provided much needed analytical and research support for the negotiating agenda of the group. The support system provided by Australia to the Cairns Group has been extremely helpful. Similarly, technical support provided by UNCTAD to the least developed countries, by South Centre to the G-33, and by the Africa Union and the Economic Commission for Africa offices to the African Group has been critical. Such support systems do not need to be formal or governmental. For example, the Friends of the Development Box took good advantage of the substantive support provided by some nongovernmental organizations.
- Another crucial factor has been the political commitment of coalition members to their negotiating objectives. When shared and expressed at the highest level, such commitment increased the internal cohesion of the group. It also allowed coalitions to selectively use blocking strategies in the negotiations. Such strategies, or the credible threat to use them, can be a helpful tool in tough negotiations. The Cairns Group demonstrated this during the Uruguay Round. More recently, the African Group has shown this commitment on the issue of Trade-Related Aspects of Intellectual Property Rights (TRIPS) and public health.
- Finally, sometimes factors and actors outside the coalition facilitated the success of the group, such as differences among the major powers, which left room for a third force to emerge, and the support of at least one of the major powers, such as of the U.S. to the Cairns Group during the Uruguay Round. More recently, the compromise between the United States and the European Union in August 2003, which presented the unwelcome prospect of another Blair House agreement, prompted the establishment of the G-20 (which was also partly the outcome of a broader political solidarity movement among developing countries that had been strengthened by changes in some Latin American governments).

These lessons should guide developing countries in using alliances and coalitions to achieve their negotiating objectives in the Doha Round of agricultural negotiations. The Doha Ministerial Declaration of 2001 strengthened the mandate for multilateral negotiations on trade in agriculture and set an ambitious deadline to finish the negotiations by January 1, 2005. The failure at the Fifth Ministerial Conference of the WTO in September 2003 was a major setback that also meant that the original deadline to conclude the negotiations would not be met. (The Cancún setback was reversed to some extent by the adoption of the Framework Agreement in the summer of 2004.) Recognizing that movement in the agricultural negotiations is essential to unlock the current stalemate in the Doha Round of negotiations, all attention should be on reaching agreement on agricultural modalities in time to allow the Doha Round to finish before the existing "Fast Track" authority granted to the U.S. President by the Congress expires in mid-2007.

As a result, the agricultural negotiations have moved into an intensive phase. Developing countries must participate effectively in these negotiations if they want to safeguard their interests and avoid having their fate decided by a deal between the major powers. The identification of their negotiating objectives in the earlier phases of these negotiations, and their experiences with alliances and coalitions, should guide them in this endeavor.

Without trying to define the exact shape and nature of possible strategies for effective alliances and coalitions for developing countries, the following sections outline some of the essential principles that can guide them in these efforts.

Balancing Holistic and Specific Agendas

Various alliances and coalitions of developing countries have already identified their interests and concerns and have elaborated their objectives for the current round of agricultural negotiations. The effort now should be to support each other on issues of common concern and to accommodate internal differences in a spirit of give and take. There is enough common ground among developing countries to build a large coalition on some basic interests while allowing various subgroups to pursue their specific interests as well. While the members of the Cairns Group and some members of the G-20 focus more on market access, they also acknowledge that developing countries experiencing difficulties with the fast pace of liberalization should not have change imposed on them. The reform of subsidy disciplines, on the other hand, is of interest to almost all developing countries, since they lack the means to use this instrument. Coalitions and alliances can support each other on the broad strategic direction of agricultural negotiations while pursuing their own specific agendas on selected issues.

The agenda needs to be proactive. Developing countries have already presented many forward-looking negotiating proposals in the earlier phases of the negotiations. The set of proposals by the Friends of the Development Box very early in the negotiations was probably the most ambitious proposal for agricultural trade reform. Similarly, recent proposals by the G-20 cover almost all aspects of agricultural negotiations and often provide a middle ground between the positions of the United States and the European Union. This proactive stand should be maintained in the final give and take that may allow agreement on modalities.

Flexible Structures and Effective Internal and External Coordination

As the negotiations move into a more intensive phase, the need for effective coordination mechanisms for coalitions will increase. There are advantages to both having some minimal formal mechanisms and maintaining the flexibility inherent in informal procedures. This should allow the coalitions to become a group with a common negotiating agenda while pursuing information exchange and collaboration with other countries and groups. Membership of developing country groups often overlaps—the African Group, the ACP countries, and the least developed countries have many common members; the G-33 and G-20 also share a common core of members. This overlapping membership should facilitate informal coordination among these groups. Developing countries might also consider a more regular mechanism for this purpose, such as fortnightly meetings of the coordinators of various alliances and coalitions for information exchange and collaboration.

The structures and internal coordination of coalitions should also be useful for pooling resources. Research and analytical support to provide technical backup to the political negotiating objectives will be essential if developing country coalitions wish to continue the successful transformation from agenda-setting to negotiating groups that has been achieved in the recent past, particularly through the G-20 and G-33. The resources of individual developing countries are quite limited, and coalitions and alliances should give countries the opportunity to pool resources and direct them to priority areas. Bigger developing countries in the groups, such as Argentina, Brazil, and India in the G-20; Egypt, Nigeria, and South Africa in the African Group; and Indonesia in the G-33 can contribute more to the substantive support systems. So can the intergovernmental and nongovernmental organizations engaged in this exercise.

Finally, the leaders of developing country coalitions will have an important role to play, as they have in the past. Their commitment, diplomatic skills, sincerity, and respect can add to the internal cohesion of the coalitions as well as to their effectiveness in the negotiations. Leaders will also be expected to invest resources to support the needs of the group.

Maintaining and Exercising Political Commitment

Developing countries should not be defensive about their interests and concerns. They are not free riders in the multilateral trading system. Because of the comprehensive coverage of the WTO agreements and application of the single undertaking principle, developing countries have made important concessions to their developed country partners. Getting paid back in agriculture is long overdue. Hence they should have the confidence of an equal partner in the system.

The multilateral trading system is based on the interdependence of all countries and on trade-offs. Two important implications are that all economies, even the United States and the European Union, need other economies and the WTO to benefit from globalization and liberalization, and that all countries should benefit from the final outcome of negotiations by trading their gains in one area for concessions in another area. It is perfectly legitimate for developing countries to demand benefits in agriculture, where many of them have a comparative advantage, in exchange for concessions in other areas.

WTO negotiations relate to important national interests, and developing countries should not shy away from using any strategy to safeguard these interests. Developing countries constitute almost three-quarters of the members of the WTO and have several well-functioning alliances and coalitions in the agricultural negotiations. That situation, together with the WTO principle of decision making by consensus and the political commitment of developing countries at the highest level, should give developing countries more influence in the agricultural negotiations. Political commitment will be particularly important in making selective use of blocking tactics, as the Cairns Group did during the Uruguay Round. The G-20 and other developing country coalitions should be ready to stand up for their fundamental interests and refuse to accept any agreement that fails to support them.

Changing Power Dynamics in the Negotiations

One of the most important overall objectives for coalitions and alliances of developing countries should be to change the power dynamics in WTO negotiations. Despite the composition of membership and the decision making principle, the United States and the European Union often have an iron grip on agenda setting and negotiations. To alter this power dynamic, developing countries will need to build and maintain effective coalitions inside the WTO and collaborate with important actors outside the WTO.

Public opinion sometimes plays a more important role than good negotiating skills and technical arguments. It was the fear of adverse public opinion that forced the major developed countries to accept developing country demands on TRIPS and public health at the time of the Doha Ministerial Conference. The G-20 and G-33, and the Friends of the Development Box before them, have demonstrated that this can be done in agriculture as well. Collaboration and coordination with nongovernmental organizations, media, academics, parliamentarians, and others should therefore be an integral part of the strategy of developing countries.

Finally, the United States and the European Union are often more attentive to their own domestic constituencies than to developing country requests, no matter how legitimate. Therefore, it should be useful to work with like-minded groups in the United States and the European Union to create domestic lobbies there in favor of developing country requests. For that, too, the media, nongovernmental organizations, and academia can play a useful role.

CONCLUDING REMARKS

Often in the multilateral trading system the final deals have been crafted between the United States and the European Union. This pattern is especially clear in agricultural negotiations. As a consequence, the outcome of these negotiations has not benefited developing countries as was expected and promised. The situation is now changing. The major objective of developing countries in the current negotiations should be to emerge as an effective third force, an equal partner in the negotiating process and with equal benefits from the final outcome of the negotiations. Their alliances and coalitions should be directed toward achieving this end. They can hope to achieve this objective by building their own platform with an active agenda, by balancing the power of the major developed countries with their own numerical strength in the WTO and through alliances with civil society actors outside the WTO, and by selectively supporting each other.

NOTES

This is a revised version of the paper presented at the 2002 International Agricultural Trade Research Consortium (IATRC) Symposium. The author is grateful to his colleagues in the South Centre; in the secretariats of the World Trade Organization, the United Nations Conference on Trade and Development, and the Food and Agriculture Organization; and member of civil society organizations for their helpful insights and contributions. Special thanks are also due to IATRC, in particular to Richard Barichello, for providing the opportunity to present the initial draft of this paper, and to John Nash of the World Bank for the opportunity to revise that paper. The useful comments by Prof. Barichello and Hugo Cayrus (former delegate of the Uruguay Mission in Geneva) on the earlier draft of the paper are gratefully acknowledged. However, the author is solely responsible for any mistakes that remain.

1. Current members of the Cairns group are Argentina, Australia, Bolivia, Brazil, Canada, Chile, Colombia, Costa Rica, Fiji, Guatemala, Indonesia, Malaysia, New Zealand, Paraguay, the Philippines, South Africa, Thailand, and Uruguay.
2. Special and differential treatment concerns provisions in the WTO's legal texts that seek to provide for a lower degree or level of obligations or commitments from developing countries than from developed countries in recognition of the lower level of economic development of developing countries.
3. However, the contractual nature of the WTO means that final responsibility for assuming responsibilities and claiming rights rests with individual countries.
4. "Criteria based" seems to best captures this group's characteristics: the least developed countries, which meet certain clearly defined criteria established by the United Nations, and the African, Caribbean, and Pacific countries, which have a special nonreciprocal preferential relationship with the European Union.
5. There are currently 41 WTO members who are part of the African Group: Angola, Benin, Botswana, Burkina Faso, Burundi, Cameroon, Central African Republic,

Chad, Congo, Congo (Democratic Republic), Côte d'Ivoire, Djibouti, Egypt, Gabon, the Gambia, Ghana, Guinea, Guinea Bissau, Kenya, Lesotho, Madagascar, Malawi, Mali, Mauritania, Mauritius, Morocco, Mozambique, Namibia, Niger, Nigeria, Rwanda, Senegal, Sierra Leone, South Africa, Swaziland, Tanzania, Togo, Tunisia, Uganda, Zambia, and Zimbabwe. See www.wto.org/english/tratop_e/agric_e/negs_bkgrnd04_groups_e.htm#key.

6. Current members of the Caribbean Regional Negotiating Mechanism are Antigua and Barbuda, Bahamas, Barbados, Belize, Dominica, Grenada, Guyana, Jamaica, Montserrat, Trinidad and Tobago, Saint Kitts and Nevis, Saint Lucia, Saint Vincent and the Grenadines, Suriname, and Haiti. Cuba and Dominican Republic are contributing members.
7. Currently, 50 countries are designated as least developed by the UN Economic and Social Council. Of these, 32 are members of the WTO and another 11 have WTO observer status. A complete list of least developed countries is available at www.unctad.org/Templates/webflyer.asp?docid=2929&intItemID=1634&lang=1.
8. The framework approach for agricultural negotiations was first proposed by the United States and the European Union in the run-up to the Cancún Ministerial Conference when it became clear that full negotiating modalities would not be established by that time. Their proposal consisted of a set of parameters to guide the subsequent negotiations for the full negotiating modalities. There is no agreed definition of the term framework, though there is a general understanding that a framework does not include numerical targets for commitments in the three pillars (export competition, domestic support, and market access) of agriculture negotiations.
9. Article 5 of the URAA on special safeguards allows WTO members to impose additional duties on imports of agricultural products when the volume of imports exceeds a specific threshold or when prices fall below a specified reference price. The special safeguard is available only for products for which such safeguards have been reserved in the schedule of commitments made by individual members. Members do not need to prove injury or threat of injury to the domestic industry to invoke the measure (as is required under the general safeguard provision of Article XIX of GATT 1994). The special safeguard is triggered automatically. Only a few developing countries that undertook tariffication during the Uruguay Round have access to the special safeguard. As a consequence, developing countries, especially the G-33, have attempted to establish a special safeguard mechanism to allow developing countries to respond effectively to import surges and price depressions.
10. Currently, the ACP consists of 79 countries, 54 of them WTO members. A complete list of ACP member countries is available at http://europa.eu.int/scadplus/leg/en/lvb/r12100.htm.
11. The countries that sponsored the proposal on a development box in the WTO were Cuba, Dominican Republic, El Salvador, Haiti, Honduras, Kenya, Nicaragua, Pakistan, Sri Lanka, Uganda, and Zimbabwe.
12. Current members of the G-20 (which has not always had precisely 20 members) are Argentina, Bolivia, Brazil, Chile, China, Cuba, Egypt, Guatemala, India, Indonesia, Mexico, Nigeria, Pakistan, Paraguay, Philippines, South Africa, Tanzania, Thailand, Uruguay, Venezuela, and Zimbabwe.
13. Currently G-33 has the following as members: Antigua and Barbuda, Barbados, Belize, Benin, Botswana, China, Congo, Cote d'Ivoire, Cuba, Dominican Republic, Grenada, Guyana, Haiti, Honduras, India, Indonesia, Jamaica, Kenya, Republic of Korea, Madagascar, Mauritius, Mongolia, Mozambique, Nicaragua, Nigeria, Pakistan, Panama, Peru, Philippines, Saint Kits and Nevis, Saint Lucia, Saint Vincent

and the Grenadines, Senegal, Sri Lanka, Suriname, Tanzania, Trinidad and Tobago, Turkey, Uganda, Venezuela, Zambia, and Zimbabwe.

14. These concepts pertain to defensive interests in the area of market access under the agricultural negotiations. The concept of special products would allow developing countries to exempt certain products from further tariff reductions, while the special safeguard mechanism would give developing countries an opportunity to take protective action against harmful import surges or price drops by increasing tariffs or applying quantitative restrictions.
15. The term "modalities in the agricultural negotiations" refers to the numerical targets for reduction commitments under the three pillars, as well as the rules elements framing the context within which trade under the agreed commitments will take place.

BIBLIOGRAPHY

Bergsten, C. Fred. 1998. "Fifty Years of GATT/WTO: Lessons From the Past for Strategies for the Future." Working Paper 98-3, Institute for International Economics, Washington, DC.

Durrant, Nigel. 2000. "Report on Participation in UNCTAD Expert Meeting on the Impact of the Reform Process in Agriculture on LDCs and Net Food Importing Developing Countries and Ways to Address Their Concerns in Multilateral Trade Negotiations." Paper presented at UNCTAD, Geneva, July 24–26.

Eglin, Michaela. 1999. "Recent Developments in the WTO." Paper presented to the International Chamber of Commerce, Commission on Trade and Investment Policy, Geneva, May 18.

European Commission, Directorate-General for Trade. 2000. "Improving the Functioning of the WTO: Suggestions for a Way Forward." Note for the attention of the 133 Committee, Brussels.

Finger, J. M., and P. Schuler. 1999. "Implementation of Uruguay Round Commitments: The Development Challenge." Policy Research Working Paper 2215, World Bank, Washington, DC.

Finlayson, Jock A., and Ann Weston. 1990. *The GATT, Middle Powers, and the Uruguay Round.* Ottawa: North-South Institute.

Fowler, Penny. 2000. "WTO Institutional Reform: Taking Stock of Proposals Made So Far." Paper presented at the workshop on WTO Institutional Reform: A Development Perspective, Geneva, Feb. 2.

Hamilton, Colleen, and John Whalley. 1989. "Coalitions in the Uruguay Round." *Weltwirtschaftliches Archiv* 125 (3): 547–56.

Higgot, Richard A., and Andrew Fenton Cooper. 1990. "Middle Power Leadership and Coalition Building: Australia, the Cairns Group, and the Uruguay Round of Trade Negotiations." *International Organization* 44 (4): 589–632.

Hoekman, Bernard, and Will Martin. 1999. "Preparing for WTO 2000 Negotiations: A Proposal to Enhance Developing Country Participation." World Bank Development Research Group and World Bank Institute, Washington, DC.

Krueger, Anne. 1999. "The Developing Countries and the Next Round of Multilateral Trade Negotiations." *World Economy* 22 (7): 909–32.

Narlikar, Amrita. 1998. "Divided They Fell: The South in Trade Negotiations." MPhil thesis, University of Oxford, Oxford.

———. 2000. "Bargaining Together in Trade: Developing Countries in Coalitions." DPhil dissertation, University of Oxford, Oxford.

Panagariya, Arvind. 2000. "The Millennium Round and Developing Countries: Negotiating Strategies and Areas of Benefit." G-24 Discussion Paper Series 1, UNCTAD, Geneva.

Ricupero, Rubens. 1998. "Integration of Developing Countries into the Multilateral Trading System." In *The Uruguay Round and Beyond: Essays in Honour of Arthur Dunkel,* Jagdish Bhagwati and Mathias Hirsch, eds. Ann Arbor, MI: University of Michigan Press.

South Centre. 2001. "WTO Decision-Making and Developing Countries." Trade-Related Agenda, Development, and Equity (TRADE) Working Paper 11, Geneva.

———. 2004. "South-South Cooperation in the Multilateral Trading System: Cancun and Beyond." Trade-Related Agenda, Development, and Equity (TRADE) Working Paper 21, Geneva.

———. 2000b. Workshop report, Workshop on WTO Institutional Reform: A Development Perspective, Geneva, Feb. 2

———. 2005. "State of Play in Agriculture Negotiations: Country Groups' Positions." SC/TADP/AN/AG/10, Geneva.

Tussie, Diana. 1995. "Holding the Balance: The Cairns Group in the Uruguay Round." In *The Developing Countries in World Trade: Policies and Bargaining Strategies,* Diana Tussie and David Glover, eds. Boulder, CO: Lynne Rienner.

WTO (World Trade Organization). 1994. *The Results of the Uruguay Round.* Geneva: WTO.

———. 2001a. "Ministerial Declaration." WT/MIN(01)/DEC/W/1, WTO, Geneva.

———. 2001b. "Implementation-Related Issues and Concerns." WT/MIN(01)/W/, WTO Geneva.

CHAPTER SIX

Domestic Management of Price Risk in the Context of Trade Reform in Developing Countries

William Foster and Alberto Valdés

This chapter addresses continuing trade reform and the management of price risk that originates in world markets and affects farmers in developing countries. The chapter focuses specifically on national border measures related to international price fluctuations. It does not examine safety net policies (such as revenue insurance), international assistance measures (such as food aid and compensatory financing), or the effects of food price movements on real wages and their potential macroeconomic repercussions. The chapter takes the perspective that the price risk management problem arises not so much from the instability of international prices themselves, but rather from the difficulties associated with periods of low and politically unsustainable price levels.

The governments of many developing countries understandably have little confidence in the current ability of their domestic markets and institutions to manage the risks to farmers of extended periods of low prices. This lack of confidence and the associated political pressures from producers—especially those competing with imports—reduces any enthusiasm for further trade liberalization. Distortions in world prices and transmission of price risk become critical issues in the political commitment to deepen reforms in developing countries.

Thus, the central politically sensitive issues for developing countries in the process of expanding or deepening trade liberalization are these:[1]

- Enhanced transmission to domestic markets of international price movements due to trade reforms, especially the elimination of quantitative restrictions, and the limited policy tools available in the current environment of trade commitments.
- The definition of price risk in periods of very low prices facing producers in import-competing sectors.
- Resistance in developing countries to lowering trade barriers on imports due to developed country subsidies that artificially lower world prices, which are in turn transmitted to domestic markets. Some developing countries argue that activities that would be competitive at world prices without distortions are not sustainable in the current environment of distorted international prices.
- The stochastic nature of world prices, with occasional periods of prices persistently below trend, which limits the type of policies that might be used to manage price risk.
- The practical relevance of enhanced price transmission, because the price risk facing farmers is not caused by world price movements alone, but by other factors as well, such as exchange rate fluctuations. That price transmission is not the only important question implies the reduced effectiveness of border instruments to manage price risk.
- In an environment of World Trade Organization (WTO) commitments and integrated world markets, what policy options are available for managing price risk?

GREATER PRICE TRANSMISSION AND THE LIMITS TO MANAGING INTERNATIONAL PRICE VARIABILITY UNDER TRADE LIBERALIZATION

In the mid-1980s several developing countries, particularly in Latin America, began a series of economic reforms. During the 1990s larger numbers of developing countries and eventually the transition economies of Eastern and Central Europe also began to reform, through trade liberalization, privatization, and deregulation. The degree and depth of these reforms varied. Chile was an early and deep reformer, beginning with a radical change in its trade regime in the mid-1970s. In contrast, Venezuela and the Caribbean countries began reforms in the mid-1990s, coinciding with the emergence elsewhere of the transition from command economies.

In a protectionist economic environment—with high tariffs, quantitative restrictions, variable levies, and state trading monopolies—there is less transmission of international price variability than under a system that emphasizes the use of (low) tariffs only. And even without quantitative restrictions, high tariffs reduce the practical importance of international price fluctuations and cushion the effect of any shocks transmitted from international to domestic markets.

Trade liberalization meant the reduction in direct price interventions, the lowering of tariff levels, and the convergence of tariff rates across commodities. Perhaps most critical to price transmission, trade liberalization meant the elimination of most quantitative restrictions on imports and the end to state trading, policies that had insulated domestic consumers and producers from the vicissitudes of world markets and international trade. The decline of trade-restricting policies magnified the transmission of price signals across borders as the determinants of a country's allocation of resources. Consequently, both price risk and policies to counteract possible distortions in international prices have featured prominently in domestic policy debates.

The policy instruments available to governments today are restricted largely to tariffs and surcharges (including safeguards), and their levels are limited.[2] For many developing and transition economies the current trade and policy environment has amplified political pressures to counteract the transmission to internal markets of the debilitating effects of distorted world prices caused by external interventions.

The Importance of Price Risk during Periods of Low Prices for Producers in Import-Competing Sectors

The adverse effect on developing country exporters of agricultural products of the high levels of protection in developed countries (addressed in the following section) is widely recognized. In practical political terms, the problem of access to export markets is not a contentious issue in internal debates over domestic policies in developing countries, although it is clearly an important foreign relations issue. But what generates the most complex domestic policy debates in many developing countries is the pricing of importables.

Price risk is often understood, in the simplest terms, as the variance in prices. But in the context of trade liberalization and efforts to encourage governments to move toward a world price regime, price levels as well as price variance have to be considered. For countries that have opened their markets significantly to trade, the major dilemma today is dealing with episodes of excessively low border prices for some import-competing activities. These concerns over low-price episodes are reinforced by the long-term decline in world prices.

Trade liberalization, by reducing border protection on importables and removing export taxes and restrictions on exportables, has reduced the bias against export agriculture. So while both importables and exportables are now increasingly influenced by world price regimes, the beneficiaries of trade liberalization have tended to be producers in export-oriented sectors (and consumers). With respect to policy issues, however, producers of importables tend to be better organized, more vocal, and stronger lobbyists than producers of exportables. Not only does this political reality reinforce the prominence of importables in policy debates, but the policy tools still available for protection are straightforward and bureaucratically remunerative (such as increasing tariffs) for importables. For exportables, however, there is not much that a fiscally limited developing country can realistically do, unlike richer countries, where export subsidies are a relatively minor burden on taxpayers.

Evidence That Greater Price Transmission Is Perceived to Increase the Vulnerability of Producers

The 1992 study of the political economy of agricultural price policies in 18 developing countries by Schiff and Valdés shows that governments tend to insulate domestic sectors more during periods of volatile world prices. If price stability was the goal, then governments overall succeeded in achieving it, primarily through direct interventions. Relative to world prices, protective policies managed to reduce domestic price variability by an average of 25 percent—and by even more for products with highly volatile world prices. In a cross-country analysis of the transmission of world agricultural price shocks, Quiroz and Soto (1995) found that in 67 of 76 countries it took at least two years to transmit 50 percent of international price shocks to domestic markets.

Governments' past policy decisions can be interpreted as evidence that governments think that reducing price transmission reduces the vulnerability of producers. This is the expected reaction in a welfare and public-choice perspective where commodity prices are politically sensitive. On the producer side governments in developing countries tend to be sensitive to price instability because farmers tend to be risk averse, there are few opportunities to hedge risk, credit markets are less developed, and governments do not have the fiscal resources to subsidize farmers in years of low prices. On the consumer and labor market side, because governments lack the fiscal resources to provide broad coverage of safety net programs, variation in food prices can significantly affect real wages and real household income.[3]

For politicians and farmers in import-competing sectors, then, the policy problem relates to the difficulties associated with price levels falling below long-term trends rather than to the volatility of domestic prices because of world price fluctuations. Aggravating the political pressure to "do something," producers and politicians in developing countries tend to attribute these low-price episodes to the distortions in world prices brought about by developed countries subsidies.

THE ROLE OF DEVELOPED COUNTRY SUBSIDIES IN LOWERING WORLD PRICES

Developing countries resist lowering their trade barriers in part because they believe that developed country subsidies artificially and significantly lower world prices. Many industries in developing countries argue that they would be competitive in world markets without these price distortions. For developing countries this means that price risk management tools must not merely guard against low prices but must also compensate for the downward shift in the long-term pattern of prices caused by developed country subsidies.

Is this a reasonable argument? What is known about how developed country policies distort the price levels around their long-term trends? It is an open question to what degree commodity price levels and the declining trend in prices are due to protection in developed countries and to what degree to productivity levels, factor use, income growth, and population.[4]

The argument is often made that producers in developing countries should be compensated for the absolute value of the export subsidies, without making a clear distinction between measurable subsidy levels and their overall effect on world prices. From an economist's perspective, of course, what matters is the final effect of subsidies on world prices, not the absolute subsidy levels. The focus on absolute subsidy levels leaves the question of the appropriate compensating tariff or surcharges with an unrestricted upper limit.[5]

Practically all quantitative analyses of agricultural subsidies based on steady-state comparisons derived from modeling efforts conclude that such policies depress world prices relative to the case under less protection. As McCulloch, Winters, and Cirera (2002, pp. 175–76) comment: "Agricultural markets are among the most distorted in the world, with both developed and developing countries maintaining high levels of intervention."

It is important, however, to distinguish the impacts of interventions in developing countries and developed countries. Developed countries usually protect their agricultural sectors, and developing countries usually tax it. The historical evidence suggests that developed country policies have depressed world prices, while developing country policies have raised them.[6] In addition, exchange rate misalignment and industrial protection in developing countries have been shown to depress the internal prices of agricultural tradables.

It is well recognized today that domestic price and trade interventions among the major producing and trading countries continue to have a significant effect on world prices. The higher the level of protection on importables and the higher the export subsidies, the lower will be the world prices facing exporting and importing developing and transition economies. From a welfare analysis point of view it is recognized that consumers in the country imposing these policies suffer the main costs of intervention. But for agricultural sectors developed country policies can also impose high costs on developing countries because agriculture is a relatively more important sector for these economies and rural poverty is of considerably greater social importance.

Several efforts have been made to quantify the effects of these interventions on world prices and trade flows (see Goldin and Knudsen 1989 for a review of the literature for the Organisation for Economic Co-operation and Development [OECD]). The modeling efforts by the Global Trade Analysis Project (GTAP) and the OECD are particularly significant. Keeping certain methodological caveats in mind,[7] these studies can be used as points of reference to provide orders of magnitude for world price distortions.

Valdés and Zietz (1995) and Ingco (1996) summarize the findings of several published studies on predicted world price effects of partial agricultural trade reform. Ingco reports estimates of world price effects on the order of 5 percent or less for rice and coarse grains, and roughly 6 percent for wheat, with six estimates ranging from 1.2 percent to 10 percent. The effects are lower for tropical products.

Goldin, Knudsen, and van der Mensbrugghe (1992) use the Rural-Urban North-South (RUNS) model to simulate both partial and full agricultural reforms and multisectoral reforms.[8] Under partial agricultural reforms tariff equivalents are reduced by 30 percent. Under full agricultural reforms all tariffs are eliminated, including those on inputs. The effects of partial reforms are similar to those mentioned by Ingco, but for full agricultural reforms the world price effects are considerably and surprisingly higher, especially compared with similar simulations. For example, sugar prices rise from 10.2 percent under partial agricultural reforms to 59.3 percent under full agricultural reform. Wheat prices rise 5.9 percent under partial reform and 39.2 percent under full reform. For multisectural reform the price effects in general are lower, due to both demand and supply effects in a hypothetical world of more efficient use of resources. Practically all studies conclude that the largest effects are for sugar and dairy, with increases of at least 10 percent under partial reform and higher under full agricultural reforms.[9]

WHAT DO WE KNOW ABOUT PRICE VARIABILITY AND THE PERSISTENCE OF LOW PRICES? THE STOCHASTIC NATURE OF WORLD PRICES

Measurement of price instability in world agricultural markets is well researched. Sarris (1997a,b), for example, has done comprehensive work on measurement for cereals. He finds no trend toward greater world price instability. Harwood and others (1999) come to the same conclusion for corn, using data for 1920–96.

Coefficients of variation of world prices for corn, rice, sugar, and wheat for 1960–97 show that sugar is considerably more unstable than the three cereals throughout the period (Quiroz, Foster, and Valdés 1999; table 6.1). A much higher coefficient of variation is found for 1973–85 than for the preceding and following periods, and wheat and sugar exhibit a decline in price instability for the period 1986–97 (consistent with the conclusions of Sarris). Evidently, the coefficient of variation for these commodities changes with time.

A related question is whether instability is due to the "system" of protection (see, for example, Josling 1980). Certainly, variable levies and quotas with a targeted domestic price for importables shift domestic instability to world markets. As quantitative restrictions and variable levies are removed, the contribution of distortions in developed countries to world price instability would

Table 6.1 Coefficients of Variation of World Prices of Corn, Rice, Sugar, and Wheat, 1960–97

Period	Corn	Rice	Sugar	Wheat
1960–72	0.11	0.09	0.60	0.25
1973–85	0.31	0.44	0.81	0.42
1986–97	0.18	0.20	0.22	0.17
1960–97	0.37	0.46	0.90	0.44

Source: Quiroz, Foster, and Valdés (1999).

lessen. Uruguay Round tariffication in developed countries and developing countries should reduce world price instability but increase the transmission of instability to domestic producers and consumers. Tyers and Anderson (1992, p. 264) conclude from policy simulations of tariffication in developed countries that "[t]he effect of tariffication is to reduce [world] price volatility substantially" during the 1990s. Tariffication in developed countries contributes to less instability in wheat, dairy products, and beef, among others. For some commodities, however, such as rice and sugar, reduced instability derives primarily from the tariffication policies of developing countries.

More important than instability itself for the price risk facing agricultural producers in developing economies is the persistence of low prices. In an open economy a central problem in the design of policy instruments for dealing with instability is understanding the nature and duration of price cycles in world markets. Do shocks to international prices dissipate rapidly, or do they persist for several years?

There is now a rich literature on the times-series properties of commodity prices. Early research, often framed within the context of unit-root analysis, concluded that prices exhibited a significant degree of persistence to shock. Gersowitz and Paxon (1990) show that the hypothesis of a unit root could not be rejected for commodity prices of a number of African exports. Later studies have been more cautious in deducing unit roots from simple measures of persistence (Caner and Hansen 1997; Perron 1989; and Zivot and Andrew 1992). Leon and Soto (1995) conclude that real world prices do not exhibit unit roots, but rather are trend stationary processes. Nevertheless, there remains the stylized fact that commodity prices exhibit considerable shock persistence (see also Deaton 1992).

Cashin, Liang, and McDermott (2000) present empirical evidence that the distribution of commodity prices is not symmetric—low prices endure longer than high prices (table 6.2). They find in the case of wheat, for example, that international price shocks have a median half-life of 44 months, with a 90 percent confidence interval that implies a range from an extreme low half-life of 14 months to a high of "infinity." There is a 50 percent probability that prices below the expected value (declining over time) will prevail for more than 44 months.

Table 6.2 Statistics on Prices of Corn, Rice, Sugar, and Wheat, 1960–97

	Corn			Rice		
Period	Skewness	Kurtosis	Jarque–Bera	Skewness	Kurtosis	Jarque–Bera
1960–72	–0.34	2.34	5.87	–0.51	1.87	15.14
1973–85	1.01	3.58	28.50	1.59	5.53	107.30
1986–97	1.14	4.73	47.76	1.25	4.73	51.64
1960–97	0.65	3.77	42.60	1.21	6.30	310.64

	Sugar			Wheat		
Period	Skewness	Kurtosis	Jarque–Bera	Skewness	Kurtosis	Jarque–Bera
1960–72	1.88	6.47	170.7	0.35	1.65	14.39
1973–85	2.05	8.51	306.98	1.69	6.06	134.79
1986–97	0.62	3.12	8.85	0.43	2.22	7.86
1960–97	3.25	17.66	4835.00	1.41	6.10	325.08

Source: Quiroz, Foster, and Valdés (1999).

Low prices have a tendency to persist for many months, with occasional spikes of shorter duration (figure 6.1). These characteristics of world price movements lead to notable difficulties for policy design. The use of futures markets can reduce the effect of short-term uncertainty but cannot guard against the effects of consecutive years of low prices. Minimum import price schemes were popular in the past, and several developing countries still have systems of price bands. Safeguards are always a contingency measure, but under WTO rules they are limited in duration and frequency of application and involve compensation.

THE PRACTICAL RELEVANCE OF PRICE TRANSMISSION TO THE PRICE RISKS FACING FARMERS

World price distortions due to developed country subsidies and the stochastic nature of world prices make price transmission—endogenously determined by policies such as trade barriers—a relevant policy question in developing countries. There has been a lively debate in the literature on the degree of price transmission. For European producers Tyers and Anderson (1992) demonstrate a transmission rate of world price variation of less than 10 percent in the short run and 20 percent in the long run. More generally, Sarris (1997b) estimates transmission coefficients of 0.24 in the short run and 0.58 in the long run. In a controversial paper Mundlak and Larson (1992, p. 419) conclude that "the deviation from unitary elasticity is, on the whole, surprisingly small." In

Figure 6.1 Average Annual Real Price of Corn, Rice, Sugar, and Wheat, 1960–97 (US cents, as of July 1997)

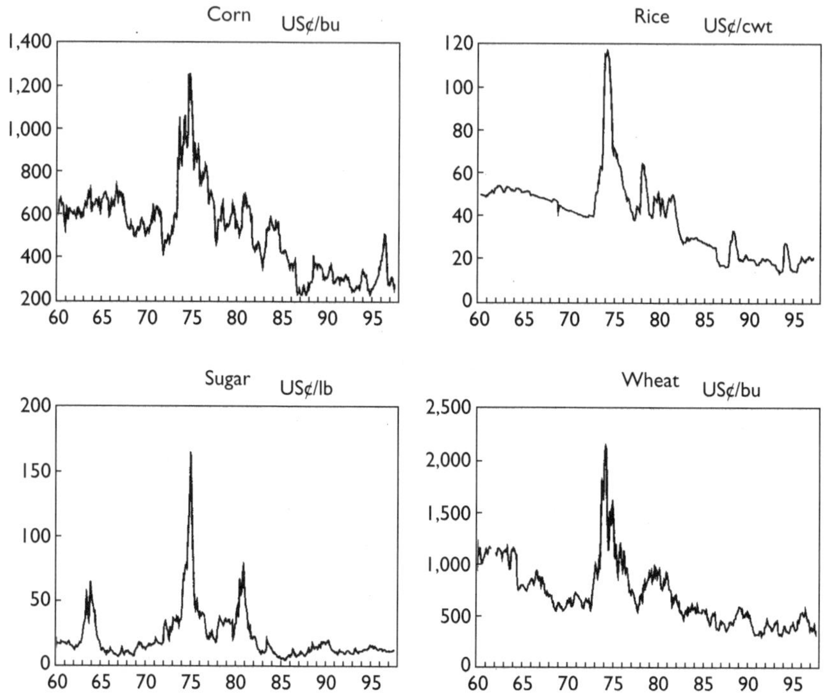

Source: Quiroz, Foster, and Valdés (1999).

their judgment, while policies affect price levels, policies appear ineffective at insulating to any great degree domestic prices from world price changes. Mundlak and Larson also assert that variations in world prices are the major contributor to variations in domestic prices, a conclusion at odds with the evidence from the price decompositions presented below.

In contrast to Mundlak and Larson, who use Food and Agriculture Organization (FAO) average unit export values, Quiroz and Soto (1995) use both spot prices and an error-correction specification of the relationship between world and domestic prices. Covering 78 countries, Quiroz and Soto (1995, p. 14) conclude: "In an overwhelming majority of cases transmission of international price signals in agriculture is either non-existent or low, by any reasonable standard." The degree of transmission from world prices varies from the transmission within one year of 50 percent or more of any given shock for Australia, Canada, New Zealand, and Uruguay, to transmission over five years or longer for half of any world price shocks for 30 countries, to virtual isolation from international price signals for another group of 30 countries.

A major caveat is that the data in these mentioned studies reflect trade regimes before the Uruguay Round. So, with tariffication and the removal of quantitative restrictions, transmission could be higher today.

Different approaches can be taken in specifying the relevance of price transmission. The regression-oriented decomposition of Mundlak and Larson (1992), for example, results in an isolated elasticity of world price transmission, controlling for the variability of other factors—an elasticity derived from partial correlations underlying regression analysis.

In itself, however, that decomposition says little about the magnitudes of the absolute effects of world price changes on domestic producer prices. In a practical sense the isolated, *ceteris paribus* effect of price transmission itself might not be the most important issue facing farmers in developing countries. The practical impacts of world prices on domestic prices are, at a minimum, filtered through fluctuations in exchange rates, which are much more volatile in developing economies. In addition, changes in border protection have also been important during the 1990s in many countries, influencing the ultimate effects of changes in world prices on domestic producers. Thus, another approach is to decompose the total variation of domestic prices as a sum of changes in world prices, exchange rates, and border protection.

Consider the extreme case of countries with fixed exchange rates and dollar convertibility, such as Argentina until recently. In such cases, and where the rate of inflation would be close to zero, a price transmission elasticity of one would be expected. Moreover, any decomposition of domestic price changes would show a near one-to-one correlation between domestic prices and world prices (setting aside marketing margin changes). In contrast, a country such as Chile has had substantial fluctuation in its real exchange rate, despite a stable macroeconomic environment (an inflation rate of less than 3 percent, a fiscal deficit less than 1 percent of GDP, and ample foreign exchange reserves). This has been due mainly to movements in capital accounts and the inherent instability associated with emerging economies related to the "neighborhood effect"—the Asian financial crisis, the Tequila Effect, the Brazilian devaluation, and the Argentine crisis. Even if the price transmission elasticity were one for Chilean exported fruits and wine (which is likely the case), the final effect of world price changes on real domestic prices might be overwhelmed by the accumulated influence of exchange rate variation.

Or consider the example of real price trends in wheat in the transition economies of Bulgaria, Romania, Russia, and Ukraine (Valdés 2000), which have experienced large annual variations in real producer prices. Decomposition of these fluctuations for 1994–97 permits examination of the contribution to price changes of changes in border prices, real exchange rates, and policy interventions (table 6.3). Decomposition shows an imperfect correlation (sometimes negative) between border price changes and domestic producer prices. For example, in Bulgaria the domestic prices of wheat increased 25 percent

Table 6.3 Decomposition of Real Producer Price for Wheat in Transition Economies, 1994–97 (percentage change)

Country	Period	Domestic price	Border price	Real exchange rate	Residual policies
Bulgaria	1994–95	2	6	–8	4
	1995–96	25	6	20	–1
	1996–97	–2	–18	22	–6
	1994–97	25	–6	34	–3
Poland	1994–95	–8	–14	–8	14
	1995–96	13	28	–2	–13
	1996–97	–9	–24	3	12
	1994–97	–4	–10	–7	13
Romania	1994–95	–8	–6	–1	–1
	1995–96	13	3	4	5
	1996–97	–13	–13	–3	3
	1994–97	–8	–16	0	8
Russia	1994–95	17	14	–4	7
	1995–96	16	7	–2	11
	1996–97	–6	–12	2	4
	1994–97	27	9	–4	22
Ukraine	1994–95	–30	–5	–35	10
	1995–96	–9	7	–20	4
	1996–97	–4	–12	–5	12
	1994–97	–43	–10	–60	27
Germany	1994–95	–4	14	–5	–12
	1995–96	1	11	3	–12
	1996–97	–4	–10	6	–1
	1994–97	–7	14	4	–26

Source: Valdés (2000a).

while border prices fell 6 percent, with the domestic increase owing primarily to a 34 percent increase in the real exchange rate.

The evidence for various agricultural commodities in Argentina, Chile, and Colombia shows a similar pattern of the alternating relative weight of border prices movements to the final determination of domestic real producer prices (tables 6.4, 6.5, and 6.6). In short, price transmission itself is not the whole story.

POLICY IMPLICATIONS FOR MANAGING PRICE RISK IN THE CONTEXT OF WTO COMMITMENTS

In summary, there are five points to keep in mind with respect to managing price risk in developing countries:

Table 6.4 Decomposition of Producer Price Changes in Argentina for Selected Exportable Commodities, 1960–95 (cumulative percentage change)

Product	Period	Real domestic prices	Real border prices	Real exchange rate	(1+Ti) tariffs	Others factors and policies	(1+Ti) + others
Beef	1960–69	–43.55	–30.97	–244.19	—	—	231.61
	1970–79	22.29	43.58	–67.67	—	—	46.38
	1980–84	–33.97	–104.29	87.20	—	—	–16.88
	1985–89	32.68	13.16	39.36	–19.62	–0.22	–19.84
	1990–93	–91.35	13.28	–132.01	27.75	–0.38	27.38
	1994–95	2.45	–3.31	–2.02	—	—	7.78
Maize	1960–69	2.57	–21.54	–14.42	—	—	38.52
	1970–79	–102.78	4.04	–83.34	—	—	–23.49
	1980–84	54.93	–33.69	89.39	—	—	–0.77
	1985–89	–38.40	–38.74	14.36	4.65	3.52	9.23
	1990–93	–68.28	–38.88	–61.98	28.61	3.97	32.58
	1994–95	25.97	13.08	–2.02	—	—	14.92
Sorghum	1960–69	–4.51	–24.07	–14.42	—	—	33.98
	1970–79	–38.49	4.86	–58.54	—	—	15.19
	1980–84	–4.69	–23.41	64.60	—	—	–45.88
	1985–89	–15.72	1.86	–35.62	2.65	15.39	18.04
	1990–92	–89.00	–47.73	–54.70	25.28	–11.85	13.43
Soybeans	1960–69	—	—	—	—	—	—
	1977–79	–112.07	–51.20	–55.40	—	—	–5.47
	1980–84	7.60	–60.75	80.42	—	—	–12.07
	1985–89	–41.02	10.87	–48.30	–3.52	–0.07	–3.59
	1990–93	–58.64	–39.38	–61.98	38.67	4.04	42.72
	1994–95	–41.36	–52.61	–2.33	—	—	13.58
Sunflowers	1960–69	—	—	—	—	—	—
	1977–79	–89.08	–24.34	–55.40	—	—	–9.33
	1980–84	22.02	–59.88	80.42	—	—	1.48
	1985–89	–56.64	–17.50	–35.62	–2.01	–1.51	–3.52
	1990–92	–67.65	–46.14	–54.70	32.93	0.27	33.19
Wheat	1960–69	–3.77	–18.09	–14.42	—	—	19.51
	1970–79	–87.73	6.85	–92.60	—	—	–33.80
	1980–84	–64.03	–62.15	9.18	—	—	–11.06
	1985–88	–3.72	–19.11	–12.32	20.18	7.53	27.71
	1991–93	–24.76	–35.94	–26.64	31.64	1.42	37.82
	1994	–2.61	–5.93	–1.44	—	—	4.77

Source: Valdés (1996).
—Not available.

Table 6.5 Decomposition of Producer Price Changes in Chile for Selected Tradable Commodities, 1960–93 (cumulative percentage change)

Product	Period	Real domestic prices	Real border prices	Real exchange rate	(1+Ti) tariffs	Others factors
Exportables						
Apples, red	1960–70	133.77	41.02	30.94	17.14	44.67
	1971–74	–2.40	–21.22	44.77	–10.38	–15.58
	1975–83	6.40	–8.40	46.47	–6.77	–24.90
	1984–89	30.48	–4.10	36.11	0.00	–1.53
	1990–93	–429.10	–64.88	–14.79	0.00	–349.43
Grapes, Thompson	1960–70	99.29	21.53	30.94	17.14	29.67
	1971–74	54.35	4.37	44.77	–0.59	5.80
	1975–83	41.51	20.91	46.47	–16.55	–9.31
	1984–89	–4.70	–30.47	33.67	0.00	–7.91
	1990–94	22.24	21.37	–16.80	0.00	17.67
Importables						
Beef	1960–70	41.20	9.57	30.94	0.00	0.69
	1971–74	87.27	42.14	44.77	0.00	0.36
	1975–83	–51.72	–76.06	46.47	0.00	–22.12
	1984–89	136.69	64.93	33.67	13.98	24.12
	1990–95	–30.05	16.88	–26.84	–3.54	–16.54
Maize	1960–70	—	—	—	—	—
	1971–74	—	—	—	—	—
	1975–83	—	—	—	—	—
	1984–89	–4.24	–45.12	25.27	–7.84	23.46
	1990–93	–22.18	–23.84	–16.25	–3.54	21.44
Milk	1960–70	3.29	–5.37	30.94	0.00	–22.28
	1971–74	77.44	14.27	44.77	0.00	18.40
	1975–83	–0.18	–2.39	46.47	0.00	–44.26
	1984–89	–6.25	9.46	33.67	13.98	–63.35
	1990–93	–16.51	–19.66	–16.25	–3.54	22.94
Sugarbeets	1960–70	—	—	—	—	—
	1971–74	—	—	—	—	—
	1975–83	—	—	—	—	—
	1984–89	–1.35	39.16	25.27	–7.84	–57.93
	1990–93	–7.57	18.72	–16.25	–3.54	–6.50
Wheat	1960–70	6.33	–13.15	26.76	0.00	–7.28
	1971–74	53.81	80.13	9.89	0.00	–36.21
	1975–83	35.51	–88.39	81.35	0.00	42.55
	1984–89	–0.42	–32.83	37.84	–7.84	2.41
	1990–95	–27.80	–12.84	–26.84	7.84	4.04

Source: Valdés (1996).
—Not available.

Table 6.6 Decomposition of Producer Price Changes in Colombia for Selected Tradable Commodities, 1960–95 (cumulative percentage change)

Product	Period	Real domestic prices	Real border prices	Real exchange rate	(1+Ti) tariffs	Others factors
Exportables						
Beef	1960–69	—	—	—	—	—
	1970–79	—	—	—	—	—
	1980–89	–6.45	–40.26	63.16	–29.22	–0.13
	1990–92	27.68	–35.73	4.94	75.43	–16.96
	1993–95	–24.77	15.87	–32.89	—	–7.74
Coffee	1960–69	–6.12	–27.89	20.90	–6.76	7.63
	1970–79	47.24	78.81	–21.43	–34.88	24.75
	1980–89	–33.07	–108.98	65.31	61.82	–51.22
	1990–92	–47.12	–61.91	4.94	28.45	–18.60
	1993–95	28.07	74.80	–32.89	—	–13.83
Cotton	1960–69	–7.30	–20.82	20.90	0.13	–7.52
	1970–79	13.46	40.04	–21.43	–0.09	–5.06
	1980–89	4.43	–52.62	65.31	0.11	–8.37
	1990–92	–25.87	–38.25	4.94	13.02	–5.58
Importables						
Rice	1960–69	–21.60	–16.70	20.90	0.00	–25.80
	1970–79	–29.05	2.89	–21.43	0.00	–10.51
	1980–89	10.62	–109.06	65.33	41.30	13.05
	1990–92	–30.75	–23.45	–12.18	6.86	–1.99
Maize	1960–69	—	—	—	—	—
	1970–79	—	—	—	—	—
	1980–89	–5.08	–46.55	63.37	–26.47	4.57
	1990–92	–36.69	–10.01	4.94	–20.01	–11.60
	1993–95	–33.53	–15.22	–32.89	—	14.58
Milk	1960–69	—	—	—	—	—
	1970–79	—	—	—	—	—
	1980–89	–15.58	–42.41	63.16	–44.87	8.54
	1990–92	–16.62	–29.41	4.94	25.61	–17.76
	1993–95	10.09	16.50	–32.89	—	26.48
Sorghum	1960–69	—	—	—	—	—
	1970–79	—	—	—	—	—
	1980–89	4.38	–54.42	63.03	–6.74	2.52
	1990–92	–21.28	–5.49	–12.02	–2.61	–1.16
Soybeans	1960–69	—	—	—	—	—
	1970–79	—	—	—	—	—
	1980–89	26.89	–45.34	63.03	10.55	–1.35
	1990–92	–43.95	–32.51	–12.02	–7.74	8.32
Wheat	1960–69	–11.40	–39.52	20.90	0.00	7.22
	1970–79	–25.40	17.64	–21.43	0.00	–21.61
	1980–89	31.22	–69.92	65.17	41.84	–5.87
	1990–92	–39.74	–31.59	–12.02	2.28	1.59

Source: Valdés (1996).
—Not available.

First, perhaps the central concern is whether the price level is very distorted—and excessively low—because of subsidies in developed countries, a problem that is intensified in the context of falling real prices.

Second, for developing countries and transition economies world price distortions and the possibility of facing periods of low world prices are now more important in determining domestic producer price risk as a result of their trade liberalization and the resultant enhanced price transmission. Reduced protection and the change in the system of protection brought about by decisions in developing countries augmented the importance of the possibly distorted price levels and the stochastic nature of world prices.

Third, while world price instability itself might be a concern, especially in developing countries, the biggest political difficulty in developing countries is the possibility of extended periods of low prices. And the persistence of low prices exacerbates any attempt to resolve it without resort to border measures.

Fourth, an important question is what can be done to deal with the low-price problem for developing countries? Special safeguards, a potential solution, cannot be used by most developing countries in the current WTO environment because they replaced quantitative restrictions with tariffs before the Uruguay Round (see Konandreas 2000).

Fifth, while the emphasis has been on direct price transmission, there are other effects of trade liberalization on the welfare of the poor that are not captured by looking simply at price effects. There are important questions about the proper definition of transmission. Normally, it refers to transmission from border prices to domestic prices of tradables. But from the perspective of poor farmers second-order transmissions are also important—of world market changes through labor markets and capital markets and the influence of missing staple markets (Taylor 2002). Imperfectly functioning capital markets and high transaction costs—including costs associated with access to markets for new products—tend to isolate poor farmers and rural areas. Rural households that would lose under trade liberalization could conceivably move their resources—primarily labor—to other economic sectors where transaction costs are lower and access to capital is less expensive. Many do, but for some the net benefits of migration are low, especially for older people and those with human capital specific to farming.

There seems little question that world prices have been affected by government policies in both developed and developing countries, but the degree to which such policies have distorted prices is subject to debate. Also, the recent global movement toward liberalization may have changed these distortions, but certainly not the negative direction of their effect on world prices. Liberalization in developing and transition economies has enhanced the transmission of prices and thus the importance of the distortions that continue to exist.

In this period of major policy reform toward more open economies, there are valid political and economic arguments for governments and the farming community in developing countries to seek effective interventions to deal with enhanced price transmission, especially in the context of persistent low world prices. The movement toward trade liberalization, toward allowing market price signals to determine the use of resources, could be frustrated by the reluctance of governments to further expose their farming constituents, especially those in import competing sectors, to the risks of price instability and periods of persistent low prices associated with additional reforms.

Those who believe in the benefits of freer world trade have an interest in facilitating policy adjustments in developing economies. But adjustments must be designed so as to overcome the political resistance likely to result from the exposure of large agricultural sectors, with their large concentrations of poor people, to the risks of sustained low prices.

Perhaps the first question an economist would ask is: "What about using market-oriented policies?" If problems associated with price risk were related merely to year-to-year resource allocations, then futures and other derivative markets would likely be the most efficient solution for overcoming the risk-related political costs of further trade reform that arise from risk aversion, underdeveloped capital markets, and other possible institutional problems. If private hedging were not feasible, then a government policy based on futures would serve. An expected low price would simply signal a decrease in resource use devoted to the commodity. And if a realized low price in the previous year led to an expectation that prices would eventually rise, then resources would merely wait to reenter production of the commodity until price realizations signaled their expected profitable use.

Resource decisions, however, are usually matters of multiple year commitments. The stochastic nature of world prices suggests a high probability that low-price events come grouped together in distinct episodes of months, if not years. In that case futures and options markets would be inadequate to ensure completely against the unfavorable effects of exposing import-competing farm sectors to world price declines. Other strategies are called for to smooth income fluctuations across years, such as the use of credit or equity markets, long-term contracts, vertical integration, and other means. In developing countries, however, the resources for implementing these market-based strategies are often lacking or are only slowly becoming available. Therefore, it is worthwhile considering other government price stabilization plans to reduce resistance to reform by reducing the effects of what seems to be the most disturbing characteristic of world commodity prices: their periodic tendency to persist at values below trend.

Border Measures and Domestic Support Measures within the WTO Framework

While there are many possible instruments for this purpose, there are questions of both effectiveness and legality under the current WTO legal framework and potential revisions. Konandreas (2000) classifies permissible policies under the current framework into two broad categories: border measures through tariffs (within the tariff ceiling bounds) and domestic support measure (price and nonprice programs within the limits of WTO commitments).

Border Measures

Most countries have bound their tariffs at a relatively high rate—100 percent and higher. A few countries (Argentina, Chile, Malaysia, the Philippines, and Thailand) have bound their tariffs at about 30 percent. In many countries, applied rates are lower than the bound tariff. In Konadreas's (2000) assessment a high bound tariff might be insufficient to avoid the politically difficult situation of very low prices. More significantly, however, the lack of other instruments under the WTO has encouraged governments to commit to overly high bound tariffs, giving them considerable discretion in choosing tariff levels and creating greater uncertainty about the effective trade regime at any point in time.

In practical political terms few countries have access to the special safeguard clause, an exemption to tariff ceiling levels. From earlier commitments eligibility is limited to the tariffication process, and because the majority of developing countries did not "tariffy," but instead offered ceiling bindings, very few can use the special safeguards option.

Domestic Support Policies

There are both bound supports under nonexempt policies subject to commitments of aggregate expenditure ceilings (the aggregate measurement of support established during the Uruguay Round) and nonbound supports, exempt from limits, operating within the green box. In addition, developing countries have access to a special category of exemptions under special and differential treatment, such as investment subsidies and input subsidies to low-income farmers. Of 71 developing countries, 61 reported zero aggregate measurement of support levels—for the remaining 10 countries these levels are very small. In part this is due to fiscal limitations (Konandreas 2000). The implication is that most developing countries are limited in their support options to action under the *de minimis* clause and the definitions of the green box, and are thus restricted in their use of nonborder support policies. In contrast developed countries (and a few developing countries) reported high aggregate measurement of support levels.

Developing countries now have fewer fiscal resources to manage price risk and aid their farmers through domestic supports and fewer alternative market instruments to compensate for the higher probability of periods of low domestic prices that might result from further moves toward trade liberalization. This tempts many governments in developing countries to seek protection of their import-competing sectors through border measures. From the perspective of increasing the welfare gains from trade and facilitating liberalization, future WTO negotiations might well consider allowing greater flexibility to developing economies to use well-defined and disciplined tariffs and surcharges, by permitting the application of price bands or price floors, modifying the general WTO safeguards, and—perhaps the most promising—altering the special safeguard clause for countries with low bound tariffs.

Price Bands

Several Latin American countries have used price bands, which resemble price floors, but with several important differences. Price bands stabilize prices between a floor and a ceiling, which are both typically based on moving averages of past world prices, not a domestic target price. For example, Chile uses a 60-month moving average for wheat and a 120-month moving average for sugar, with 25 percent of the highest and lowest prices eliminated in calculating the moving average.

In the past the announced goal of price bands has been stabilization, not the avoidance episodes of extremely low prices. In fact, the automatic determination of the price bands can lead to floor prices that would be difficult to justify as protection against the risk of unsustainable low prices. For example, in the case of Chilean sugar there have been periods when the floor price in dollars has exceeded the price ceilings in other periods (figure 6.2). It is difficult to rationalize the narrowing over time of the price bands for sugar and edible oil (figure 6.3), except by reference to the way in which international price formation affects the mechanical determination of the floor and ceiling.

The price floors associated with price bands as they have been typically applied are simply moving averages, reducing near-term volatility but not offering an ensured minimum level as a fixed point of reference. Indeed, the adjusting price floor in a price band scheme is in many cases merely a means of deferring price changes that must inevitably occur. For example, the 1998 floor price for Chilean wheat was $150 per ton, implying a minimum price of $175 per ton, well above the long-term minimum average production cost in neighboring Argentina. Certainly, there is nothing in such price band schemes that automatically protects producers against some long-term worst case scenario for their income levels and ability to service debt. From recent experience with a relatively high price supported in the short term by the price floor, it is difficult to assess whether the policy has caused greater investment in the wheat sector (or generated more long-term financing) than would otherwise have been the case. Productivity certainly has grown in wheat and sugar, but not at a notably faster rate than in nonprotected activities such as maize.

Price Floors

One option for eliminating the worst-case scenarios associated with several concurrent years of especially low world prices would be to replace such moving price bands with a simplified *fixed* price floor scheme. For "sensitive" commodities a minimum world price or threshold level might be defined, below

Figure 6.2 Price Band of Edible Oil in Chile, 1986–97

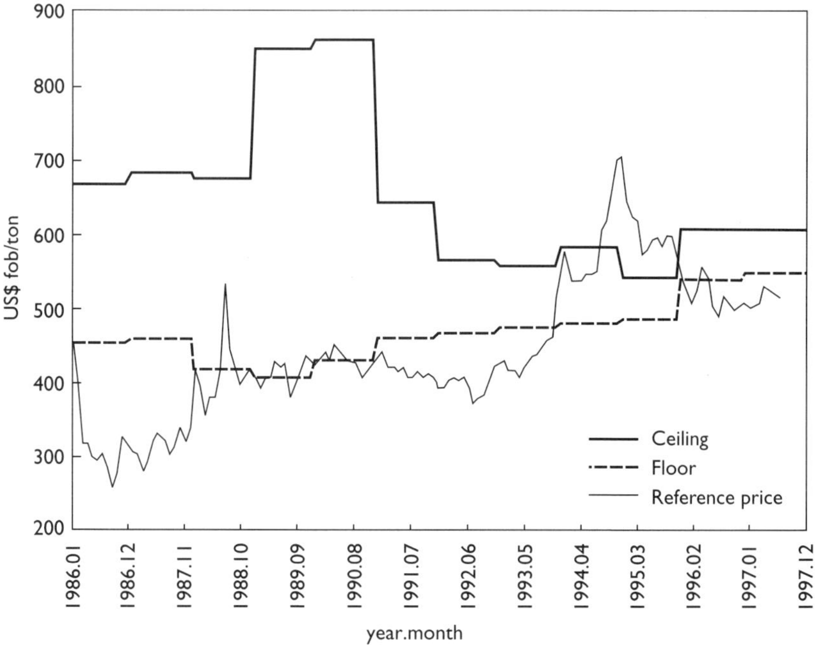

Source: Quiroz, Foster, and Valdés (1999).

which a government agrees to intervene to maintain the domestic price at that level.[10] For international acceptability this threshold price should be based on the minimum average cost of the least cost international exporter, making it unmistakably transitory, in the sense that prices would almost certainly rise in the future. For example, when sugar prices reached $250 per ton in 1985, sugar production was unprofitable even in Australia, one of the most cost-efficient sugar producers in the world; one could have concluded that world prices were unmistakably low and would rise in the future and that resources would certainly move from sugar production. In fact, two years later, prices increased to approximately $400.

The objective of the type of floor price policy discussed here is more narrowly defined than that of price stabilization as pursued by most current stabilization schemes. A price floor based on some fixed, internationally recognized, most-efficient average cost of production would be meant to ensure against the lowest prices. While this would likely reduce the variance of the domestic price, the objective would not be to insulate domestic prices in any general sense. Indeed, a simple floor price policy would allow the flow of information between international and domestic markets through price signals in all periods except those with extremely low prices and transitory low prices.

Figure 6.3 Price Band of Sugar in Chile, 1986–97

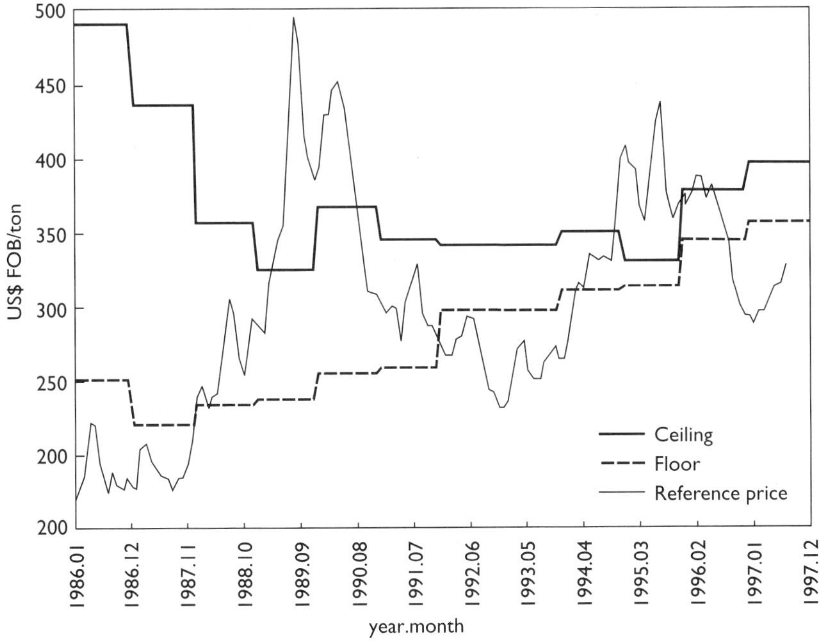

Source: Quiroz, Foster, and Valdés (1999).

Such a policy would not impede the development of risk markets, the use of futures, and other activities the way that price stabilization has tended to do.

While the principal advantage of a price floor would be the protection of producers in long-run viable sectors that might not otherwise survive extremely low prices in the short run, there are other advantages. One is to encourage investment in promising sectors. In an immature economy not yet able to diversify away by other means, a price floor based solely on the most efficient world producer would not distort long-run returns to investment or protect long-run uncompetitive sectors. Another is that, unlike variance-stabilizing policies such as moving-average price bands, a fixed floor price has the advantage of an easily referenced and guaranteed forecast of a minimum worst-case scenario, improving the ability of lenders to scrutinize producers' cash flows and thus to extend credit.

There are practical implementation benefits as well. For import-competing commodities a price floor policy could be implemented through a system of variable surcharges that are triggered by a predetermined international reference price along the lines of the WTO safeguard mechanism.[11] A basic criterion for establishing a feasible floor price policy should be to limit the nature of the interventions. The record of most ad hoc price stabilization programs is one of a proliferation of distortions and indiscriminate protections that are difficult to justify.[12] A second criterion should be to limit eligibility to standardized commodities that are a near-perfect substitute for the commodity on international markets.[13] These two criteria would guard against both the protection of goods that are not economically profitable in the long run and the tendency of governments to manipulate for short-term objectives programs that ought to be transparent and based on long-term economic feasibility.

General WTO Safeguards and Contingency Measures

When there is either a large and abrupt surge in imports or a sudden decline in import prices that threaten a country's import competing sector, WTO safeguards or contingency measures are applicable. These measures permit the suspension of WTO obligations. There are several categories of general safeguard measures (see Konandreas 2000 and Hoekman and Kostecki 1996):

- Antidumping measures are used to counteract the effects of exports sold below home market prices. The legal test is material injury to a domestic industry. Although the United States has been the most notorious user of antidumping measures, they have been used by some developing countries, although with indifferent success. Of the 469 antidumping investigations initiated during 1987–97 by Latin American and Caribbean countries, 60 were related to agriculture. Only 199 of the investigations resulted in further action, and only 3 applied to agricultural products (Paz Cafferata and Valdés 2000).[14]
- Countervailing duties, applicable in response to government subsidies of export products, are also based on material injury to a domestic industry.
- Emergency safeguards, explicitly temporary and limited in frequency of use, are immediately applicable without formalities when imports threaten the serious injury of domestic industries. The use of this measure does not presume any "unfair" behavior on the part of exporting firms or governments.
- Measures related to balance of payments, limited in availability to the least developed countries, are used to safeguard a government's external financial position.
- Countries may ask for "general waivers," which require formal authorization by the WTO Council.
- Modifications of schedules and renegotiations of tariffs are a permanent measure.

Special Safeguards

Special safeguards are applicable to agricultural producers under the Uruguay Round Agreement on Agriculture but are restricted to products that were included in the Uruguay Round tariffication process. Many developing countries are not eligible to use special safeguards because they set bound tariffs outside of the tariffication mechanism. The future status of special safeguards is precarious, particularly considering the heavy criticism from the Cairns Group. But the special safeguard clause could be modified to allow effective border measures to protect farmers from the risk of low world prices in the absence of a sufficiently flexible (and WTO legitimate) standard tariff system or where domestic supports are inadequate.

Modification of the special safeguard scheme would have to be clearly limited to permitting countries to apply tariffs beyond their bound ceilings only when otherwise competitive domestic producers face severe injury during periods of extremely low prices. While access would not apply for any modification for commodities with bound tariffs that are considerably above applied rates, Konandreas (2000, p. 12) notes that with "no apparent relationship" between access to special safeguards and low bound tariffs, eligibility to the existing [special safeguards] clause has very little relationship to the problem that presumably it was meant to address."

One modification would be to allow special safeguards only for commodities and countries for which bound tariffs are below some threshold (Konandreas suggests 70 percent; 35 percent would be better). Alternatively, the upper limit to variable safeguards could be inversely related to the bound tariff. This would induce governments to set lower bound tariffs because they would have access to additional border protections in emergencies.

The triggering of variable safeguards would have to be specified in terms of well-defined low-price events, applicable to all countries, developed and developing. This would necessarily involve negotiations within a WTO framework to determine coverage of importables that qualify for variable special safeguards. It would also require registration.

A third possible modification would make access contingent on domestic support transfers. Countries able to use other safety net mechanisms, such as farm revenue insurance along the lines of Canada's Net Income Stabilization Account, to protect producers during periods of low prices would be excluded. Konandreas (2000) suggests, for example, that special safeguards be limited to countries with domestic support below 15–20 percent of the value of domestic production.

These issues are being discussed at the WTO and elsewhere. The specificity of such measures and their legality, operational implementation, and relative effectiveness require research attention by economists and others committed to improving the performance of the international trade system.

NOTES

Parts of this paper related to world price distortions and transmission were developed in preparation of a paper delivered at the Organisation for Economic Co-operation and

Development Global Forum on Agriculture, Agricultural Trade Reform, Adjustment, and Poverty, May 15–16, 2002, Paris.

1. While this chapter emphasizes the relationships between further policy reforms and price risk and developing country farmers, price risk is obviously relevant for consumers as well, particularly low-income consumers. With trade reforms and world prices largely determining domestic prices, lower food prices would benefit consumers, although prices might be more volatile and some people are concerned about increased import dependence. But those are issues of food supply management and are often examined in the context of food security.
2. With policies restricted to tariffs, an important choice is between differentiated and uniform tariffs. While most trade economists favor low uniform tariffs, technical economic arguments can always be found for applying higher or lower tariffs in some products. But the process is almost always corrupted, a captive of special interests. Harberger (1984, p. 431) asserts that "some types and patterns of trade restrictions are far worse than others . . . [and] [t]he only sure way to guarantee against catastrophic variations in rates of effective protection . . . is to make the rate of nominal protection uniform across all products. . . . Only a given uniform rate of tariff can automatically avoid capricious and distorting variations in the effective rates of protection actually achieved." Elsewhere Harberger (2001, p. 549) comments that in overwhelmingly supporting uniform tariffs "practicing professionals . . . would be expressing not the implications of neoclassical theory but rather what they think of as practical wisdom derived from long experience . . . a political-economy argument for uniformity, not a neoclassical one."
3. Not considered here are the effects of trade liberalization and price transmission on agricultural value added. In Brazil after the 1991 reforms, border protection on tradable inputs fell rapidly, benefiting the producers of exportables (export taxes were eliminated) and partially compensating producers of importables for lower tariffs. Reductions in the prices of purchased inputs and machinery tended to favor mid-size and larger farmers.
4. Of course, productivity and factor use are endogenous and not independent of policy, but this issue is beyond the scope of the present discussion.
5. In Chile farm lobbies proposed, with considerable political support from legislators, a surcharge on imported milk products that would compensate one-for-one the EU export subsidy on milk. The surcharge would bring internal Chilean prices to the internal EU price, a gross overestimate of the true distortion in world prices.
6. See, for example, Zietz and Valdés (1989) for Organisation for Economic Co-operation and Development countries, and Tyers and Anderson (1992) for work on developed and developing countries.
7. There are three notable methodological questions regarding estimates of the effects of trade liberalization derived from these models. First, what is assumed in estimation models about price transmission is an important issue and not always clear (Coleman 1995; Taylor 2001). There is a complex interaction between domestic policies and the transmission of world prices to domestic markets. For example, prices in remote areas tend to exhibit independence from prices in major trading centers. Notwithstanding, various parameters can be drawn on to estimate export demand and supply in order to predict the overall sector's response—even if some subsets of producers are not well integrated in the markets for tradables. This question is one of distributional welfare. Second, how realistic are the assumptions about price transmission? Some earlier work (for example, Valdés and Zietz 1980) assumed perfect transmission, but more recent studies (such as Tyers and Anderson 1992) have allowed for the possibility of lower transmission elasticities. This is

an empirical question grounded in the nature of the available data and the econometric subtleties required to give flexibility to the analysis. Third, what about the interdependence across products, both horizontally and vertically? Processed agricultural products (such as orange juice concentrate, tomato paste, processed frozen and canned products, and wine) are rarely considered. Adequately accounting for cross-product effects is a complex analytical problem, involving a proliferation of parameters. Some authors consider a fixed-proportion world, others are inclined to an Armington-style approach. This issue has not been resolved yet in a satisfactorily rigorous way.

8. RUNS was developed as a joint OECD–World Bank project. It includes 22 regions and 20 sectors, 15 in agriculture, and covers 1985–2002.
9. For more recent analysis, see OECD (2001) and Burfisher (2001).
10. A government's commitment to intervene at very low prices should probably be reserved to one or a few commodities, whose long-term international competitiveness is highly probable. This basic criterion of long-term comparative advantage of selected commodities would preclude encouraging commodity production for self-sufficiency or other goals inconsistent with developing patterns of free trade based on underlying differences in the costs of production. For example, supporting rice production in Chile would not be consistent with this criterion, nor would promoting the production in tropical climates of commodities associated with temperate zones, as has been the case with crops such as wheat in Colombia or sorghum in Venezuela.
11. For exported commodities a fund built up of producer contributions when the floor policy is dormant could finance producers in periods of extremely low prices. Put options could complement a price floor policy in the initial years of operation before fund reserves could cover a string of low-price events.
12. Not only does the floating nature of price bands undermine the use of any floor for guaranteeing medium-term agricultural loans (and tend to preclude alternative market developments that could reduce the consequences of price risk), as a broad rule price bands have been applied indiscriminately to various commodities and products. This has been notable in the cases of Colombia, Ecuador, and Venezuela, where the policy covers more than 120 importable goods. Administration of such a system of price bands has been cumbersome at best and has tended to make the structure of incentives and effective protection almost unpredictable (Quiroz 1996, 1997).
13. This criterion precludes stabilization programs for agro-industrial products derived from basic commodities, which in effect become indistinguishable from crude protectionism, as has been the experience during the 1990s with price bands for "derivatives" in Colombia, Ecuador, and Venezuela.
14. Argentina, Brazil, and Mexico initiated 87 percent of all Latin American and Caribbean antidumping investigations during 1987–97, and 88 percent of the investigations related specifically to agriculture (Paz Cafferata and Valdés 2000).

BIBLIOGRAPHY

Burfisher, M. E., ed. 2001. "Agricultural Policy Reform in the WTO: The Road Ahead." Agricultural Economics Report 802, Economic Research Service, Market and Trade Economics Division, U.S Department of Agriculture, Washington, DC.

Caner, M., and B. Hansen. 1997. "Threshold Autoregression with a Unit Root." Working Papers in Economics 381, Boston College, Boston.

Cashin, P., H. Liang, and J. McDermott. 2000. "How Persistent Are Shocks to World Commodity Prices?" *IMF Staff Papers* 47 (2): 177–217.

Coleman, D. 1995. "Problems of Measuring Price Distortion and Price Transmission: A Framework for Analysis." *Oxford Agrarian Studies* 23 (1): 3–13.

Deaton, A. 1992. "Commodity Prices, Stabilization, and Growth in Africa." Research Program in Development Studies, Centre for International Studies, Woodrow Wilson School, Princeton University, Princeton, NJ.

Gersovitz, M., and C. Paxon. 1990. "The Economics of Africa and the Prices of Their Export." Studies in International Finances 46. Princeton University, Princeton, NJ.

Goldin, I., and O. Knudsen. 1989. *Agricultural Trade Liberalization: Implications for Developing Countries.* Paris: OECD.

Goldin, I., O. Knudsen, and D. van der Mensbrugghe. 1992. *Trade Liberalisation: Global Economic Implications.* Paris: OECD.

Harberger, A. C. 1984. *World Economic Growth: Case Studies of Developed and Developing Nations.* San Francisco: Institute of Contemporary Studies.

———. 2001. "The View from the Trenches: Development Processes and Policies as Seen by a Working Professional." In *Frontiers of Development Economics: The Future in Perspective,* G. M. Meier and J. E. Stiglitz, eds. New York: Oxford University Press.

Harwood, J., K. Coble, R. Hefner, J. Perry, and A. Somwaru. 1999. "Managing Risk in Farming: Concepts, Research, and Analysis." Agricultural Economic Report 774, Economic Research Service, U.S. Department of Agriculture, Washington, DC.

Hoekman, B., and M. Kostecki. 1996. *The Political Economy of the World Trading System: From GATT to WTO.* New York: Oxford University Press.

Ingco, M. D. 1996. "Progress in Agricultural Trade Liberalization and Welfare of Least-Developed Countries." World Bank, Washington, DC.

Josling, T. 1980. "Developed Country Agricultural Policies and Developing Countries' Supplies: The Case of Wheat." International Food Policy Research Institute, Washington, DC.

Konandreas, P. 2000. "The Need for Effective Safeguards Against Very Low World Market Prices in the Context of the WTO Negotiations on Agriculture." FAO Informal Expert Consultation, Rome, Dec. 7–8.

Leon, J., and R. Soto. 1995. "Structural Breaks and Long-Run Trends in Commodity Prices." Policy Research Working Paper 1406, World Bank, Washington, DC.

McCulloch, N., L. A. Winters, and X. Cirera. 2002. *Trade Liberalization and Poverty: A Handbook.* London: Centre for Economic Policy Research.

Mundlak, Y., and D. Larson. 1992. "On the Transmission of World Agricultural Prices." *World Bank Economic Review* 6 (3): 399–422.

OECD (Organisation for Economic Co-operation and Development). 2001. *A Forward-Looking Analysis of Export Subsidies in Agriculture.* Paris: OECD.

Paz Caferata, J., and A. Valdés. 2000. "Interests and Options in the WTO 2000 Negotiations: Latin America and the Caribbean." In "Agricultural Trade Liberalization in a New Trade Round: Perspectives of Developing Countries and Transition Economies," M. Ingco and A. Winters, eds., Discussion Paper 418, World Bank, Washington, DC.

Perron, P. 1989. "The Great Crash, the Oil Price Shock, and the Unit Root Hypothesis." *Econometrica* 57 (6): 1361–401.

Quiroz, J., and R. Soto. 1995. "International Price Signals in Agricultural Prices: Do Governments Care?" Documento de Investigación 88. Programa de Postgrado en

Economía, Instituto Latinoamericano de Doctrina y Studios Sociales/Georgetown University, Santiago.

Quiroz J., W. Foster, and A. Valdés. 1999. "Agricultural Price Instability and Price Floors: A Proposal." World Bank, Washington, DC.

Sarris, A. 1997a. "¿Ha aumentado la inestabilidad de los mercados internacionales de cereales?" *Revista Española de Economía Agraria* 181 (Sept.–Dec.): 157–82.

———. 1997b. "Risk Management in Cereal and Oilseed Markets." Paper prepared for the Commodity Risk Management Group, World Bank, Washington, DC.

———. 1999a. "Commodity Risk Management for Developing Countries: Towards Implementing a New Approach." Paper prepared for the Commodity Risk Management Group, World Bank, Washington, DC.

———. 1999b. "Price and Income Variability." Paper prepared for the Commodity Risk Management Group, World Bank, Washington, DC.

Schiff , M., and A. Valdés. 1992. *The Political Economy of Agricultural Pricing Policy.* Vol. 4, *A Synthesis of the Economics in Developing Countries.* Baltimore: Johns Hopkins University Press.

Taylor, J. E. 2002. "Trade Integration and Rural Economies in Less Developed Countries: Lessons From Micro Economy-Wide Models, With Particular Attention to Mexico and Central America." Latin America and the Caribbean, World Bank, Washington, DC.

Tsetsekos, G., and P. Varangis. 1999. "The Structure of Derivatives Exchanges: Lessons From Developed and Emerging Markets." Paper prepared for the Commodity Risk Management Group, World Bank, Washington, DC.

Tyers, R., and K. Anderson. 1992. *Disarray in World Food Markets: A Quantitative Assessment.* New York: Cambridge University Press.

Valdés, A. 1996. "Surveillance of Agricultural Price and Trade Policy in Latin America During Major Policy Reforms." Discussion Paper 349, World Bank, Washington, DC.

———. 2000. "Agricultural Support Policies in Transition Economies." Technical Paper 470, World Bank, Washington, DC.

Valdés, A., and W. Foster. 2002. "Reflections on the Policy Implications of Agricultural Price Distortions and Price Transmission for Producers in Developing and Transition Economies." Paper presented at the OECD Global Forum on Agriculture, Agricultural Trade Reform, Adjustment and Poverty, Paris, May 23–24.

Valdés, A., and J. Zietz. 1980. "Agricultural Protection in OECD Countries: Its Cost to Less-Developed Countries." International Food Policy Research Institute, Washington, DC.

———. 1995. "Distortions in World Food Markets in the Wake of GATT: Evidence and Policy Implications." *World Development* 23 (6): 913–26.

Zietz, J., and A. Valdés, 1989. "International Interactions in Food and Agricultural Policies: The Effect of Alternative Policies." In *Agricultural Trade Liberalization: Implications for Developing Countries,* I. Goldin and O. Knudsen, eds. Paris: OECD.

Zivot, E., and D. Andrews. 1992. "Further Evidence on the Great Crash, the Oil Price Shock, and the Unit Root Hypothesis." *Journal of Business and Economic Statistics* 10 (3): 251–70.

CHAPTER SEVEN

Implications of Food Import Regulations and Market Access for Developing Countries

Tim Josling

Food import regulations are often significant impediments to market access. Developed countries have been revising their regulations in recent years in response to growing consumer demands for safe and healthful foods and the increasing complexity of global food supply chain networks. Developing countries find such regulations particularly burdensome, as they are likely to require expensive procedures at both the production and processing stages.[1]

Other chapters in this volume examine the impact of tariffs on market access opportunities for developing countries. This chapter concentrates on food import regulations that focus on human, plant, and animal health. The evidence examined comes from the discussion of market access issues within the World Trade Organization (WTO) Sanitary and Phytosanitary (SPS) Committee, where developing countries have challenged the import regulations of developed countries and other developing countries when they believed that those regulations unnecessarily impeded trade.

OBLIGATIONS UNDER THE AGREEMENT ON THE APPLICATION OF SANITARY AND PHYTOSANITARY MEASURES

The Agreement on the Application of Sanitary and Phytosanitary Measures (the SPS Agreement), negotiated in the Uruguay Round, marked a turning point in the development of multilateral trade rules in an area of trade that had long been contentious. By attempting to define rules that would encourage the adoption of "trade-friendly" health and safety measures and discourage measures that were acting as disguised protection, the SPS agreement aimed to reduce trade tensions. However, numerous complaints are still being brought before the WTO SPS Committee, and the issue of questionable trade barriers is still high on the grievance list of exporting firms and governments.[2] This chapter looks at whether the SPS Agreement has changed the way countries design and apply their sanitary and phytosanitary measures, both to improve market access for developing countries and to maintain adequate protection of human, animal, and plant health.

Two conflicting views have emerged on the market access effects. One view holds that the SPS Agreement has benefited trade by disciplining national sanitary and phytosanitary measures, making them less trade distorting and ensuring that they are based on scientific analysis. If this view is correct, there should be evidence of policy changes attributable to the SPS Agreement that remove or reduce trade distortions. The other view is that the SPS Agreement has had no discernable effect, with countries continuing their previous policies, or has impeded trade by requiring or encouraging stronger regulations and disadvantaging countries without the administrative infrastructure to reach those standards.

The primary function of the SPS Agreement was to clarify the meaning of Article XX of the General Agreement on Tariffs and Trade, which established the right of countries to use trade measures to protect animal, plant, and human health. The SPS Agreement reaffirms that right but elaborates on the procedures that countries should follow so as not to unduly restrict market access for other countries. It sets up a framework for national sanitary and phytosanitary measures so that countries do not infringe on the rights of trade partners. And it offers a notification and review process that allows countries to challenge measures that appear to infringe on their rights or on those of others.

There are at least six elements of the SPS Agreement that could have an impact on trade flows in agricultural and food products (table 7.1).

Transparency

Transparency refers to the requirement to notify changes in sanitary and phytosanitary measures to the SPS Committee. Measures in place before the SPS Agreement came into force do not need to be notified. This requirement would be expected to have a positive impact on trade. Such notification, including single access points for information, makes it easier for foreign firms to gain market entry. Under certain circumstances, however, transparency could induce countries to implement policies that are more restrictive of trade. The need to notify and to subject policies to international scrutiny might encour-

Table 7.1 Elements of the Sanitary and Phytosanitary Agreement That Could Affect Market Access for Developing Countries

SPS Agreement element	Possible trade impact
Transparency, notification, and establishment of inquiry points	Reduction of transaction cost where developing country exporter gains better information about access conditions. Will normally lead to improved market access.
Risk-based approach for all measures	Reduction of overprotection by regulations stricter than necessary on the basis of scientific evidence. However, trade flows may be reduced if the encouragement of risk assessment leads to stricter regulations.
Harmonization on international standards, regionalization, and equivalence	Removal of cost of meeting separate standards in different markets. However, there may be high cost in meeting the harmonized standards. Developing countries may also feel that they have little say in setting international standards. Equivalence and mutual recognition are also more difficult for developing countries to negotiate.
Science-based justification for standards that are not based on international norms	Removal of "economic protection" of domestic industry by obliging that standards not based on multilateral norms be justified in scientific terms.
Counternotification by other members	Removal of trade barriers by the importing country in response to a request for change or clarification by the exporter.
Dispute settlement	Increase in trade flows resulting from the resolution of a particularly difficult trade conflict, or the introduction of sanctions where the importer declines to change policies.

Source: Author's analysis.

age policies that are less trade friendly. But such an outcome is unlikely in practice. Commonly, the nontransparent measure may have been applied in an ad hoc way by customs agents or domestic sanitary authorities. The requirement to be transparent will not in itself guarantee that the more visible regulation is less trade restricting, though that is likely to be the case in most instances.

Risk Assessment

To ensure that no additional protection is built into the domestic standard or regulation that unduly impedes trade, measures must be based on risk assessments. By discouraging countries from implementing or maintaining frivolous trade restrictions, this requirement will in general have a positive impact on trade. But it might encourage measures that are too costly by overstressing riskiness at the expense of affordability and consumer choice. Risk assessment will not always lead to more trade-friendly standards, especially when the previous standards were too lax for the risks involved. However, the overall benefit of a risk-based system presumably outweighs occasional overprotection arising from the introduction of more objective standards.

Harmonization, Regionalization, and Equivalence

The encouragement of harmonization, regionalization, and equivalence is intended to facilitate trade by reducing the number of standards to be met. Harmonization on an internationally agreed standard is particularly encouraged and is deemed to have met the requirements of the SPS Agreement. Harmonization will generally have a positive impact on trade if it removes arbitrary differences in regulations and cuts transaction costs.

But harmonization is not always beneficial to trade. Harmonization may encourage adoption of the most restrictive standards even where they may not be necessary based on risk assessment. Some international standards may be inappropriate for developing country importers, though the advantages of using them may outweigh the costs of the lack of country specificity. For exporters, the benefits of harmonization are more clear-cut by facilitating access to foreign markets. For the exporting country the issue of the appropriateness of such standards for the domestic market may be less important.

Regionalization, equivalence, and mutual recognition are other ways of removing trade barriers arising from arbitrary differences among standards. Regionalization will tend to increase market access by reducing the areas from which goods cannot be exported and reducing the likelihood of any negative trade impacts for the exporter. Equivalence also will tend to facilitate trade. An agreement between exporter and importer that the exporter's standards are equivalent to standards in the importing market will tend to reduce transaction costs. The exporter may have to modify domestic practices to reach an equivalence agreement, but the result should be better market access. Mutual recognition also reduces transaction costs, including mutual recognition of test results and certification. Few negative consequences for trade are likely from these agreements.[3]

Science-Based Standards

Stricter-than-international standards, if used, must be justified by scientific evidence, to prevent the use of strict regulations that reduce market access but that are not justified by scientific evidence. The need for scientific justification is in general a positive development for trade relative to an unregulated system in which countries can introduce their own standards without justification. But there is no guarantee that the strict application of the SPS Agreement will not result in "overprotection." Science-based standards are not in themselves a guarantee against trade distortions, nor do they take the benefits of trade into account. Thus strict standards justified by scientific studies on the impact of the spread of animal and plant disease, for example, can also be costly to an importing country even if disease risk is present. In human health cases the trade-off is less apparent or appealing, but even in these cases sound public policy must account for the cost to the economy of alternative ways of promoting health.

Counternotification

Counternotification allows SPS Committee members to comment on each other's sanitary and phytosanitary measures and to bring evidence before the committee of possible violations of the SPS Agreement. This is a relatively inexpensive and low-key way of raising issues without going at once to the dispute settlement process and one of the most powerful ways of facilitating trade. Exporters can bring to the attention of WTO members instances of sanitary and phytosanitary measure used by an importing country that are likely to be problematic for trade and inconsistent with the obligations under the SPS Agreement. Negative trade impacts can arise from counternotification in certain circumstances where modification of an import measure is imposed on a country by commercial or political pressures.

Dispute Settlement

The incorporation of the SPS Committee in the "single undertaking" of the WTO allows the procedures of the dispute settlement understanding to be used in sanitary and phytosanitary disputes and facilitates resolution of disputes that have not been resolved in earlier levels of consultation. This incorporation was a major advance for the resolution of trade conflicts. The more structured legal system would be expected to yield positive trade benefits. Negative trade impacts might arise, however, if the panels examining disputed measures adopt a perspective that undermines consumer confidence or weakens the acceptance of the WTO and its trade disciplines.

THE SPS COMMITTEE AND TRADE DISPUTES

The establishment of the SPS Committee within the WTO has facilitated the exchange of views on the operation of sanitary and phytosanitary policies. The process of notification and counternotification has given countries the opportunity to probe each other's actions while maintaining respect for the

Figure 7.1 Stages of Counternotification and Dispute Procedures through the Sanitary and Phytosanitary Committee

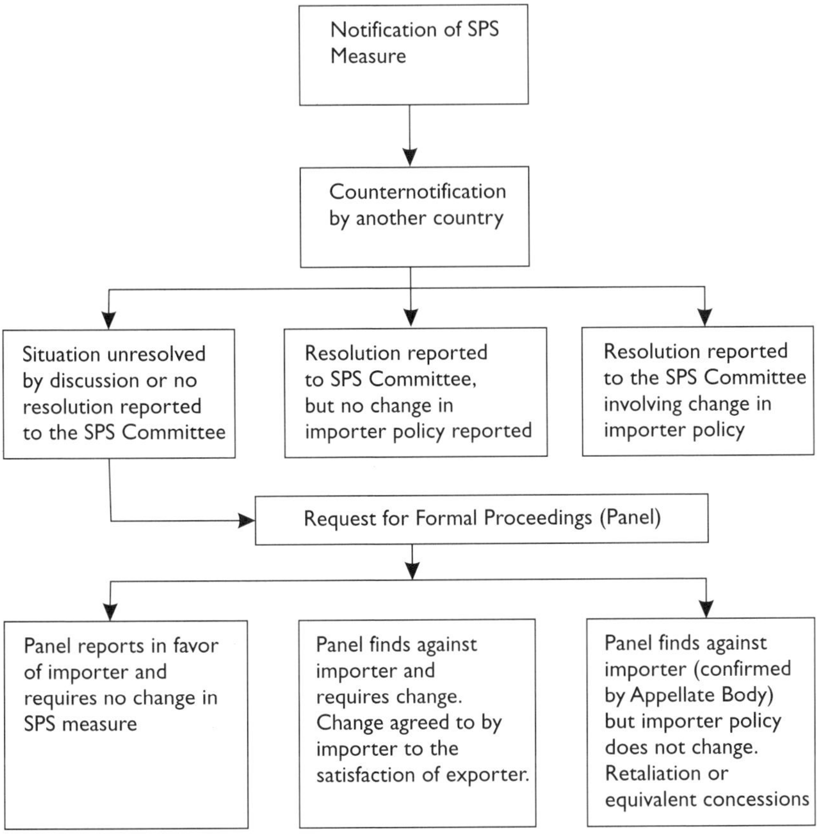

Source: Author's analysis.

SPS Agreement. Figure 7.1 shows the procedures that are associated with the committee.

About a third of developing country WTO members (39 countries) have either raised or supported a sanitary and phytosanitary case. Argentina alone has raised 17 cases and supported 10 others. Other countries involved in multiple cases include Brazil (5 raised and 8 supported), Chile (4 and 11), the Philippines (5 and 3), and Thailand (9 and 3). The members of Mercosur and ASEAN have been particularly active in lodging complaints and supporting statements, and 10 of the 14 members of the Cairns Group have raised complaints.

The majority of the cases raised or supported by developing countries have targeted developed countries (figure 7.2). The European Union was the respondent in 44 percent of cases, either collectively or as individual countries, fol-

Figure 7.2 Incidence of Developed Countries as Respondent in Sanitary and Phytosanitary Cases Raised by Developing Countries, 1995–2003

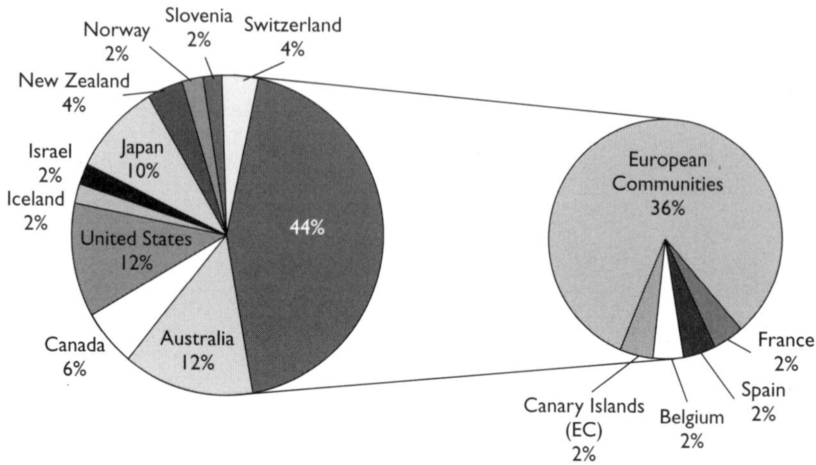

Source: Author's analysis based on WTO Sanitary and Phytosanitary Committee documents.

lowed by the United States and Australia (12 percent each) and Japan (10 percent). One-third of the cases raised or supported by developing countries have targeted other developing countries. Seventeen developing countries (10 percent of all developing countries) have been respondents in cases raised or supported by developing countries. The Republic of Korea was the respondent in five cases, followed by the Czech Republic, Indonesia, Mexico, Slovak Republic, and Turkey in two cases each.

Nature of Disputes

Of the 69 cases in which developing countries raised or supported the counter-notification, almost two-fifths are related to animal health regulations, about one-third to plant health, and about one-quarter to human health and safety (figure 7.3).[4] The predominance of animal health cases is largely the result of widespread concern about the spread of foot and mouth disease and bovine spongiform encephalopathy (BSE). The foot and mouth disease cases were in reaction to outbreaks in Taiwan, China, and the United Kingdom and the resurgence of the disease in Argentina and Uruguay after its near eradication in those countries. It has become common practice to ban imports from countries in which there are outbreaks. Removing the bans seems to take some encouragement from the SPS Committee. In the case of BSE, and the broader class of diseases called transmissible spongiform encephalopathy, the newness of the disease, and the fact that it had not before been considered either a communicable cattle disease or a threat to humans, left countries uncertain as to

Figure 7.3 Nature of Sanitary and Phytosanitary Cases Raised or Supported by Developing Countries, 1995–2003

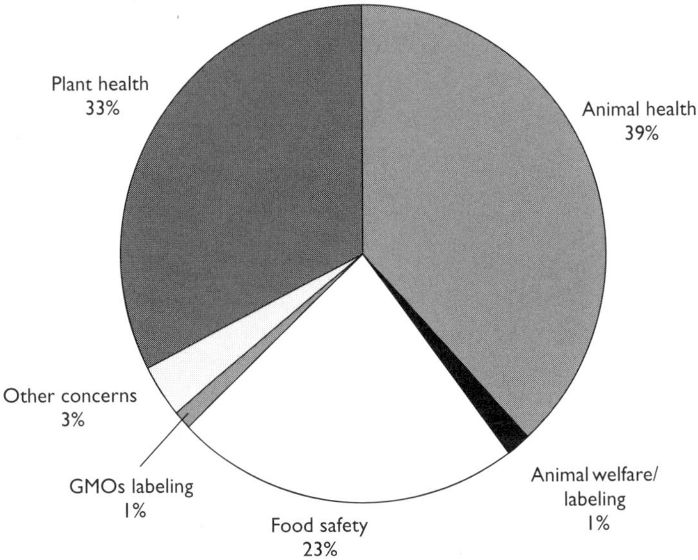

Source: Author's analysis based on WTO Sanitary and Phytosanitary Committee documents.

how to regulate trade. Again, most of the discussion in the SPS Committee revolved around requests by exporters for removal of bans imposed by importers as a reaction to the emergency.[5]

In many ways the food safety and the plant health cases are more typical of the trade barriers facing developing countries. In food safety the main developing country challenges have concerned the tight EU regulations on exports of fruits, vegetables, and nuts to the European Union and restrictions on fish and poultry exports. Some cases concerned the supposed contamination of exports with aflatoxins or other natural substances. Other cases concerned residues of pesticides and other chemicals from the production process. The plant health issues are more diverse, reflecting the greater number of pest and plant diseases that are the subject of international controls.

Dispute Grounds

What were the grounds on which the sanitary and phytosanitary measures were contested? Half the cases involved a challenge by a developing country that the respondent had not completed a risk assessment (figure 7.4). In well over half the cases no international standards existed, confirming that standards are still incomplete. Where international standards exist, disputes are less common—only 6 percent of the 69 cases identified here were about the dis-

Figure 7.4 Issues Addressed in Sanitary and Phytosanitary Cases Raised or Supported by Developing Countries, 1995–2003

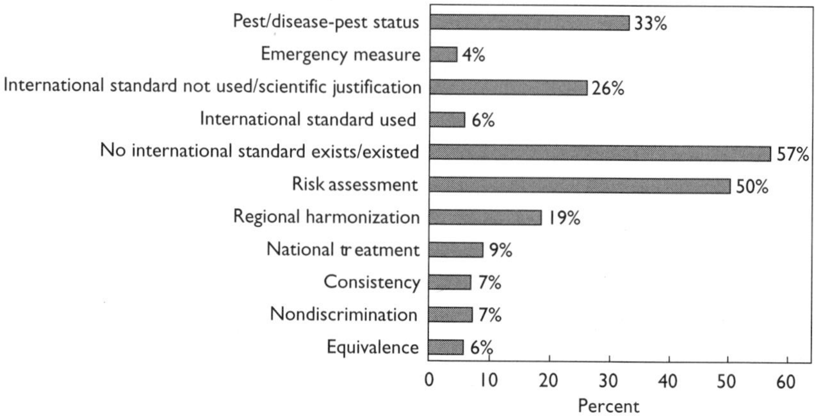

Source: Author's compilation.

puted use of international standards. In somewhat more cases (26 percent) the importer had used the provision in the SPS Agreement concerning use of a standard more rigorous than the international norm. In these cases the challenging country claimed that there was no scientific basis for such standards. Several cases appeared to be related to the harmonization of regional standards, where an importer had raised import requirements as a consequence of regionalization. The continuing process of adopting EU-wide rules that are stricter than those that some members had in place has contributed to this. The joint food standards of Australia and New Zealand were also challenged in some cases as being more restrictive than one of the countries had in place before the common standards were introduced.

Complaints of violating nondiscrimination and national treatment provisions, common sources of trade complaints to the WTO, were infrequently cited as the reason for complaints. Similarly, few complaints were related to equivalence agreements and consistency of risk assessment among measures.

Dispute Outcomes

What were the outcomes of these 69 cases of challenge by developing countries? The record is neither clear nor particularly encouraging for developing countries. In 60 percent of cases no solution had been reported to the SPS Committee (figure 7.5). In 30 percent a solution was reported though it was often not clear from the report that all challengers had agreed with the solution.[6] More worrying, in only 20 percent of cases did the developing country challenger clearly achieve its objective, and in several cases the problem has persisted after a solution had been agreed on.

Figure 7.5 Outcomes of Sanitary and Phytosanitary Cases Raised or Supported by Developing Countries, 1995–2003

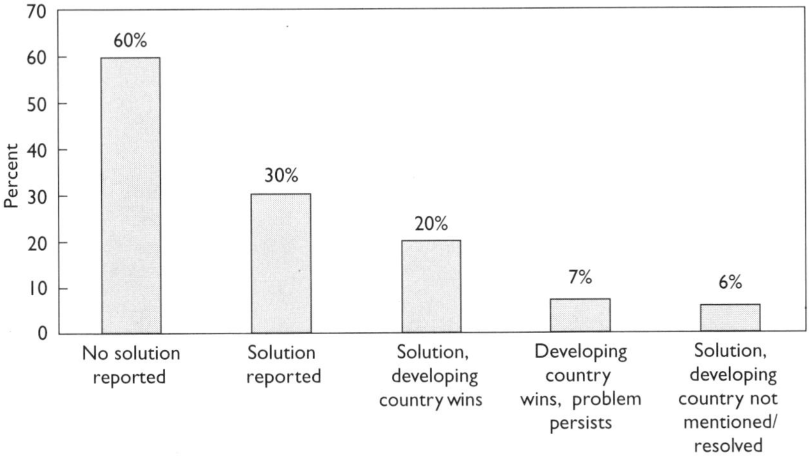

Source: Author's compilation.

The solutions themselves give some concern for the way the system is working. In only 7 percent of the cases did the developed country importer adjust its measures or their application (figure 7.6). In almost twice as many cases a developing country importer made an adjustment as a result of a challenge by other developing countries. The developing country exporter was reported to have modified policies as a result of the dispute in almost 10 percent of cases. In a few cases the developing country exporter appeared to receive technical assistance to help with the adjustment. Some 6 percent of the cases discussed in the SPS Committee ended with a decision to initiate formal dispute settlement proceedings.[7]

Developing countries have not made wide use of the formal dispute settlement process beyond counternotification in the committee. Only four formal disputes (7 percent) have been raised or supported by developing countries. In three of these cases consultations under dispute settlement were initiated; in the fourth formal consultations have been requested but no panel has been established (table 7.3). In each case the respondent is a developing country.

EXPERIENCE OF DEVELOPING COUNTRIES IN RESOLVING DISPUTES

Four examples illustrate the range of issues and solutions: EU standards on aflatoxins in imported foods, EU restrictions on fish and fish products from East Africa, and Czech and Korean restrictions on Thailand's poultry and meat exports.

Figure 7.6 Solutions in Sanitary and Phytosanitary Cases Raised or Supported by Developing Countries, 1995–2003

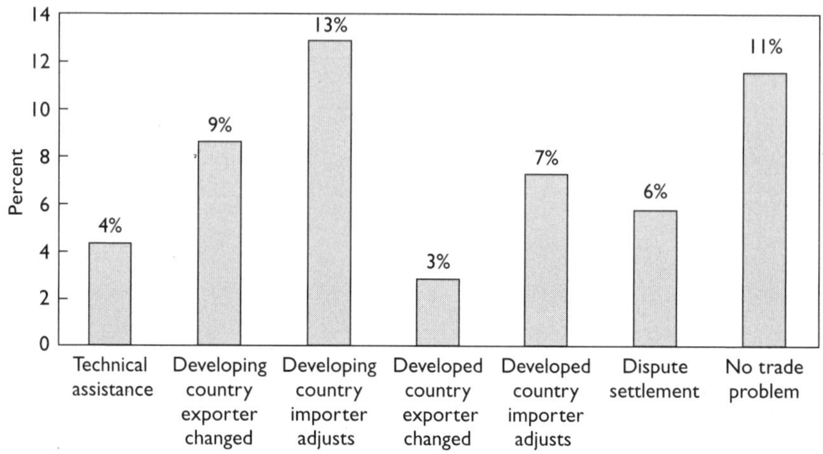

Source: Author's compilation.

EU Standards for Aflatoxin in Foodstuffs

Mycotoxins are naturally occurring substances produced by fungi that infest certain food crops. Allowing infested plant material into the food chain poses a health risk to consumers. The most prevalent mycotoxin is aflatoxin, found on cereals, nuts, vegetables, and fruits. The aflatoxins considered most harmful to humans have been identified in corn and corn products, peanuts (groundnuts) and peanut products, cottonseed, milk, and tree nuts (including Brazil nuts, pecans, pistachios, and walnuts).[8] In 1997 the Joint Food and Agriculture Committee–World Health Organization (FAO-WHO) Expert Committee on Food Additives concluded that "aflatoxins should be treated as carcinogenic food contaminants, the intake of which should be reduced to levels as low as reasonably achievable" (Otsuki, Wilson, and Sewadeh 2001, p. 504).

The expert committee also illustrated the dilemma in determining what level was "reasonably achievable" when it concluded that the difference between two hypothetical standards of 10 parts per billion (ppb) and 20 ppb could translate into the difference between 39 and 41 cancer cases per billion people from exposure to the aflatoxin. The stricter standard was achievable but might not be reasonable if the cost of achieving it were excessive. One estimate noted that the cost of reducing the likely incidence of cancer from this cause by two in a billion could be very considerable in lost trade opportunities for developing countries (Otsuki, Wilson, and Sewadeh 2001). This implies the strong possibility of overprotection of consumers, who would pay higher prices for these products, and negative impacts on overseas suppliers, who may have few

Table 7.3 Sanitary and Phytosanitary Disputes Raised or Supported by Developing Countries, 1995–2003

Respondent	Issue	Raised or supported by	Actions / results	Category
Egypt	Restrictions on canned tuna	Thailand	Egypt agreed to report back to the committee. Thailand requested formal consultations.	Food safety
Korea, Rep.	Shelf-life requirements	Australia, Canada, United States, Argentina, European Union	Formal dispute settlement: United States-Korea and Canada-Korea. US-Korea mutually agreed solution notified in July 1995. Canada-Korea notified a mutually satisfactory solution in April 1996.	Food safety
Korea, Rep.	Import clearance measures and practices	United States, several delegations	Consultations initiated under dispute settlement (WT/DS3, WT/DS41); mutually satisfactory solution found.	Other concerns
Turkey	Restrictions on banana imports	Ecuador	Formal consultations requested by Ecuador on September 10, 2001 (DS237).	Plant health

Source: Author's compilation based on data from WTO Sanitary and Phytosanitary Committee documents.

alternative crops to sell and for whom the loss of income could lead to deprivations of a wider magnitude.

The main controversy has centered on strict health standards imposed by the European Union, which replaced a variety of standards in individual member states.[9] For aflatoxin B1 in goundnuts the range of tolerances had been from 1 ppb in France and Denmark to 25 ppb in Portugal (Otsuki, Wilson, and Sewadeh 2001). The initial EU regulation in 1997 set the standard at 10 ppb for groundnuts for further processing and 4 ppb for groundnuts for direct consumption. This was amended in 1998 to a somewhat less restrictive standard of 15 ppb for processing groundnuts and a specific standard for aflatoxin B1 of 8 ppb for processing groundnuts and 2 ppb for groundnuts destined for direct consumption.

While the regulation was in draft form, a number of countries argued in March 1998 that the EU proposal would impose severe restrictions on trade without significantly reducing health risks to consumers.[10] These countries argued that the EU proposal did not seem to be based on a proper risk assessment. There was no international standard at that time, though the Codex Alimentarius Committee on Food Additives and Contaminants was considering the matter. But the European Union made it clear that its proposed measure reflected the desired level of protection, as allowed by the SPS Agreement, and that it did not support the norm that the Codex was considering. The European Commission planned to evaluate the comments received and formalize the proposal in June 1998. The regulation was enacted with minor modifications and came into effect on January 1, 1999.[11]

Bolivia's experience with the EU standard illustrates some of the issues involved for developing countries. In September 1998 Bolivia informed the SPS Committee that the proposed EU measure would have severe effects on Bolivian exports of Brazil nuts. Bolivia entered into bilateral discussions with the European Commission (EC) to find a mutually agreeable solution. In November 1998 the committee chairman reported that "the discussions had been very fruitful, and had helped Bolivia to better understand the rationale behind the EC measures, as well as the EC procedures followed. They had also helped the EC understanding of the potential effect of some of its measures on the Bolivian industry."

In March 1999 Bolivia argued for application of the principle of special and differential treatment in favor of a low-income country. Bolivia outlined the socioeconomic and ecological implications of the EU measure for the Brazil nut industry and for the economy overall. The European Commission countered that the problems in Bolivia stemmed from needed improvements in the production chain and the equipment used. It noted that a project to improve production and storage processes and the livelihood of nut collectors had been included in the 2002 EU aid program and that it had also proposed a certification procedure for Bolivian exports.

The study by Otsuki, Wilson, and Sewadeh (2001) used a gravity model of trade to estimate the potential effect of the regulations on the exports of nuts (groundnuts and groundnut products) and cereals (corn and corn products) from African countries to the European Union. The study found that the European Union's stricter aflatoxin regulations relative to the proposed Codex standards could have resulted in $380 million in lost export revenue by African countries, or 76 percent of the value of their cereals and cereal products. The trade impact of reduced exports of edible nuts was estimated at $287 million, or 53 percent of potential trade. Thus the total export effect was estimated at $670 million a year. Though the additional risk (estimated at two more deaths per billion people) from increased exposure to aflatoxins might be undesirable in itself, it ought perhaps to be assessed against the possibility that the additional export earnings from not imposing the stricter standard could generate enough income to fund health improvement programs that would reduce mortality by more than the aflatoxin standard would.

The controversy over aflatoxins illustrates an important aspect of health standards. Developing countries that have actual or potential export interests in agricultural and food goods clearly see the tendency toward tighter health requirements in developed countries as a problem. While countries can air such problems in the SPS Committee, regulators and politicians in developed countries have little room to maneuver in relaxing such regulations. Where such rules contravene WTO rules, such as by discriminating among suppliers or artificially restricting imports in favor of domestic production, the dispute settlement process is at hand to explore the case in detail. But such action is costly and not always successful. In cases such as the aflatoxin standard, the main hope is to secure assistance from the importing country in meeting the high standards.

EU Trade Restrictions on Imports of Fish in Response to a Cholera Outbreak in East Africa

In March 1998 the European Union informed the SPS Committee that it had restricted imports of a range of fruit, vegetable, and fish products from Kenya, Mozambique, Tanzania, and Uganda following outbreaks of cholera in those countries.[12] The European Union undertook to develop a policy on imports from countries with cholera outbreaks based on a risk assessment. In this instance international scientific evidence collected by the WHO helped to illuminate if not to bridge the gap between the parties.

WHO guidelines on control of cholera indicate that the risk of cholera transmission through food imports is very low and suggest means of control other than import bans. Fish products, in particular, which are not generally consumed in raw form in Europe, are deemed by the WHO to pose no significant risk. Initially, the European Union argued that the WHO was not the appropriate body to suggest standards in this case and denied that its ban violated Article 2.2 (not based on scientific principles). In its defense it invoked Article 5.7 (allowing temporary measures while evidence is collected) of the SPS Agreement. The EU also pointed out that it was attempting to help the affected exporting countries to introduce stricter controls before export. But eventually the EU authorities declared that they were satisfied with the procedures installed for testing exports and lifted the ban in 1997.

Lifting the ban seems to have had a positive impact on at least some African food exports to the European Union. Tanzanian exports of fish fillets have increased sharply since 1997, especially to the EU market (figure 7.7).[13] EU demand for such fillets was rising during 1995–98, and the Tanzanian share of that market was increasing. This suggests that the impact of the cholera-linked ban on fish imports from Tanzania was of short duration. Consultation in the SPS Committee can be assumed to have assisted in the resolution of that dispute. The situation is somewhat different in the case of exports of fish fillets from Kenya to the European Union (figure 7.8). Export sales from Kenya continued to slide even after the resolution of the cholera dispute.[14] By 2000 the EU market for Kenyan fish fillets had virtually disappeared.

The experience of Tanzania and Kenya suggests that raising an issue in the SPS Committee may indeed help to get a trade conflict resolved. But the resumption of trade cannot be assumed. Other factors, including the response of the food regulatory authorities in both the importing and the exporting countries, can affect trade recovery after a period of restriction.

Czech Ban on Poultry Imports from Thailand

Trade in poultry meat is rife with accusations of unsubstantiated sanitary barriers to imports. One dispute exemplifies how the SPS Agreement apparently led to a change in importer policy. In September 1998 Thailand raised in the SPS Committee the Czech Republic's ban on poultry meat from Thailand on the grounds of unacceptable levels of arsenic acid. The Czech government was asked to supply the scientific justification, as mandated by the SPS Agreement. After consultations at a technical level and a visit to Thailand by Czech experts in September 1999, the Czech Republic notified the SPS Committee that the ban had been lifted.

Trade flows show the significance of the ban to Thailand (figure 7.9). Thai exports of chicken had been rising since 1996 and had begun to capture a substantial share of the Czech market for poultry. Imports from Thailand seem to have increased dramatically in 1998 even though total Czech imports were down. Though the Czech Republic was not a major destination for Thai poultry, the prospect of losing such a rapidly growing market may have prompted Thai concern over the import regulation. Though precise data are not available for the following two years, both Czech imports and Thai exports of poultry continued to climb. When available, bilateral trade figures will show whether there was any trade impact from the lifting of the ban.

Figure 7.7 Trade in Fish Fillets between Tanzania and the EU-15

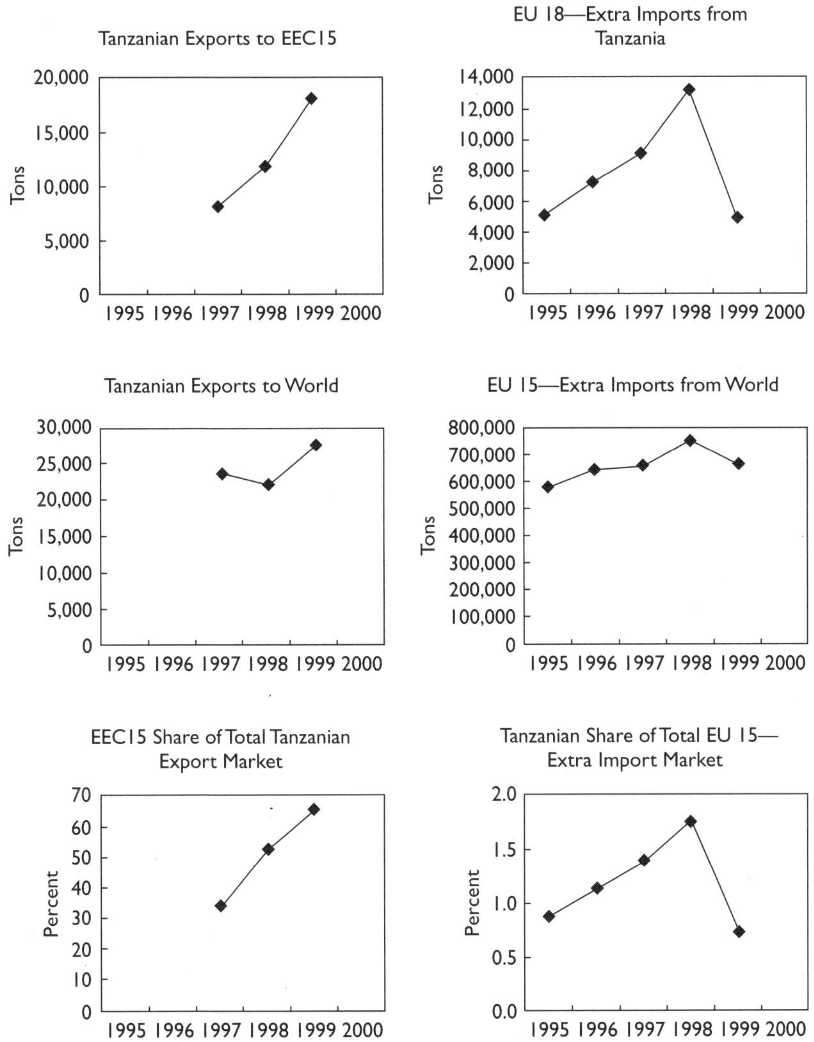

Source: OECD ITCS Harmonized System 2001.

Korean Import Ban on Frozen Poultry from Thailand

Exports of chicken from Thailand to the Republic of Korea were the subject of another counternotification in the SPS Committee. In October 1997 Thailand questioned a Korean ban on poultry imports to prevent the risk of listeriosis. Thailand claimed that the ban breached Article 7 of the SPS Agreement (ensur-

Figure 7.8 Trade in Fish Fillets between Kenya and EU-15

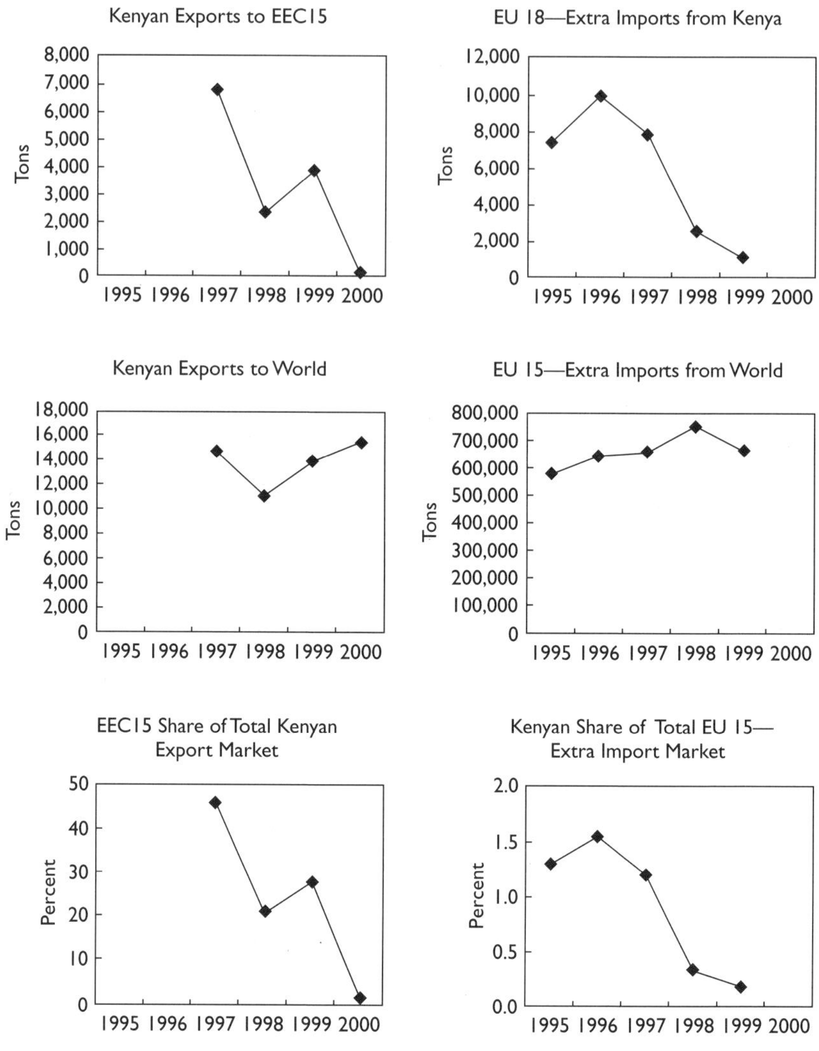

Source: OECD ITCS Harmonized System 2001.

ing transparency) as Korea had not provided justification for the ban and the incidence of listeria in Asia was in any case very low. Korea replied that the regulation was temporary, to remain in effect only until the new Korean food code, harmonized to international norms, was in place. The new code exempted frozen chicken destined for further processing and cooking from the zero-tolerance test for listeria. Thailand was satisfied with the explanation, and the problem was resolved.

Figure 7.9 Trade in Poultry between Thailand and the Czech Republic

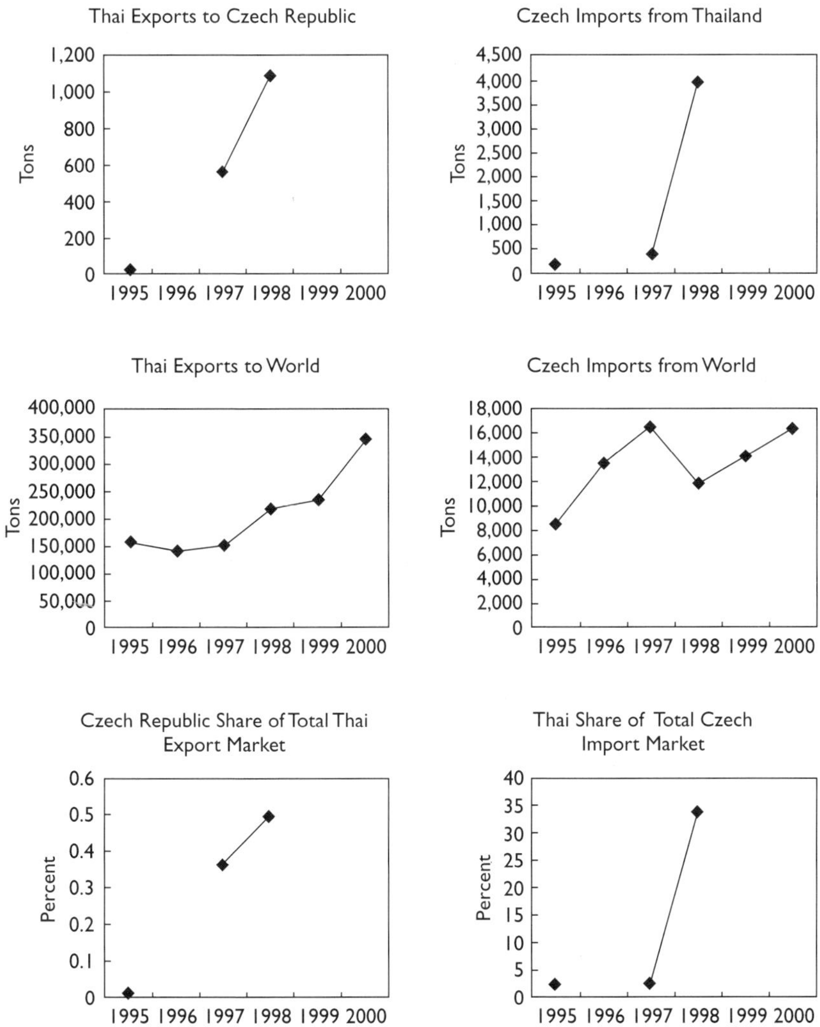

Source: OECD ITCS Harmonized System 2001.

The upward trend in Thai exports of chicken to Korea hesitated in 1997, as the share of Thai chicken exports accounted for by the Korean market fell, though Korean import data show the trend continuing (figure 7.10). In 1998 Thailand noticeably increased its share of the Korean market at a time when Korea's total poultry imports were lower. The resumption of the upward trend in 1998 suggests that the counternotification in the SPS Committee may have played a role.

Figure 7.10 Trade in Poultry between Thailand and Korea

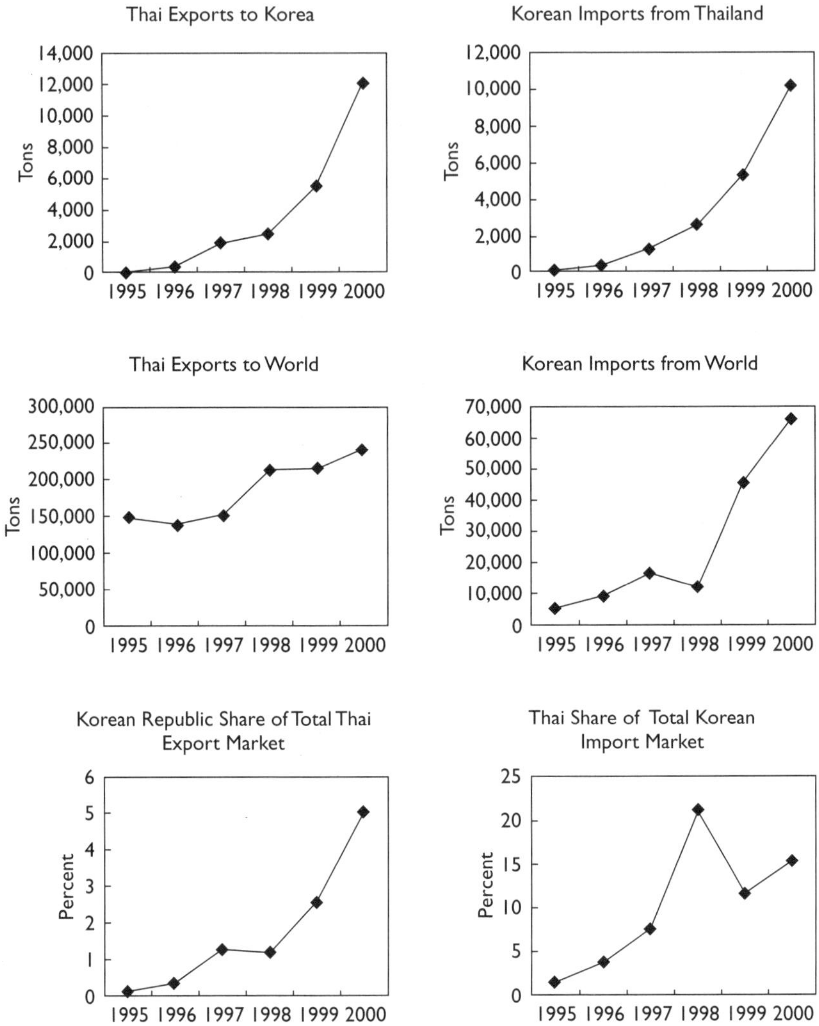

Source: OECD ITCS Harmonized System 2001.

SUGGESTIONS FOR IMPROVING MARKET ACCESS

Developing countries face a formidable challenge in meeting the norms and standards set by the major developed country markets and by international standard-setting organizations. The way in which the SPS agreement affects the ability of developing countries to use trade as an engine for development and growth is naturally of interest and concern. Improvements in this aspect of the integration of developing countries into the global trade system could have significant implications for poverty reduction and sustainable growth.

To sell food and agricultural goods into developed country markets (and increasingly into other developing country markets), developing country exporters must meet or exceed the standards set for those markets. But reaching those standards requires infrastructure and production conditions that are often lacking, making this an uphill task for developing exporters. As the complexity of these standards increases, the disparity can be expected to widen.

The international community as a whole must address this issue if developing countries are not to be left behind. Seeking exemptions from these standards is to brand exports from developing countries as inferior or unsafe. That approach has little merit. Requesting assistance with the infrastructure to meet the standards is the more constructive approach. Together with the monitoring of the standards themselves to ensure that they do not contain additional impediments to the exports of developing countries, such an approach can more fully integrate developing countries into the international trade system.

What lessons can be drawn from the operation of the WTO framework for improving market access by developing countries? One clear conclusion from the first few years of experience with the SPS Agreement is that harmonization around international standards is proceeding slowly. Although the standard setting bodies—Codex, World Organization for Animal Health, and the International Plant Protection Convention—have been active, they have also been slowed in their progress by their newfound importance in the trade system. Now that their standards are recognized as meeting the risk-assessment criteria of the SPS Agreement, the specification of standards has become a more sensitive task. Developing countries need to become more active in this area of standard setting, to ensure that standards do not reflect merely the desires of developed countries.

To be more representative and responsive to the needs of developing countries, standard-setting bodies should ensure broad geographic representation. Coordination among developing countries on a regional or trade-interest basis could also be strengthened. Rotating responsibilities for representation and designated scientific support groups for particular sanitary and phytosanitary issues could reduce the resource and financial burden on individual countries. The standard-setting bodies could take the initiative by preparing an inventory of standards and allowing time on the agenda for their consideration. Some acceleration of the time taken to agree on standards could be contemplated for issues of specific interest to developing countries.

As an alternative to harmonization, equivalence and regionalization offer promise for developing countries. But as with harmonization on multilateral standards, equivalence and regionalization have not been easy to achieve in practice.[15] Developing countries frequently lack the capacity to negotiate equivalency agreements. Assistance from the international community could be of value here. Technical agencies could identify situations where equivalent levels of protection could be provided by different means and assist the developing country to prepare the supporting documentation for negotiating such agreements. The SPS Committee should periodically review the success of such negotiations and provide a forum for discussing grievances.

Preparing the documentation for negotiations on regionalization is also difficult for smaller developing countries with limited scientific and administrative capacity. The international community could assist countries with monitoring and certification schemes. As appropriate, developing countries could designate export enclaves where biosafety was ensured through special monitoring and testing. Enclaves would be open for inspection by importing countries, which could certify that production from these regions was acceptable on sanitary or phytosanitary grounds. Such preclearance could also be advantageous for the importing country.

Many of the difficulties that developing countries face in making use of the benefits of the SPS Agreement stem from inadequate capacity to participate fully in the SPS Committee. The main constraints are the costs of preparing challenges and following through with a complaint rather than the lack of information or opportunity for complaints. Though assistance is now available for countries initiating disputes, help with preparing challenges to notifications of others could be useful. As there are similarities between the issues facing groups of countries in the same region, such help could involve coordination among delegations.

A new round of WTO trade negotiations is well under way, and developing countries will have a major say in shaping the outcome. Though the SPS Agreement itself is not on the negotiating table, several countries have made suggestions for improving it.[16] The Doha Implementation Decision instructed the SPS Committee to address some of these issues. A World Bank–WTO launched initiative in September 2002 links aid to trade opportunities to help in the fight against poverty and established a fund called the Standards and Trade Development Facility. Agreement on further reform of agricultural trade is unlikely to enjoy the support of developing countries if the restrictions on market access arising from discriminatory use of health and safety regulations by developed countries is not adequately addressed.

ANNEX TABLES

Table 7.A1 Sanitary and Phytosanitary Cases Raised or Supported by Developing Countries

	Country	Raised	Supported	Respondent
1	Argentina	17	12	1
2	Bolivia	1	1	1
3	Brazil	5	10	1
4	Bulgaria	1	1	—
5	Chile	4	11	1
6	Hong Kong, China	—	1	—
7	Colombia	—	3	—
8	Côte d'Ivoire	1	—	—
9	Croatia	1	—	—
10	Cuba	—	—	1
11	Czech Republic	1	1	2
12	Ecuador	2	1	—
13	Egypt, Arab Rep.	1	—	1
14	El Salvador	—	—	1
15	Estonia	1	—	—
16	Gambia, The	1	—	—
17	Hungary	3	1	—
18	India	—	1	—
19	Indonesia	2	2	2
20	Kenya	—	1	—
21	Korea, Rep.	—	3	5
22	Latvia	1	—	—
23	Malaysia	1	4	—
24	Mexico	—	—	2
25	Pakistan	—	2	—
26	Paraguay	—	1	—
27	Peru	2	1	—
28	Philippines	5	3	—
29	Poland	2	—	1
30	Romania	1	—	1
31	Senegal	1	—	—
32	Slovak Republic	1	—	2
33	South Africa	—	3	—
34	Sri Lanka	—	—	—
35	Thailand	9	3	—
36	Turkey	—	1	2
37	Ukraine	—	—	1
38	Uruguay	3	6	—
39	Venezuela	—	—	1
	Total	**67**	**73**	**26**

Source: Author's calculations based on WTO Sanitary and Phytosanitary Committee documents.

—, Not applicable.

Table 7.A2 Developing Country Proposals Related to Product Attribute Regulation in the Agricultural Negotiations

Country and document number	Proposal
Mexico W/138	Sanitary and phytosanitary measures should be addressed only under the SPS Agreement
Kenya W/136	All exported products should comply with international standards or with the national requirements of the exporting country to prevent dumping of substandard products in countries without national standards; arbitrary imposition of sanitary and phytosanitary measures by developed countries has hampered market access opportunities
Congo, Dem. Rep. W/136	Developing countries should receive technical and financial assistance in standardizing products
Nigeria W/130	Members should apply a unified set of international measures that reflect the specific constraints of developing countries, to eliminate the misuse of sanitary and phytosanitary measures for protective purposes
Turkey W/106	Developed countries should consider ways to modify current uses of sanitary and phytosanitary and technical barriers to trade that continue to hamper market access for developing countries
India W/102	Developed countries should not be allowed to use sanitary and phytosanitary measures for protectionist purposes by prescribing overly stringent trade restrictive measures for denying market access to developing countries
Caricom W/100	The negotiations should deal with nontariff measures so that unjustified use of technical barriers and sanitary and phytosanitary measures does not hinder market access
Korea, Rep. W/98	Genetically modified organisms must be addressed because of increasing consumer concerns over food safety, health, environment, and biotechnology; the need for precautionary measures to protect human health and the environment as well as consumers' increasing demand for informed choice should be dealt with in the negotiation
Small Island Developing States[a] W/97 Mauritius W/96	Developing countries should have access to appropriate technology to meet increasingly stringent sanitary and phytosanitary requirements, receive assistance so that they can participate in standard setting bodies, and be exempt from requirements for a detailed risk assessment when refusing entry of products that threaten biodiversity; geographic indications should also be extended to a wider range of agricultural products

Source: IATRC (2001).

a. Includes Dominica, Jamaica, Mauritius, St. Kitts and Nevis, St. Lucia, St. Vincent and the Grenadines, and Trinidad and Tobago.

NOTES

The author is Professor Emeritus, Food Research Institute and Senior Fellow, Institute for International Studies, Stanford University. Paper presented to the IATRC Summer Symposium, Whistler, BC, June 16-17, 2002. Research assistance from Rachel Anderson is gratefully acknowledged. Comments from participants at the meeting and from the editors have been helpful in revising the paper.

1. For a more detailed discussion of the problems that developing countries face in adapting to the Agreement on the Application of Sanitary and Phytosanitary Measures see Jensen (2002), Henson and others (1999), and Henson and Wilson (2002).
2. See for instance the report on trade barriers to processed agricultural goods by the US International Trade Commission (USITC 2001) and the information gathered by the OECD (2002).
3. Regionalization, equivalence, and mutual recognition do, of course, increase the disparity between the exporters that are involved in such agreements and those that are not. This form of "trade diversion" can best be offset by expanding these agreements rather than discouraging them.
4. In addition, developing countries raised two food-related issues in the Technical Barriers to Trade Committee. These are not considered here.
5. For further discussion of the disputes over animal health see Josling, Roberts, and Orden (2003).
6. Countries are encouraged to report to the committee the outcome of the challenge but have no obligation to do so. Many of the cases may be resolved, but the solutions may not have been reported, although it is not clear why countries would wish to hide that fact. Or the dispute may still be unresolved at the time of the committee meeting but the parties may not wish to report on progress. Presumably, the WTO lacks the resources to follow up on these cases.
7. In a handful of cases the parties agreed after consultations that the measure in question had no trade impact and therefore no solution was required.
8. A detailed account is given in Otsuki, Wilson, and Sewadeh (2001).
9. This raises two significant points. First, many of the contentious EU standards that countries have challenged have resulted from the harmonization of such standards in the European Union's single market. In many cases the European Union decided on standards that were stricter than those existing in some individual member states. This increased the likelihood that some exporters would face stricter standards as a result of harmonization. Second, the European Commission in effect has faced the same dilemma as has the multilateral trade system: how to maintain support for standards without distorting trade patterns by overprotection. The commission is generally more favorable to risk-based regulatory systems with scientific credibility than the member states that wish to keep some (political) control.
10. This case draws on WTO (2001). The countries concerned were Argentina, Australia, Bolivia, Brazil, the Gambia, India, Indonesia, Malaysia, the Philippines, Senegal, Thailand, supported by Canada, Colombia, Mexico, Pakistan, Paraguay, Peru, the Philippines, South Africa, Turkey, the United States, and Uruguay.
11. An additional problem was the proposed sampling procedure for aflatoxin, which exporting countries regarded as "unduly costly, burdensome and unjust." The European Union argued that since contamination appeared in a small percentage of kernels, a simple sample was not sufficient to minimize risk to consumers. The directive on sampling went into effect on April 5, 2002.
12. This case is also discussed in Henson, Loader, and Brouder (2000).

13. EU import statistics (extra-EU 15 trade flows), however, appear to show a sharp decline of fish fillets from Tanzania in 1999.
14. There was apparently an increase in exports to the European Union from Kenya in 1999, as reported in Kenyan export data, though the EU import statistics show a decline in 1999 in imports of fish fillets from Kenya.
15. More detail on the success of harmonization, equivalence, and regionalization is given in Josling, Roberts, and Orden (2003).
16. The International Agricultural Trade Research Institute (IATRC 2001) lists suggestions for changes in the sanitary and phytosanitary regulations made by developing countries in the current agricultural trade negotiations. The list is reproduced as annex table 7.A2.

BIBLIOGRAPHY

Henson, Spencer, and John S. Wilson. 2002. "A National Capacity to Maintain Sanitary and Phytosanitary Standards: What Is Required?" World Bank, Washington, DC.

Henson, Spencer, Rupert Loader, Alan Swinbank, and Maury Bredahl. 1999. "The Impact of Sanitary and Phytosanitary Measures on Developing Country Exports of Agricultural and Food Products." Paper presented at the World Bank/WTO Conference on Agriculture and the New Trade Agenda in the WTO 2000 Negotiations, Geneva, Oct. 1–2.

Henson, Spencer, Rupert Loader, and A. Brouder. 2000. "Food Safety Standards and Exports of Perishable Products From Developing Countries: Fish Exports From East Africa to the European Union." *American Journal of Agricultural Economics* 82 (5): 1159–69.

IATRC (International Agricultural Trade Research Institute). 2001. "The Role of Product Attributes in the Agricultural Negotiations." Commissioned Paper 17, Minneapolis, MN.

Jensen, Michael Friis. 2002. "Reviewing the SPS Agreement: A Developing Country Perspective." Working Paper 02.3, Centre for Development Research, Copenhagen.

Josling, Tim, Donna Roberts, and David Orden. 2003. *Food Regulation and Trade: Toward a Safe and Open Global System.* Washington, DC: Institute for International Economics.

OECD (Organisation for Economic Co-operation and Development). 2001. "International Trade by Commodities Statistics, Harmonized System Trade Data." OECD, Paris.

———. 2002. "Agro-Food Products and Technical Barriers to Trade: A Survey of Issues and Concerns Raised in the WTO's TBT Committee." COM/TD/AGR/WP (2002)70/FINAL, Joint Working Party on Agriculture and Trade, OECD, Paris.

Otsuki, Tsunehiro, John S. Wilson, and Mirvat Sewadeh. 2001. "Saving Two in a Billion: Quantifying the Trade Effect of European Food Safety Standards on African Exports." *Food Policy* 26 (5): 495–514.

USITC (U.S. International Trade Commission). 2001. *Processed Foods and Beverages: A Description of Tariff and Non-Tariff Barriers for Major Products and Their Impact on Trade.* Washington, DC: USITC.

WTO (World Trade Organization). 2001 "Special Trade Concerns." G/SPS/GEN/204. Sanitary and Phytosanitary Committee, WTO, Geneva.

CHAPTER EIGHT

Implications of Multifunctionality for Developing Countries

Philip L. Paarlberg, Maury Bredahl, and John G. Lee

The interests of developing countries received limited attention in the Uruguay Round Agreement on Agriculture and little consideration in discussions of multifunctional services—the nonmarket joint products generated by agricultural production, such as, food security, rural development, rural landscapes, cultural heritage, rural lifestyles, and biodiversity. This chapter examines how policies to address multifunctionality might affect developing countries through two links. One is through spillover effects on developing countries when developed countries support agriculture under the guise of multifunctionality, and the other is through developing country use of multifunctionality. Any spillover effects through international price transmission depend critically on the policy regimes in both developed and developing countries. Policy instruments that interrupt price transmission can mitigate spillovers. Developing countries may have an interest in applying policies to foster multifunctionality, but difficulties with cost and implementation limit their ability to subsidize agricultural production systems in that way.

THE MULTIFUNCTIONALITY DEBATE

Differences over acceptable policy instruments to support the multifunctionality of agricultural production have caused friction in World Trade Organization (WTO) negotiations. Some European and Asian countries claim that minimally distorting policy instruments (green box) are inadequate to the demands for multifunctional services (Bohman and others 1999; Cahill 2001; OECD 2001). These countries argue that securing multifunctional services requires production-linked subsidies and trade interventions, instruments that are subject to limits under the Uruguay Round Agreement on Agriculture. Prior to the agreement, trade and domestic policy instruments were used to achieve the level of output necessary to generate the demanded amounts of multifunctional outputs. Reinstrumentation and reduction of border measures under the Agreement on Agriculture risk lowering production of joint outputs from agriculture. Proponents of multifunctionality want such spending to be exempted from limits.

Countries exporting agricultural products, the United States and the Cairns Group in particular, have a much different view. They argue that reinstrumentation of policy instruments from amber box to green box can adequately provide the multifunctional outputs demanded. Trade intervention is inappropriate and subsidies to agriculture should be decoupled from production decisions.

Paarlberg, Bredahl, and Lee (2002) propose a framework for bridging differences over the provision of joint outputs. They argue that while border measures to promote multifunctionality are never justified, production-linked subsidies sometimes are. To prevent multifunctionality from becoming disguised protection, they propose several criteria for exempting production-linked support to agriculture from reduction commitments.

PROPOSED FRAMEWORK FOR HANDLING MULTIFUNCTIONALITY

Broadly, multifunctionality includes food security, rural development, and attributes produced jointly with agricultural outputs, such as biodiversity, cultural heritage, and rural lifestyles. Paarlberg, Bredahl, and Lee (2002) propose a framework for including joint products of agriculture in WTO negotiations based on classic analysis of policy intervention by Johnson (1972) and Bhagwati (1981). Many analyses of multifunctionality focus on the joint production aspect of agriculture and multifunctional services without considering demand (social welfare) or trade impacts (Hodge 1999; Romstad 2000). The Paarlberg, Bredahl, and Lee framework retains the joint production characteristic of agriculture, but shifts the focus to the social welfare function. They argue that multifunctional services demanded by some societies are externalities that appear in the social welfare function. A society derives value from a set of externalities, which may be positively or negatively linked to the production of specific agricultural commodities or not linked at all. The value placed on the individual externalities can differ across countries.

Solving for the welfare optimizing policy intervention rules using this framework shows that standard Pareto-optimality conditions are obtained with one exception. With externalities, $E_j j = 1, \ldots, k$ in the social welfare function, U, the marginal rate of transformation for commodity i exceeds the marginal rate of substitution, as follows:

$$\sum_j \frac{(\partial U/E_j)(\partial E_j/\partial Q_j)}{(\partial U/\partial C_0)} \text{ for all } i = 1, \ldots n, \quad (1)$$

where Q_i is output of the ith good and C_0 is consumption of a numeraire good. The first term in the numerator is the impact of the jth externality on the country's welfare, and the second term is the impact of agricultural production of commodity i on externality j. Several conclusions follow.

First, externalities in the social welfare function do not justify trade interventions, even when linked to output. The optimal tariff story due to international market power remains, but nothing additional is revealed by including multifunctionality.

Second, production-linked subsidies can emerge as appropriate policies if certain conditions are met. One condition is that society values the externality —$\partial U/\partial E_j > 0$. A second condition is that the externality is positively linked to output—$\partial E_j/\Delta Q_i > 0$. If the externality rises as output expands, the appropriate policy is a subsidy. If the externality worsens as output expands, $\partial E_j/\partial Q_i < 0$, the appropriate policy is a tax. When changes in output do not affect the externality, even with a positive social value for the externality, production-linked intervention is not appropriate.

Third, the intervention is the sum across all externalities, both positive and negative, because interactions among externalities must be considered. This means that a country cannot select only the positive aspects of agricultural production to justify intervention, but must also recognize the harmful effects. Gains in landscape preservation from producing rice must be weighed against any pollution caused.

Fourth, intervention is not harmonized across countries since the intervention in each country reflects the social valuation in that country. Harmonization emerges as a special case.

Finally, recognition that production-linked subsidies can be justified based on multifunctionality suggests that a country's producers have the incentive to inflate the importance of multifunctionality to win extra subsidies. To limit the ability of countries to use multifunctionality to disguise protection, Paarlberg, Bredahl, and Lee (2002) propose three criteria.

- Countries using multifunctionality to support production-linked intervention must explicitly identify the externalities. Broad, imprecise amenities like *cultural heritage* are insufficient and simply cloud the issue.
- The value to society must be measured for each externality, and there are several ways to accomplish this (Santos 2001). Although there are difficulties in valuing externalities, it can be done.

- The measures of the social values of the externalities must be linked to output changes. If that connection cannot be demonstrated, the rationale for production-linked subsidies cannot be supported. Country positions on multifunctionality submitted to the Organisation of Economic Co-operation and Development (OECD) indicate weak links to commodity outputs (Abler 2001).

IMPLICATIONS FOR DEVELOPING COUNTRIES

If adopted, the Paarlberg, Bredahl, and Lee (2002) proposal would affect developing countries in two broad ways: through spillover effects occurring through the world market if developed countries subsidize their agricultural systems and through developing country use of multifunctionality as justification for subsidies.

Spillover Effects

Consider the case of developed country use of multifunctionality to justify production-linked subsidies. Because most countries advocating such subsidies affect world prices for agricultural goods, there may be spillover effects on developing countries.

The potential presence of spillover effects can be demonstrated. Assume that the world consists of two countries that trade two goods: an agricultural good, denoted by subscript *a*, and a nonagricultural good. Country 1 is a developed country that imports the agricultural good. Country 2, denoted by an asterisk, is a developing country that exports the agricultural good. In the developed country the agricultural good provides an externality, *E*, while the nonagricultural good does not, so the price of the nonagricultural good is the numeraire. The developed country is assumed to impose a constant specific tariff, *t*, so the change in welfare incorporates a trade contraction effect. A subsidy, *s*, is paid on agricultural output to capture any difference between the actual subsidy and a subsidy equal to the difference between the marginal rate of substitution and marginal rate of transformation, as shown in expression 1. Differentiating the social utility functions and the national budget constraints at world market prices provides the normalized change in national welfare for the two countries, dy and dy^*:

$$dy = tdM_a - M_a dP^* + \{[(\partial U/\partial E)(\partial E/\partial Q_a)/(\partial U/\partial C_n)] - s\}dQ_a \quad (2)$$

$$dy^* = M_a dP^* \quad (3)$$

where $M_a = C_a - Q_a$ and C_a and C_n are the quantities of the agricultural good and nonagricultural good consumed. The relative world price of the agricultural good is denoted P^* and the output of the agricultural good is Q_a.

When the developed country increases the agricultural subsidy, equation 2 shows that there are three impacts on its welfare. First, output of the agricultural good rises and imports fall, $dM_a < 0$. Second, the world price of the agricultural good falls, $dP^* < 0$. The trade contraction generates a welfare loss for the developed country, but the improved terms of trade generate a welfare gain. Third, if subsidy s is less than the welfare optimum subsidy, an increase in the subsidy will raise welfare through the last term in equation 2.

The effect on the developing country, equation 3, depends only on the terms of trade effect and is negative as $dP^* < 0$. Further insight can be gleaned if country 2 is recognized as an aggregate of many countries and is decomposed. Countries exporting the agricultural good suffer a welfare loss from the terms of trade change. Countries importing the agricultural good experience a welfare gain as the relative price of their import falls.

The impact on global welfare is found by adding equations 2 and 3. The impact of the increased subsidy on global welfare is ambiguous because the terms can conflict. The trade contraction due to the subsidy increase lowers world welfare. If the actual initial subsidy, s, is less than the wedge between the marginal rate of substitution and the marginal rate of transformation then an increase in the subsidy adds to global welfare as agricultural output expands. In this case the total change in global welfare is ambiguous, and there is a global optimum subsidy. If the actual subsidy exceeds the wedge, an increase in the subsidy unambiguously lowers global welfare. If the subsidy matches the optimum, any change in the subsidy lowers world welfare.

This formulation leads to the conventional wisdom that exporting developing countries would suffer an adverse change in their terms of trade and a welfare loss if subsidies based on multifunctionality are allowed. Importing developing countries would experience a terms of trade gain and a welfare improvement.

Yet, there are reasons to be cautious about asserting the sign of the spillover effects on individual developing countries and on developing countries as a group. The policy environment and trading institutions in both developed and developing countries affect the outcome. The formulation here assumes no policy intervention by the developing country, and the importing developed country its assumed to apply a fixed specific tariff and production subsidy. If these assumptions change, the welfare effects can differ from those shown.

One argument for production-linked subsidies is that green box instruments do not secure provision of externalities. The terms of trade argument made above assumes that subsidies for multifunctional purposes are additional to existing amber box instruments. Allowing production-linked subsidies for multifunctional objectives could enable developed countries to shift farm support from amber box instruments to green box instruments, which could facilitate reinstrumentation. This can be seen in equation 2 by assuming that the total subsidy, s, consists of two parts. One part is a traditional output subsidy, s_t, with the subsidy due to multifunctionality denoted s_m, so that $s = s_t + s_m$. If the traditional subsidy declines exactly as the multifunctional subsidy rises, $ds_m = -ds_t$, then there is no change in s and no spillover effect. The total subsidy on the commodity could even fall if the reduction in s_t exceeded the increase in s_m. Then the international price would be higher. Developing country exporters would experience a terms of trade improvement and a welfare gain. Importing countries would be harmed.

The formulation assumes a fixed tariff. If increases in an output-linked subsidy for multifunctional purposes are accompanied by tariff reduction, the world price could be unaffected or even rise.

Recall that the multifunctional intervention for a commodity is the sum of the effects across all externalities. The assumption usually made by proponents of multifunctionality is that the intervention would be positive, hence a subsidy would be the appropriate policy intervention. But that might not be the case for many agricultural commodities since negative externalities, like pollution or soil erosion, could overwhelm the positive externalities, so that the net intervention would be a tax. The developed country's output of the commodity would fall. Developing countries that exported the commodity would have a welfare gain through the terms of trade effect. Countries that imported would see an adverse terms of trade effect.

The argument that exporting developing countries suffer a welfare loss and importing developing countries experience a welfare gain when a developed country introduces subsidies for multifunctional purposes assumes price transmission between the developed country's domestic price and the world price. Different types of policy regimes by the importing developed country have different implications for price transmission and hence alter spillover effects.

The importance of the developed country's policy regime to the spillover effects arising from a multifunctional subsidy in that country can be illustrated through the developed country's domestic demand and supply relations. The developed country is assumed to introduce a subsidy based on multifunctionality that rotates the supply relation from S_0 to S_1 in figure 8.1. This subsidy also rotates the excess demand by the developed country from ED_0 to ED_1. Developing countries are part of the excess supply facing the developed country.

Import quotas sever the link between domestic prices in the importing country and the world market, shown by the perfectly inelastic excess demand at Q in figure 8.1. Increased output in the importing developed country using quotas or state trading lowers that country's domestic price, from P_0 to P_1 but does not affect the world price, P_0^*, because imports remain at Q unless the subsidy is large enough to drive the domestic price in the developed country below P_0^*. This means that there will be no welfare changes in developing countries.

If the importing developed country uses a variable tariff, then added output due to multifunctional subsidies is reflected in a lower world price (figure 8.2).

Figure 8.1 Multifunctional Subsidy with an Import Quota

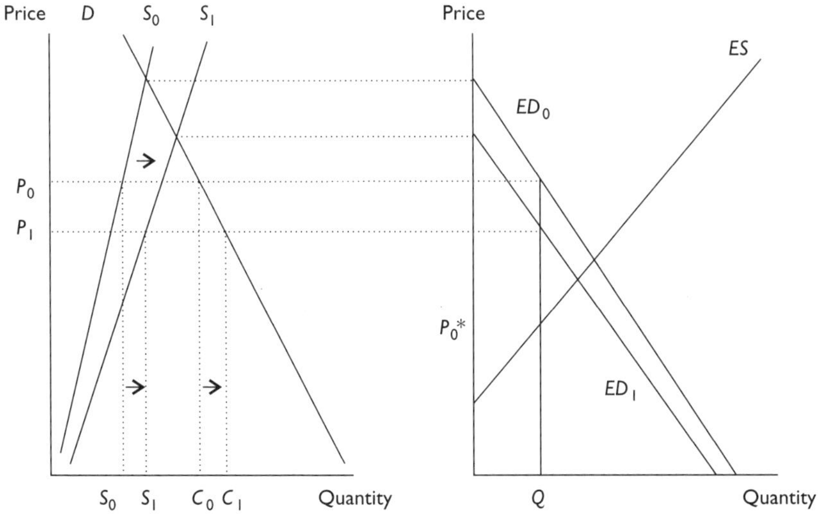

Figure 8.2 Multifunctional Subsidy with a Variable Tariff

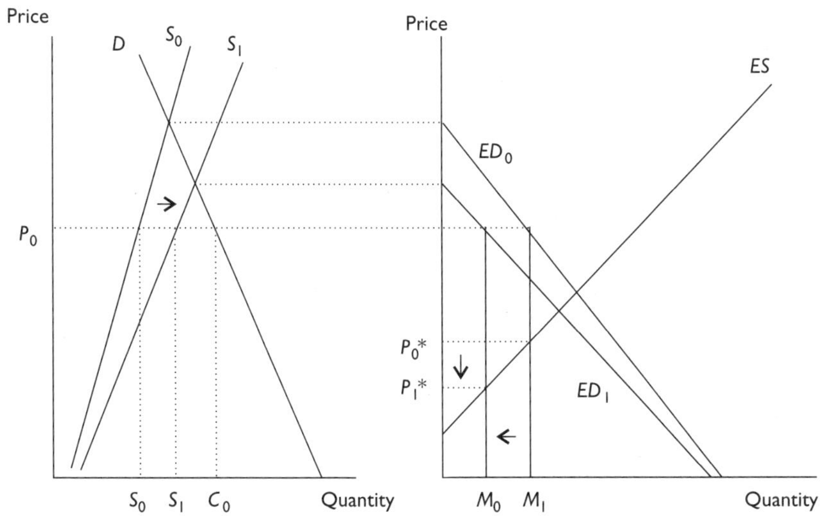

The perfectly inelastic section of the excess demand relation shifts along with the undistorted section to maintain a constant domestic price in the developed country, P_0. Increased output induced by the multifunctional subsidy is reflected in reduced imports, from M_0 to M_1. That induces a lower price in the world market and for developing countries P_1^* in place of P_0^*.

Other policy instruments can be analyzed with a similar framework. A tariff rate quota has a mix of tariff and quota effects on price variability (Abbott and Paarlberg 1998). When a tariff rate quota is used, multifunctional subsidies also have a mix of quota and tariff effects on price. The multifunctional subsidy shifts the excess demand inward. With a tariff rate quota there can be a regime switch from a tariff to a pure quota that is reflected in the world price transmission. If the excess demand is such that the tariff rate quota acts like a tariff, or if the subsidies induce a regime switch, the world price will be affected and there will be a spillover effect. But if excess demand always intersects the quota portion of the tariff rate quota-distorted excess supply, the world price will not change and there is no spillover.

Domestic policies play a role in determining any spillover. Tariffs may vary to maintain a minimum domestic price, as in figure 8.2. Other policies to consider include target prices, land retirement, and stockholding. A target price allows spillover from the multifunctional subsidy to the world price. Land retirement has an opposing effect and in concept could be designed to exactly offset the subsidy. Increased stockholding could also absorb the subsidy-induced output.

It is also critical to examine the entire package of multifunctional subsides. The formulation by Paarlberg, Bredahl, and Lee (2002) applies subsidy rules to a vector of agricultural outputs. That multifunctional subsidies expand the output of traded agricultural goods such as grains cannot be taken for granted. If subsidies were based on multifunctionality, there would likely be shifts among agricultural products. Output reductions would be possible for many major traded goods. Whether that would happen is an empirical question.

Price transmission from the world market to the developing country is also important. Unlike the situation depicted by equation 3, changes in welfare cannot be inferred from movements in the world market price.

The impacts of various policy regimes in a developing country when a developed country adopts a subsidy based on multifunctionality can also be understood using an open country demand and supply model such as that in figures 8.1 and 8.2. Because the subsidy is imposed by a developed country, for importing developing countries it is the excess supply it faces that shifts, while for exporting developing countries it is the excess demand relation that moves in response to the subsidy.

When the developing country uses an ad valorem import tariff, a multifunctional subsidy introduced by a developed country creates excess supply at the initial world price, increasing the excess supply relation facing the developing country. Imports expand, and both the price in the developing country and the world price fall. Tariffs allow price transmission, and falling world prices are a net benefit as consumer surplus expands by more than producer surplus falls. Because the developing country does not alter its tariff and imports expand, tariff revenues rise in most cases.

A much different outcome occurs if the developing country uses an import quota. Import quotas sever the link between the developing country's domestic price and the world price by creating a perfectly inelastic portion in the excess demand relation. There is the same rotation of excess supply, but under the quota imports remain frozen. Thus, the domestic price in the developing country remains unchanged, and there are no changes in producer and consumer surplus. The adjustment to the multifunctional subsidy is forced entirely on the world price, which falls. A falling world price causes the quota rent to expand. The degree of benefit depends on what kind of mechanism the importing developing country has to capture quota rents.

Some developing countries have adopted tariff rate quotas (Abbott and Morse 2000). Consider the case where excess demand triggers the outside-quota tariff before the subsidy is introduced. Introducing the multifunctional subsidy shifts the true excess supply, and the domestic price falls. If initial imports are at the quota, the shift in the excess supply can also cause the domestic price in the developing country to fall if it results in outside-quota imports. If the multifunctional subsidy-induced shift in the excess supply is so small that imports remain at the quota, there would be no domestic price impact, just as with a pure quota. When there is underfill, the low tariff initially applies. Introduction of the subsidy causes the domestic price to fall, but the decline could be by less than for a pure tariff because imports could expand to the quota level. In this situation the tariff rate quota dampens the spillover effect. An interesting aspect of this solution is that whereas before the subsidy there were no quota rents, introduction of the subsidy creates a new equilibrium with quota rents. If the developing country is not capable of capturing those rents, it could experience a welfare loss.

Once domestic policies are introduced, further complications can arise. A falling world price can hurt importing developing countries. If a developing country is running a price support system at a price above the world market level, a lower world price increases the cost of that policy. For example, assume that the developing country has a price objective. Before the multifunctional subsidy is introduced, a tariff provides adequate protection. Introduction of the subsidy lowers the world price. If the tariff is WTO bound, the developing country may not be able to raise the tariff to offset the falling world price. It must then defend the price objective using either costly direct payments or stocks purchases or both.

For an exporting developing country imposing an export tax, the additional output in the developed country lowers the price in the developing country and reduces the export volume on which that tax applies. A multifunctional subsidy introduced by a developed country rotates to the left the excess demand facing the exporting developing country. Exports by the developing country contract, and world and domestic prices fall. Consumers in the developing country experience a welfare gain, while producers suffer a welfare loss. The producer welfare loss dominates the consumer welfare gain, and export tax revenue is lower.

When an export marketing board in the exporting developing country sets the export quantity, the excess supply relation may have a perfectly inelastic section. The shift in the excess demand as a result of the subsidy does not alter the export volume. The price received for exports falls, but the domestic price does not change. The marketing board sees reduced rents from international trade.

A conventional trade model ignoring policy institutions suggests that spillover effects from a multifunctional subsidy in a developed country hurts developing country exporters and benefits developing country importers. But once trade and domestic policies are recognized, spillover effects are more complicated. Policy instruments that allow price transmission, like pure tariffs, variable tariffs, export taxes, and sometimes tariff rate quotas, have such spillover effects. Quantity instruments, like import quotas, state trading, and export marketing boards, may not allow price transmission or spillover effects unless the instruments adjust endogenously.

Would adoption of subsidies for multifunctionality based on the identified criteria generate spillover effects? Many of the most vocal advocates of multifunctionality are in European countries that tend to rely on variable tariffs and export subsidies as well as tariff rate quotas. Such policy instruments would generate spillover effects on world prices. Developing countries use policy instruments that can sever the link between world and domestic prices. A broad generalization might be that importing developing countries most frequently use policies that sever price transmission and would not see many benefits from lower world prices. Exporting developing countries have instruments that allow more price transmission and could be harmed.

It is important to recognize that multifunctional subsidies may not result in increased agricultural output in developed countries. It is not certain that multifunctional subsidies based on the suggested criteria for avoiding disguised protection would be positive once all externalities are considered. There would be output shifts among agricultural commodities, and some outputs could fall. Multifunctional subsidies could allow reinstrumentation toward green box policies and would be established in the context of a wider round of trade liberalization negotiations. Offsetting reductions in other policies could truncate or even reverse spillovers.

Developing Country Use of Multifunctionality

Discussions of multifunctionality have focused on developed country use of subsidies to provide externalities those countries value. But agriculture could have joint product characteristics in developing countries as well. If agriculture contributes to the preservation of a rural heritage in Norway, why would it not help preserve rural heritage in Indonesia? Could preserving cultural heritage be more important to developing countries than to developed countries, as suggested by the Korean report to the OECD (Abler 2001)? If flood and avalanche control are important multifunctional benefits from agriculture in Austria and Switzerland, why would they not be important in the Philippines? Developing countries also have an interest in subsidizing agriculture to gain externalities that they value, perhaps even more than developed countries. Are they capable of using the proposed framework to introduce subsidies?

While the externalities tied to agricultural outputs have considerable overlap between developed and developing countries, valuation and ranking of specific externalities differ. Identification of such differences is an advantage of focusing on the social welfare function instead of the agricultural production process. The difference between the marginal rate of transformation and the marginal rate of substitution is tied to the value of each externality—$\partial U/\partial E_j$. Perhaps rural poverty and rural to urban migration have more importance in developing countries? The framework allows such differences, and measuring these values is a key criterion.

Because multifunctional subsidies would not be harmonized across countries, some producers will feel disadvantaged. Under the intervention rule payments vary across countries because countries attach different social values to different externalities. Another source of differences in payments could occur because the links between the externalities and commodity outputs differ across countries. Countries with lower subsidies will argue that producers in other countries receive unfair subsidies.

A constraint to using multifunctional subsidies in developing countries is the cost. Drake (1992) estimates willingness to pay for landscape preservation in Sweden as $130 per hectare of grain, $250 per hectare of pasture, and $315 per hectare of woodland. Santos (2001) cites studies measuring valuation for several individual externalities in OECD countries, and the estimates are quite large in total value. Developing countries have limited funds, and many are under pressure from international institutions and donor governments to reduce public spending. Operation of a system of multifunctional subsidies in a developing country would likely require outside financing as part of development aid.

However, there is an equivalency between subsidies and taxes. The intervention is the difference between the marginal rate of substitution and the marginal rate of transformation. That difference can be implemented through subsidies or taxes. If developing countries cannot afford to subsidize activities that generate multifunctional benefits, might they be able to tax activities that do not generate multifunctional benefits?

An alternative to subsidies and taxes could be regulatory multifunctionality. For example, proposed legislation in Iowa would use regulations to favor livestock facilities having "family farm" characteristics at the expense of large, outsider-owned enterprises. Proponents claimed special value to livestock raised on smaller family units compared with large commercial units that may be investor-owned.

The literature on the differences between a regulatory system and price-based instruments, especially concerning environmental policy, is well developed. While economists tend to prefer price-based interventions for their flexibility, often policy intervention relies on a regulatory approach that sets specific standards. Examples include land-use restrictions, select zoning ordinances, livestock waste storage and disposal requirements, and total maximum daily load requirements for improved water quality. These regulations can occur at the local, state, or national level, and several have direct impacts on agricultural output.

The proposed criteria require an extensive, functioning system of implementation. Satisfying the criteria requires precise determination of the joint products from agricultural production. Comprehensive surveys may be required to estimate willingness to pay at varying levels of commodity outputs. The complexity of the task is evident in a survey of measurements of social values for externalities in OECD countries (Santos 2001). To what extent can countries implement multifunctional subsidies? Do countries have the capability to identify and measure the externalities? Can they develop the links between externalities and commodity outputs required under the criteria? If estimates are obtained, do the institutions exist to distribute the funds? Implementing the proposed criteria could prove difficult for many countries, both developed and developing. Regulatory multifunctionality might be easier to implement but could also be less effective in generating the desired levels of external benefits.

Another issue concerns the interactions between agricultural output interventions based on multifunctionality and existing policies that try to tap the "agricultural surplus." Many developing countries continue policy regimes with origins in dual-sector models that tax agriculture and promote industrialization. Subsidies to encourage agriculture could conflict with that policy environment.

Multifunctionality in a European country or in Japan could be argued to be intended to freeze the rural economy's structure, or at least to resist further structural change. Mellor (1976) argues that a key initiator of economic growth in developing countries is rising agricultural productivity and subsequently scale economies. Would intervention based on multifunctionality truncate or retard that process and sacrifice development objectives? Not necessarily, if the intervention is based on social welfare because the social value of all externalities such as rural culture, rural heritage, and economic development should be reflected in any intervention.

Food security is important to developing countries and is identified as an aspect of multifunctionality (Bredahl, Nersten, and Prestegard 1999). Does food security have an option value (the value of having a secure food supply in the future) or existence value (value of knowing that a country is currently food secure) that could be used to establish an intervention? The Norway report to the OECD cited by Abler (2001) suggests that an option value exists. Is food security related to a country's commodity output? The country reports prepared for the OECD indicate that of all the externalities considered, food security has the strongest link to output (Abler 2001). This may imply a stronger case for multifunctionality in developing countries than in developed countries. Yet food security is broader than the simple externality model presented here. Food security raises issues of trade policies, domestic policies, stockholding policies, and diversified suppliers. How do these attributes alter policy intervention in the context of the model that generates expression 1? Perhaps food security should be divorced from the idea of externalities and production-linked subsidies and addressed in a separate food security agreement.

The framework discussed here covers only local and national externalities. What about transnational or global externalities? Should developed country views about preserving indigenous cultures, rain forests, and biodiversity or shifting production to more traditional crops be reflected in interventions? Transnational externalities involve recognizing that domestic preferences can differ from those of the international community and reconciling differences in preferences when determining intervention. Could this be a way for developed country agricultural exporters to retard competition from developing countries? Might the United States, for example, argue for subsidies for landscape preservation in Brazil to hinder expansion of Brazilian soybean production? How might such subversion of multifunctionality be mitigated?

CONCLUSIONS

Using subsidies to achieve multifunctional goals is a contentious issue in WTO negotiations. Paarlberg, Bredahl, and Lee (2002) propose a means of bridging differences between proponents and opponents of multifunctional support. That framework demonstrates that there may be a role for production-linked subsidies. To mitigate disguised protection three criteria are proposed: explicit identification of the positive and negative externalities associated with agricultural production, estimates of the social value of the externalities, and explicit links to output.

Developing countries have had a limited presence in the multifunctionality discussion. This chapter considers the effect on developing countries of allowing multifunctional subsidies within the proposed rules. The conventional wisdom is that exporting developing countries would be hurt by lower world commodity prices caused by increased developed country output while importing developing countries would benefit.

Two types of broad effects are identified: spillover effects and developing country use of multifunctionality.

The spillover effects on developing countries transmitted through world market prices are uncertain. If multifunctional subsidies allow developed countries to shift more current support to green box instruments, overall support to agriculture could fall. Since a multifunctional subsidy on a commodity should recognize positive and negative externalities, it is not ordained that commodity support would rise. However, there would be shifts in support among agricultural outputs. When domestic and trade policies are introduced, spillover effects become uncertain. Policy instruments allowing price transmission have spillover effects. Policy instruments that sever price transmission truncate spillovers. Countries pressing for multifunctional subsidies use policy instruments that tend to allow spillover effects. But many importing developing countries use instruments that sever domestic to world price links, so spillover effects might not alter their welfare. Exporting developing countries are more likely to experience a spillover, and that would generally imply welfare losses.

Developing countries themselves also have multifunctional concerns, but they have additional difficulties in setting a policy based on multifunctionality. A major issue would be the cost of subsidies. An alternative might be tax equivalents or regulatory policies. The proposed criteria are difficult to implement. They require the capacity to identify and measure the social values of a set of externalities and their linkages to output. Multifunctional subsidies could be in conflict with policies that implicitly tax away agricultural surplus. Multifunctionality could be used to freeze and preserve the existing agricultural structure, which risks sacrificing agriculture as an engine of development. Some externalities in developing countries are transnational, so there could be differences between local and global preferences. There is a general concern that multifunctionality arguments could be coopted by groups in developed countries to stifle competition from developing countries.

BIBLIOGRAPHY

Abbott, P. C., and B. A. Morse. 2000. "Tariff Rate Quota Implementation and Administration by Developing Countries." *Agricultural and Resource Economics Review* 29 (1): 115–24.

Abbott, P. C., and P. L. Paarlberg. 1998. "Tariff Rate Quotas: Structural and Stability Impacts in Growing Markets." *Agricultural Economics* 19 (3): 257–67.

Abler, D. 2001. "A Synthesis of Country Reports on Jointness Between Commodity and Non-Commodity Outputs in OECD Agriculture." Paper presented at the Workshop on Multifunctionality, OECD, Directorate for Food, Agriculture, and Fisheries, Paris, July 2–3.

Bhagwati, J. N. 1981. "The Generalized Theory of Distortions and Welfare." In *International Trade: Selected Readings*, J. N. Bhagwati, ed. Cambridge, MA: MIT Press.

Bohman, M., J. Cooper, D. Mullarky, M. A. Normile, D. Skully, S. Vogel, and E. Young. 1999. "The Use and Abuse of Multifunctionality." White Paper, Economic Research Service, U.S. Department of Agriculture, Washington, DC.

Bredahl, M. E., N. K. Nersten, and S. S. Prestegard. 1999. "Multifunctionality: Concepts and Applications to the Cultural Landscape of Norway." Notat 1999: 21, Norsk Institutt for Landbruksokonomisk Forskning, Oslo.

Cahill, C. 2001. "The Multifunctionality of Agriculture: What Does It Mean?" *Euro-Choices* (Spring): 36–40.

Drake, L. 1992. "The Non-Market Value of Swedish Agricultural Landscape." *European Review of Agricultural Economics* 19 (3): 351–64.

Hodge, I. 1999. "Agri-Environmental Relationships and the Choice of Policy Mechanism." Department of Land Economy, University of Cambridge, Cambridge, U.K.

Johnson, H. G. 1972. "Optimal Trade Intervention in the Presence of Domestic Distortions." In *Aspects of the Theory of Tariffs.* Cambridge, MA: Harvard University Press.

Mellor, J. W. 1976. *The New Economics of Growth: A Strategy for India and the Developing World.* Ithaca, NY: Cornell University Press.

OECD (Organisation for Economic Co-operation and Development). 2001. *Multifunctionality: Towards an Analytical Framework.* Paris: OECD.

Paarlberg, P. L., M. Bredahl, and J. G. Lee. 2002. "Multifunctionality and Agricultural Negotiations." *Review of Agricultural Economics* 24 (2): 322–35.

Romstad, E. 2000. "Public Goods from Agriculture: Production and Provision Mechanisms." Department of Economics and Social Sciences, Agricultural University of Norway, Ås, Norway.

Santos, J. M. L. 2001. "A Synthesis of Country Reports on Demand Measurement of Non-Commodity Outputs in OECD Agriculture." Paper presented at the Workshop on Multifunctionality, OECD, Directorate for Food, Agriculture, and Fisheries, Paris, July 2–3.

CHAPTER NINE

Managing Import Competition When Developing Countries Liberalize Trade: India's Experience

Ashok Gulati and Sudha Narayanan

Since the Uruguay Round Agreement on Agriculture (URAA) was signed in 1994, there has been considerable concern in developing countries as to whether liberalization would be beneficial or detrimental to domestic agricultural sectors.

One fear is that a deluge of cheap imports would wipe out the production base of a large section of domestic agriculture, threatening food security and increasing the dependence on food aid. Also, liberalization could expose small and resource-poor farmers to dramatic fluctuations in prices, pushing them to the brink of destitution. These concerns assume even greater significance in the context of heavy export subsidization by many developed countries and the questionable food aid policies of some. Indeed, much resistance to import liberalization by developing countries has come in response to such developed country policies.

Against this backdrop, the key policy questions are:

- How can developing countries pursue liberalization while minimizing any adverse impact on domestic agricultural sectors?

- How can developing countries ensure fair competition in world agricultural trade so that when they liberalize they are not threatened by inflows of cheap subsidized exports from developed countries?

Unless ways are found to help developing countries manage import competition, further reform in agricultural trade could well be in jeopardy.

This chapter examines these questions within the context of India's liberalization experience, beginning in the second half of the 1990s. It addresses the competitiveness of Indian agriculture and India's experience with agricultural liberalization, looking at the role of domestic pressures from different quarters. The chapter then tries to answer the central question of how developing country governments can manage import competition when they liberalize.

INDIA'S POLICY BEFORE THE URUGUAY ROUND

Indian agriculture long thrived in an autarkic environment, with a panoply of controls governing international trade. Since the early 1960s, India had invoked the balance of payments exception of the General Agreement on Tariffs and Trade (GATT) to impose quantitative restrictions on imports, particularly on agricultural products. Imports and exports of several major agricultural commodities were channeled through state trading enterprises.

As part of a broader reform agenda, India began a unilateral effort to liberalize trade policy in the early 1990s but largely in nonagricultural sectors. Following the signing of the URAA in 1994, some limited adjustments were made in agriculture. India maintained quantitative restrictions rather than converting them to tariffs, invoking Article 4.2 of the URAA, which allowed for restrictions under balance of payments considerations. India was also exempted from the requirement of providing minimum access to exports from other countries.

In making its tariff commitments, India took advantage of the flexibility provided to developing countries to bind agricultural tariffs at ceiling levels that were among the highest in the world: 100 percent for raw commodities, 150 percent for processed products, and 300 percent for edible oils (except soybean oil). Preexisting commitments were retained for tariff lines on which tariff commitments had been made during earlier rounds or under Article XXVIII for renegotiations. In India's tariff schedule at the Uruguay Round all 686 lines at the six-digit level of the Harmonized System (HS) falling within the purview of the URAA were subject to tariff commitments.

INDIA'S LIBERALIZATION EXPERIENCE, 1995–2002

Given the limited change that the URAA implied initially, agricultural trade liberalization did not cause major problems during the early years of implementation. During this period average tariffs on agricultural products declined, and India unilaterally liberalized imports of some commodities. High world prices in 1995–97 meant that despite these policy reforms agricultural imports were not large enough to generate concern.

Recent Policy Changes

All this changed, however, in 1997 when the United States challenged India's persistent use of quantitative restrictions, citing improvement in the balance of payments situation.[1] The World Trade Organization (WTO) Appellate Body report (WTO 1999, p. 37) of August 23, 1999, recommended that "India bring its balance-of-payments restrictions, which the Panel found to be inconsistent with Article XI:1 and XVIII:11 of GATT 1994, and with Article 4.2 of the Agreement on Agriculture, into conformity with its obligations under these agreements." India agreed to eliminate the restrictions on 1,429 six-digit tariff lines in two installments in 2000 and 2001. The last quantitative restrictions on 715 six-digit HS tariff lines were eliminated on April 1, 2001, including 147 tariff lines pertaining to agriculture. After that, quantitative restrictions could be imposed or maintained on imports only for protection of health and morals (Article XX of GATT 1994). Such restrictions include imports of certain animal fats, prohibited for religious reasons.

When the last quantitative restrictions were abolished in 2001, a standing group of secretaries of concerned ministries and the director general of foreign trade was established as a kind of war room for tracking, collating, and analyzing data on imports of 300 sensitive items, some two-thirds of them agricultural products.[2] The national government also began to explore options for imposing temporary quantitative restrictions to counter surges of cheap imports. Further, the 2001 budget required that imports of certain agricultural commodities receive biosecurity and phytosanitary permits and meet other packing and labeling conditions already provided for in legislations.[3] In early May 2001, the government declared that imports of the 300 sensitive commodities could be routed only through designated ports and airports in India.[4]

These measures represented a shift to nontariff protection measures, apparently designed to counter the perceived threat of an import flood. While the biosecurity permit requirement remains in force, the port-of-entry restrictions caused an uproar among importers who had invested heavily in facilities at other ports. The order was withdrawn within less than a month.[5]

With the phasing out of import restrictions in 1999, India renegotiated tariff rates for some critical commodities that had been bound in earlier rounds.[6] Bound tariffs were raised from 0 to 60 percent for skimmed milk powder and to 60–80 percent for cereals and from 45 to 75 percent for rapeseed, mustard, and colza oils (table 9.1). Soybean oil, however, continued to have a bound rate of 45 percent. The renegotiated tariffs introduced tariff rate quotas, with lower

Table 9.1 Goods for Which Bound Rates Were Renegotiated

HS code	Description	Old bound rate	New bound rate	Comments
0402.10	Milk, concentrated or containing added sugar; in powder, granule, or other solid form, of a fat content not exceeding 1.5 percent by weight	0	60	A global tariff rate quota of 10,000 metric tons at a within-quota tariff of 15 percent applicable cumulatively to tariff lines 0402.10 and 0402.21
0402.21	Milk not containing added sweeteners	0	60	
806.1	Grapes, fresh	30	40	
Ex1001.90	Spelt	0	80	
1005.10	Maize, seed	0	70	
1005.90	Maize, other	0	60	A global tariff rate quota of 350,000 metric tons in 2000/01 rising to 500,000 metric tons in 2004/05 at a within-quota rate of 15 percent
1006.10	Rice in the husk (paddy or rough)	0	80	
1006.20	Husked (brown) rice	0	80	
1006.30	Semimilled or wholly milled rice	0	70	
1006.40	Broken rice	0	80	
1007.00	Grain sorghum	0	80	
1008.20	Millet	0	70	
1514.10	Rapeseed, colza, and mustard oils, crude	45	75	
1514.90	Rapeseed, colza, or mustard oil and fractions thereof; other	45	75	A global tariff rate quota of 150,000 metric tons at a within-quota tariff rate of 45 percent
1901.10	Preparations for infant use, retail sale	17.5	50	

Source: Government of India, Ministry of Commerce data, 2001.
Note: HS, Harmonized System.

Figure 9.1 India's Bound Tariff Rate and Effective Customs Duty, 2002–03

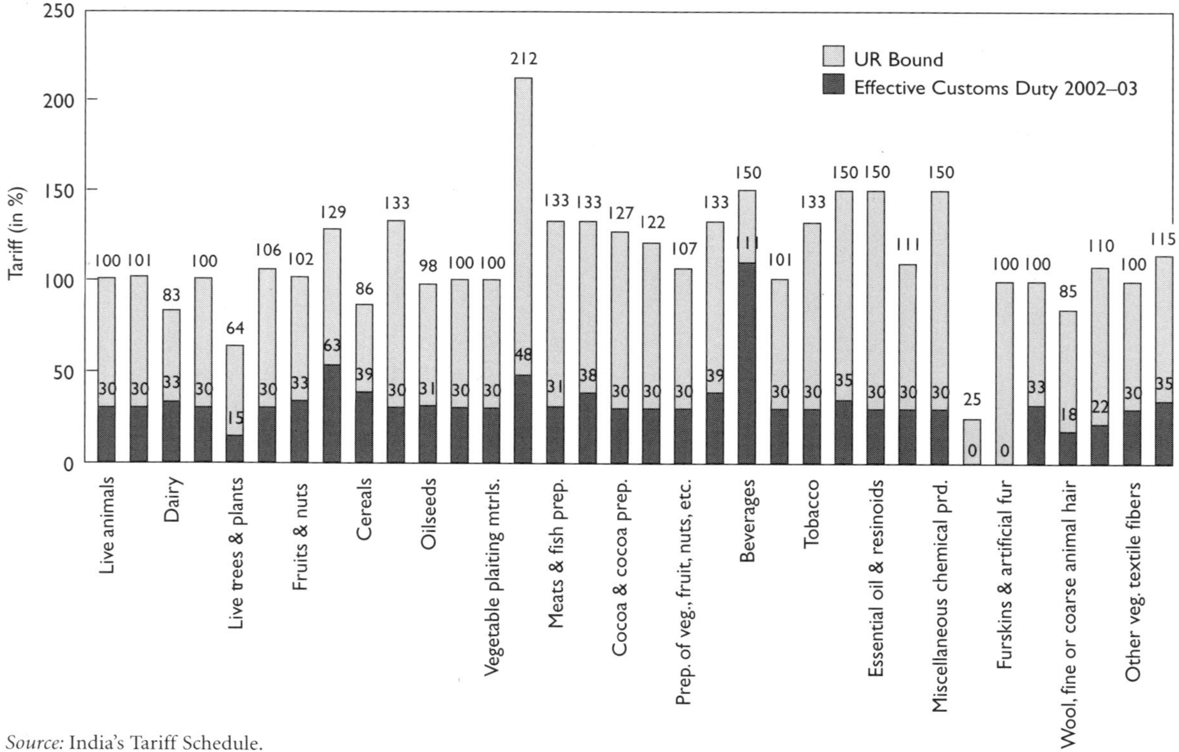

Source: India's Tariff Schedule.

within-quota rates for maize, skimmed milk powder, and rapeseed, colza, and mustard oils.

The Export and Import Policy for 2002–07 includes no quantitative restrictions for agricultural products, barring those for reasons of security and religion. The simple average bound tariff on agricultural products was 114.97 percent, and the average applied tariff as of April 1, 2002, was 34.5 percent.[7] The gaps between bound rates and applied rates are thus enormous (figure 9.1). Imports of a few critical commodities, including several cereals and edible oils, continue to be controlled by state trading enterprises (table 9.2).

India's Experience With Import Competition

Until well into the 1990s, agricultural imports were not so large as to cause panic (figure 9.2), despite declining tariffs (import weighted averages), because quantitative restrictions remained in place. Even after some imports were liberalized, imports were not a problem because of the high international prices during 1995–97. When international prices crashed thereafter to extraordinarily low levels, imports rose. Following removal of remaining quantitative restrictions during 1999–2000, imports registered a decline, perhaps owing to the increased tariff levels.

Table 9.2 List of Items to Be Imported Only by State Trading Enterprises

HS number	Export-import code	Item
1	100100 00.20	Durum wheat, other than seed quality
2	100190 02	Wheat for human consumption
3	100190 03.90	Meslin, other than seed quality
4	100200 00.20	Rye, other than seed quality
5	100400 00.20	Oats, other than seed quality
6	100590 00.20	Maize, other than for use for poultry or animal feed or as seed
7	100610 00.90	Rice, other than seed quality
13	100700 00.20	Grain sorghum, other than seed quality
14	1008	Buckwheat, millet, and canary seed and other cereals, other than seed quality
20	120300 00	Copra
21	151311 00	Coconut (copra), crude oil
22	151319 00	Coconut (copra), other

Source: Goyal (2002).

Note: Includes imports allowed only through specified state trading enterprises under paragraph 4.8 of the Export and Import Policy.

HS, Harmonized System.

Figure 9.2 Agricultural Imports and Tariffs in India, 1991/92–2002/03

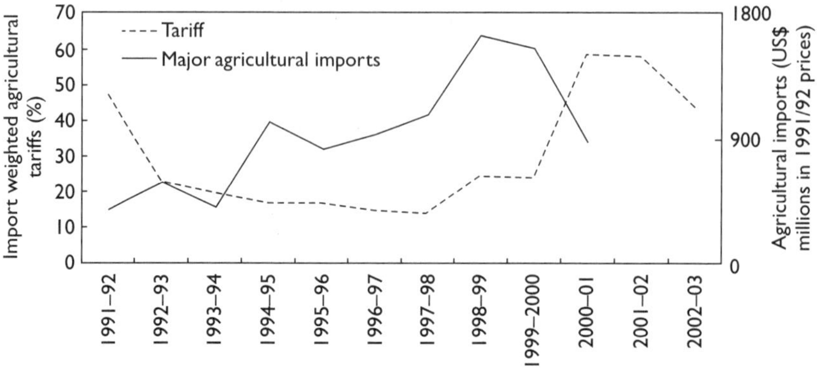

Source: Computed by the authors.

The real story of India's liberalization lies in the details, however. That requires examining the major imports and how they behaved. In the late 1990s, India's major agricultural imports were wheat, maize, pulses, oilseeds and edible oils, and milk.

At the time of the Uruguay Round negotiations, Indian agriculture was reasonably competitive (Gulati and Kelley 1999; Gulati and others 1994), so trade liberalization would not necessarily be expected to have an adverse impact. Commodities such as rice and wheat, India's major staples, turned out to be efficient import substitutes and export competitive for several years (figures 9.3a and 9.3b). Most other pulses and coarse cereals appeared to be efficient import substitutes, although not export competitive. The only major uncompetitive commodity seemed to be oilseeds and edible oils, which are produced at high cost in India. Milk was also of concern, although trends in the 1990s were encouraging (Sharma and Gulati 2002).

The study by Gulati and Kelley (1999) predicted that with liberalization India would be exporting 3–4 million tons of rice, about 5 million tons of wheat, and half a million tons of cotton, while importing some 1.5–2 million tons of edible oils. Other research concluded that India would be a major importer (36–64 million tons by 2020) of grains in the long run (Bhalla, Hazell, and Kerr 1999). The Gulati and Kelley study was based on filling the wedge between domestic and external prices (f.o.b. for rice, wheat, and cotton and c.i.f. for oilseeds and other commodities) for 1990–93 and making certain assumptions about world prices, such as they would be at a level that prevailed during 1990–93, and trade policies, which were free from any export/import controls. In the event, volatile world prices and India's evolving trade policy regime meant that things turned out a bit differently from their predictions.

Figure 9.3a Nominal Protection Coefficients for Selected Agricultural Commodities, 1991–97

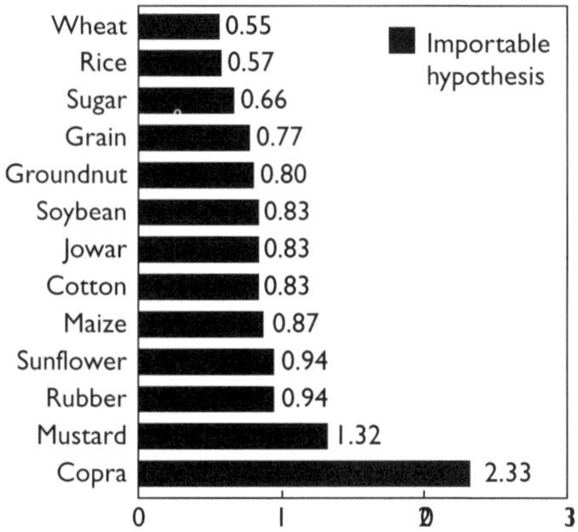

Figure 9.3b Nominal Protection Coefficients for Selected Agricultural Commodities, 1992–97

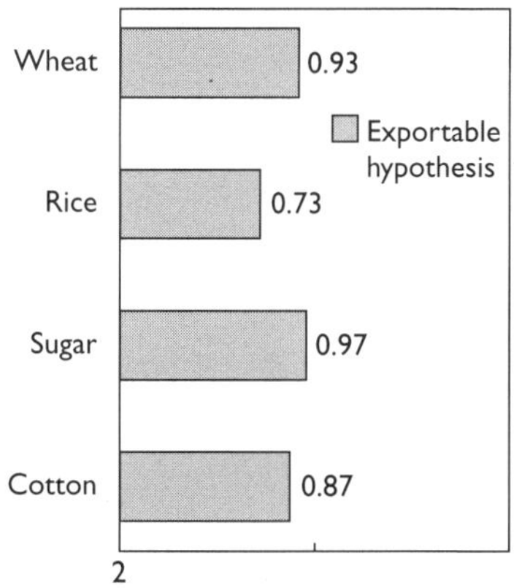

Source: Gulati and Pursell (2000).
Note: Under importable hypothesis, domestic prices are compared with the import parity prices, that is, cost, insurance, and freight (c.i.f.), while under exportable hypothesis, domestic prices are comapred with the export parity prices, that is, free on board (f.o.b.). For more details, see Gulati and Kelley (1999).

Edible Oils

Perhaps the most dramatic illustration of the impact of import liberalization on domestic sectors in India is edible oils. India had followed a rather successful import substitution strategy through the 1980s, using nontariff barriers to protect the nascent oilseed sector. As a result of protection, oilseed production grew more than 100 percent between 1980 and 1993–94 (from 10 million tons to 21 million tons). By the 1990s India was competitive enough to export oil meal (World Bank 1999). The protection also brought greater production stability by promoting diversity in crops and across regions. India did import some oils during the 1980s, though this was tightly controlled through the State Trading Corporation and the Hindustan Vegetable Oil Corporation. Imports of oilseeds, also through state trading enterprises, were practically nonexistent.

Protection was targeted to protect oil crushers rather than oilseed farmers. Oil processors were less efficient than oilseed farmers, as shown by nominal protection coefficients (figure 9.4). Oil processors were unable to take advantage of economies of scale because processing of groundnut and mustard, India's two largest oilseeds, was reserved for small-scale industries. By the early 1990s India had almost achieved self-sufficiency in edible oils, but domestic prices were about 60 percent higher than world prices because of protection.

Figure 9.4 Competitiveness of Oilseed Cultivators and Edible Oil Processors, 1990–95

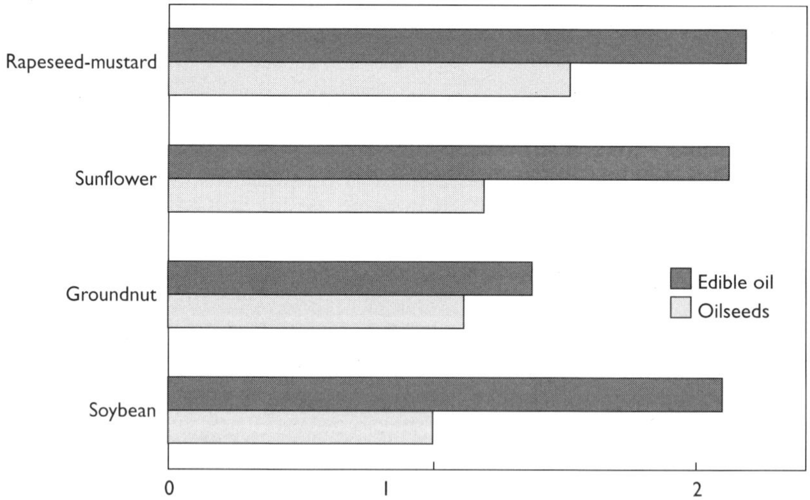

Source: Gulati and Kelley (1999).
Note: Nominal protection coefficients are much larger for edible oil than for oilseeds, implying that oil processors are less competitive than oilseed farmers.

Starting in 1994 far-reaching reforms were undertaken. The government began to liberalize imports of major edible oils (palmolein first, others a year later, with the exception of coconut oil) and to reduce import duties; that is, from 65 percent in 1994 to 30 percent, then to 20 percent, and finally to 15 percent on crude oils by December 1999 (table 9.3). International prices were high until 1997, so imports were low. When world prices crashed soon after, imports flooded in, reaching 5 million tons in 1999 and 4 million tons each in 2000 and 2001 (figure 9.5).[8] India's self-sufficiency in oils eroded drastically, from 97 percent in 1993 to 55 percent in 2001. Of all vegetable oil imports in the three year period ending in 2000/01 (4.57 million tons per year), palmolein and palm oil together accounted for 65 percent, soybean oil (degummed and refined) for 20 percent, sunflower oil for 10 percent, and rapeseed oil for 3 percent (figure 9.6).

Some sections of the industry felt that the government should not have lowered duties so drastically, especially for palmolein, particularly since the bound rates were considerably higher. Some argued that the duties had been lowered only as part of a deal with Malaysia for concessions in other sectors and to secure a rail contract (Hegde 2002).

Soybean oil imports, too, were cause for complaints. While bound rates were renegotiated for some oils and raised from 45 to 75 percent, soybean oil's

Table 9.3 Border Protection on Edible Oils, Pre-1994–2004

Period	Protection measure
Pre-1994	Quantitative restrictions
April 10, 1994	Quantitative restrictions removed, 65 percent tariff (concessional rate of 20 percent for state trading enterprises)
March 1, 1995, to February 1997	30 percent tariff
March 1, 1997, to September 16, 1997	20 percent + 2 percent
September 16, 1997, to May 31, 1998	20 percent + 5 percent
July 10, 1998, to December 1999	15 percent +1.5 percent
December 30, 1999	15 percent for crude oils for actual users
November 21, 2000	25 percent crude palm oil; 70 percent for refined palm oil
March 1, 2001	75 percent for crude palm oil; 90 percent for refined palm oil
August 3, 2001	Specific duties on selected oils
October 30, 2001	65 percent for crude palm oil

Sources: Solvent Extractors Association of India (2000); Indian government Economic Survey 2001–02.
Note: Tariff rates are those for actual users (such as refiners, vanaspati manufacturer). Typically, duties are higher for imports by traders.

Figure 9.5a Vegetable Oil Imports in India, 1980–2001

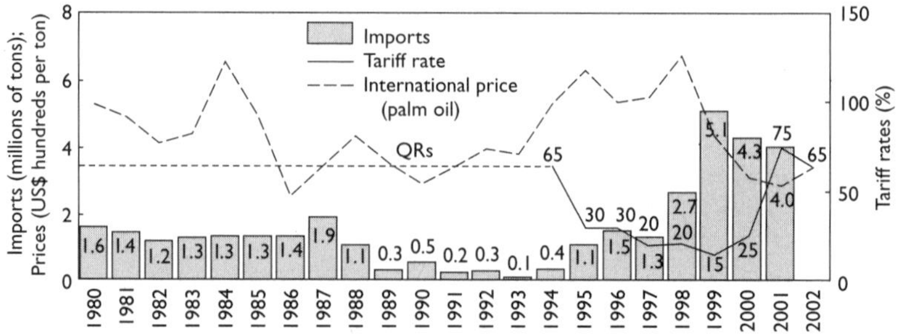

Source: Solvent Extractors Association of India (2002).

Figure 9.5b Net Imports of Palm Oil in India, 1980–2002

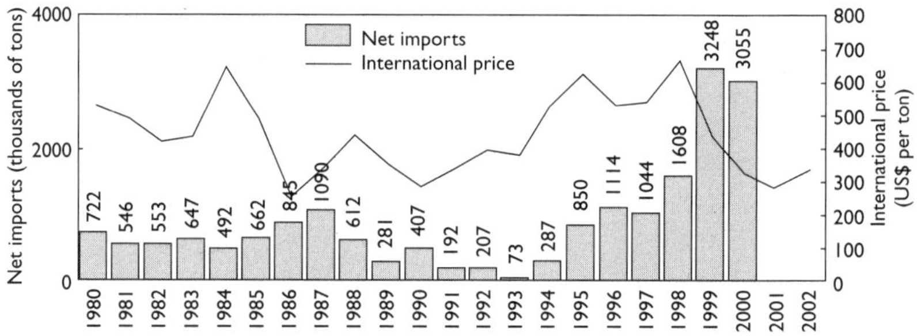

Source: Solvent Extractors Association of India (2002).

Figure 9.5c Net Imports of Sunflower Oil in India, 1980–2002

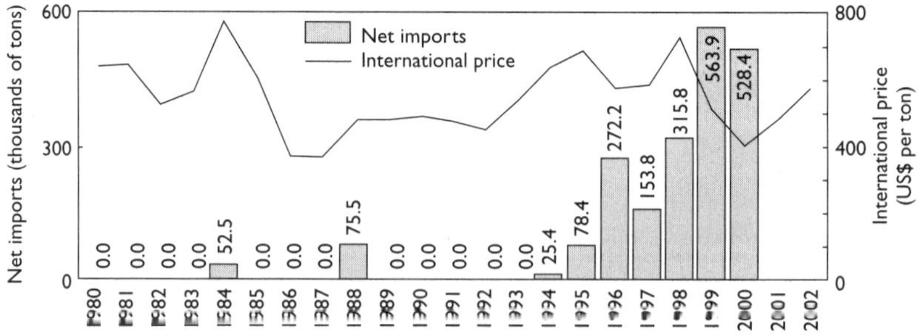

Source: Solvent Extractors Association of India (2002).

Figure 9.5d Net Imports of Soybean Oil in India, 1980–2002

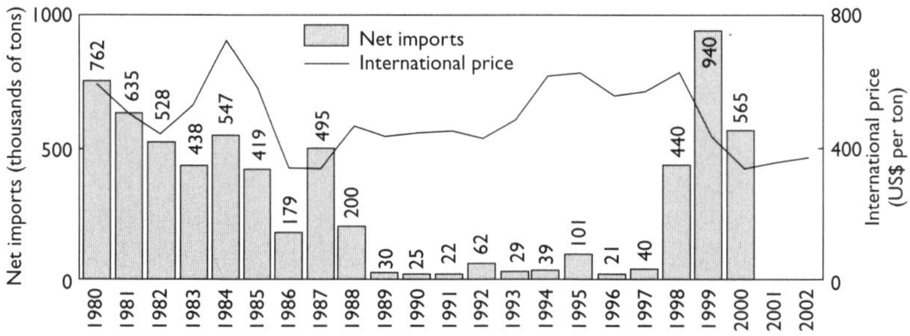

Source: Solvent Extractors Association of India (2002).

Figure 9.6 Composition of India's Vegetable Oil Imports, 2000–01 (average 4.57 million tons)

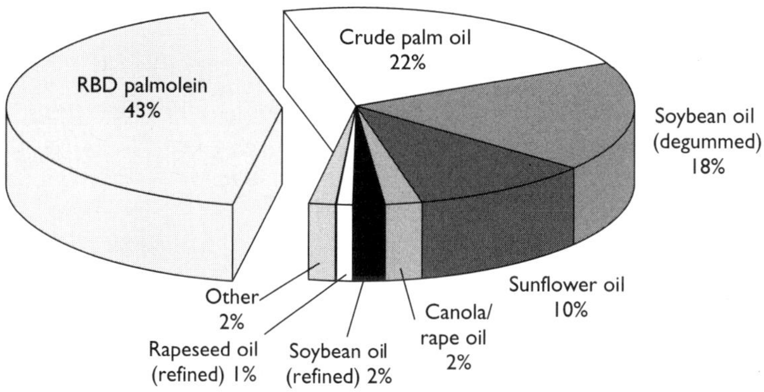

Source: Solvent Extractors Association of India (2002).
Note: Years refer to November–October.

bound rate remained 45 percent. With dramatic increases in soybean oil imports, demand grew for renegotiation of the bound rate.[9]

As domestic pressure from the vegetable oil industry rose, the government hiked the import duty on oils to 25 percent in November 2000 and to 75 percent in the 2001 budget, and then reduced it to 65 percent in October 2001 (see table 9.3). With these changes, and a good oilseed harvest, imports of vegetable oils declined between November 2001 and April 2002, to 27 percent less than the previous year's imports for the same period (Solvent Extractors Association of India 2002).

While oil imports were generally along expected lines, if somewhat higher than initially anticipated, cereal imports were more unpredictable.

Rice

Trade policy reform in the cereals sector also started in 1994/95, when India liberalized exports of common rice. The following year India's rice exports shot up from less than 1 million tons to about 5 million tons, making India the second largest rice exporter in 1995/96 (figure 9.7). During this time domestic prices were far lower than international prices. However, when international prices crashed in the late 1990s, India's rice exports turned sluggish. In 1999/2000 and 2000/01 India even began to import some rice, as domestic prices were comparable to international prices, blunting India's competitive edge. This change is reflected in the nominal protection coefficients during this period.[10] Although nominal protection coefficients remained broadly below 1, they do not take into account domestic taxes on rice (such as the purchase tax and mandi tax) of almost 12 percent, which make exports more difficult than the nominal protection coefficient would imply.

Wheat

Encouraged by the phenomenal growth in rice exports soon after export liberalization, India opened up exports of wheat in 1995. But as exports started picking up, pressure built on domestic prices. In 1996 the government hastily banned wheat exports and opened up imports of wheat at zero import duty.

Figure 9.7 Net Exports of Rice from India, 1980–2000

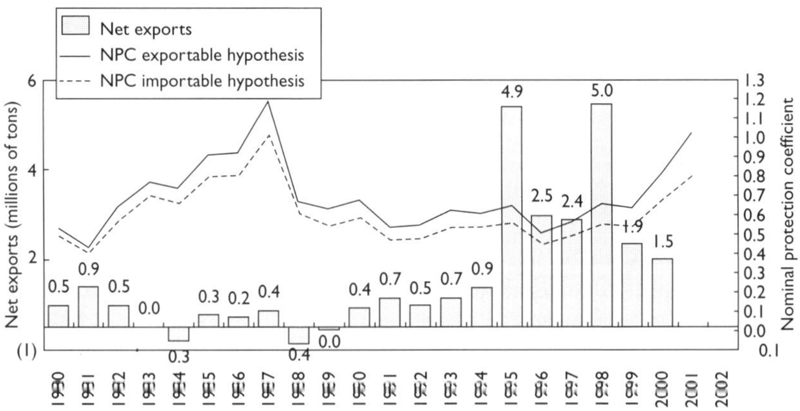

Source: Computed by the authors.

The motivation behind this policy change reflects an interesting aspect of the political economy of trade policy. Owners of roller flourmills in southern India (primarily a rice-growing region) have always complained about the constraints they face in procuring wheat (grown mainly in the north), arguing that the northern industry, which is closer to the center and has stronger bargaining power, gains from discriminatory pricing of the Food Corporation of India's open market sale of wheat (*Business Line* 2001). In 1997 this powerful lobby secured the right to import wheat freely for all roller flourmills.[11] Initially, this had little practical relevance since domestic prices were so far below world prices. But from 1998 onward, when the world prices of wheat and most other agricultural commodities collapsed, wheat imports increased dramatically, despite bumper crops at home (figure 9.8).

Thus imports were coming in even as government foodgrain stocks procured from farmers accumulated, reaching an unprecedented level of 60 million tons as of July 1, 2001. The government was forced to raise the import duty from 0 to 50 percent on December 1, 1999. The government also started offloading wheat stocks to private traders for export at concessional rates.[12]

Maize

Indian imports of maize have traditionally been controlled by state trading enterprises. Domestically, there is a minimum support price, although state procurement is rare. Unlike wheat and rice, which are staple foods, maize is used primarily as feed. Pressure to liberalize imports came from a strong lobby of industrial users of maize, which increasingly complained about the high cost of maize inputs. The feed industry is an important link to the poultry and livestock sectors, which are among the fastest growing sectors in India. The government, responding to domestic pressure, allowed the feed industry to import maize for direct use without a license, subject to registration of the import con-

Figure 9.8 Wheat Imports and Exports of India, 1980–2000

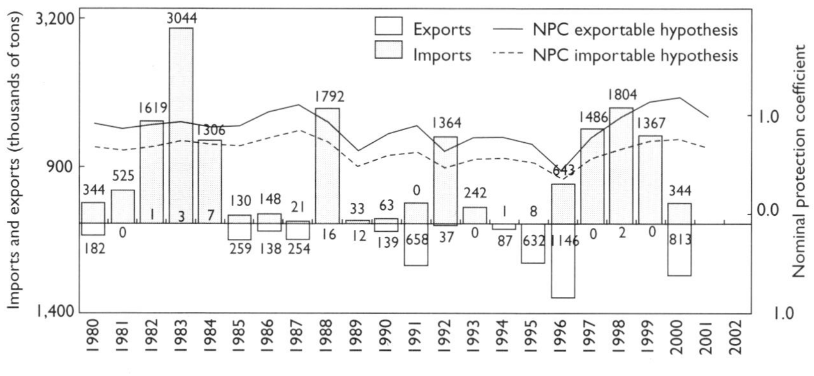

Source: Computed by the authors.

tract or letter of credit with the Agricultural Processed Exports Development Authority. However, imports of maize for other uses and imports of maize flour continue to be routed through state trading enterprises such as the Food Corporation of India.

While little maize was imported throughout the 1990s, when world prices started to collapse in 1997 feed manufacturers in India actively imported maize. In 1999 imports reached a peak of more than 200,000 tons, tapering off thereafter (figure 9.9).

A tariff rate quota was established when the bound tariff rate for maize was renegotiated. The within-quota rate was set at 15 percent and the outside-quota rate at 60 percent (the effective basic duty was 50 percent). The quota is distributed among eligible importers. Quota limits were set at 350,000 tons in the first year, gradually increasing to 500,000 tons in the fourth year. This implies potential annual imports of half a million tons.

The important dimension in the maize story is what happened on the domestic front. As was the case for wheat, bumper crops of maize in the southern states of Andhra Pradesh and Karnataka caused domestic prices to plunge, and farmers demanded that the state governments procure supplies to support prices. The states did so in 2000/01, but it was feared that such large-scale procurement could set a precedent and signal the beginning of regular procurements by state agencies in times of excess maize supply.[13] This would send the wrong price signals to farmers, who would begin to respond to the fixed minimum support prices rather than to actual market conditions. Moreover, with the tariff rate quota in place, there is increasing demand from farmers to institutionalize maize procurement to protect them from price crashes.

This, like the case of wheat, clearly illustrates the dilemmas facing developing country governments at the national and subnational levels: on the one hand imports of cheap maize and on the other hand domestic prices propped up through government procurement.

Figure 9.9 India's Maize Imports, 1980–2000

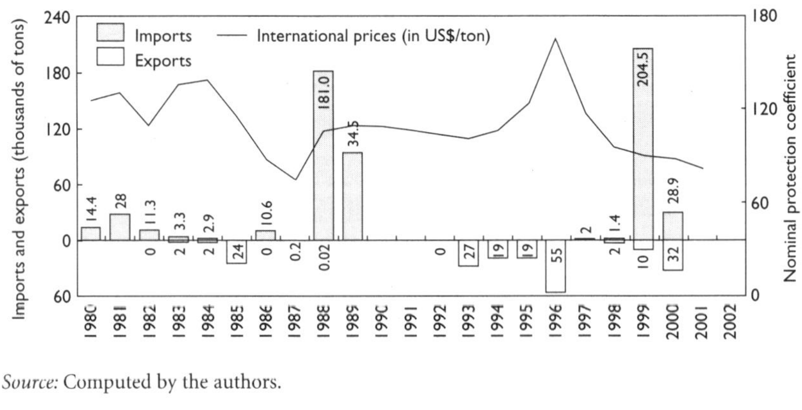

Source: Computed by the authors.

Onions

The case of onions also shows the interplay of political economy and trade policy and highlights the link between import and export policies. India has traditionally been an exporter of onions. In 1998 the onion crop in Maharashtra failed, but exports continued unabated, putting severe upward pressure on domestic onion prices. Onion prices rose tenfold in urban markets. Because onions are an important part of the Indian consumer's food basket, the so-called onion crisis became a politically charged issue. Onion exports were banned, and the government was subsequently forced to airlift onions from Iran and sell them to consumers, particularly in Delhi, at a subsidized rate (Desai 1999).

Dairy Products

During the early 1970s imports of dairy commodities accounted for about 50–60 percent of total output. Imports of most dairy products declined significantly in the 1980s and 1990s, except for milk powder and butter, which increased substantially in the 1990s owing mainly to low import duties (Sharma and Gulati 2002). Imports of dry milk spiked in 1999 (figure 9.10).

India had renegotiated its tariff binding for milk powder, setting it at 60 percent. A tariff rate quota is now in place, with a quota of 10,000 tons at a 15 percent tariff rate. The issue of import competition is essentially a question of policies in other countries. The dairy sector is heavily protected in many developed countries, and dairy exports from these countries receive high export subsidies, which make them artificially competitive. Even with distorted international prices, Indian skim milk powder has been reasonably competitive, especially since 1994. India's competitiveness would be even greater, however, if international prices were free of distortion. The case of dairy products highlights the need to look into the question of whether import liberalization of commodities that are highly distorted in world markets is a wise step.

Figure 9.10 Imports of Dry Milk in India, 1980–2000

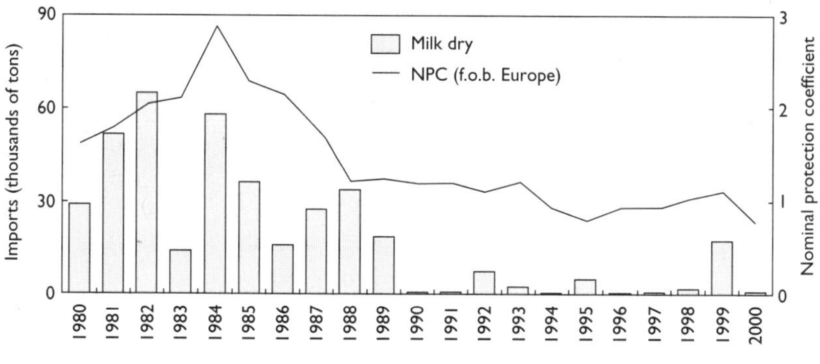

Source: Computed by the authors.

MANAGING IMPORT COMPETITION

India's experience with liberalization in agriculture reveals that managing import competition is a multidimensional problem and often sector specific.

As imports of vegetable oils suggest, an inefficient domestic sector can be significantly undermined by import competition. While this is to be expected with trade liberalization, it imposes significant adjustment costs on developing countries. While there may be efficiency gains for the economy overall, the losers (in this case the oil processing industry) will cry foul. To manage a smooth transition, governments need to acknowledge that and determine how to minimize the adverse impact of import competition without sacrificing efficiency.

Liberalization of the cereals sector highlights three distinct issues. First, even commodities that are efficient import substitutes can occasionally turn uncompetitive, particularly when world prices fluctuate substantially. A key issue is how developing countries can deal with such a situation, so that farmers, particularly small and resource-poor farmers, are protected from devastating price declines. Second, because of the link between domestic pricing and trade policies, trade policies are often held hostage by domestic lobbying groups, and developing countries need to know how to negotiate such conditions. Third, as the case of wheat clearly demonstrates, there is a need to recognize the link between import liberalization and export policy and to coordinate the two, particularly for commodities that are importables in some years and exportables in others. The experience with wheat and onions is relevant here.

Finally, as the case of dairy imports shows, sometimes managing import liberalization depends at least partly on the policies of other countries. The central issue here is how developing countries can influence policies in other countries and use the multilateral trade negotiations to advance their concerns for managing import liberalization.

Border Protection Policies

Perhaps the most important aspect for developing countries to consider is border protection to buffer domestic markets against dramatic drops in world prices that lead to import surges. Even when production in a country is competitive and imports pose little threat during times of normal prices, import surges can occur when world prices collapse. Under such circumstances the production base of vulnerable sections of the farm population can be wiped out. In the United States, Congress authorized four emergency packages of market-loss assistance payments during 1997–2001 totaling more than $34 billion (Gulati and Hoda 2002) to cope with the sharp fall in prices.[14] Developing countries, unlike the United States, do not have the resources to compensate farmers in that way. Thus they need to look to other measures.

Bound tariff rates, when set high enough above applied rates, offer some scope for raising tariffs when prices crash. When applied rates and bound rates do not differ, there may still be some scope for renegotiating tariffs (as India did), although compromise is often required. For instance, although edible oils are generally bound at 300 percent in India, soybean oil continues to be bound at 45 percent, which acts as an anchor on the overall tariff that can be imposed on other edible oils. However, in cases of dramatic and persistent price declines, as during the late 1990s, more effective measures are needed.

India and other developing countries might negotiate in the WTO for the right to use special safeguards. Countries can invoke special safeguard provisions to raise tariffs above bound rates when there is an import surge. Under the URAA, the right to use special safeguards has been claimed primarily by developed countries. The special agricultural safeguards provision is far simpler to administer in developing countries than are general safeguard measures, which require proof of serious injury to domestic industry. Also helpful for developing countries using special safeguards would be the ability to impose countervailing duties without establishing material injury (Gulati and Hoda 2002). Many developing countries lack the administrative capacity to prove that their countervailing duties against actionable subsidies are justified. Also important is abolition of the "peace clause," so that countries can impose countervailing duties equivalent to the export subsidy.

Other instruments for managing import competition in agriculture are tariff rate quotas, variable levies, and price bands. Though effective in offering import protection, these instruments have numerous problems. With tariff rate quotas it is doubtful that developing countries could administer the quotas in a transparent manner, without giving in to political influence. Moreover, it is in developing countries' interest to press for phasing out tariff rate quotas, whose use by developed countries has been found to severely restrict market access for developing country exports. Variable levies are incompatible with the WTO provisions, and a WTO panel has ruled that Chile's price band system was inconsistent with the provisions of the WTO since it acted as a variable import levy and often exceeded Chile's bound rate (WTO 2002).

Another possibility is seasonal tariffs, as proposed by the edible oil and oilseeds sector in India. Higher tariffs during the domestic harvest season and lower tariffs in the domestic lean season would protect the interests of both consumers and producers.

India's experience also highlights the need to coordinate import and export policies. While import liberalization tends to lower the prices of importables, export liberalization tends to increase the prices of exportables.

"Behind the Border" Reforms

Often neglected but equally important are domestic policy reforms. Domestic pricing and marketing reforms continue to be the weakest link in Indian agriculture. Thus, while the government holds mammoth stocks of food (estimated at about 60 million tons in January 2002), a large number of Indians suffer from poverty and malnutrition.

Because of political pressures from various interest groups, the government often ends up pursuing economically unsound policies. India's experience with maize shows what can happen. When maize was being imported following import liberalization, domestic prices crashed and farmers lobbied for state governments to procure maize. Two states bent to this pressure and procured close to 2 million tons of maize in less than a year to prop up domestic prices. When this happens repeatedly, farmers' production decisions are guided by administered prices rather than market forces, undermining the very logic of trade liberalization.

Rather than buckling to pressure for procurement, governments need to encourage the use of other domestic instruments and institutional innovations. Hedging instruments to ensure against price risks can help to protect farmers. Greater vertical integration of farmers with user industries could also help (oilseed farmers with vegetable oil industry, maize farmers with feed industry, wheat and rice farmers with the millers, and so on). Commodity futures trading would also mitigate risks arising from volatile prices.

At the Negotiating Table

A major problem for developing countries is continuing subsidization of exports and heavy support of domestic agricultural sectors by several developed countries, making their exports artificially competitive. Developing countries need to use multilateral negotiations to put pressure on developed countries to end such practices.

There is considerable skepticism about whether the URAA has resulted in liberalization in any of the most heavily protected agricultural products. Many Organisation for Economic Co-operation and Development (OECD) countries had protection levels in 1997–99 that were comparable to pre-Uruguay Round levels (figure 9.11). The European Union, for example, continues to rely heavily on export subsidies. Of the 25 countries reporting export subsidies to the WTO, the European Union accounts for almost 90 percent of the total, with the highest subsidies in livestock sector products such as meat and milk, followed by grains and sugar (figure 9.12).

Further trade liberalization by developing countries, particularly in heavily distorted markets, would be detrimental to their production base as well as being unfair. In the negotiations, developing countries could seek to gain substantial ground on the following points:

- They could pursue proposals to eliminate export subsidies that are scheduled in specific commitments.

Figure 9.11 Producer Support Estimates for Organisation for Economic Cooperation and Development Countries, 1986–88 and 1997–99

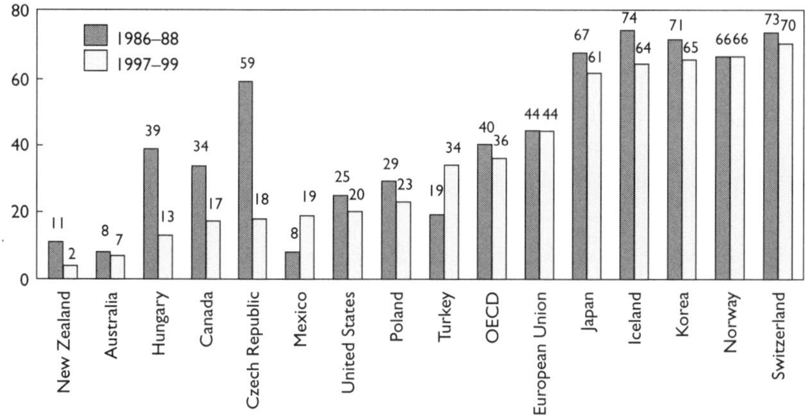

Source: OECD (2001).

Figure 9.12 Weighted Average Export Subsidy per Ton of Notified Subsidized Exports, Selected Commodities 1995–99

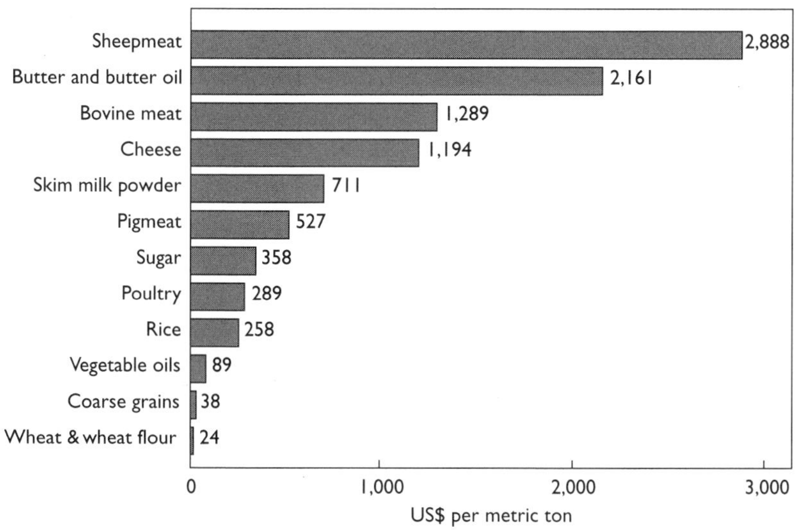

Source: Gulati and Narayanan (2002).

- In view of the large overhang of unutilized budgetary outlays and volume commitments in the United States and the European Union, a substantial down payment in terms of large cuts in export subsidy outlays and volumes could be sought up front, with no rollover facility of unutilized funds permitted.
- Other forms of export subsidy also need attention, since they provide a ready means to circumvent commitments on explicit export subsidies.
- The misuse of food aid as an instrument for disposing of surpluses should stop, without undermining the humanitarian objectives of food aid. One solution is to establish a multilateral institution to manage food aid operations. The institution could receive cash donations from donor countries and purchase food on the international market (Gulati and Hoda 2002).
- In addition to greater transparency of operations for state trading enterprises, their export monopolies must end and private firms must be allowed to compete with them. Stricter rules on export taxes and restrictions are needed to alleviate the food security concerns of countries that rely on imports.
- Domestic support in OECD countries must be substantially curtailed. If anything, movement seems to be in the opposite direction. The 2002 U.S. Farm Bill, for instance, represents a step backward on the road to liberalization (USDA 2002).

Experience shows that in multilateral negotiations, only the mighty count. Uruguay Round negotiations were overshadowed by bilateral understandings between the United States and the European Union. If developing countries are to influence the outcome, they would need to align with a potentially powerful third force, such as the Cairns Group, although how effective and cohesive a group it is remains to be seen. Also interesting is to see where China aligns. At the threshold of new negotiations, it seems that a negotiating group that included China, India, and the Cairns Group would be a force to reckon with, a crucial partnership for ensuring that developing countries do not face unfair import competition when they liberalize trade.

NOTES

1. The WTO provisions relating to the use of quantitative restrictions for balance of payments support requires that a member announce publicly the schedule for eliminating quantitative restrictions. India presented a case for a schedule of nine years for elimination of quantitative restrictions. Although it was acceptable to most developing countries, several developed countries objected to a phase-out period of even seven years. The United States, European Union, Canada, Australia, New Zealand, and Switzerland (and Japan as a third party) started dispute settlement proceedings against India. India reached mutual accords with all but the United States, agreeing to phase out its quantitative restrictions over a six-year period (1997–2003). The United States filed a dispute against India, and a panel was constituted in November 1997 to examine U.S. allegations that the quantitative restrictions were inconsistent with India's obligations under the WTO.

2. These 300 items covered a range of products whose production is reserved for small-scale industries in India.
3. For instance, imports of primary products of plant and animal origin are subject to biosecurity and sanitary and phytosanitary permits issued by the ministry of agriculture as set out in the Plants, Fruits, and Seeds (Regulation of Import into India) Order of 1989. Imports of meat and poultry products are subject to conditions regarding manufacture, slaughter, packing, labeling, and quality laid down in the Meat Food Products Order of 1973. Imports of food products whose domestic manufacture and sale are governed by the Prevention of Food Adulteration Act of 1954 must comply with the quality and packaging requirements of the Standards of Weights and Measures Rules of 1977.
4. The designated ports include Chennai, Mumbai, Kolkata, Vishakapatnam, Kochi, and Jawaharlal Nehru Port Trust; airports at Mumbai, Chennai, Delhi, and Kolkata; and the Inland Container Depot at Tughlakabad. Notification 11 (RE-2001)/1997–2002.
5. Notification 13 (RE-2001)/1997–2002 dated May 21, 2001.
6. At the time of the Uruguay Round tariffs were already bound at 0 percent for milk, spelt wheat, rice, grain sorghum, and millet. Zero percent tariff bindings were committed in 1947 for some commodities, like rice, plums, fresh grapes, and dried skimmed milk; at the Torquay Protocol in 1951 for maize, millet, and spelt; and at the Dillon Round in 1962 for sorghum. Negotiations were concluded in September 1999 with the European Union and in December 1999 with Australia and the United States and duly communicated to the WTO.
7. Almonds (0802.11 in shell and 0802.12 shelled) were excluded in these calculations because tariffs were specific rather than ad valorem.
8. These refer to vegetable oils (edible and nonedible) including castor oil, coconut oil, cotton oil, groundnut oil, linseed oil, maize oil, mustard oil, olive oil, olive residues oil, palm and palm kernel oil, rapeseed oil, rice bran oil, safflower oil, sesame seed oil, soybean oil, sunflower oil, tung oil, and other vegetable oils.
9. Curiously, the issue of soybean oil imports was hijacked by some nongovernmental organizations in a completely different context. Around the time when imports of soybean oil began increasing, in August 1998, cases of dropsy occurred in northern India, caused by adulteration of mustard oil, leading to a temporary government ban on oil crushing. This was seen by many as a conspiracy by foreign soybean oil traders to gain entry to Indian markets.
10. The nominal protection coefficients computed here use the minimum support price as the surrogate domestic price for 1981–2001. For the importable hypothesis the minimum support price is compared with seasonal international prices valued at the shadow exchange rate. For the exportation hypothesis the minimum support price for a product is marked up by a marketing margin (internal transport and handling costs), so that the f.o.b. Indian price is compared with the f.o.b. price of efficient exporting countries. Internal transport costs were calculated as the average rail freight rate per ton (from Ludhiana, Punjab, to Kandla port during 1990/91–2000/01) relative to the minimum support price for rice and wheat, or 9.3 percent for rice (paddy) and 13.2 percent for wheat. Handling charges were estimated as 5 percent of freight costs. As international prices recover to their long-run average, India is expected to regain its competitiveness in rice exports and emerge as an important exporter. Removal of rice milling from the small-scale industry list in the mid-1990s and modernization of the industry have also helped make India an emerging rice exporter.

11. Public Notice 31 of August 12, 1997, permitted wheat imports on behalf of Roller Flour Mills by the State Trading Corporation (STC) and the Projects Equipments Corporation (PEC). Public Notice 45 of October 5, 1998, permitted Roller Flour Mills to freely import wheat directly under the actual user condition or through STC, PEC, or Minerals and Metals Trading Corporation (MMTC) for milling only.
12. There has been some debate on whether this constitutes an export subsidy on wheat. The government of India claims that it is merely defraying the costs of internal transport, which is permissible under the URAA (Gulati and Hoda 2002).
13. For instance, in November 2000 the Andhra Pradesh Marketing Federation decided to procure maize directly from the farmers to ensure the minimum support price since the Food Corporation of India's purchases of maize had little impact on prices. Subsequently, as much as 100,000 tons were to be procured from farmers at the announced minimum support price. The situation was the same in neighboring Karnataka, where excess production caused the price of maize to plummet to Rs3,100 per ton. There were reported suicides by farmers. The Food Corporation of India started procurement operations in mid-November, continuing to end-March. By mid-March it had purchased 2.8 million tons of maize. This had a dramatic impact on the price of maize, which rose to Rs3,800 per ton (Narayanan and Gulati 2002).
14. In four consecutive emergency packages during 1998–2001 the U.S. government sanctioned payments of $6 billion, $8 billion, $15.3 billion, and $5.5 billion. The 2000 package included $8.2 billion in subsidies for crop insurance. A substantial portion of these annual payments was designated as market loss assistance to farm producers after the fall in world prices of food grains, undermining the decoupled nature of the production flexibility contract payments.

BIBLIOGRAPHY

Ahluwalia, Montek. 2002. "Economic Reforms in India Since 1991: Has Gradualism Worked?" *Journal of Economic Perspectives* 16 (3): 67–88.

Bhalla, G. S., Peter Hazell, and John Kerr. 1999. "Prospects for India's Cereal Supply and Demand to 2020, Food, Agriculture and Environment." Discussion Paper 29, International Food Policy Research Institute, Washington, DC.

Business Line. 2001. "The Southern Roller Flour Mills." www.thehindubusinessline.com.

Desai, Ashok. 1999. *The Price of Onions*. New Delhi: Penguin India.

Goyal, Arun. 2002. *Easy Reference: Customs Tariff 2002–03*. New Delhi: Academy of Business Studies.

Gulati, Ashok, and Anwarul Hoda. 2002. "Negotiating Beyond Doha: Indian Agriculture and the WTO." International Food Policy Research Institute, Washington, DC.

Gulati, Ashok, and Tim Kelley. 1999. *Trade Liberalization and Indian Agriculture*. New Delhi: Oxford University Press.

Gulati, Ashok, and Sudha Narayanan. 2002. *Subsidy Syndrome in Indian Agriculture*. New Delhi: Oxford University Press.

Gulati, Ashok, and Garry Pursell. 2000. "Trade Policies and Indian Agriculture." World Bank, Washington, DC.

Gulati, Ashok, Anil Sharma, Kailash Sharma, Shipra Das, and Vandana Chhabra. 1994. *Export Competitiveness of Selected Agricultural Commodities*. New Delhi: National Council for Applied Economic Research.

Hegde, D. M. 2002. "Oilseeds: Measures to Turn Self-Reliant." In *Survey of Indian Agriculture 2002*. Chennai: *The Hindu*.

Narayanan, Sudha, and Ashok Gulati. 2002. "Maize Policy in India." International Food Policy Research Institute, Washington, DC.

OECD (Organisation for Economic Co-operation and Development). 2001. *Agricultural Policies in OECD Countries: Monitoring and Evaluation 2001*. Paris; OECD.

Reserve Bank of India. 2001. *Handbook of Statistics on the Indian Economy*. Mumbai: Reserve Bank of India.

Sharma, Vijay Paul, and Ashok Gulati. 2002. "Trade Liberalization, Market Reforms, and Competitiveness of Indian Dairy Sector." International Food Policy Research Institute, Washington, DC.

Solvent Extractors Association of India. 2000. *SEA Millennium Handbook on Indian Vegetable Oil Industry and Trade*. Mumbai: Solvent Extractors Association of India

———. 2002. "Latest Updates Flash News." Solvent Extractors Association of India, Mumbai.

USDA (U.S. Department of Agriculture). 2002. *Farm Bill 2002: Frequently Asked Questions*. Washington, DC: USDA.

World Bank. 1999. "India: The Oilseed Complex: Capturing Market Opportunities." South Asia Region, Rural Development Sector Unit, World Bank, Washington, DC.

WTO (World Trade Organization). 1999. "India—Quantitative Restrictions on Imports of Agriculture, Textile, and Industrial Products." Report of the Appellate Body. WT/DS90/AB/R (99–1329), WTO, Geneva. www.ejil.org/journal.curdevs/sr4.html.

———. 2002. "Chile–Price Band System and Safeguard Measures Relating to Certain Agricultural Products: Report of the Panel." WT/DS/207/R, WTO, Geneva.

CHAPTER TEN

The Breadth of Policy Reforms and the Potential Gains from Agricultural Trade Liberalization: An Ex Post Look at Three Latin American Countries

Alberto Valdés and William Foster

If agricultural trade liberalization is so desirable, what explains the perception that liberalization has not been successful? This perception is particularly prominent in Latin America, a region of early developing country reformers.

Two factors seem to underlie the perception of lack of success. One is the expectation that trade liberalization would provide a tremendous impetus to the farm sector, without adequate consideration of the influence of other policies and external factors. The other is that much of the literature that has reinforced the opinion that trade liberalization, and policy reforms more generally, was a false promise based on a false premise. Although most of Latin America has significantly reoriented policy toward a more open trade regime, in several countries agricultural market and trade liberalization have been incomplete or have occurred in fits and starts, sometimes with backtracking and the reemergence of protectionism. Thus the true effects of unadulterated trade liberalization are difficult to measure.

Liberalizing trade was certainly a leading element in the reorientation of the economic policies of many Latin American countries. But it was only part of the story. Trade reforms took place in a context of larger structural reforms, macroeconomic adjustments, deregulation and privatization, and a general redefinition of the role of the state in the economy. When the economic policy shift began, most Latin American countries were suffering from low growth and serious macroeconomic disequilibria—high inflation, fiscal deficits, current account deficits, and financial sectors in critical trouble. Not only were economic reforms pushed by an ideological impulse toward smaller government, but agricultural trade reforms were implemented in this context of fiscal deficits and large foreign debt. These macroeconomic constraints induced large budget cuts, including cuts in subsidized credit, marketing programs, and infrastructure that affected agriculture. Thus agricultural performance over the past two decades and the impacts of reforms on farmers, particularly lower income farmers, were affected not only by trade liberalization but also by the macroeconomic constraints on government budgets.

Edwards (1986, pp. 185–87) noted early in the reformist drive in Latin America that "liberalization has always been attempted at a time when a major stabilization program, aimed at reducing inflation and solving a serious balance of payments problem, is underway. As a result of this, the costs of the liberalization process are confused with the stabilization program, with the consequent resistance to the liberalization effort." Moreover, as if speaking of Colombia and Argentina in the 1990s, Edwards added, "sometimes the transition between a repressed and liberalized economy is mismanaged at the macroeconomic level, generating additional costs, which can be associated with the liberalization process itself."

The gloomy assessment of trade liberalization is of practical concern today because developing countries are in the midst of a new round of multilateral trade negotiations. Both in their domestic policies and in their negotiating positions in the Doha Round, governments are being influenced by the perception of the unsatisfactory outcomes of previous reforms. Especially in many developing countries there is a reluctance to liberalize agricultural trade unilaterally, given the uncertain benefits from further liberalization.

Contributing further to such pessimistic perceptions are the uninspiring results of some large-scale trade liberalization models aimed at projecting the results of further reforms. Some models show gains for all, and some show gains for some and losses for many. From these simulations it is not clear that a country gains from unilateral liberalization after all. Why should developing countries liberalize, if the likely gains are so small?

To gauge the success of past and future trade liberalization, analyses should focus both on external and internal reforms and on the context in individual countries, not merely on the narrower aspects of trade reform. This chapter reviews the concerns about the results of past reform efforts and the projections of large-scale models. It also examines experience with reforms in Latin

America generally in the past two decades, especially as they relate to agriculture. The chapter then presents a detailed analysis of Argentina, Chile, and Colombia. Each country at one time committed itself to agricultural policy reform, but each country shows a distinct history of the breadth and depth of reforms, of the short- and medium-term outcomes of those reforms, and of the ability to sustain them. The chapter examines the historical data on performance indicators and emphasizes the importance of the quality and persistence of sectoral and macroeconomic reforms that would allow agriculture to find its place in world markets in the context of an open economy. There is a clear message for aid agencies on the importance of a comprehensive evaluation of the major constraints to greater flexibility in an economy and of facilitation of continuous adjustments in farm structure, output mix, and other factors in an environment of more open markets.

COMPLAINTS ABOUT THE RESULTS OF PAST TRADE LIBERALIZATION AND MODEL ESTIMATES OF FUTURE GAINS

Complaints about the results of the structural reforms in Latin America as they have affected agriculture center on several related perceptions:

- Growth in the agricultural sector following the reforms has been less dynamic than historical rates.
- Imports have been growing faster than exports.
- The sector has become polarized, with dynamic growth among a few producers and little or no growth for the majority, particularly small farmers.
- Agricultural employment has stagnated, and youths continue to leave agriculture.
- Poverty has not improved and may even have worsened.

One explanation for these problems—advanced, for example, by the World Bank (2001a) draft Action Plan 2001 for Latin America—is that the macroeconomic and trade reforms were not accompanied by a sufficient emphasis on a "micro agenda." These micro reforms would have mitigated deep-seated structural distortions in the rural sector, improving factor and goods markets and reducing the inequalities that limit the access of the poor to expanding urban and international product markets.

Others emphasized that the deregulation associated with the reforms accentuated the differences between commercially oriented farmers and those less prepared to take advantage of economic liberalization. What micro agenda there was led to the elimination of subsidies and services associated with credit and extension. Markets did not fill the gap equally for all, producing a degree of exclusivity in the distribution of the benefits of reform and leaving many smaller farmers unable to access the services that previously had been partially underwritten by the government. The divide between viable and nonviable producers grew with the unfolding of the consequences of the reforms, and there were no policies to mitigate the human costs of economic adjustment and the aggravation of rural poverty (Spoor 2000).

As the director of the UN Economic Commission for Latin America, José Antonio Ocampo (2001, p. xv), asserted:

> After a decade or more of structural reforms and adjustment policies, the expectations for a rapid and vigorous growth in the agricultural sector and for the resolution of the sector's principal problems are still far from being satisfied. . . . [O]ne observes a strong dynamism among a small group of regionally concentrated producers and a lack of dynamism among the majority of producers, especially the small and less capitalized. As a result, the aggregate statistics show production growing at a lower rate than in the past.

On top of these complaints about the results of liberalization, recent estimates of the gains for developing countries from further trade liberalization have been uninspiring (see chapter 8).

The study by Dimaranan, Hertel, and Martin (chapter 6 in volume 2) using the Global Trade Analysis Project (GTAP) model finds that if all countries liberalize agricultural trade there is an overall net gain of $30 billion annually but developing countries lose $4.8 billion. The study by Vanzetti and Sharma (chapter 5 in volume 2) finds total welfare gains from agricultural trade liberalization of all commodities by all countries of $24 billion, with developing countries capturing only $6 billion. Moreover, the majority of countries are welfare losers: 109 out of 161. Most of the countries experiencing welfare losses are developing or transition economies, a result primarily of rising commodity prices for imported food following the elimination of export subsidies and output-enhancing domestic support programs. Most developing countries experiencing gains produce commodities subsidized in developed nations. In contrast to these studies, a recent World Bank (2001a) study finds very large potential welfare benefits to developing countries from global agricultural trade reform of more than $140 billion annually, mostly a result of developing countries' own reforms ($114 billion).

Are the Complaints about Weak Results Justified?

Several questions need to be answered to determine whether the complaints directed against past trade reforms are justified: Are they based on a correct interpretation of the facts? Are the indicators implicit in these complaints the correct measures for assessing the impacts of structural reforms? Is any evaluation of such a diverse region premature, with less than a decade of data since the beginning of reforms for the majority of countries and even less for some countries? Should evaluation be restricted to the few early reformers?

There were some common expectations across countries about the impacts of policy changes. Reforms were expected to improve the economic climate for investment and the efficiency of resource use, resulting in better economic performance. By accelerating economic performance, reforming countries could expect faster growth in employment, higher incomes, and more resources to fund public social expenditures.

For agriculture, expectations were less optimistic about the sector's performance under the new economic regime. Sectoral reforms were to be implemented in the context of broader adoption of economywide market-oriented policies, therefore contributing to an improved economic environment overall. Nevertheless, for the farm sector the changes in economywide and sectoral policies would not necessarily guarantee increased exports, faster agricultural growth, or increased sectoral income. Sectoral outcomes would depend on the sector's potential efficiency at the start of reforms and on changes in the opportunity costs of resources as the economy adapted to the new economic regime.

Several analysts had emphasized the evidence of widespread "plundering" of agriculture prior to reforms through a policy-induced transfer of income from the farm sector to nonfarm sectors and government.[1] Economic reform and the removal of the antiagricultural bias of policy-distorted incentives (particularly associated with trade) were expected to unleash the farm sector, leading to faster growth as more investments were drawn into a now more profitable sector. After the fact, the evidence suggests that this expectation was correct for some countries. But for others the evidence is far from clear, in part because of the confused nature and depth of the reforms and, perhaps more important, because of changes in two key prices that are particularly influential for agriculture: the exchange rate and the interest rate.

The debates leading to the policy changes seem to have given little attention to whether the proposed new model of rural development was exclusionary or inequitable within the agricultural sector. The reforms were expected to have a differential impact within agriculture for producers of exportable, importable, and nontradable crops, but concerns about equity were diffuse. Broadly speaking, the reforms would end the policy-induced implicit and inequitable income transfers out of agriculture.

In addition, the removal of the anti-export bias was expected to have a positive effect on employment and wages by expanding the production of exportables, with their relatively higher labor intensity. Thus workers, at least in the longer term, would benefit more than capitalists. Another equity concern was the possible adverse effects on low-income consumers. The reforms were expected to result in higher prices of food, which makes up a larger share of expenditures in lower income households. The initial evidence, however, tended to mitigate this concern early in the debate,[2] and the results of the reforms have all but eliminated this equity concern.

The Shift in Emphasis in the Debate over Reforms: Were Reforms Exclusionary?

The emphasis of the debate over structural reforms has shifted from the productive and export potential of agriculture to the difficulties resulting from a liberalized economy for import-competing farmers, and from consumers and farmers broadly defined to the more specifically defined rural and farming poor. While the reforms were expected to result in greater competition for farmers producing import-competing goods, this received little attention because of the belief that Latin America's status as a predominately net food and net agriculture exporting region would persist following the reforms.

This sanguine disinterest in the effects of reform on the import-competing sector is now understood to have been based on a misinterpretation of the evidence.[3] Furthermore, the difficulties of import-competing farmers and specific regions have now gained greater political visibility simply from the contrast of their plight with the successes of other farmers and regions. Whether farmers benefited from the reforms depended strongly on their ability to change cropping patterns, adapt new technologies, increase capital intensity, and integrate into marketing chains that might benefit from reform, especially agro-industrial chains oriented toward export markets.[4]

Producers of importables, generally protected before the reforms, had much less protection after the reforms. Who are these farmers today? Many are smaller farmers or regionally concentrated farmers, as in Chile, the Dominican Republic, and parts of Brazil. In some countries, however, such as Colombia, small farmers tend to produce nontradables for local markets and so were neither helped nor harmed directly by trade liberalization.[5] But beyond the simple fact of whether a farmer produces an importable good is the question of why a farmer would remain in a sector that had lost out in the new environment of open-market-oriented policies. Examination of this issue reveals the difficulties and stagnation of the import-competing sector and the unresolved problems of the rural and farming poor, both discussed in the following sections.

The criticism that the structural reforms led to an exclusionary model of agricultural development, with a few commercially successful large operations and many poor small farmers—is almost certainly an exaggeration. Nevertheless, it is worth asking whether agricultural development would have been any less exclusionary without the reforms.

Unrelated to the processes of reform, changes disproportionately favoring larger commercial operations were already occurring in agriculture. The diffusion of new technologies had contributed to increases in the returns to more capital-intensive methods of farming and to complementary tradable inputs. The increasing capital intensity of agriculture had already made the sector more sensitive to interest rates and to credit constraints and less sensitive to the cost of labor (Mundlak 1999) the main cost advantage of being a small farmer.[6]

Before the structural reforms, subsidized credit relieved some of the pressures related to this increasing emphasis on capital, including human capital, while import restrictions raised the price of tradable inputs potentially used more intensively by larger commercial enterprises. To the extent that smaller producers specialized in import-competing activities, trade restrictions in product markets also held back an uneven development in the sector.[7] With the reforms, subsidized credit was reduced, the relative price of tradable inputs fell, and the price of exportables relative to importables rose. These conditions would be expected to result in an increasing concentration of production in the commercial farm sector.

A REVIEW OF REFORM EFFORTS AND AGRICULTURAL PERFORMANCE IN LATIN AMERICA

This analysis of the effects of reforms in Latin America looks at the differences between early and late reformers, at differential impacts within the agricultural sector, and at the effect on food security.

A Comparison of Early and Late Reformers

One way to measure the speed and breadth of the reform process is to compare early and late reformers, as in the case of trade reform (table 10.1). Trade reforms in Latin America have been well documented (see, for example Edwards 1993) and include tariff reduction, the lessening of tariff dispersion, and the reduction (or elimination) of nontariff barriers in almost every country since the mid-1980s (table 10.2). Trade reforms affect all tradables, however, not just agriculture.

There is less information on other policy reforms affecting Latin American agriculture. There has been some systematic work on economywide reforms in Latin American countries, notably by Lora (1997) and Morley, Machado, and Pettinato (1999). Morley, Machado, and Pettinato develop an index of structural reforms covering five policy areas (trade, tax, finance, the capital account, and privatization). They find significant differences among Latin American countries in the timing and extent of reforms. While most countries reduced tariffs and liberalized the domestic financial sector (important reforms for agriculture), fewer countries moved to decontrol the foreign capital account and even fewer agreed on privatization and tax reform (table 10.3).

For analyzing agriculture, however, the Morley, Machado, and Pettinato index is of limited applicability. The index does not capture such less easily observed reforms as port management or reforms in factor and service markets (other than in finance) that affected agricultural performance directly, through factor price changes, and indirectly, through marketing and transport costs. In Chile, for example, land, labor, and water market reforms produced incentives for investment attached to land, and port and transport reforms were extremely important for the growth of exports, especially perishables.

Table 10.1 Degree of Trade Liberalization in Selected Latin American Countries, 1980s and 1990s

Degree of liberalization	Mid to late 1980s	Mid to late 1990s
High	Bolivia, Chile, Mexico	Argentina, Bolivia, Chile, Peru
Medium	Colombia, Costa Rica	Brazil, Colombia,[a] Costa Rica, Mexico
Minimal	Argentina, Brazil, Peru	

Source: Spoor (2000, p. 151).

a. Colombia experienced a significant turn toward free markets in the early 1990s, but by 1995 had retreated nearly to prior levels of protectionism for the agricultural sector.

Table 10.2 Changes in Tariffs and Nontariff Barriers in Latin America, 1985–92 (percent)

	Average tariff protection[a]		Average nontariff barrier coverage	
Country	**1985**	**1991–92**	**1985–87**	**1991–92**
Early reformers				
Bolivia	20.0	8.0	25.0	0.0
Chile	36.0	11.0	10.1	0.0
Mexico	34.0	4.0	12.7	20.0
Recent reformers				
Costa Rica	92.0	16.0	0.8	0.0
Uruguay	32.0	12.0	14.1	0.0
Very recent reformers				
Argentina	28.0	15.0	31.9	8.0
Brazil	80.0	21.1	35.3	10.0
Colombia	83.0	6.7	73.2	1.0
Guatemala	50.0	19.0	7.4	6.0
Nicaragua	54.0	—	27.8	—
Paraguay	71.7	16.0	9.9	0.0
Peru	64.0	15.0	53.4	0.0
Venezuela	30.0	17.0	44.1	5.0
Other				
Ecuador	50.0	18.0	59.3	—
Average	51.8	13.8	28.9	4.2

Source: Edwards (1993, table 5.2).

Note: Country classification is based on Edwards (1993). All averages are unweighted.

—Not available.

a. The unweighted average of total charges (tariffs plus paratariffs).

Table 10.3 Economywide Reforms in Latin America by Period and Type

Period	Trade	Tax	Financial	Capital account	Privatization
1970	None	None	None	Costa Rica Venezuela Argentina	Paraguay Peru El Salvador Guatemala Honduras Uruguay Argentina Brazil Colombia Costa Rica Dominican Republic
1970–85	Chile Bolivia El Salvador	Uruguay Chile	Colombia Uruguay Chile	*Backsliding in Costa Rica Venezuela Argentina*	*Backsliding in Paraguay Peru, Costa Rica, Colombia*
1986–90	Argentina Colombia Costa Rica Guatemala Mexico Paraguay Uruguay Venezuela	Bolivia Brazil	Paraguay Bolivia El Salvador Brazil Argentina Mexico Costa Rica	Bolivia Costa Rica Guatemala Jamaica	Paraguay Peru
1991–95	Brazil Dominican Republic Ecuador Honduras Jamaica Peru	Costa Rica El Salvador Paraguay	Peru Dominican Republic Ecuador Guatemala Honduras Jamaica	Argentina Dominican Republic Ecuador El Salvador Honduras Peru Venezuela	Brazil Chile Colombia Costa Rica Mexico

Source: Morley, Machado, and Pettinato (1999).

Moreover, their index of trade reform does not capture the effects of trade preferences, particularly significant for agriculture.

For a sample of 14 Latin American reformers, the growth rate of agricultural exports exceeded that of agricultural GDP during the decade of the 1990s for all countries except the Dominican Republic and Honduras (table 10.4). The average growth rate of agricultural GDP for Chile, the earliest reformer in Latin America, exceeded that of all other Latin American countries in both the

Table 10.4 Agricultural Performance of Early and Later Reformers in Latin America

Country	Year of reform	Growth rates of agricultural GDP[a] 1980–89	Growth rates of agricultural GDP[a] 1990–99	Growth rates of agricultural exports[b] 1980–89	Growth rates of agricultural exports[b] 1990–99
Earliest reformer					
Chile	1975	5.81	4.74	11.98	11.81
Early reformers					
Bolivia	1985	1.11	3.28	14.16	15.19
Costa Rica	1986	3.33	3.38	3.48	9.36
Mexico	1985	0.31	1.92	5.84	11.48
Average early reformers		1.58	2.86	7.83	12.01
Later reformers					
Argentina	1990	0.65	3.69	1.42	8.74
Brazil	1990	3.35	2.82	1.10	4.45
Colombia	1990	2.71	1.59	0.31	4.28
Ecuador	1991	4.30	2.57	3.45	10.48
El Salvador	1989	−2.17	2.02	−10.00	8.92
Guatemala	1988	1.01	2.95	−2.14	6.86
Peru	1990	3.27	3.99	4.31	10.18
Uruguay	1990	0.70	2.45	6.51	5.15
Honduras, all years	1990	2.99	1.66	0.73	−1.02
Honduras, excluding 1999[c]			2.82		2.83
Average later reformers[d]		1.87	2.77	0.63	6.88
Others					
Dominican Republic	?	1.44	2.62	0.04	−1.42
Average, all		2.19	2.93	1.61	6.57

Source: Authors' compilation based on data from the Inter-American Development Bank.
— Not available.
a. Agricultural GDP includes crops, livestock, forestry, and fisheries.
b. Includes only crops and livestock.
c. The year Honduras was devastated by Hurricane Mitch.
d. Uses Honduran data excluding 1999.

1980s and 1990s, consistent with the hypothesis that early and comprehensive reforms can have a positive, sustained effect on agricultural growth.

There is an obvious positive correlation between reform and growth of the agricultural sector overall and of agricultural exports. Following reforms, growth rates of agricultural GDP increased in the 1990s in all countries except Brazil, Colombia, Ecuador, and Honduras.

The impact of the reforms is even more striking for agricultural exports. Agricultural exports expanded in all countries but the Dominican Republic and Uruguay (and excluding Honduras, whose results are skewed by the devastation caused by Hurricane Mitch in 1999). The increase in export growth rates is striking between the 1980s and the 1990s. Average export growth rates rose from 7.83 percent a year to 12.01 percent a year among middle reformers, and from 0.63 percent to 6.88 percent a year for later reformers.

Trade liberalization also appears to have encouraged diversification of exports. Exports of fruit grew considerably in Brazil, Chile, Costa Rica, Dominica, Mexico, Panama, and St. Lucia. And while traditional tropical fruit exports grew, liberalization also spurred an increase in nontraditional export crops (such as soybeans in Argentina and Brazil) and led to experimentation in export products, with several successes (asparagus in Peru, tomatoes and mangos in Mexico; see Paz and Valdés 2000).

The expansion of agricultural exports, especially of perishables, occurred in an environment of simultaneous changes attributable to multiple economy-wide reforms: modernization of ports, deregulation and privatization of telecommunications, domestic and foreign direct investments in processing and marketing channels, and the adoption of new technologies for processing, storage, and shipment.[8] It would be difficult to isolate the effects of trade liberalization from the myriad impacts of general economic reforms, deregulation, and privatization on the supply chain of agricultural products.

Nonetheless, it is clear that reforms in Latin America led to an increase in the "tradability" of agriculture—the ratio of agricultural trade (exports and imports) to total agricultural GDP (table 10.5). For 18 Latin American countries the tradability index rose from an average of 74 percent in 1990 to 87 percent in 1996. Tradability increases were particularly large in Argentina, Costa Rica, Chile, Ecuador, El Salvador, Mexico, and Venezuela. For all countries except Brazil and Peru tradability in 1996 was close to or above 50 percent.[9] With the increase in tradability agricultural sectors become more exposed to changes in world prices and exchange rates and to shifts in foreign market conditions generally.

Differential Impacts within Agriculture

Reforms affected agricultural subsectors in different ways. Perhaps the most useful way to distinguish effects is by production of exports, of import-competing goods, and of home or nontradable goods (often produced predominantly by small farmers) and by farm size and geographic region. There are at least three well-documented studies that show that policy reforms affected producers differently according to these characteristics and over time: Helfand and Castro de Rezende (2000) for Brazil, Jaramillo (1998) for Colombia, and the World Bank (2003) for Nicaragua.

Producers of exportables generally gained, as did wage-earners in agriculture and processing, because export products tend to be the most labor intensive. All else being equal, the farmers who could take advantage of the expanding export sector were those who were able to invest and to bear the price risks

Table 10.5 Tradability Indices in Agriculture in Latin America and the Caribbean (percent)

Country	1990	1996
Argentina	45	68
Brazil	17	24
Colombia	30	48
Costa Rica	82	130
Chile	53	80
Ecuador	58	89
El Salvador	45	71
Guatemala	33	48
Honduras	121	99
Jamaica	206	161
Mexico	52	79
Nicaragua	81	84
Panama	70	73
Paraguay	55	55
Peru	32	38
Dominican Republic	46	50
Uruguay	79	86
Venezuela	36	65
Simple average	74	87

Source: Quiroz (2000).
Note: The tradability index is the value of agricultural exports plus agricultural imports divided by agricultural GDP.

associated with export markets. These were mainly larger, commercial operations. As documented for Chile in the early reform process, only a minor share of small farmers could participate as producers in the expanding export growth of fruits and vegetables (Carter and Mesbah 1993), although many participated as wage earners, especially in postharvest activities (for example, in packing houses).[10]

Import competing producers likely lost in the short run, but their welfare in the longer run depends on their capacity to increase productivity and change cropping patterns. In some regions farmers had little flexibility to increase productivity and adjust their output mix, and as a consequence these farmers remain critical of trade liberalization. One such group was the *ejidatarios* in central Mexico, who were harmed by the reduced protection of traditional grains resulting from NAFTA. The Mexican government instituted a compensation scheme (Pro Campo) that provides decoupled income transfers to producers, in addition to a program of investment and technical assistance (ALIANZA). By contrast, milk producers in Chile, who traditionally competed with imports and had been protected prior to liberalization, managed to take advantage of the modernization of the economy and the availability of new dairy technologies and genetic lines. The sector grew in efficiency and has now become an export sector. But, again, those who could take advantage of the new environment were generally larger farm operators.

The third group, nontradable producers, has been less directly affected by trade reform. These producers may be harmed indirectly if consumers switch to lower priced importables or may benefit indirectly from the higher price of exportables. Producers of nontradables are mainly small farmers, and members of these households tend to be relatively more involved in rural nonfarm labor. In Colombia small farm households benefited during the reform process mainly from increased employment opportunities that became available in the rural nonfarm economy (Jaramillo 1998). But whether this was a direct result of trade liberalization is unclear.

In addition to being more technologically advanced and more flexible in adapting to changing market conditions, commercial farms also tended to use more imported inputs, whose prices fell with trade liberalization. The reduction or elimination of government subsidies on inputs also increased the relative advantage of larger farms. With the change in market environment, many governments tried to lessen the impacts of economic reforms through targeted extension and credit programs for small farmers and social programs for the poor in rural areas, including farmers. Examples include Brazil's National Program to Strengthen Family Farming (PRONAF) and Chile's Agricultural Development Institute (INDAP) for extension and credit services, and Mexico's Program for Education, Health and Nutrition (Progresa), Peru's Social Fund (FONCODES), and Brazil's Previdencia for social programs.

The secular trend toward greater capital intensity in farming would also be expected to heighten the differential impact of reforms by farm size. A cross-country study by Mundlak, Larson, and Butzer (1999) of 37 countries for 1970–90 illustrates the increasing importance of capital and the declining importance of land and labor to improved sectoral performance. For the countries studied, the average growth rate was 4.25 percent a year for fixed capital but near zero for labor and land. Thus small farmers who depend more on labor and land than on capital could have been disadvantaged by this structural trend toward capital-intensive farming combined with the higher price risk associated with trade liberalization and a production orientation toward import-competing and nontradable goods (see box 10.1 for Brazil's experience).

Effects on Food Security

Food security, an imprecise term, is defined here as the ability of food-deficit countries, regions, or households to meet target levels of consumption on a year-to-year basis. Reaching target levels, which could be trend levels, does not guarantee the avoidance of chronic malnutrition. For most of Latin America chronic malnutrition is associated with persistent poverty, a long-term problem that lies beyond the ability to meet aggregate targets.

Box 10.1 A Case Study of the Differential Effects of Reforms and Trade Liberalization

Evidence from Brazil, for which there are good disaggregated data on the distribution of production across types of farms, clearly shows how reforms disadvantaged smaller, low-technology farmers (World Bank 2001b). Changes in government policy and in market conditions reinforced the advantages of technologically advanced commercial producers.

First, technical assistance appears to have benefited larger farmers more than others, especially those engaged in import substitution. Second, commercial farmers used purchased inputs more intensively than did small farmers. Because input prices fell more rapidly than output prices after reforms, for larger commercial farms costs fell more than revenues and proportionally more than for smaller farms. Per hectare returns were negative for low-technology, small, and subsistence farmers, who used no purchased inputs and so did not benefit from lower input prices, and who experienced falling output prices. Third, changes in processing and markets raised quality standards and led to the development of sophisticated systems of production financing and marketing, again advantaging larger commercial enterprises. As the government reduced subsidized credit, capital-intensive farmers could turn to the private sector for investments to meet the increased demand for higher quality products. Entry into marketing channels for higher quality products brought the benefit of access to a more sophisticated production financing system.

The share in the value of production has been declining for smaller farms (100 hectares or less) and increasing for larger farms (see table). In 1970 smaller farms produced 57.8 percent of production, and the largest farms (more than 1,000 hectares) produced 12.6 percent. By 1985 the contribution of smaller farms had fallen below half of total production, and by 1995 the largest farms had increased their proportion of total output by two-thirds, reaching a 21 percent share.

Other countries in the region probably experienced similar changes associated with the reform process. In Chile, especially as the second phase of reforms unfolded in the mid-1980s, the demand by commercial, export-oriented enterprises for new varieties and more sophisticated production techniques and financing instruments was met by both the public and private sectors. To some extent, this was balanced by the targeting of public technical and financial assistance toward smaller and poorer farmers. But because private sector participation increased rapidly, the technological and financial support from all sources grew faster for larger commercial farms than for smaller farms.

Share of Production Value by Farm Size in Brazil, 1970–95 (percent)

Year	0–9 hectares	10–99 hectares	100–1,000 hectares	More than 1,000 hectares
1970	17.8	40.0	29.3	12.6
1980	13.0	37.7	33.2	16.0
1995	12.2	34.4	32.3	21.0

Source: World Bank (2001b).

Aggregate Food Supplies

Stable food supplies in the aggregate, including national food self-sufficiency, are not synonymous with consumption stability for large segments of the population. If a country lacks the means to transfer food or income to some regions or households, they might remain exposed to food insecurity. Despite no aggregate deficit in the food supply in Argentina and Brazil, for example, there are households suffering from hunger and malnutrition, principally because of poverty and inadequate social programs.

In middle-income countries aggregate food supply is less relevant in the context of an open economy. With a few exceptions, in Latin America the goal of attaining a target level of food self-sufficiency is no longer an influential consideration. Arguments over grain reserves or food security stocks have almost disappeared from informed policy debate. Practically all Latin American countries are price takers in world food markets, with perhaps two exceptions.[11] Food supply management has become a matter primarily of foreign exchange and the capacity of infrastructure (mainly ports) and logistics to deliver food imports to consumers.

Thus, trade policy has been decoupled from political discussion of food policy, because trade policy instruments are considered inadequate for increasing household income and food consumption in the poorest households. A large proportion of the poor are net buyers of food, and thus border protection on food imports would increase domestic food prices for all consumers, including the poor, and there would be a decline in real income. Also, governments are increasingly free of food supply management responsibility now that food trade is almost exclusively in the hands of the private sector, and price controls have been eliminated.[12] True, governments would still face severe political consequences in the event of a major food shortage, but such shortages now occur only as a consequence of contradictory signals sent to private producers and traders by inept or corrupt governments.

Food Security at the Household Level

In Latin America, with some exceptions like Haiti, caloric intake is not a good indicator of food security. For the region as a whole caloric intake, after a long period of stagnation, has risen steadily since 1990, coincidental with the initiation of reforms in most countries (FAO, 2001, figure 22). At the household level, particularly in middle-income countries, food security is more properly associated with nutritional status and health, based on anthropometric and health indicators. Latin America has by far the lowest prevalence of underweight, stunted, and wasted children—standard measures of nutritional status —in the developing world (table 10.6).[13]

Health status depends in part on nutritional status. A health production function can be envisioned that is determined by nutritional status, privately provided inputs (clean water and perhaps boiling capability, refrigeration, the

Table 10.6 Prevalence of Underweight, Stunted, and Wasted Children in Developing Countries, 1995–2000 (percent of population falling below minus two standard deviations of reference value)

Region or country group	Underweight	Stunted	Wasted
Latin America and the Caribbean	9	17	2
Developing countries	29	33	10
Least developed countries	40	45	12

Source: FAO (2001, table 5).

healthful characteristics of food selection, and time preparing food), publicly provided inputs (potable water, sewage, electricity, nutritional information, and others), and socioeconomic variables. Thus income gains could reduce malnutrition even if they have but a small or insignificant effect on a simple measure of nutrient intake at the household level. Families may decide to allocate additional income to improve the infrastructure in their home (electricity, refrigeration, sewage, potable water) rather than to buy more calories, and this could improve their nutritional and health status inputs (Schiff and Valdés 1990). Agricultural growth in a more open and dynamic economy could be one source of income growth at the household level and indirectly a source of government revenue for the provision of publicly provided health inputs.

The principal policy concerns following the reforms of the past two decades appear to have been household income, health, and sanitation, in conjunction with targeted nutritional programs as part of broader social safety net schemes. Social programs include food stamp programs, school lunch programs, and direct cash and in-kind transfers as part of an integrated policy of nutrition and health systems. With adequate domestic policies targeted to the poor, trade liberalization in agriculture has not been inconsistent with food security, but rather has likely lowered the price of food.

What About Price Shocks?

But does trade liberalization increase the risk of shocks that might precipitate a food crisis? At a national level is agricultural liberalization associated with increased volatility in production and prices? Diets in Latin America have become more diversified and less dependent on one or two products. The removal of price controls and the deregulation of markets contributed to this diversification by ending artificially low prices for only a few staples. This in turn has made the poor less vulnerable to food supply or price shocks in specific products.

Nevertheless, tariffication has increased the transmission of world price variability to domestic markets. The spikes in international prices, however, tend to be of short duration, whereas periods of low commodity prices tend to persist. Thus tariffication has exposed consumers to momentary price spikes but has also allowed them to benefit from extended periods of low prices. The enhanced price transmission resulting from trade reform appears not to have generated major consumer problems associated with price volatility.

But what of small farmers producing food? Those producing nontradables are not affected by trade policy, but those producing importables are harmed by the reduction in border protection of food. However, as documented for farmers of Northeastern Brazil (López and Romano 2003), small farmers are often net buyers of importables (not only food), which could compensate them for part of their loss on the output price side. In most cases small farmers qualify for social safety net schemes as well. Distant rural areas often present a problem, however, for the delivery of social programs, and much improvement is needed.

THREE CONTRASTING CASES: AGRICULTURAL REFORMS IN ARGENTINA, CHILE, AND COLOMBIA

This section reviews policy reforms and their consequences for the illustrative cases of Argentina, Chile, and Colombia. Each country shows a distinct history of reforms, of the short- and medium-term outcomes of those reforms, and of the ability to sustain reforms. The focus is primarily on agriculture-specific reforms, although macroeconomic and other reforms also affected the performance of the farm sector.

Argentina is an example of reforms initially limited to trade and macroeconomic policies in the early 1980s, which were discontinued and then restarted in the early 1990s, with a broader and deeper program of policy changes. Argentina experimented early with reforms in an attempt in 1976 to restore macroeconomic stability after a period of crisis with high fiscal and current account deficits and hyperinflation. There was little specific emphasis on agricultural sectoral policy reform. Both internal price controls and some restrictions on short-term capital flows were relaxed. There was also some trade liberalization, although with little effect on agriculture. The episode of market-oriented reforms was brief, and by 1978 the emphasis shifted to antiinflationary measures (Corbo, de Melo, and Tybout 1986). Reform was renewed in earnest in 1989–90 with trade liberalization and the removal of export taxes, followed by deregulation and privatization. Mercosur was established in 1991 (Sturzenegger 1999; Ghezan, Mateos, and Elverdin 2000). Following several years of success, the country faced a major economic crisis at the end of the 1990s, understood as the result primarily of a failure of macroeconomic management. In the ensuing drastic currency devaluation in late 2001, export taxes were reinstated.

Chile is an example of early, broad, deep, and sustained reforms. Chile was the earliest adopter of market-oriented, open-economy reforms in the developing world. Its macroeconomic structural reforms begin in earnest in 1975–76, following a period of economic crisis. Although most reforms were implemented between 1976 and 1978, Chile experienced later phases of policy innovation. After 1983 Chile introduced a number of adjustments aimed at stabilizing farm prices for wheat, sugar, and oil seed, and in 1991 credit and extension assistance services were expanded to small farmers (Hurtado, Valdés, and Muchnik 1990; de la Cuadra and Hachette 1991).

Colombia is an example of ambitious plans for reforms that were briefly implemented and then withdrawn in response to unfavorable domestic political reaction to the macroeconomic and world price environment in which the reforms were implemented. Colombia introduced reforms in 1990 to liberalize trade and deregulate the economy. Between 1993 and 1995 it introduced sectoral reforms, but soon thereafter the process of reform was discontinued (García-García and Montes 1989; Perry 2000; Jaramillo 1998, 1999).

Reforms in Argentina

Reform of Argentine agriculture involved trade, deregulation and privatization, and tax and credit policies. The policy changes that began in 1991 emphasized economywide policies and a shift away from sectoral policies (see Sturzenegger 1999 and Ghezán, Mateos, and Elverdín 2000). While trade reforms had the most direct impact on agriculture, deregulation and privatization of important elements of infrastructure, particularly in transport, were also important to the country's export-oriented farm sector. Transport was opened to private domestic and foreign investment, spurring greater competition in ports, sea and river shipping, and internal freight (Sturzenegger 1999).

Tariffs were reduced from an average of 50 percent in 1988 to 10–39 percent in 1992. By 1996 the average tariff on agriculture was 13 percent plus a "statistical tax" of 3 percent. Taxes on imported agrochemicals (15 percent) and fertilizers (25–35 percent) were eliminated, and machinery tariffs fell from 50 percent to 15 percent. An important policy change was the reduction and elimination of export taxes between 1991 and 1993, with three exceptions: oil seeds were still taxed at 3.5 percent, processed leather at 5 percent, and raw leather at 15 percent. Other export taxes were also eliminated, including taxes on exchange rate transactions. Overall more than 120 quantitative restrictions, permits, and prior authorization on exports were eliminated. With some exceptions quantitative restrictions on imports were also abolished. In 1991 a South American customs union, Mercosur, was proposed with the goal of the free movement of trade and a common external tariff by 1995 (Laird 1997). This ambitious goal was not fulfilled, although Mercosur continues with a number of exemptions (such as sugar) from the regional free-trade goal.

Deregulation and privatization, which began in 1989, were strengthened in 1991 with the establishment of a legal framework for state reform. State trading agencies had long controlled domestic and foreign marketing of grains, beef, sugar, milk, yerba mate, fisheries, forestry, and other sectors. The reforms of 1991 eliminated all these agencies, and their assets were sold. Ports, rail freight branches, and grain elevators at seaports were privatized, and licenses for transport between Argentina and neighboring countries were eliminated. The government instead took on a regulatory role and retained responsibility for statistical services and export promotion.

Tax reforms involved the adoption of a value-added tax (VAT) and the elimination of 24 separate taxes. These taxes had included items especially important for agriculture: gas, oil and tires, new vehicles, and financial services. A drawback of the VAT for exporters was also introduced.

Several programs for small- and medium-scale agriculture were introduced to compensate for economywide policy changes that were expected to be detrimental to the farm sector. The Cambio Rural program of 1993 supported the conversion of land to other uses. The Programa Social Agropecuario provided technical assistance and credit to small land owners (*minifundistas*). There was also a conversion program to aid tobacco farmers, regionally specific programs for the northeast, a special program for development of the forestry sector, and reforms in the system of research and extension.

Reforms in Chile

One of the earliest reformers, Chile began radical structural and sectoral policy changes oriented toward open trade, privatization, and economic deregulation some two years after the end of the Allende regime in 1973. The reforms of the 1970s were a radical departure from Chile's economic policies of the previous decades (see Hurtado, Valdés, and Muchnik 1990; Valdés, Hurtado, and Muchnik 1991; and Jarvis 1985).

During the Alessandri administration of 1958–64 the three main goals of economic policy important to agriculture were controlling inflation, reducing the budget deficit, and improving net foreign exchange earnings. To stabilize prices the government fixed nominal farm prices for essential products, nominal exchange rates, and marketing margins at the retail level. Certain exports were prohibited (wheat, flour, lamb, and others), while others (fruit) were promoted. After a brief attempt at trade liberalization in 1961, tariffs were increased and import quotas and licenses were revived. In addition there were agricultural development programs with subsidies for milk producers, subsidized credit, and subsidized rail transportation for wheat, cattle, and forages. A marketing board was established, first for wheat and later for other products, in an attempt to guarantee a "normal supply." The board also had a monopoly on imports. A small-scale land reform program, based on voluntary sales at market prices, attempted to promote small-scale farms.

The Frei administration of 1965–70 introduced a more explicit agricultural policy oriented toward self-sufficiency and the coordination of relative prices to increase overall production. The interventionist price regime was intensified to more specifically direct production and consumer patterns. For the major staple crops (wheat, flour, milk, and beef) restrictive tariffs were applied, with fixed prices established for consumers and minimum prices for producers, along with fixed marketing margins, export quotas, licenses, and prohibitions. Tax rebates were introduced for certain exports. A crawling peg system for exchange rates was adopted, to avoid overvaluation.

Recognizing the importance of relative prices to encourage production, the government allowed farm prices to rise more quickly than nonagricultural prices. To reduce marketing margins, the government intervened in marketing channels: it increased storage and processing facilities, improved transport systems, increased food security stocks, and operated marketing boards to support the prices of wage goods. Tension emerged between the policy objective of increasing production through higher prices and raising rural wages relative to urban wages, and the objective of restraining wages in the nonagricultural sector. A massive land reform program began in 1967, based on expropriations and partial compensation, determined by the state and oriented toward the establishment of large, cooperative farms (*asentamientos*).

During the Allende administration (1971–73) the expropriation-based land reform program was expanded to 40–50 percent of farmland resources (as measured by productive equivalents).[14] Interventionist economic policies intensified. Inflation accelerated, and under the logic of the prevailing economic model, the government responded with even more severe price controls. Food shortages broke out, and black markets emerged. The government moved to establish monopolies in fertilizer, wheat, maize, milk, sugar, and other products. The government accentuated the protectionism of the previous administration, fixing the nominal exchange rate and imposing stricter controls on imports and exports.

Following the overthrow of the Allende government in 1973, the military government of Gen. Augusto Pinochet began a radical change in economic and agricultural policies toward market-based resource allocations. The role of the government in the economy was reduced, trade was liberalized, and private property rights were strengthened. During the first phase of reforms during 1973–83, general economic reforms were put into effect quickly and sector-specific reforms were deferred. In the face of hyperinflation and large deficits in internal and external accounts macroeconomic stabilization was a key consideration, as was making the reforms credible.

Agricultural reforms reduced government involvement in services and privatized input and product markets. A new land policy provided strong protection of private property. Land titles were given to the beneficiaries of the previous land reform program, establishing small farms. Government expenditures on agriculture fell dramatically: in real terms in 1980–83 the government spent one-third of what it spent in 1965–74 (Valdés, Hurtado, and Muchnik 1991, pp. 125–30). The marketing board and price control agencies were closed down, and price controls were lifted except on wheat, milk, and oilseeds. Legal ceilings on interest rates were raised and then removed, and preferential credit rates for agriculture were abolished.

Beginning in 1975 almost all nontariff barriers were eliminated, and tariffs on most imports were rapidly reduced. A uniform tariff was introduced, beginning at 90 percent in 1975 and falling to 20 percent in 1977 and to 10 percent in 1979. Export restrictions were eliminated, and a crawling peg system was put in place until 1979, when a fixed exchange rate system was reintroduced.

Despite the ambitious nature of reforms, delays in implementation adversely affected the agricultural sector. Elimination of price controls was slow for some products, and realization of reforms in land and water rights took longer than expected. Labor market reforms were also postponed. Nevertheless, privatization and deregulation of airlines and telecommunications significantly improved the quality of services and lowered costs, particularly important to the agricultural export sector.

Despite attractive relative prices, other conditions necessary to stimulate private investments in agriculture were absent. As would be repeated with Colombia's trade liberalization in the early 1990s, Chilean farmers were disadvantaged during 1978–82 by exchange rate appreciation and falling world commodity prices. During this period farm lobbies representing import-competing activities sought selective protection, and the question of special treatment for the agricultural sector reemerged.

A second phase of reforms began in 1984, following a deep recession. The government reversed the currency appreciation with nominal devaluations, fiscal restraint, and restrictions on short-term capital inflows. A price stabilization mechanism was established for the importables wheat, sugar, and oilseeds, based on a variable levy, commonly referred to as price bands. A scheme of minimum customs valuations for dairy products was introduced. Partly as the result of government policies, the real exchange rate (tradables relative to home goods) increased between 1984 and 1991, and a new episode of currency appreciation began, again creating political tension in the farm sector. For producers of import-competing products the decline in profitability became even more pronounced when Chile joined Mercosur as an associate member and was obligated to grant trade preferences to Argentina and Uruguay, countries with competitive exports in wheat, maize, oilseeds, and beef.

Reforms in Colombia

During the initial phase of reforms in Colombia in 1991 and 1992 the government attempted to address major bottlenecks (World Bank 1995). It sought to achieve neutrality of incentives with respect to border protection and credit and to reorient government away from direct interventions in markets toward the provision of public goods and the creation of conditions to encourage private investment in credit, marketing, technology, and land improvements.

Decentralization and community participation were also sought, especially in research and extension and irrigation investments.

During 1991 and 1992 nontariff barriers were eliminated, including the state monopoly on grain imports. The activities of the grain marketing board (IDEMA) were restricted to marginal areas, with a system of minimum guaranteed prices for grains. The number of tariff positions was reduced from seven to four, and tariffs declined from 0–50 percent to 0–20 percent, with an average tariff on farm goods of 15 percent in 1991. Tariffs on agricultural inputs fell from 15 percent to 2 percent. Export taxes were eliminated, except on coffee. A price band scheme was introduced for eight products and their derivatives and substitutes (a total of 112 items). Reforms were also implemented as part of Colombia's commitments under the Andean Pact.

Attempts were also made to reform the credit system. Forced loans to the farm sector were replaced by incentives for private banks to increase agricultural lending. The government planned to reduce and then eliminate subsidies on interest rates and to restructure the large state-supported, nearly bankrupt agricultural bank, Caja Agraria, which had a history of persistent losses. These attempts failed, however, in the face of strong pressures from farm lobbies and labor unions (Jaramillo 1998, pp. 46–47). A similar fate met attempted reforms in the research and extension system to promote competition and decentralization.

Reforms to domestic transport infrastructure were particularly important for Colombia, where the terrain makes overland transport costs between production zones and ports relatively high. While external transport costs were lowered through privatization of ports in 1990 and elimination of flag restrictions (World Bank 1995), internal transport costs remained high, in part because of high insurance costs (hijacking is a persistent problem) and poor road conditions. Ports were congested, and investments were low relative to the volume of export trade.

A decline in profitability as falling international prices coincided with a severe drought in 1992 led to strong pressure from farm lobbies to slow or reverse the movement toward market liberalization (World Bank 1995). In response, IDEMA was authorized to intervene in some product markets to support prices at higher than guaranteed minimums. Quantitative restrictions were imposed on some imports, notably affecting milk and chicken parts.

In 1993 antidumping and countervailing duty laws were adopted, and in 1994 safeguards were made available to industries suffering because of imports. At the end of 1994 the government began a series of negotiated procurement agreements. Farmers, processors, and government officials reached agreements on prices and on volumes of domestic output that would be absorbed by industry. In exchange for these commitments, processors received import quotas at lower tariffs. Drawbacks on exports were eliminated, and a stabilization fund was created for exports. The procurement agreements, price bands, and contingency measures such as safeguards provided the government with considerable flexibility in implementing border protection and price supports.

The agricultural crisis was an important issue in the presidential campaign of 1994. The new Samper administration (1994–98) initiated further interventions, beginning with purchase agreements for wheat, sorghum, maize, barley, and oil palm. IDEMA engaged in price support activities in grain markets, subsidies were introduced for cotton and soybeans and for banana exports, and new price bands were added for pork, raw sugar, soybean and palm oils, and chicken parts. New import controls were established for rice, along with storage subsidies (Jaramillo 1999).

By the end of the 1990s the incentive framework and the role of the government were very different from what had been envisioned at the beginning of the reform process. The government was once again heavily involved in managing trade and prices.

Overall Performance Indicators: Growth Rates, Agricultural Production, and Trade Flows

The performance indicators discussed here for Argentina and Colombia are separated into periods before and after the reforms, with the reforms further divided into an early and a later phase. For Chile the data distinguish three subperiods following the years of heavy government intervention in 1971–73, with 1974 considered as prior to the introduction of true market-oriented reforms.

Argentina

The agricultural sector overall and agricultural exports grew slowly in Argentina in the period immediately before the reforms (table 10.7).[15] Growth accelerated as reforms were introduced, outpacing agricultural growth rates as far back as the 1960s.[16] Agricultural exports grew at an average annual rate of 11 percent during the 1990s, well above the 8 percent average for the previous three decades, including the 1970s, a decade of high growth and high prices.

Imports grew as well. Average annual import growth more than doubled in the period immediately following the reforms, later averaging four times higher than before the reforms. Average annual growth of imports was 48 percent immediately following the reforms and then stabilized at about 9 percent after 1995. More recently, however, export growth has outpaced import growth. The overall tradability index (exports plus imports as a share of total agricultural GDP) increased from 45 percent before the reforms to 68 percent recently.

Chile

Agricultural production and exports, which declined during 1970–73, grew at a strikingly high rate after the introduction of reforms (see table 10.7). Between

Table 10.7 Performance Indicators for Agriculture for Argentina, Chile, and Colombia, 1960–98 (percent, unless otherwise indicated)

Country	Period	Economy wide GDP growth rate	Production value growth rate	Agricultural GDP growth rate	Value added (percent of GDP)	Rural population (percent of total)	Labor force (percent of total)	Exports index (1961 = 100)	Imports index (1961 = 100)	Trade (percent agricultural GDP)	Export growth rate	Import growth rate	Value added per worker (constant 1995 US$)
Argentina	1960–69	10.3	2.9	0.9	10.4	24.2	18.5	139	117	11.7	5.9	9.0	8,044
	1970–79	4.8	2.1	1.8	9.2	19.6	14.6	319	282	22.8	17.4	18.8	9,174
	1980–89	–1.3	–0.3	0.1	8.2	15.4	12.6	589	414	37.1	1.2	–2.8	10,740
	1990–94[a]	17.4	4.3	4.6	6.4	12.7	12.2	787	898	45.9	9.4	48.1	11,628
	1995–98	2.6	4.2	3.8	5.8	11.2	—	1,231	1,726	62.9	13.2	9.0	13,634
Colombia	1960–69	6.0	2.7	4.9	30.3	47.4	46.2	115	98	9.7	4.1	4.8	1,691
	1970–79	6.5	4.1	4.5	27.5	39.7	41.0	359	275	19.7	19.1	19.2	2,069
	1980–89	5.7	2.1	2.7	20.6	33.4	34.0	690	653	29.8	2.5	3.1	2,579
	1990–94[a]	2.1	2.1	–2.4	17.3	29.6	26.6	748	949	28.9	9.2	30.4	3,146
	1995–98	3.5	1.9	0.9	13.3	27.6	—	1,012	2,421	51.9	3.4	13.8	2,698
Chile	1960–70	5.2	2.4	2.2	8.2	28.4	27.2	107	122	10.1	4.4	3.7	2,512
	1971–73	—	–5.5	–6.5	7.5	23.5	23.5	126	211	16.9	–8.9	23.2	2,513
	1974	–12.7	19.2	26.8	5.7	22.2	22.8	249	540	36.2	149.8	120.0	2,805
	1975–83[b]	–0.4	2.1	2.2	7.2	19.5	21.3	966	417	33.3	23.0	4.4	3,053
	1984–89	3.2	4.7	8.0	8.1	17.2	19.5	2,456	238	31.0	19.6	–4.6	3,747
	1990–98	8.4	3.9	2.5	8.3	15.8	18.8	6,622	701	59.8	12.3	18.0	4,946

Source: Calculated by authors from World Bank and FAO data.

—Not available.

a. Reforms initiated in 1990–91.

b. Reforms initiated in 1975–76.

1975 and 1983 overall growth rates for agriculture returned to their average of the 1960s, while export growth rates soared. After 1983 aricultural growth increased faster than overall economic growth, so that agriculture's share in GDP rose. Liberalization altered the composition of production and trade in agriculture. Exportables (fruits, vegetables, and forestry) increased in importance, while livestock and field crops (primarily wheat) declined (see also de la Cuadra and Hachette 1991, p. 264). Following reform, agricultural export growth rates increased across the board (yearly growth rates averaged 10 percent or greater for two decades), although growth has slowed recently.

Colombia

Colombia's agricultural performance following reforms differed from that of Argentina and Chile (see table 10.7). In the first reform phase production value continued to grow at the same rate as before the reform. The value-added measure shows a decline in agricultural performance. The second reform phase shows a recovery in agricultural GDP, with a slight deceleration in the growth of production value. Export performance appears not to have been affected, while growth in agricultural imports increased considerably. Although production value grew, agricultural value added stagnated immediately after reforms through 1992 (Jaramillo 1998). A severe drought in 1992 (the worst on record) led to a dramatic drop in annual crop production; a sharp increase in permanent crops excluding coffee, which continued its unstable growth pattern; and a moderate increase in livestock overall, with a large increase in poultry.

Colombian agriculture experienced a crisis in growth indicators during the 1990s. Annual crop production had negative growth in 1996 and 1997. Growth in permanent crops slowed after 1995. Cultivated land, excluding coffee, shrank by more than 600,000 hectares—a loss of 800,000 hectares in annual crops and a gain of 200,000 in permanent crops (see Perry 2000, p. 21).

Following reforms, export growth rates increased across the three aggregate groups of crops and livestock, forestry, and fisheries. Coffee also experienced strong export growth of more than 9 percent immediately after the reforms, but growth then slowed to its rate during the 1980s. After 1994 export growth slowed considerably, with fisheries experiencing a decline. Sugar exports, which showed strong growth in the 1970s and 1980s, continued to grow at a slower rate of 16–17 percent. There was no significant change in the composition of exports or in the rate of export growth generally.

Growth in agricultural imports following reforms shows a pattern similar to that of Argentina. Imports grew on average 30 percent a year immediately following reform, then slowed. During 1995–98 imports averaged four times their level in the 1980s. The tradability index grew by more than 50 percent, from 30 percent before the reforms to 48 percent later. After an initial period when imports grew more rapidly than exports, export growth overtook import growth.

Evidence on Factor Use and Productivity

Argentina

Consistent with the hypothesis that reduced government intervention would lead to an increase in productivity, value added per worker increased considerably following reforms, with agricultural GDP per worker returning to its pre-1980s trend line (figure 10.1). Land productivity has continued to increase at a fairly constant rate since the 1970s. Fueling the rise in production and labor productivity since the reforms has been the rapid increase in fertilizer (figure 10.2), pesticide, and purchased seed use, spurred by the decline in domestic prices following reform (Ghezán, Masteos, and Elverdín 2000, table 14). Between 1991 and 1997 herbicide use grew at an average annual rate of 21 percent, insecticide use at 19 percent, and fertilizer use at 28 percent (figure 10.3). The increase in machinery use, which began slightly before the reforms, may also have contributed to the production increase (figure 10.4). Average annual sales of tractors increased about 15 percent in 1993–97 over 1984–88, with sales accelerating in the 1990s. The increased use of inputs is reflected clearly in rising yields: maize yields doubled in the 1990s over the 1980s, and sunflower yields grew 73 percent (Ghezán, Masteos, and Elverdín 2000).

Chile

Agricultural value added per worker began to recover after 1973, following a period of political and sectoral instability (figure 5). Although the recovery was remarkable considering the initial conditions (half of the agricultural land in productive-capacity equivalents had been expropriated), the immediate agri-

Figure 10.1 Agricultural Value Added per Worker in Argentina

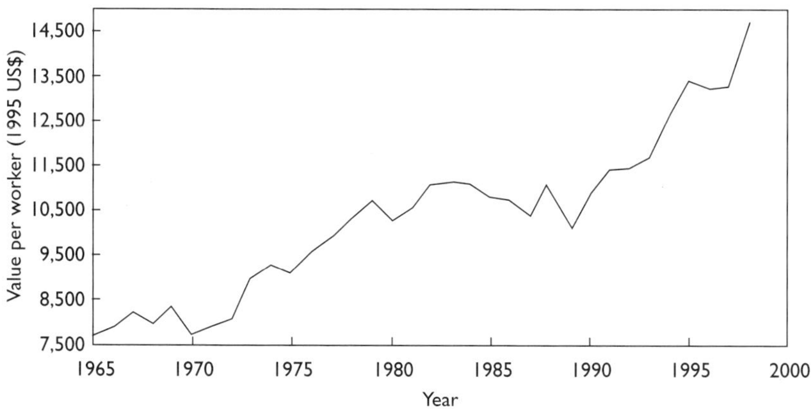

Source: World Bank (2001c).

Figure 10.2 Fertilizer Use in Argentina, Chile, and Colombia, 1960–2002 (kilograms per hectare)

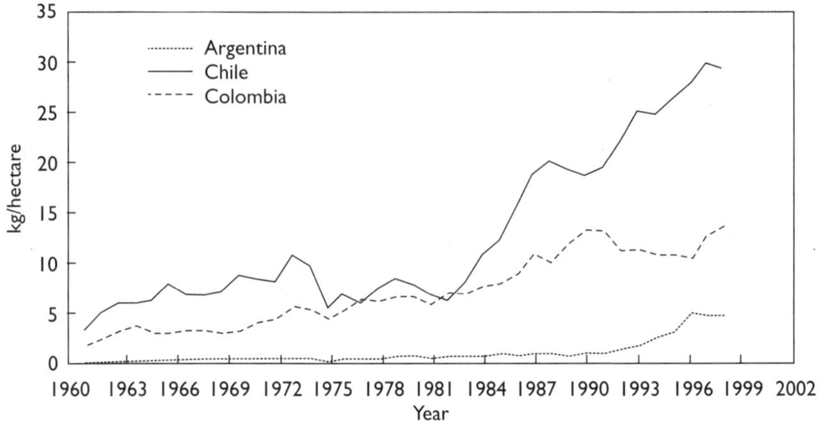

Source: World Bank (2001c).

cultural growth response to market-oriented reforms might be characterized as "too low" (Barahona and Quiroz 1990)[17] considering the increases in relative prices to producers that followed. After two years of decline in 1983 and 1984 associated with rising exchange and interest rates, growth in production and labor productivity began to increase in 1985. This growth is correlated with increased use of fertilizer, expansion of irrigated area, increased machinery use (figures 2 and 6), and the introduction of new varieties and nontraditional crops. Increases in land productivity were also notable.

Figure 10.3 Sales of Selected Inputs in Argentina, 1986–97

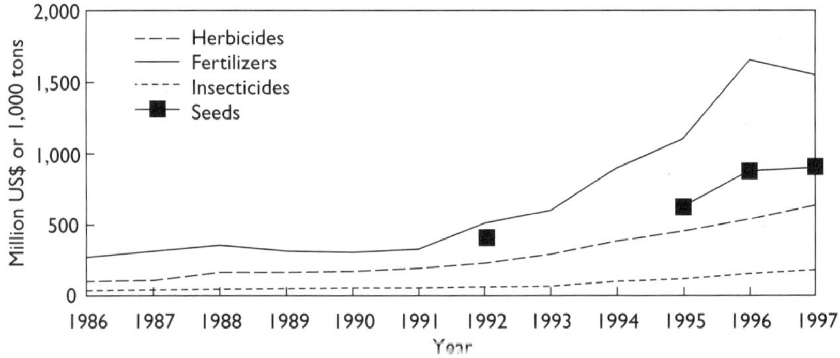

Source: Ghezán, Mateos, and Elverdín (2000).

Figure 10.4 Indices of Factor Use in Argentina, 1960–2000

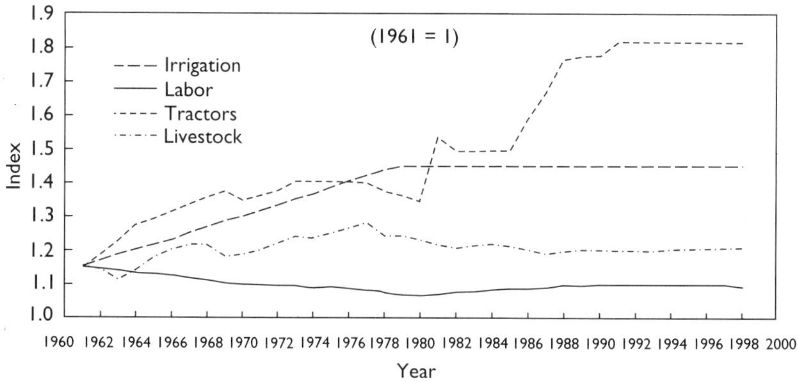

Source: World Bank (2001c).

Arnade (1998) and Gardner (1995) suggest that Chile also experienced a postreform gain in overall productivity. A simple regression analysis of aggregate production value on input use for 1961–98 indicates a large jump in overall productivity following the initiation of reforms in 1974–75.[18] There is less evidence for a shift in the annual rate of productivity increase after 1974, and the data suggest that the gains in production are explained by increased input

Figure 10.5 Agricultural Value Added per Worker in Chile, 1965–99

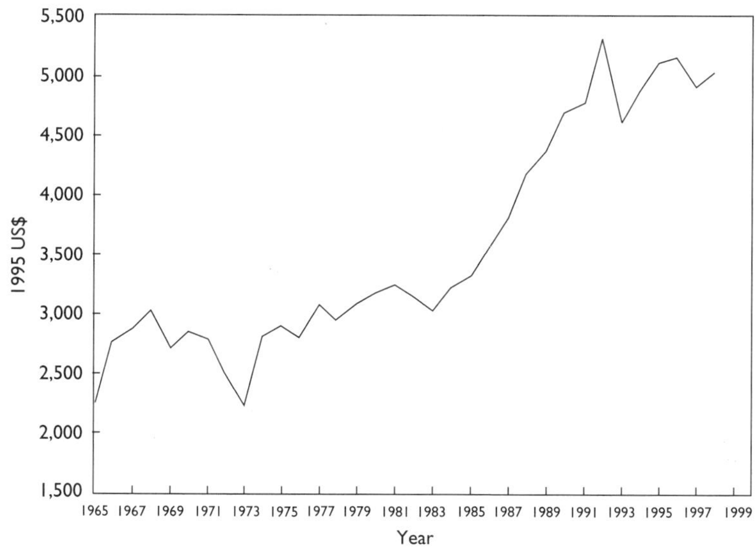

Source: World Bank (2001c).

Figure 10.6 Indices of Factor Use in Chile, 1960–2000

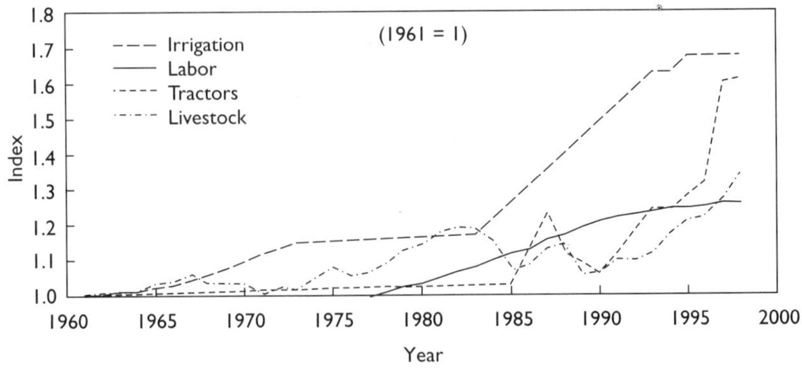

Source: World Bank (2001c).

use alone. These are tentative results, however, and much work is yet to be done on the connection between structural reforms and productivity gains.

Colombia

In Colombia the rate of growth of the value of production per worker declined following reform (figure 10.7). After more than two decades of almost steady growth, GDP per worker fell by 14 percent between 1990–94 and 1995–98 (see table 10.7). Measures of land productivity show a similar pattern. The worst drought on record, which reduced yields and plantings of rain-fed crops in 1992, explains the short, sharp decline in productivity for 1993 and perhaps 1994 (Jaramillo 1998). But it leaves unexplained the continuing low levels thereafter of both production and productivity growth.

The slowdown in production and declines in productivity were related to the decline in domestic prices of farm products, which affected production decisions and input use. An obvious source of the slackening in production is to be found in the use of fertilizers (see figure 10.2). Fertilizer use, which had grown by 8 percent a year in 1961–90, declined 3 percent a year on average in 1991–96. Fertilizer use dropped 15 percent from 1991 to 1992. Only in the late 1990s did fertilizer use begin to grow again, returning to prereform highs. Since 1990 there has also been a significant decline in machinery use and a slight increase in livestock (figure 10.8). Only irrigation, which is to a large extent a public investment, has increased significantly since 1990. Land use for crops fell significantly after reform, especially for annual crops. Private sector investment stagnated after reform, except for some permanent crops in the initial years after the reform (Perry 2000).

Arnade's (1998) evidence suggests that Colombia experienced a sharp decline in production, but an even faster decline in input use, leading to an increase in productivity. However, a simple regression analysis of the natural log of aggregate

Figure 10.7 Production Value per Worker in Colombia, 1960–2000

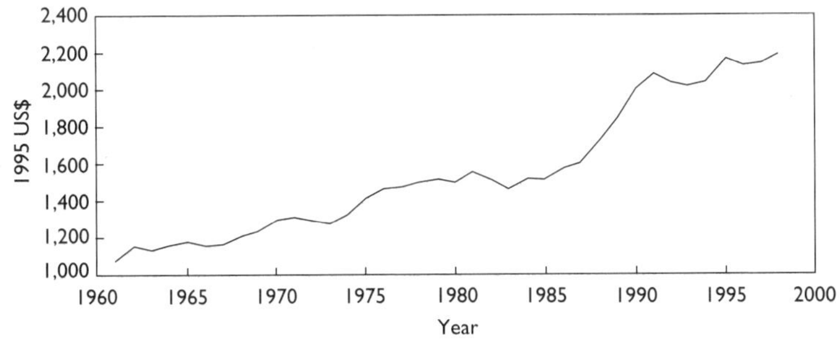

Source: World Bank (2001c).

production on input use between 1961 and 1998 does not corroborate this finding. The results show no major difference between pre- and postreform productivity growth. A regression of labor productivity on input use, in contrast, does suggest a gain in productivity per worker of some 6 percent after the reforms. The evidence is therefore mixed. The possibility remains, as Gardner (1995) notes for Hungary, of a postreform gain in productivity in a once-protected agricultural sector, despite the poor results in terms of overall production.

Reforms and Changes in Incentives: Protection, Exchange Rates, and Real Farm Prices

This section briefly discusses protection indicators, the effect of the exchange rate regime, and the evolution of domestic farm price in real terms, which captures the interaction between protection, exchange rates, and border prices.

Figure 10.8 Indices of Factor Use in Colombia, 1960–2000

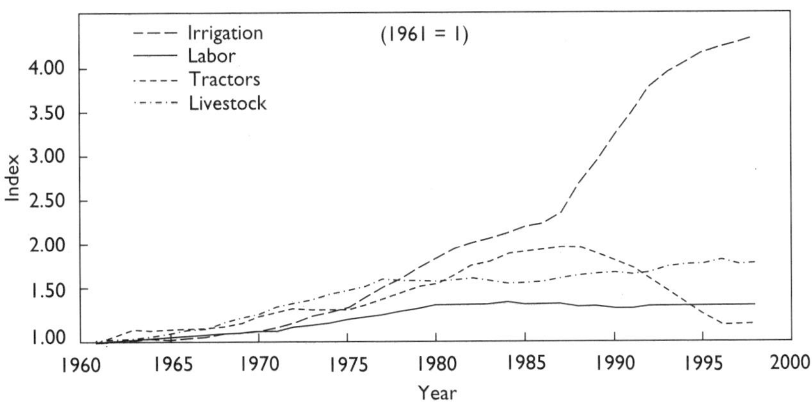

Source: World Bank (2001c).

Argentina

Before the 1990–91 reforms Argentina had a policy of taxing export agriculture (table 10.8). During the 1980s average agricultural export taxes ranged from 9 percent (cotton) to 22 percent (sunflowers). Taxes rose in 1990, reaching 19 percent for beef, 30 percent for wheat and maize, and 35 percent for sunflowers. With the introduction of reforms, average tax rates fell by 55 percent for soybeans and 80 percent for wheat, corn, and sorghum.[19] The effective nominal tax fell 76 percent for beef and 79 percent for wheat. Declines for other crops were similar. After 1992 tax rates became virtually insignificant, and wheat, maize, and sorghum began to receive slight subsidies of 1–2.5 percent because of reimbursements.[20]

An analysis focusing only on agricultural trade policy changes would lead, as Sturzenegger (1999) stresses, to the conclusion that agricultural producer prices should have increased significantly. However, a broader perspective incorporating changes in exchange rates and border prices shows that real domestic prices of exportables fell immediately after the initiation of reforms. In 1990–93 real domestic prices fell for all crops due to a substantial appreciation in the exchange rate and a notable decline in border prices. The virtual elimination of the export tax would otherwise have been expected to contribute to a large increase in domestic prices. Consider the case of maize in 1990–93. Real domestic farm prices fell by a cumulative 68 percent, reflecting a 39 percent decline in border prices and a 62 percent appreciation of the currency, only partially counteracted by a cumulative decline in export taxes of 29 percent.

Chile

Before 1974 there was some export promotion of fruit and policies favored most import-competing crops (beef, maize, milk, sugarbeets, and wheat; table 10.9). Thereafter, export promotion was discontinued, as reflected in the decline in the nominal rates of protection for exportables. Since the second phase of reforms in the early 1980s, nominal rates of protection for exports have effectively been zero. For import-competing crops, however, nominal rates of protection were relatively high during 1984–89 as the government responded to the strains on the traditional farm sector arising from low international prices and a strong appreciation of the currency in 1979–82.[21] (Nominal rates of protection jumped when Chile instituted price bands for wheat, sugar, and oilseed and minimum import prices for milk.) Although there was a currency depreciation in the late 1980s, protection remained. When the currency appreciated again during the 1990s, price bands, already in place, cushioned the effects on producers of traditional crops. The high nominal rates of protection for beef during 1984–89 reflect hoof and mouth disease-related restrictions on imports from other countries in the region.[22]

Again, focusing on trade instruments alone does not tell the full story. During the initial phase of reforms in 1975–83 the real border prices of most products (except grapes) declined substantially (see table 10.9). For example, the 0.18 percent average decline in the real farm price of milk during this period was the result of a 2.4 percent decrease in the real border price, a 46 percent increase in the real exchange rate, and a 44 percent decrease in price supports. Real domestic prices rose for fruits and wheat and declined for beef and milk. What benefited producers was the average increase in the real exchange rate, although there was notable volatility and a decline in the real exchange rate in 1979–81, when the nominal rate was fixed at 39 pesos to the dollar as part of the government's stabilization program. In December 1977 a 10 percent uniform tariff was established as a goal to be reached by June 1979 (de la Cuadra and Hachette 1991). Except for wheat, producers faced falling tariffs during the initial phase of reforms. Thus, before 1979 lower real border prices and lower tariffs were offset by a favorable movement in the exchange rate.

During the second phase of the reform, 1984–89, real domestic prices fell for all products considered, except beef and apples. Real domestic prices declined for wheat, maize, and fruits despite a steady increase in the real exchange rate because of declines in border prices. After 1990 real domestic prices fell for all products except grapes, due to an appreciation of the currency and, for four of the products, a decrease in real border prices.

To the extent that the changes in the real domestic prices of these products approximate changes in the returns to farming, the main forces behind agriculture's price incentives were the exchange rate and border prices, both beyond the control of sectoral policy.

Colombia

All products except beef suffered significant declines in real domestic prices immediately following the reforms (table 10.10). Before the reform, in 1980–89, there was a substantial increase in the real exchange rate, favoring agriculture. Beginning with the initiation of the reforms, there is substantial appreciation of the currency and notable declines in border prices for all crops except coffee. For example, the 31 percent decrease in the real domestic price of rice between 1990 and 1992 reflects a 23 percent fall in real border prices and a 12 percent decline in the real exchange rate, compensated only slightly by a 5 percent increase in the net effects of tariff protection and other variables.

Jaramillo (1998, table 6.10), who decomposes changes in farm returns following the reforms beginning in 1990, finds declines in returns to most crops during 1994–97. Despite border protection for most crops, real farm returns fell as a result of large declines in real exchange rates and border prices. Changes in input prices and wage rates had little influence. In the case of maize, an importable and important for small farmers, Jaramillo found that

Table 10.8 Decomposition of Producer Price Changes for Exportables in Argentina, 1960–95 (cumulative percentage change)

Product	Period	Real domestic prices	Real border prices	Real exchange rate	(1+Ti) tariffs	Other policies and effects	(1+Ti) + Others
Beef	1960–69	–43.55	–30.97	–244.19	—	—	231.61
	1970–79	22.29	43.58	–67.67	—	—	46.38
	1980–84	–33.97	–104.29	87.20	—	—	–16.88
	1985–89	32.68	13.16	39.36	–19.62	–0.22	–19.84
	1990–93	–91.35	13.28	–132.01	27.75	–0.38	27.38
	1994–95	2.45	–3.31	–2.02	—	—	7.78
Maize	1960–69	2.57	–21.54	–14.42	—	—	38.52
	1970–79	–102.78	4.04	–83.34	—	—	–23.49
	1980–84	54.93	–33.69	89.39	—	—	–0.77
	1985–89	–38.40	–38.74	14.36	4.65	3.52	9.23
	1990–93	–68.28	–38.88	–61.98	28.61	3.97	32.58
	1994–95	25.97	13.08	–2.02	—	—	14.92
Sorghum	1960–69	–4.51	–24.07	–14.42	—	—	33.98
	1970–79	–38.49	4.86	–58.54	—	—	15.19
	1980–84	–4.69	–23.41	64.60	—	—	–45.88
	1985–89	–15.72	1.86	–35.62	2.65	15.39	18.04
	1990–92	–89.00	–47.73	–54.70	25.28	–11.85	13.43

Soybeans	1960–69	—	—	—	—	—	—
	1977–79	–112.07	–51.20	–55.40	—	—	–5.47
	1980–84	7.60	–60.75	80.42	—	—	–12.07
	1985–89	–41.02	10.87	–48.30	–3.52	–0.07	–3.59
	1990–93	–58.64	–39.38	–61.98	38.67	4.04	42.72
	1994–95	–41.36	–52.61	–2.33	—	—	13.58
Sunflowers	1960–69	—	—	—	—	—	—
	1977–79	–89.08	–24.34	–55.40	—	—	–9.33
	1980–84	22.02	–59.88	80.42	—	—	1.48
	1985–89	–56.64	–17.50	–35.62	–2.01	–1.51	–3.52
	1990–92	–67.65	–46.14	–54.70	32.93	0.27	33.19
Wheat	1960–69	–3.77	–18.09	–14.42	—	—	19.51
	1970–79	–87.73	6.85	–92.60	—	—	–33.80
	1980–84	–64.03	–62.15	9.18	—	—	–11.06
	1985–88	–3.72	–19.11	–12.32	20.18	7.53	27.71
	1991–93	–24.76	–35.94	–26.64	31.64	1.42	37.82
	1994	–2.61	–5.93	–1.44	—	—	4.77

Source: Author's computations based on FAO data.
—Not available.

Table 10.9 Decomposition of Producer Price Changes in Chile (cumulative percentage change)

Product	Period	Real domestic prices	Real border prices	Real exchange rate	(1+Ti) tariffs	Other policies and effects
Exportables						
Apples, red	1960–70	133.77	41.02	30.94	17.14	44.67
	1971–74	–2.40	–21.22	44.77	–10.38	–15.58
	1975–83	6.40	–8.40	46.47	–6.77	–24.90
	1984–89	30.48	–4.10	36.11	0.00	–1.53
	1990–93	–429.10	–64.88	–14.79	0.00	–349.43
Grapes, Thompson	1960–70	99.29	21.53	30.94	17.14	29.67
	1971–74	54.35	4.37	44.77	–0.59	5.80
	1975–83	41.51	20.91	46.47	–16.55	–9.31
	1984–89	–4.70	–30.47	33.67	0.00	–7.91
	1990–94	22.24	21.37	–16.80	0.00	17.67
Importables						
Beef	1960–70	41.20	9.57	30.94	0.00	0.69
	1971–74	87.27	42.14	44.77	0.00	0.36
	1975–83	–51.72	–76.06	46.47	0.00	–22.12
	1984–89	136.69	64.93	33.67	13.98	24.12
	1990–95	–30.05	16.88	–26.84	–3.54	–16.54
Maize	1960–70	—	—	—	—	—
	1971–74	—	—	—	—	—
	1975–83	—	—	—	—	—
	1984–89	–4.24	–45.12	25.27	–7.84	23.46
	1990–93	–22.18	–23.84	–16.25	–3.54	21.44
Milk	1960–70	3.29	–5.37	30.94	0.00	–22.28
	1971–74	77.44	14.27	44.77	0.00	18.40
	1975–83	–0.18	–2.39	46.47	0.00	–44.26
	1984–89	–6.25	9.46	33.67	13.98	–63.35
	1990–93	–16.51	–19.66	–16.25	–3.54	22.94
Sugarbeets	1960–70	—	—	—	—	—
	1971–74	—	—	—	—	—
	1975–83	—	—	—	—	—
	1984–89	–1.35	39.16	25.27	–7.84	–57.93
	1990–93	–7.57	18.72	–16.25	–3.54	–6.50
Wheat	1960–70	6.33	–13.15	26.76	0.00	–7.28
	1971–74	53.81	80.13	9.89	0.00	–36.21
	1975–83	35.51	–88.39	81.35	0.00	42.55
	1984–89	–0.42	–32.83	37.84	–7.84	2.41
	1990–95	–27.80	–12.84	–26.84	7.84	4.04

Source: Author's computations based on FAO data.
—Not available.

Table 10.10 Decomposition of Producer Price Changes in Colombia, 1960–95 (cumulative percentage change)

Product	Period	Real domestic prices	Real border prices	Real exchange rate	(1+Ti) tariffs	Other policies and effects
Exportables						
Beef	1960–69	—	—	—	—	—
	1970–79	—	—	—	—	—
	1980–89	–6.45	–40.26	63.16	–29.22	–0.13
	1990–92	27.68	–35.73	4.94	75.43	–16.96
	1993–95	–24.77	15.87	–32.89	—	–7.74
Coffee	1960–69	–6.12	–27.89	20.90	–6.76	7.63
	1970–79	47.24	78.81	–21.43	–34.88	24.75
	1980–89	–33.07	–108.98	65.31	61.82	–51.22
	1990–92	–47.12	–61.91	4.94	28.45	–18.60
	1993–95	28.07	74.80	–32.89	—	–13.83
Cotton	1960–69	–7.30	–20.82	20.90	0.13	–7.52
	1970–79	13.46	40.04	–21.43	–0.09	–5.06
	1980–89	4.43	–52.62	65.31	0.11	–8.37
	1990–92	–25.87	–38.25	4.94	13.02	–5.58
Importables						
Rice	1960–69	–21.60	–16.70	20.90	0.00	–25.80
	1970–79	–29.05	2.89	–21.43	0.00	–10.51
	1980–89	10.62	–109.06	65.33	41.30	13.05
	1990–92	–30.75	–23.45	–12.18	6.86	–1.99
Maize	1960–69	—	—	—	—	—
	1970–79	—	—	—	—	—
	1980–89	–5.08	–46.55	63.37	–26.47	4.57
	1990–92	–36.69	–10.01	4.94	–20.01	–11.60
	1993–95	–33.53	–15.22	–32.89	—	14.58
Milk	1960–69	—	—	—	—	—
	1970–79	—	—	—	—	—
	1980–89	–15.58	–42.41	63.16	–44.87	8.54
	1990–92	–16.62	–29.41	4.94	25.61	–17.76
	1993–95	10.09	16.50	–32.89	—	26.48
Sorghum	1960–69	—	—	—	—	—
	1970–79	—	—	—	—	—
	1980–89	4.38	–54.42	63.03	–6.74	2.52
	1990–92	–21.28	–5.49	–12.02	–2.61	–1.16
Soybeans	1960–69	—	—	—	—	—
	1970–79	—	—	—	—	—
	1980–89	26.89	–45.34	63.03	10.55	–1.35
	1990–92	–43.95	–32.51	–12.02	–7.74	8.32
Wheat	1960–69	–11.40	–39.52	20.90	0.00	7.22
	1970–79	–25.40	17.64	–21.43	0.00	–21.61
	1980–89	31.22	–69.92	65.17	41.84	–5.87
	1990–92	–39.74	–31.59	–12.02	2.28	1.59

Source: Author's computations based on FAO data.
—Not available.

real returns fell 47 percent due to a 28 percent decline in the real exchange rate and a 32 percent decline in world prices, which were only partially compensated for by a 16 percent increase in border protection.

The importance of the exchange rate in determining the effects of reform is also documented in Jaramillo (1999), Perry (2000), and Quiroz (1997). Perry notes that the trade reforms were expected to benefit agriculture, especially exports, but that instead the reforms brought a harmful strengthening of the currency and increased costs of capital. He attributes the difficulties suffered by the agricultural sector to the reduction in the competitiveness of commercial farming resulting from the combination of currency appreciation and increased real interest rates.

While one could argue about the cause and effect relation between reforms and currency appreciation, it is difficult to deny that these two key prices, the exchange and interest rates, were at the heart of Colombian agriculture's difficulties following the reforms.

Have Reforms Exacerbated Rural Poverty? Some Evidence from Colombia and Chile

The effects of the policy reforms on agriculture flow from five main components of reform: macroeconomic stabilization, trade liberalization, deregulation, privatization, and a more explicit commitment to the targeting of social policies. Some elements of reform were implemented more rapidly than others, most notably macroeconomic stabilization and trade liberalization. Building up the institutions and information systems needed for implementation of the other components requires time, which makes evaluation of the impact of reforms on poverty difficult for countries such as Argentina and Colombia that have initiated reform more recently. Even for Chile, where there is a greater amount of longitudinal and cross-sectional household data, there is little information prior to 1987 at the micro level on which to base a comparative analysis of the impacts of reform on poverty.[23]

Even with the best of data, it would be difficult to isolate the partial effect of any one of these components of reform from the net effect of the general shift toward market-oriented policies.[24] With the data actually available, analysis is particularly problematic for the rural sector, because household surveys have had a strong urban bias in design and coverage. The weaknesses of the time-series data on rural poverty in the region are acute, leading to wide differences in estimated levels of poverty at any point in time and to distrust of estimated trends in rural poverty rates.

Reliable data on rural household income and poverty are available for specific years for some countries (Argentina in 1996, Brazil in 1996, Chile biannually since 1987, Colombia in 1993 and 1997, El Salvador in 1995, Honduras in 1994, Mexico in 1994 and 1997, Nicaragua in 1993 and 1998, Paraguay in 1994, and Peru in 1994 and 1997). While these snapshots of individual country situations are useful for cross-sectional analysis, they say little about the evolution of poverty rates and their determinants over time.

Colombia

Following the initiation of reforms in Colombia, rural per capita income fell an average of 5.7 percent annually between 1991 and 1995. As Jaramillo (1999) notes, this striking rate of decline masks great diversity in income changes across income strata (table 10.11). The deterioration in income levels during this period was concentrated in the richest 10 percent of rural households. On average, poorer households experienced income gains (1.4 percent a year for deciles 1–9). Income change was inversely related to income strata, suggesting that in the five years following the reforms rural income became less skewed. The poorest quintile experienced the greatest annual growth rate (4.1 percent). Difficulties in the postreform period experienced by the farm sector overall—declining world prices, rising exchange rates, and other factors—were thus apparently not translated into overall hardship for the majority of the rural population.

Data in Jaramillo (1999) on levels of rural poverty are consistent with proportionately greater rates of increase in income for the poor: per capita rural poverty rates fell from 36 percent in 1988 to 26 percent in 1995 (table 10.12). By contrast, data from the Economic Commission for Latin America (ECLAC) show poverty rates essentially stagnant over this period (Ocampo 2001). The data in Wodon (2001) show an increase in rural poverty between 1995 and 1998. From these sources it is difficult to conclude that reforms have had a negative impact on rural poverty.

Table 10.11 Average Annual Rural Income Growth Rates in Colombia, 1978–95 (percent)

Decile or decile group (1 poorest, 10 wealthiest)	1978–91	1991–95
1–2	–0.1	4.1
3–5	–0.4	2.1
6–8	–0.7	1.1
9	–0.7	0.4
1–9	–0.6	1.4
10	3.3	–14.3
All	1.1	–5.7

Source: Jaramillo (1999, table 6).

Table 10.12 The Evolution of Poverty Rates in Colombia, 1986–98 (percent)

Source of estimate	1986	1988	1989	1991	1992	1993	1994	1995	1996	1997	1998
Urban											
Jaramillo (1998)[a]	—	—	—	11.0	10.7	8.4	8.0	7.5	—	—	—
Ocampo (2001)[b]	—	—	—	53.0	—	—	45.0	—	—	45.0	—
Wodon (2001)	61.5	—	53.6	—	49.9	—	—	46.3	47.1	—	54.8
Rural											
Jaramillo (1999)	—	36.0	—	31.4	30.8	30.0	28.5	26.2	—	—	—
Ocampo (2001)	—	—	—	61.0	—	—	62.0	—	—	60.0	—
Ocampo (2001)[c]	42[d]			55			57			54	
Wodon and others (2001)	—	—	—	—	—	—	—	77.4	75.6	—	80.0

Note: The two most reliable household surveys for poverty measures in Colombia are the National Socioeconomic Characteristics Survey (CASEN) 1993 and the Living Standards Measurement Study (LSMS) 1997. They are not strictly comparable because of differing sample designs.

—Not available.

a. Based on a survey by the National Department of Statistics (DANE), which includes a module on rural income.

b. Based on per capita income data from the Economic Commission for Latin America and the Caribbean.

c. Expressed as the proportion of households based on Economic Commission for Latin America and the Caribbean data.

d. De Janvry and Sadoulet (1999) based on Economic Commission for Latin America and the Caribbean data.

ECLAC data show an increase in poverty between 1986 and 1991, however, a period that included high rates of protection and high agricultural growth rates before reform. Apparently, during the prereform period of high levels of protection agricultural output grew but rural poverty increased. By contrast, during the postreform period agricultural protection declined, the sector did poorly in terms of growth, but again paradoxically according to Jaramillo and not contradicted by other data, rural poverty declined.

Chile

With the same micro-level data derived from reliable and consistent surveys in Chile, poverty measurements vary considerably (table 10.13).[25] Nevertheless, the four measures presented in table 10.13 show a degree of consistency in basic

Table 10.13 The Evolution of Poverty Rates in Chile, 1987–98 (percent)

Source of estimate	1987	1990	1992	1994	1996	1998
Urban						
World Bank (2000)	35.2	29.1	20.7	19.3	15.6	13.5
De Janvry and Sadoulet (1999)[a]	38.0	33.0	28.0	23.0	19.0	—
Wodon (2001)	45.3	48.3	41.2	27.4	24.1	23.6
Ocampo (2001)[a]	—	38.0	—	28.0	22.0	21.0
Rural						
World Bank (2000)[b]	63.5	50.6	40.1	42.1	42.5	37.3
De Janvry and Sadoulet (1999)[a]	45.0	34.0	28.0	26.0	26.0	—
Wodon and others (2001)	57.0	60.8	60.4	44.6	42.5	42.5
Ocampo (2001)[a]	—	40.0	—	32.0	31.0	28.0
Poverty deficit[b]						
Total	15.7	12.0	7.8	7.6	6.5	5.7
Urban	13.4	10.2	6.5	6.3	4.8	4.5
Rural	25.3	19.7	13.4	14.2	15.0	12.6

Note: All estimates are based on the National Socioeconomic Characteristics Survey (CASEN), a national survey of approximately 40,000 households commissioned biannually since 1985 by the Ministry of Planning and Cooperation.

—Not available.

a. Based on calculations by the Economic Commission for Latin America.

b. The poverty line was set at 37,889 pesos per month in 1998 pesos.

trends. All find a significant decline in poverty levels over time, with a slowdown in the rate of decline in later years.

World Bank (2000), perhaps the most reliable source, shows that the incidence of poverty is considerably higher in rural than in urban areas. In 1987, 64 percent of the rural population was poor compared with 35 percent of the urban population, but rural poverty declined significantly thereafter, falling to 37 percent in 1998. The reduction was more pronounced in urban areas, however. In 1998 poverty was 38 percent of its rate in urban areas in 1987 but 59 percent of its rate in rural areas. Thus, although rural households were better off in 1998 than in 1987, there was a widening of rural-urban income differentials. To what extent this growing income differential can be attributed to the reforms themselves is unknown and requires further study.

Progress in reducing both urban and rural poverty is due mainly to Chile's sustained and rapid overall economic growth, with an average annual GDP growth rate of 6.5 percent from the mid-1980s to the mid-1990s. In countries where agriculture's shares in income and employment are relatively low, as is typical in middle-income countries, and where labor markets are integrated, rapid overall growth can go a long way toward reducing rural poverty, even if agriculture does not grow very fast. Migration appears to have been a notable factor in translating overall growth into poverty reduction. De Janvry and Sadoulet (1999) find that in most of Latin America rural-urban migration has been a primary factor explaining the reduction in rural poverty during the 1990s. Although not strictly comparable, the de Janvry and Sadoulet findings are consistent with the detailed analysis of Mundlak, Cavallo, and Domenech (1989) for Argentina and Coeymans and Mundlak (1991) for Chile. Using migration functions, they report high elasticities of migration with respect to income differentials of 5.6 for Argentina and 7 for Chile.[26] The implication from these results using agricultural income data is that wage differentials should also have declined, which is interesting in light of the widening gap in poverty levels using more general income measures of rural and urban households.

From a policy point of view, the depth of poverty is more relevant than the incidence. The poverty deficit (how far income is below the poverty threshold) overall fell from 15.7 percent in 1987 to 5.7 percent in 1998, or a 64 percent improvement (see table 10.13). The poverty deficit fell less for rural households, from 25.3 percent to 12.6 percent, or 50 percent, and more for urban households, from 13.4 percent to 4.5 percent, or 66 percent. Thus for Chile both the incidence and depth of poverty declined with rapid economic growth, although poor rural households have a greater chance than poor urban households of experiencing severe poverty.[27]

Further analysis is required to determine to what extent these rural-urban differences in the decline of the poverty deficit are related to different levels of social support, the mix of income sources, demographic changes (especially important in light of the self-selection implicit in migration decisions), and other variables (see box 10.2). In Chile, which has a well-established social support system, it would be relevant for policy analysis to investigate whether coverage is biased toward urban areas.

Effects of Reforms on Farm Structure and the Concentration of Production

What can be said about the impact of reforms on the structure of farming? Even without reforms, farm structure is likely to have changed over time in most countries. Nonetheless, it is useful to explore the ways in which the new economic environment accompanying reforms might have led to different rates of change in the number of farmers and the concentration of production. All else being equal, the reduction in the bias against export agriculture would have offered greater benefit to those who could take advantage of export-related opportunities, mainly larger commercial operations. But other factors also played a role, including such external shocks as falling international prices and an appreciating exchange rate. These factors were more harmful to larger commercial farmers. The changes in relative prices following the reforms gave a degree of advantage to smaller producers of nontradable products.

Box 10.2 On Reform, Poverty, and Targeted Taxpayer Support

Open domestic markets and trade are central elements of a set of policies that facilitate growth. But how market and trade liberalization affects the poor depends on the specific package of reforms and policy changes. The detrimental effects on farmers and the rural poor who are less able to take advantage of reforms can be mitigated by targeted transfers, ideally including support to farmers of import-competing products.

The Program of Direct Rural Support (Procampo) in Mexico is a transitional mechanism designed to relieve the stress of trade liberalization (including NAFTA) on small farmers. The credit and extension programs of the Agricultural Development Institute (INDAP) in Chile are focused exclusively on small farmers. Targeted less directly to the poor, Brazil's rural pension program, set up in 1991, provides the equivalent of a highly subsidized monthly minimum wage. Reforms have often begun with macroeconomic stabilization, trade liberalization, and reduced government subsidies and intervention. The benefits of these immediate changes have often been diminished and the costs inflated by the absence of well-functioning, competitive markets, which are an intended longer term consequence of reform.

Changes in exchange rates can also have different effects across farm sizes, resulting in a new size distribution in the agricultural sector. Lopez and Romano (2001) find for Brazil that a 40 percent nominal devaluation increases real revenues by 13.4 percent for large farmers (50–2,000 hectares), by 5.4 percent for small farmers (2–10 hectares), and by 2.6 percent for very small farmers (less than 2 hectares). Smaller farmers gain less because their revenues are skewed toward nontraded goods and traded goods make up a larger share of their consumption. Larger farmers produce more traded goods and consume more nontraded goods.

A comparison of Argentina and Chile shows different effects on the number and size of farms following reform (tables 10.14 and 10.15). In the provinces for which information is available, Argentina experienced a decrease in the number of farms and an increase in the average size of farms between 1992 and 1997. The number of farms declined 31 percent in five years, with decreases across provinces ranging from 20 percent to 49 percent. Average farm sizes increased 46 percent, with increases across provinces ranging from 22 percent to 96 percent. The data appear to reflect a significant change in the overall structure of the Argentine farm sector toward larger operations, although it is unclear to what extent these results reflect migration, retirement, movement from farm operation to off-farm or on-farm work, or other factors.

Table 10.14 Number of Farms and Average Farm Size in Argentina, 1992–97

Province	Zone	Number of farms 1992	Number of farms 1997	Number of farms Change (percent)	Average size (hectares) 1992	Average size (hectares) 1997	Average size (hectares) Change (percent)
Buenos Aires	North	20,143	15,192	–25	121	161	33
	West	7,512	4,932	–34	399	618	55
	Middle	19,247	14,941	–22	248	327	32
	Southeast	8,886	6,466	–27	381	523	37
	Southwest	12,218	8,747	–28	442	615	39
	Cuenca del Salado	16,637	11,709	–30	323	492	52
Santa Fe	Middle	24,884	17,476	–30	103	170	65
	South	28,883	14,666	–49	89	174	96
Córdoba	East	13,274	8,072	–39	259	428	65
	Middle-South	10,687	8,544	–20	429	525	22
La Pampa	North and East	8,343	6,297	–25	387	512	32
All		170,714	117,042	–31	243	355	46

Source: Ghezán, Mateos, and Elverdín (2000, figure 11); Sturzenegger (1999, p. 26).

In contrast, Chile shows an apparent movement between 1976 and 1997 toward smaller farms in some regions and larger farms in others, reflecting the crop mix in various regions. The central region, where the number of farms has declined, is the heart of the fruit and wine export sector. The Metropolitan Region around the capital, which has perhaps the most sophisticated agricultural economy, shows both a large decrease in farm numbers and a large increase in average farm size. The southern region, where wheat and other traditional crops and livestock predominate, shows an increase in number of farms and a decreases in farm size. Although the farm products of the southern region (grains, milk, and beef) compete with imports, there have been notable gains in productivity, spurred in part by the market-oriented environment introduced by the reforms. These productivity gains have been especially notable for wheat and milk yields. The limited data presented here are consistent with the hypothesis that the productivity gains for traditional products have been available to small and large farmers alike, but the data to test this are unavailable.

More recent evidence suggests that the dairy sector has experienced rapid changes in production levels and in the number and size of producers. Anrique (1999) reports that the number of Chilean dairy producers is declining at 3 percent a year. Dirven (2002) summarizes studies finding a 45 percent decline

Table 10.15 Number of Farms and Average Farm Size in Chile, 1976–97

	Number of farms			Average size (hectares)		
Region	**1976**	**1997**	**Change (percent)**	**1976**	**1997**	**Change (percent)**
Arid north						
I	2,736	5,690	108	288.1	157.6	–45
II	1,341	2,042	52	86.7	56.4	–35
III	1,920	2,427	26	738.8	837.1	13
Central						
IV	17,585	17,291	–2	202.1	225.0	11
V	21,115	20,242	–4	69.2	68.8	–1
Metropolitana	20,630	15,491	–25	60.5	73.5	21
VI	36,880	30,967	–16	44.4	39.4	–11
VII	41,779	40,559	–3	58.8	53.0	–10
VIII	56,314	56,891	1	56.3	48.2	–14
IX	50,587	61,443	21	53.3	39.5	–26
X	50,557	55,045	9	72.5	66.1	-9
South						
XI	2,996	2,570	–14	602.2	601.9	0
Extreme south						
XII	1,078	1,045	-3	4,397.4	3,756.3	–15
Total	305,518	311,703	2	94.1	87.0	–8

Source: Chile, INE (1997; table 3.1).

in the number of Argentine dairy producers during the 1990s, and a nearly 50 percent decline in milk remittances to small-scale producers in Uruguay. Furthermore, the share of milk and milk products marketed through supermarket chains has been growing rapidly in Argentina, Chile, and Uruguay. Similarly, for the Chilean pork and poultry sectors the number of producers has shown a marked decline as the scale of production has increased with the adoption of new technologies and marketing methods. Between 1978 and 1998 the number of pig farms declined by 59 percent, while the number of pigs processed per grower rose more than 1,100 percent, from 472 pigs to 6,046 pigs per grower. Over the same period the number of poultry growing units declined 79 percent, while the number of broilers produced per unit grew by more than 260 percent.

There is little information on a country-by-country basis in Latin America of concentration on the buyer side. For Chile there is evidence of a high degree of buyer concentration and of increasing vertical coordination through contracts and integration. Of Chile's 16 most important agricultural products, Foster and Vargas (2000) report that only for potatoes does the market correspond to the stylized model of many market participants with activities deter-

Table 10.16 Indicators of Concentration and Growth in Chilean Markets, 2000

Product	Four-firm concentration (percent)	Herfindhal index	Market share of largest firm (percent)
Fruits and field crops			
Export oriented			
Fruit for export	34	0.04	11
Wine for export	32	0.04	14
Industrial tomatoes	90	0.23	32
Seed multiplication	47	0.8	19
Import competing			
Wheat	65	0.15	25
Maize	67	0.22	44
Durum wheat	100	0.5	50
Raps (canola)	100	1.00	100
Sugar beets	100	1.00	100
Malting barley	100	0.52	60
Few or no imports			
Potatoes	< 5	< 0.01	< 5
Animal products			
Few or no imports			
Broilers	92	0.37	55
Turkeys	100	0.42	50
Pork	61	0.18	40
Import competing			
Beef cattle	40	0.11	28
Milk	80	0.18	28

Source: Foster and Vargas (2000).

mined by spot prices generated by open markets (see table 10.16). All other product markets have a high degree of buyer concentration, are coordinated through marketing or production contracts, or are completely integrated. The degree of industrialization in Chilean agriculture appears to be high and getting higher. The export-oriented sectors of fresh fruit and wine have less processor concentration than import-competing sectors have.

POLICY IMPLICATIONS AND CONCLUSIONS

A primary goal of the trade reforms in Latin America during the 1980s and 1990s was to reverse the strong urban bias that penalized export agriculture. Domestic terms of trade between agriculture and the rest of the economy were expected to change to the benefit of the farm sector, especially for exportables. But expectations about relative prices at the farm level were not fulfilled, most notably because of currency appreciation and falling world prices. From the perspective of agricultural trade policy reforms, it would seem that agricultural producers should have experienced a significant increase in relative prices. However, as the evidence here shows, real domestic prices of farm tradables fell after the initiation of reforms in several countries, primarily because of currency appreciation and reinforced by a fall in world prices during some periods. In terms of prices, then, the main forces behind the changes in agricultural incentives were beyond the control of sectoral policies: exchange rates, border prices, and real interest rates.

Nevertheless, for Latin America generally, export agriculture did expand despite the unexpected and unfavorable change in domestic terms of trade. Moreover, exports expanded faster for countries that had early and sustained reforms. The bias against export agriculture declined: not only were export taxes eliminated and protection to importables reduced, but trade reforms were also accompanied by other policy changes, such as deregulation and privatization, that reduced the transaction costs of agricultural activities. Thus, trade liberalization was a leading element in economic policy reorientation, but it was only part of the story. Trade reforms took place in the context of economywide structural reforms, macroeconomic adjustments, deregulation, and privatization. Modernization of ports, privatization of telecommunications, airline and shipping deregulation, greater flexibility in the foreign exchange regime, and other changes were influential in determining the response of agriculture.

Even with the best of data it would be difficult to distinguish the partial effects of trade liberalization from the myriad impacts that resulted from general economic reforms. Nevertheless, some patterns are visible in the data presented here. First, in most cases trade reforms had a positive impact on agriculture, particularly exportables. Without trade reforms other reforms would likely have had a far more limited impact on the sector. Second, the breadth of the reform program matters: there is a complementarity between trade reforms and other economic policy changes. The positive impacts of trade liberalization on the agricultural sector—in changes in product mix, investments, resource mobility, and ability to adjust to changing conditions—were enhanced by deregulation, privatization, better infrastructure, and a more general reorientation of the economy toward markets.

Because reforms varied by country, there is much to be learned from the specifics of reform in individual countries, such as the three cases examined here. The farm sectors in Argentina and Chile did well after reforms, both in exports and in factor productivity, outcomes attributable to the breadth, coherence, and persistence of policy changes. Colombia is a different story. While on paper the plans for reforms were just as broad and coherent, the plans were not realized and the reforms were short-lived, perhaps partly because of mismanagement, but even more because of adverse exogenous shocks in the initial stage of reforms. By the end of 1990 the incentive framework and the role of the government were very different from what had been envisioned at the beginning of the reform process.

There is little consensus across Latin America on the impact of the reforms. This is due partly to the difficulty of separating the effects of reforms from the effects of mismanagement and exogenous shocks. Moreover, the emphasis of the policy debate on structural and sectoral reforms has shifted: from the productive and export potential of agriculture to the difficulties imposed by a liberalized economy on import-competing farmers, and from the impact on farmers and urban consumers (now nearly forgotten) to the impact on the rural poor and the small farm sector, which were presumed to have been excluded from the benefits of more open trade.

But were reforms really exclusionary? The evidence points to the exclusion of part of the small farm sector, including farms in relatively low-productivity areas. More generally, part of the small farm sector faces difficulties adjusting to several changes in the economic environment: an open trade regime (higher price risk), increasing demands of buyers for higher volumes and standards (associated with the increasing concentration of agribusiness and the dominant role of supermarkets), the general trend toward greater capital intensity, and the reduction in subsidies to agriculture. Overall, however, the reforms did not contribute to an increase in rural poverty and in some cases helped to reduce rural poverty, as in Chile and Colombia.

Economic reforms toward open trade do not guarantee that agriculture will benefit significantly in all countries. In some countries other sectors might expand. The point of such reforms is to improve the use of resources generally and to permit economic agents in agriculture and other sectors to discover their comparative advantages. Argentina, with its strong export orientation prior to reforms, probably experienced the least suffering in the adjustment of its farm sector. Trade liberalization allowed the country to capitalize on its strength. Chile had a more difficult transition following reforms, because of its initial orientation toward importables. But it discovered and developed its export potential, because of the sustained nature and cohesiveness of the reform program. In Colombia, by contrast, the export sector did not develop as expected because the politics of policy formation were dominated by the import-competing sector, stifling the reform process.

NOTES

1. As Krueger, Schiff, and Valdés (1991) document (table 1-2, p. 11 of volume I) the total nominal rate of protection (adjusted for exchange rate and other indirect effects) averaged for five countries (Argentina, Brazil, Chile, Colombia, and Dominican Republic) for 1960–84 was –28 percent, four-fifths of it due to indirect taxation. The direct nominal rate of protection shows that importables were protected (on average 13 percent) and exportables were taxed (–6.4 percent).

2. For example, Schiff and Valdés (1991) anticipated the equity question on household incomes in their simulations based on household data for 18 developing countries. They showed that the "effect of removing agricultural price interventions is not regressive. In most countries, removing direct (or total) interventions changed the real incomes of the poorer urban and rural groups by less than 5 percent (up or down). More often than not, the rural poor gained from removing the interventions."
3. As McCalla and Valdés (1999) point out for 1995–97, 13 of 32 developing countries in the Latin American and Caribbean region are net importers of both food and agricultural products. Seventeen are net importers of food.
4. "The most dynamic products are those that are the most modern and capital-intensive in commercial agriculture. The products of the small farmer, traditional crops with a high labor intensity, were stagnant or declining in terms of cultivated area" (Stallings and Peres 2000, p. 227, translated by the authors).
5. Producers of nontradables might be harmed by trade liberalization through the indirect effect of the substitution in consumption of imported foods for local products. An example is in the Sierra in Peru, where producers of traditional local (and highly nontradable) products face competition from bread, pastas, and poultry, the raw materials of which are importables (Alvarez and Valdés 1986).
6. Mundlak's findings are based on panel data covering 37 countries for 1970–90.
7. A notable exception is Colombia, where small farms tend to concentrate on the production of nontradables and commercial enterprises were harmed disproportionately by liberalized trade (Jaramillo 1998).
8. As an example, Reardon (2002) points out that trade in perishables was stimulated by the adoption of technologies permitting the profitable storage of fresh fruit on ships.
9. Brazil's low tradability index is understandable given the size of its domestic market. Peru's low tradability index suggests that the country's agriculture is relatively more oriented toward nontradables.
10. For Chile there is strong evidence from an ongoing study (Valdés and Foster 2005) that the pattern of agricultural growth following reforms had a significant effect on rural poverty reduction.
11. Exceptions might be white maize in Central America and some bean varieties in Brazil. Those products are traded within very thin markets.
12. The situation with food aid, which applies only to very few countries in the region (some in Central America, Bolivia, and Haiti), still gives governments flexibility and influence in selected food markets.
13. The slight decline in the incidence of stunting in Central America (Guatemala, El Salvador, Nicaragua) and Haiti should be viewed in the context of economies that were recovering from civil conflicts during the 1980s and early 1990s.
14. Chile's agrarian reform began with a Yugoslav-type model and moved to the increasingly centralized Soviet model (see Valdés 1978 and Jarvis 1985).
15. "Production value growth" refers to the value of production of agriculture only (crops, fruits, horticulture, and livestock). The GDP data indicate value-added measures for agriculture, fisheries, and forestry.
16. Immediately following the reforms, there was little change in animal exports but an increase in crop exports, especially maize and oil crops. For industrial crops (cotton, sugarcane) and oil seeds, the most significant increases in production began in 1994/95. In livestock production, the beef sector competed for land with crops. The expansion in grain production reduced the land available for beef cattle after 1994, and the reduction in the per capita consumption of beef and constraints

on beef exports because of outbreaks of hoof-and-mouth disease resulted in slower expansion. After a slight decline in milk production immediately following the reforms, production growth accelerated after 1993/94 (Ghezan, Mateos, and Elverdin 2000).

17. For more on the aggregate supply response to incentives in Chile, see the comments by Jarvis (1988) on the study by Quiroz and Barahona, and the follow-up discussion by Quiroz, Barahona, and Valdés (1988) and Jarvis (1988).
18. The point estimate for a positive productivity shift after 1974 is 0.157 (16 percent) with a standard error of 0.072 (p-value of 0.036). This is a shift upward in the productivity trend measured by a simple year index over the entire period of estimation, estimated at 2.3 percent a year.
19. These results are representative of the exportable sector, but Argentina has several other commodities, such as tobacco and sugar, that have experienced protection.
20. Argentina reintroduced export taxes after the large devaluations of December 2001.
21. Measured nominal rates of protection during the Allende years are not very meaningful, given the price controls, hyperinflation, shortages, and rampant black market activity.
22. The large increases in domestic beef prices are due largely to prohibitions on imports of live cattle and meat on the bone from traditional suppliers, such as Argentina and Uruguay, during 1984–89. This prohibition followed the eradication of hoof-and-mouth disease in Chile and the sanitary protections instituted to maintain the country's status as free of the disease.
23. Comparisons of poverty measures using pre- and postreform data are difficult given the dubious nationwide representation of pre-1985 data.
24. While there is a literature on estimating the partial effects of individual policy components of reform (for example, Schiff and Valdés 1992), these simulations take into account only trade liberalization and exchange rate changes, however.
25. Analyses of household surveys require many adjustments, such as whether to use per capita or per household measurements or adult equivalents, whether and how to adjust for regional prices and household production, how to adjust income levels for consistency with national income accounts data, and even whether there is reliable data to adjust the poverty line to the rural sector, considering differences in prices between sectors.
26. The data in the Mundlak, Cavallo, and Domenech (1989) study covered 1913–84, and the date in the Coeymans and Mundlak (1991) study covered 1962–82. Income differentials are measured as the ratio of sectoral average labor productivity for Argentina. For Chile income differentials are measured as the ratio of wages in nonagriculture to average labor productivity in agriculture, adjusted for differences in the cost of living and unemployment in the nonagricultural sector.
27. For a discussion of poverty in Latin America, see López and Valdés (2000).

BIBLIOGRAPHY

Alvarez, E., and A. Valdés. 1986. "Government Policy and Food Supply Management in Peru, 1950-1981." Inter-American Development Bank, Washington, DC.

Anrique, R. 1999. "Caracterización del Chile lechero." In *En producción animal 1999*, ed. L. Latrille. Valdivia, Chile: Universidad Austral de Chile.

Arnade, C. 1998. "Using a Programming Approach to Measure International Agricultural Efficiency and Productivity." *Journal of Agricultural Economics* 49 (1): 67–84.

Barahona, P., and J. Quiroz. 1990. "Policy Reforms and Agricultural Response: The Case of Chile." In *Agriculture and Governments in an Interdependent World,* Proceedings of the International Conference of Agricultural Economists (IAAE), A. Maunder and A. Valdés, eds. Hanover, NH: Dartmouth Publishing.

Chile, INE (National Institute of Statistics). 1997. *VI Censo Nacional Agropecuario.* Santiago: Chile, INE.

Coeymans, J. E., Y. Mundlak. 1991. "Agricultural Aggregate Response: A Multisectoral Analysis of the Chilean Case." *Food Policy* 16 (1): 17–22.

Corbo, W., J. de Melo, and J. Tybout. 1986. "What Went Wrong With the Recent Reforms in the Southern Cone." *Economic Development and Cultural Change* 34 (3): 607–40.

De Janvry, A., and E. Sadoulet. 1999. "Rural Poverty and the Design of Effective Rural Development Strategies." Paper presented at the annual meeting of the Junta Interamericana de Agricultura, Bahia, Brazil.

De la Cuadra, S., and D. Hachette. 1991. "Chile." In *Liberalizing Foreign Trade: The Experience of Argentina, Chile, and Uruguay,* Armeane Choksi, M. Michaely, and Demetrius Papageorgiou, eds. Oxford: Basil Blackwell.

Dirven, M. 2002. "Los Encadenamientos de la Agricultura Chilena: Acercamiento a Una Medición." Comisión Económica para America Latina, Santiago.

Edwards, S. 1986. "The Order of Liberalization of the Current and Capital Accounts of the Balance of Payment." In *Economic Liberalization in Developing Countries,* A. Choksi and D. Papageorgiou, eds. Oxford: Basil Blackwell.

———. 1993. "The Opening of Latin America." In *Latin America and the Caribbean: A Decade after the Debt Crisis.* Washington, DC: World Bank.

FAO (Food and Agriculture Organization). 2001. *The State of Food and Agriculture 2001.* Rome: FAO.

Foster, W., and G. Vargas. 2000. "Concentration in Chilean Agriculture." Department of Agricultural Economics, Pontifical Catholic University, Santiago.

García-García J., and G. Montes. 1989. *Trade, Exchange Rate, and Agricultural Pricing Policies in Colombia.* In *The Political Economy of Agricultural Policies,* A. Krueger, M. Schiff, and A. Valdés, eds. Baltimore: Johns Hopkins University Press.

Gardner, B. L. 1995. "Consequences of Policy Reform in Agriculture: Experience of Eight Countries." World Bank, Washington, DC.

Ghezán, G., M. Mateos, and J. Elverdín. 2000. "Impacto de las Políticas de Ajuste Estructural en el Sector Agropecuario y Agroindustrial: El Caso de Argentina." Serie Desarrollo Productivo 90, Comisión Económica para America Latina, Santiago.

Hurtado, H., A. Valdés, and E. Muchnik. 1990. *Trade, Exchange Rate, and Agricultural Pricing Policies in Chile.* In *The Political Economy of Agricultural Policies,* A. Krueger, M. Schiff, and A. Valdés, eds. Baltimore: Johns Hopkins University Press.

Helfand, S. M., and G. Castro de Rezende. 2000. "Brazilian Agriculture in the 1990s: Impact of the Policy Reforms." In *Tomorrow's Agriculture: Incentives, Institutions, Infrastructure, and Innovations,* Proceedings of the International Conference of Agricultural Economists (IAAE), G. H. Peters and P. Pingali, eds. Aldershot, UK: Ashgate.

Jarvis, L. S. 1985. *Chilean Agriculture under Military Rule: From Reform to Reactivation 1973-1980.* Berkeley, CA: Institute of International Studies.

———. 1988. "Reformas de las Políticas Económicas de la Agricultura Chilena: Otro Punto de Vista." *Cuadernos de Economía* 27 (80): 103–14.

Jaramillo, C. F. 1998. *Liberalization, Crisis, and Change in Colombian Agriculture.* Boulder, CO: Westview.

———. 1999. "Macroeconomic Reforms and Agriculture: The Case of Colombia." World Bank, Washington, DC.

Krueger, A., M. Schiff, and A. Valdés, eds. 1991. *The Political Economy of Agricultural Pricing Policy.* Vol. 1, *Latin America.* Baltimore: Johns Hopkins University Press.

Larid, S. 1997. "Mercosur: Objectives and Achievements." In *Trade: Towards Open Regionalism,* ed. S. J. Burki, G. E. Perry, and S. Calvo. Washington, DC: World Bank.

Larson, D. F., R. Butzer, Y. Mundlak, and A. Crego. 2000. "A Cross-Country Database for Sector Investment and Capital." *World Bank Economic Review* 14 (2): 371-91.

López, R., and C. Romano. 2003. "Determinants of Farm Revenues and Factors for Poor Farmers in Brazil," in *Rural Poverty Alleviation in Brazil: Toward an Integrated Strategy.* Chapter 5. World Bank Country Study. Washington, DC: World Bank.

López, R., and A. Valdés, eds. 2000. *Rural Poverty in Latin America.* New York: St. Martin's Press.

Lora, E. 1997. "A Decade of Structural Reforms in Latin America: What Has Been Reformed and How to Measure It." Working Paper 350, Inter-American Development Bank, Washington, DC.

McCalla, A. F., and A. Valdés. 1999. "Issues, Interests, and Options of Developing Countries." Paper presented at the WTO Conference on Agriculture and the New Trade Agenda from a Development Perspective, Geneva, Oct. 1–2.

Morley, S. A., R. Machado, and S. Pettinato. 1999. *Indexes of Structural Reform in Latin America. Series on Economic Reforms 12.* Santiago: Economic Commission for Latin America.

Mundlak, Y. 1999. "The Dynamics of Agriculture." In *Food Security, Diversification, and Resource Management: Refocusing the Role of Agriculture,* Proceedings of the International Conference of Agricultural Economists (IAAE), ed. G. Peters and J. von Braun. Aldershot, UK: Ashgate.

Mundlak, Y., D. Cavallo, and R. Domenech. 1989. "Agriculture and Economic Growth in Argentina, 1913–84." Research Report 76. International Food Policy Research Institute, Washington, DC.

Ocampo, J. A. 2001. "Agricultura y Desarrollo Rural en América Latina." In *Desarrollo Rural en América Latina y El Caribe,* David De Albuquerque, ed. Santiago: Comisión Económica para América Latina y el Caribe.

Paz , J., and A. Valdés. 2000. "Interest and Options in the WTO 2000 Negotiations: Latin America and the Caribbean." In "Agricultural Trade Liberalization in a New Trade Round," M. Ingco and A. Winters, eds. Discussion Paper 418, World Bank, Washington, DC.

Perry, S. 2000. "El impacto de las Reformas Estructurales en la Agricultura Colombiana." Serie Desarrollo Productivo 94, Comisión Económica para América Latina y el Caribe, Santiago.

Perry, G., and D. M. Leipziger, eds. 1999. *Chile: Recent Policy Lessons and Emerging Challenges.* WBI Development Studies. Washington, DC: World Bank Institute.

Quiroz, J. A. 1997. "Reformas Económicas y Precios Agrícolas en Colombia, 1991–96." Inter-American Development Bank, Washington, DC.

———. 2000. "Agriculture and the Macroeconomy in Latin America during the Nineties." Inter-American Development Bank, Conference at the Annual Meetings, Development of the Rural Economy and Poverty Reduction in Latin America and the Caribbean," New Orleans, LA.

———. 2001. "La Agricultura y la Macroeconomía en América Latina en los Noventa." Working paper, Gerens Consulting, Santiago.

Quiroz, J. A., P. Barahona, and A. Valdés. 1988. "Reformas Económicas en la Agricultura y Respuesta de la Producción Agregada: Chile 1960–1987." *Cuadernos de Economía* 25 (76): 319–403.

Reardon, T. 2002. "Product Market and Capital Market Trade Liberalization and Food Security in Latin America." FAO Expert Consultation on Trade and Food Security, Rome.

Schiff, M., and A. Valdés. 1990. "Poverty, Food Intake, and Malnutrition: Implications for Food Security in Developing Countries." *American Journal of Agricultural Economics* 72 (5): 1318–22

Spoor, M. 2000. "Two Decades of Adjustment and Agricultural Development in Latin America and the Caribbean." Serie Desarrollo Productivo, Comisión Económica para América Latina y el Caribe, Santiago.

Stallings, B., and W. Peres. 2000. *Crecimiento, Empleo y Equidad: El Impacto de las Reformas Económicas en América Latina y el Caribe.* Santiago: Comisión Económica para América Latina y el Caribe.

Sturzenegger, A. C. 1999. "Agriculture and the Macroeconomy in an Integrated World Economy: The Argentine Case." World Bank, Washington, DC.

Sturzenegger, A. C., W. Otrera, and B. Mosquera. 1990. *Trade, Exchange Rate, and Agricultural Pricing Policies in Argentina.* In *The Political Economy of Agricultural Policies,* A. Krueger, M. Schiff, and A. Valdés, eds. Baltimore: Johns Hopkins University Press.

Valdés, A. 1978. "Transition to Socialism: Observations on the Chilean Agrarian Reform." In *Employment in Developing Nations,* E. O. Edwards, ed. New York: University of Columbia Press.

———. 1996. "Surveillance of Agricultural Price and Trade Policy in Latin America during Major Policy Reforms." Discussion Paper 349, World Bank, Washington, DC.

Valdés, A., and W. Foster, eds. 2005. *Externalidades de la Agricultura Chilena.* Santiago: Ediciones Universidad Católica de Chile.

Valdés, A., and J. A. Mistiaen. 2001. "Rural Poverty in Latin America: Recent Trends and New Challenges." In *Current and Emerging Issues for Economic Analysis and Policy Research,* K. G. Stamoulis, ed. Rome: FAO.

Valdés, A., H. Hurtado, and E. Muchnik. 1991. "Chile." In *The Political Economy of Agricultural Pricing Policy.* Vol. 1, A. O. Krueger, M. Schiff, and A. Valdés, eds. Baltimore: Johns Hopkins University Press.

Venezian, E., and E. Muchnik. 1994. "Structural Adjustment and Agricultural Research in Chile." Briefing Paper 9, International Service for National Agricultural Research, The Hague.

Wodon, Q. T. 2000. "Poverty and Policy in Latin America and the Caribbean." Technical Paper 467, World Bank, Washington, DC.

Wodon, Q., and R. Castro-Fernández, K. Lee, G. Lopez-Alcevedo, C. Siaens, C. Sobrado, J.-P. Tre. 2001. "Poverty in Latin America: Trends (1986–98) and Determinants," *Cuadernos de Economía* 38 (114): 127–55.

World Bank. 1994. "Chile: Strategy for Rural Areas—Enhancing Agricultural Competitiveness and Alleviating Rural Poverty." Report 12776-CH, World Bank, Washington, DC.

———. 1995. "Colombia: Review of Agricultural and Rural Development Strategy." Report 13437-CO, World Bank, Washington, DC.

———. 1999. "Poor People in a Rich Country: A Poverty Report for Argentina." World Bank, Washington, DC.

———. 2000. *Chile's High Growth Economy: Poverty and Income Distribution, 1987–1998.* Country Study, World Bank, Washington, DC.

———. 2001a. "Latin America and the Caribbean Region Action Plan for Rural Development: An Input into the Revision of Vision to Action." Report Summary, World Bank, Washington, DC.

———. 2001b. "Rural Poverty Reduction in Brazil: Towards an Integrated Strategy." Policy Summary and Technical Papers, Report 21790-BR, World Bank, Washington, DC.

———. 2001c. *World Development Indicators 2001.* Washington, DC: World Bank.

———. 2002. *Chile: High Growth Economy, Poverty and Income Distribution, 1987–1998.* Washington, DC: World Bank.

———. 2003. "Nicaragua Poverty Assessment: Raising Welfare and Reducing Vulnerability." Report. 26128-NI, World Bank, Washington, DC.

CONTRIBUTORS

Maury Bredahl, University of Missouri
William Foster, Catholic University of Chile
Ashok Gulati, International Food Policy Research Institute
Bernard M. Hoekman, World Bank
Tim Josling, Stanford University
Rashid S. Kaukab, South Centre
John G. Lee, Purdue University
Alex F. McCalla, University of California, Davis
Sudha Narayanan, International Food Policy Research Institute
John Nash, World Bank
Francis K. T. Ng, World Bank
Marcelo Olarreaga, World Bank
Philip L. Paarlberg, Purdue University
Ramesh Sharma, Food and Agriculture Organization of the United Nations
Alberto Valdés, World Bank

INDEX

D

E

F

N

O

P

Q

R

U

ECO-AUDIT
Environmental Benefits Statement

The World Bank is committed to preserving endangered forests and natural resources. We have chosen to print *Reforming Agricultural Trade for Developing Countries (Vol. 1): Key Issues for a Pro-Development Outcome of the Doha Round* on recycled paper with 30% post-consumer waste. The Office of the Publisher has agreed to follow the recommended standards for paper usage set by the Green Press Initiative, a non-profit program supporting publishers in using fiber that is not sourced from endangered forests. For more information, visit www.greenpressinitiative.org.

Saved:

- 13 trees
- 9 million BTUs of total energy
- 1,127 lbs of CO_2 (carbon dioxide)
- 4,679 gallons of water
- 601 lbs of solid waste

green press INITIATIVE